Dignity and Solidarity

Dignity and Solidarity
An Introduction to Peace and Justice Education

Owen R. Jackson, O.S.A.

If you want peace, work for justice.
Pope Paul VI

A Campion Book
Loyola University Press
Chicago

Loyola University Press
3441 North Ashland Avenue
Chicago, Illinois 60657

Unless noted, Scripture passages are taken from
Holy Bible, New Revised Standard Version
© 1989 Division of Christian Education of the National Council of the
Churches of Christ in the United States of America.

Library of Congress Cataloging-in-Publication Data

Jackson, Owen R.
    Dignity and solidarity: an introduction to peace and justice
education/Owen R. Jackson.
        p. cm.
    Includes bibliographical references and index.
    ISBN 0-8294-0722-7
    1. Peace—Religious aspects—Christianity—Study and teaching.
2. Christianity and justice—Study and teaching. 3. International
education. 4. Church and social problems. I. Title.
BT736.4.J33 1992
261.8'07—dc20   91-41776
                                                            CIP

To my loving family and many supportive friends, that the quest for justice and peace may continue to energize us.

Contents

Part III   Values
What Are My Values?

Part IV   Influence
How Do I Change Things?

Foreword

Augustinian Father Owen R. Jackson sees peace and justice education "as a process that enables students to broaden their appreciation for people of other cultures, to develop a new vision based on humanitarian values, and to participate actively in creating a better world." No small educational objective! Arguably, the greatest change one can make in one's own life is to change the way one looks at the world. This book hopes to facilitate that change.

In bite-size chapters (easy to read, lots to chew on) Father Jackson gives the student organized themes around which class-room discussion can flow. The author structures his argument in four basic blocks, or parts, labeled "Inclusion," "Perception," "Values," and "Influence." The approach is personalist—encouraging a keener understanding (and appreciation) of self as preamble to reaching out to others with whom the student-self shares membership in a worldwide human community.

I first met Ray Jackson in the mid-1970s at a workshop sponsored by Bread for the World and hosted by Saint Louis University. The topic was hunger. The challenge was how to factor the hunger issue into the college curriculum, the liberal arts academic research agenda, the career choices of students, and the life-style of the typical campus community.

I next met this Villanova University priest on his own campus several years later. "Peace and Justice" was the rubric under which about two hundred activists and academics gathered for a one-day exchange of ideas ranging from anti-hunger strategies to nuclear disarmament.

And just a year or so ago, near the east steps of the United States Capitol, I ran into Ray Jackson as he was rounding up a group of Villanova students into a van for the return trip to Philadelphia after a day of lobbying—for peace and justice issues, of course—in Washington.

Out of those interests and extensive experience in classroom and campus ministry, as well as personal exposure to and reflection upon the impediments to a just and peaceful society, this book emerges. It is intended, as the author's preface says, "to equip the student with the knowledge and sensitivity to live a life worthy of the highest aspirations of humankind."

This book is the product of the Augustinian restlessness-of-spirit of a sensitive human being who remains convinced of the value of education in the ongoing struggle to achieve a just and peaceful society.

William J. Byron, S.J.
President
The Catholic University of America

Preface

Peace and justice are ideals that the human race has sought since the dawn of civilization. Within each of us there is an innate desire to live in harmony and act fairly in our dealings with each other, in spite of an equally strong desire to dominate and abuse our fellow humans. Situations of tension continually erupt into conflict and violence, yet perennially, philosophers, politicians, prophets, and princes have striven to create a world of peace and social justice.

This book is an attempt to place these ideals in an educational context in order to offer a way of learning that will help students to mature in both mind and heart. Much has been written, said, and done in the name of peace and justice over the past several years in the academic community. Specific courses dealing with problems of world hunger, the arms race, and innumerable other social ills have been offered with varying degrees of success. Unfortunately, the specialization common to the academic world has tended toward a departmentalization that forces students to study the trees without ever having observed the forest.

It should be noted here that we are talking specifically about Christian education. The word *Christian* does not imply a doctrinal or authoritarian approach to the subject matter, but rather a philosophical, value-conscious concern for the fundamental humanitarian roots of civilization. The experience of the Hebrew people and the two millennia of Christian community offer us a look at the human condition in its sanctity and sinfulness.

By way of definition, peace and justice education is a process whereby one learns to understand and accept the diversity of other people and cultures, develops a critically reflective sense of human experience based upon a humanitarian and Christian value system, and appropriates strategies and techniques for effective social change. This definition is composed of four elements: inclusion, perception, values, and influence. It suggests that these concerns are at the center of a broad educational effort intended to equip the student with the knowledge and sensitivity to live a life worthy of the highest aspirations of humankind.

Part I, "Inclusion," attempts to develop a sense of awareness and understanding on the part of the student about other races and cultures with regard to their individual histories and customs. The initial chapters look at personal identity and also sketch a broad view of life on planet Earth. Following this we look at the wide variety of people, cultures, religions, languages, and political and economic systems that, both in the past and in the present, are associated with the human family. The Inclusion section ends with chapters on interdependence, the nature of limits, and the acceptance of differences.

Part II, "Perception," deals with how we see the world. It begins with a chapter on self-perception and various explanations of human behavior, explores the problem of evil, and describes the process of social analysis. An attempt is made to establish criteria for examining social issues. Chapters on racism, sexism, classism, hunger and poverty, militarism, the arms race, and environmental concerns bring into view the history and present crises with respect to each of these issues. In its own chapter, the Holocaust receives special attention as the consummate evil of the twentieth century.

Part III, "Values," raises the question "What are my values?" Various understandings of value are presented to the reader in order to sharpen his or her sense of what is worthwhile. Other chapters explore the problem of objectivity and the clash of value systems. The key values of personal dignity and the unity of the human family are highlighted. Also examined are the various meanings of truth, justice, freedom, and peace. Included are questions about value conflicts, false values, and the importance of priorities. The concluding chapters close this section with a discussion of the significance of nonviolence and love as the highest values.

Part IV of the text, "Influence," leads to decision-making. The central question is "How can I be an instrument of change in the world?" Personal life-style and individual talents are discussed in the first chapter. Other chapters look at the major institutions of our society: the political parties, the business and labor sectors, the educational establishment, the media and advertising industries, and the organized churches. How they influence public policy and impact on our culture are questions raised and discussed in these chapters. Other chapters highlight famous historical figures who have influenced the course of events in positive ways.

We wish to acknowledge an article by Paul Deitterich, "Some Dimensions of International Affairs Education," in *Education for Justice*, which contains the seminal ideas for the format of this book. His insights on educational theory and their application to peace and justice education deserve the appreciation of all involved in these efforts.

Many students offered valuable criticisms of the preliminary drafts during the writing of the text. In particular we wish to thank Michael McGinnis, Maria Bello, Steve Liga, and Tim Bradley for their research, editing, and typing.

Kevin Ferris, Kathy Brown, and Wini Wolff were also of considerable help with their editorial comments.

January 1991

Part I

Inclusion

Who's Included in My World?

Introduction

The purpose of Part I, "Inclusion," is to introduce the reader to the variety and complexity of our world in terms of people and geography. Because we tend to limit our personal vision to the ordinary events and circumstances of our own lives, we sometimes forget the horizon. Naturally enough, a reflection on our world ought to begin with ourselves and the people with whom we have daily contact. It would be unfortunate, however, if our vision did not extend beyond our immediate surroundings. The present task then is to stretch our minds to include other people and nations in our world. In these reflections we are called to an understanding of the vastness and complexity of planet Earth as well as its problems, difficulties, and challenges.

We live in a time of great anxiety and new promise. There is an awareness that the twentieth century has witnessed both the monumental slaughter of human life and a yearning for liberation among countless millions of people who are poor and oppressed. In our own day, nuclear war threatens to claim a thousand times that number within minutes. Yet there is reason for hope. In spite of injustice and oppression, poverty and hunger, there is a new urgency to build a better world. Many people are seeking ways in which to alleviate the pressing concerns of humankind. It is hoped that a fresh awareness of the other people of the world will help us become sensitive to their needs.

In times past, people's perceptions were often limited by lack of information and a view of life that accepted the status quo. While these conditions are still true in some instances, more and more people are coming to realize the global connectedness of the human family. Spacecraft circling the planet, television programming on an international scale, and computer age communications have drawn people closer together than ever before. New hopes and aspirations for a better life have become the dream of humankind.

While most of us know that other races, cultures, religions, political and economic systems, and ideologies exist, it is important that we become more familiar with the general characteristics of these realities. The chapters in Part I are intended to offer this overview in order to set the stage for an examination of the major social problems confronting the human family at the end of the twentieth century and how we might begin to respond to them in positive and healing ways.

1

Who Am I?

All the world's a stage, and all the men and women merely players:
they have their exits and their entrances.

William Shakespeare[1]

Body/Mind/Heart

"Know thyself" has been good advice since the dawn of
civilization. Ancient Hindu and Taoist writers as well as the
better-known Greek and Roman philosophers stressed the importance of understanding the inner workings of our mind in
order to grow in appreciation of ourselves and the world around
us. This advice is as good today as it was then. Who am I? How do
I understand myself? How do others see me? We ponder these
and similar questions in our more reflective moments. In order
to cast the question of personal identity in simple format, let us
look at the present "you," then examine how that particular
identity came to exist, and conclude with a look at the future by
asking, "Where am I going with my life?"

Although it may seem obvious, it is crucial to understand
that our bodies are an integral part of our identity. The physical

characteristics of sex, race, size, and shape play a dominant role in our life. Some ancient philosophers believed that the body was a burden to the spirit within a person, while others thought that the spirit, or soul, was of little consequence. Today, modern science has helped us understand the biological uniqueness of each person through the study of genetic identity. This physical uniqueness manifests itself through our one-of-a-kind individual fingerprints.

In addition, our physical well-being, or lack thereof, further influences our identity. People who suffer various handicaps or other bodily ailments are clearly affected by these disorders. Eyes, ears, and all bodily parts were designed with a particular purpose in mind. When they malfunction, people generally undergo a change in their understanding of themselves. The argument here is simply that an appreciation of the physical dimensions of identity is essential to our understanding of who we are.

A special part of our physical makeup is our hormonal system. The type and amount of hormones secreted within our bodies generate much of our emotional behavior. On the one hand, emotional behavior can result from either an oversupply or a deficiency of one or another hormone. Chronic depression, severe emotional swings, and other abnormal behavioral patterns are often caused by glandular malfunction. Thus, we may attribute part of our emotional behavior to the internal mechanisms of the body. On the other hand, external events may trigger our hormonal apparatus. One of the most obvious examples of this is the bodily changes that occur in response to sexual stimulation.

Another integral part of identity is the mind—that part of us that can think and choose. In speaking about the mind, philosophers generally distinguish between the intellect and the will. The former governs our thought processes; the latter determines the decisions or choices that we make. In any case, the key power attributed to the mind, which differentiates us from other animal species, is the ability to reflect. This power of reflection allows us to step back from the immediacy of a situation and examine our attitudes, beliefs, and behavior in a dispassionate manner.

Furthermore, just as the body may suffer a physical disability, so too can a distraught mind affect our behavior. Internally, we can poison the mind with drugs or with thoughts that provoke anxiety. Externally, we may respond negatively to fear and threats. Conversely, the mind may be eased medicinally, or we may be affirmed by signs of care and love.

Finally, we may speak about the things of the heart. Because the heart tends to beat more rapidly when core values are threatened, the ancients designated the heart as the center of human life. Someone who was mean-spirited, nasty, or selfish was known as hard of heart, while the kindly or generous person was spoken of as gentle of heart. Today, of course, we realize that biologically the heart is simply a pump that pushes blood throughout the body. In spite of this, the heart, not as a bodily organ, but as the inner spirit of a person, retains the richness of meaning given to it by the ancients.

Our heart reflects the attitudes and beliefs that are the expressions of our values. Here again, just as the body may be handicapped or the mind distorted, so too can the heart, or better yet, our values, be perverted. We humans are good by nature and tend to seek what is good. But at the same time, we struggle against the limitations of our life and resist the limitations of others. We want our own way and are, at times, willing to harm others to get it. The heart, then, can be described as joyful, jolly, and light, or restless, ruthless, and cruel. In the continuing quest for self-identity, we need to ask what kind of heart do we have?

Needs/Tastes/Likes

According to Abraham Maslow, a renowned psychologist, several categories of needs are basic to all humans, and there appears to be a hierarchical ordering of these needs, beginning with biological necessities and concluding with transcendent needs.[2] In the first instance, we share common needs for food, shelter, clothing, etc., which support our biological life. For example, if we are deprived of proper nourishment we become ill and suffer the effects of malnutrition; without protection from the elements we develop colds or other ailments.

Following upon these elemental needs is a set of needs involving safety concerns. The need for security finds expression in the behavior of a child clinging to a parent's leg in the presence of a stranger, or, in later life, the purchase of insurance against material loss. When we feel threatened, we fight or we flee. In either case, we are responding in a way that satisfies our need for safety.

A third set of needs that we share with others is our need for belonging. Because we are social by nature, we need the affirmation and acceptance of others. Generally, we are most comfortable when we are with good friends who assure us that we are accepted. Thus, when biological, security, and belonging needs are met we have a solid foundation for further human development as adults.

Beyond these foundational needs comes the need for esteem. This involves both a healthy self-image and the knowledge that others respect us. Although youth is frequently characterized by feelings of inadequacy or overreliance upon grown-ups, the instinctual need for self-worth and the recognition of others drives us to accept responsibility for our own destiny. We learn to do our work well because we get a sense of satisfaction in completing particular tasks. We should bear in mind, however, that esteem needs are not satisfied by pseudoaccomplishments.[3] Esteem is always based upon achievements that are genuine. For example, cheating on an exam may help one get an A grade, but it can hardly be said to satisfy the need for true self-worth, since it is founded upon deception.

Finally, at the highest point of human life we find transcendent needs that are directed toward an understanding of life. It appears that as lower needs are satisfied, more spiritual, or higher, needs come into play. Indeed, since the beginning of recorded history people have offered explanations about the nature of the world, its purpose and meaning.

Much of religious and faith convictions are rooted in these explanations. As humans became more adept at understanding the world through the discovery of its underlying order and principles, a richer appreciation of creation's complexity became apparent. Consequently, a sense of awe is often associated with the satisfaction of the transcendent need for meaning and purpose.

In differentiating between needs and tastes we find that taste appears to be more culturally conditioned than instinctive. We all need to eat, but one person's hamburger may be another's sushi. Similarly, the clothing we wear and the houses we live in reflect current customs in various parts of the world. Particular tastes range throughout the hierarchy of needs. Within the orbit of safety needs, some people prefer to own a gun for their personal protection while others are willing to pay the taxes necessary to maintain quality police protection.

In the area of belonging and esteem needs, we note a variety of preferences from one person to the next. Some prefer one or a few close friends, while others enjoy the company of a larger group. Finally, at the highest level of needs the uniqueness of individual preference is most obvious. Each of us must find his or her own meaning to life. No one can live our life for us. If we understand that we are created one of a kind, we gradually cast off the yoke of conformity and live fully aware of our unique self-worth.

Set Patterns

In a painting or on a stage there is always a permanent horizon or backdrop. Similarly, the horizons of history and the immediacy of family have already established much of our identity. When and where we were born, the parents who nurtured us, our brothers, sisters, aunts, uncles, and other relatives are all a part of our family tree. The neighborhood where we lived, the schools we attended, the children with whom we played have indelibly stamped us with a richness of experiences that are a permanent part of our life.

Frequently enough, people fail to understand how influential the early years of life really are. Children who are raised by parents constantly on the move, either through job changes or transfers to different places, are affected by these dislocations. Children whose parents have divorced often suffer insecurities unknown to children from more stable homes. While it is true that as adults we make choices about our future and can adopt new attitudes toward life, nonetheless, much of our personal identity is determined by our genetic code and our early life experiences. These are set patterns in our life, and it is important to recognize them.

Equally important to recognize is the fact that many set patterns exist in the world around us and also determine our identity. For instance, we are products of the twentieth century. Those of us born in the United States were raised in a climate of freedom and individuality. The technological revolution of the past fifty years has changed the face of the economy, and the global conflict between free Western democratic nations and communist countries has determined much of the political climate. Today, our knowledge of computer science and genetic engineering is beginning to shape the world of the twenty-first century for our children. Just as part of our identity is determined by our family constellation, so, too, is our identity fixed by the age and era in which we live.

Sometimes people long for the good old days in the hope of returning to some past age when things seemed to be better. This yearning for the past, however, is as pointless as a yearning for an unlimited future. The make-believe of time machines in which people are transported to distant planets or to other ages is nothing more than a flight of fancy. While this may amuse us, it should not confuse us about the permanent realities of our world at the close of the twentieth century. A healthy identity accepts the past, acknowledges the present, and generates the future.

Also, in understanding who I am, it is important to know who I am not. The humorous caricature of the man standing with his hand tucked inside his jacket claiming to be Napoleon is a classic example of identity confusion.[4] While we do not often encounter such extreme cases, all of us at times tend to daydream our way out of present realities. In "The Secret Life of Walter Mitty," James Thurber introduces the reader to a man whose major preoccupation is imagining himself in different hero roles. Since heroes always win, Mitty, in his dreams, never encounters defeat.

The real world, on the other hand, is fraught with defeat and limitations. We may wish it otherwise, but in ordinary daily life, frustrations, failures, and fears are the lot of all people. Our ability to cope with these tensions helps us to achieve maturity. If we continually run from the physical, emotional, and intellectual limits of our identity, if we have not learned to accept ourselves, our individual histories, and the complexities of our age, we run the risk of living in complacent mediocrity or developing a messianic complex. Thus, to know who we are is to know who we are not.

Conscience

Another major aspect of our personality is our conscience. Conscience is rooted in our ability to make choices.

Although much of our behavior is based on habits, we all experience moments in life when, for no apparent reason, we choose to do things differently than before. This freedom of choice differentiates us from animals that operate on an instinctual level.

Helping and hurting others focuses the question of conscience. For example, we are all familiar with the cartoon depicting a pesky devil and a pious angel perched on the opposite shoulders of a person. They symbolize the choice between right and wrong. Listening to these inner voices represents the work of our conscience as it weighs the pros and cons of a given action. Although we are born to choose that which is good, at times we choose what appears good but is ultimately harmful to us. When we decide to speed because we are in a hurry, we may wind up in an accident. If we decide to party until 4 A.M., then cut classes and sleep until noon, we may get poor grades.

What appears as a good thing, i.e., party time, may in reality be a bad choice.

Conscience, the ability to choose right over wrong, good over bad, like all human characteristics, has a developmental pattern. Children understand right and wrong in terms of rewards and punishments; adolescents judge morality primarily within the context of group affirmation or rejection; adults, at least those who have reached a respectable level of maturity, are concerned with principles of conduct that reflect a universal quality. It is this adult level of conscience that we need to attain, even though occasionally we tend to slip back to the reward/ punishment or group approval levels of morality.

While Part III will deal with questions of values more thoroughly, it is important here to raise questions about the principles used in judging right and wrong. Is there something within us that can sense good and bad? Do we use the same set of rules in judging ourselves as we do in judging others? What are these rules? What role does law play in forming our judgments about right and wrong? Is there a higher law written in the hearts of all people? What is it? These and similar questions are aimed at establishing some sort of general criteria that may help us distinguish good from bad.

In ancient Greece, Socrates raised questions about good and bad, and we today are faced with the same task. We need to form our conscience so that it will contribute to our own well-being and the well-being of others. All too often we let bad habits or limited and short-term pleasures determine our behavior. If we are to grow in maturity and wisdom, we need to rethink our options and make choices that will benefit us and others.

We should also bear in mind that best intentions often go awry. New Year's resolutions are frequently forgotten by the end of January. The old adage "To err is human, to forgive divine" carries a wealth of wisdom. Part of the problem lies in the bad habits that we tend to accumulate over time. They may range from chewing our nails to talking incessantly. Bad habits, as we know, are difficult to break and can cause both personal and social problems.

Vision

Humans are achievers. Reviewing the centuries of recorded history, we witness an unrelenting story of human progress. Early peoples fashioned tools, tamed fire, and invented the wheel. As people began to gather in towns and cities, the rules of mathematics and the physical laws of nature were gradually discovered. Throughout the ages emperors and kings built empires and dynasties.

With the growth of society, science and literature, politics and economics, culture and religion took on sophistication and complexity. In ancient times, Archimedes jumped from a bathtub and cried "Eureka," when he discovered the relationship between mass and volume. At the dawn of the modern era, Isaac Newton intuited the gravitational attraction between bodies when he saw an apple fall from a tree. Both men struggled to unlock the mysteries of nature. We thus see that great political leaders, explorers, artists, prophets, and, indeed, all people to a greater or lesser degree, are driven to succeed. Although success has many definitions, it is one of the most common of human desires.

This disposition to succeed gives life direction and purpose. Without a goal or a vision we flounder around like fish out of water or like someone disoriented. In general terms, our educational system has built-in direction insofar as we must progressively master more knowledge before we can move on to further study. This system provides a societal mechanism that helps individuals apply their talents and abilities to particular tasks and to receive recognition when these tasks are successfully completed.

In addition, the pursuit of worthy goals provides meaning to life. If our goals are narrow and confined to self-serving ends, we will ultimately suffer disappointment and disillusionment at not having used our talents to reach worthwhile objectives. If we are true to ourselves, we will set ourselves tasks that will call forth the best of our abilities. If we are false with ourselves, we will squander our talents on superficial goals or distractedly jump helter-skelter from one goal to another. One important characteristic of a mature identity is the ability to set specific tasks for oneself and diligently pursue them.

Consequently, our tasks and goals in life are guided by our vision. Vision is that power of the mind to see beyond the present reality and to seek a better world. This ideal is most clearly seen in the vision of Jesus for the reign of God. He spoke of a new time when the blind would see, the lame walk, the deaf hear, and all people would have the Good News of God's love and forgiveness preached to them.[5] The Sermon on the Mount, which called on people to make peace and do justice, to forgive the enemy and care for the needy, offered a vision of human life that is beyond us, yet within our grasp.

It is the vision we carry in our heart that will determine life's goals and tasks. Jesus presents a vision of God's reign in sharp contrast to the reign of terror where violence, hatred, and prejudice are the orders of the day; or the reign of greed where selfishness, possessions, and power control our life; or the reign of indifference and apathy where concern for the hungry and homeless registers zero on our scale of priorities. A lofty vision, or a set of high ideals and values, should be at the core of our identity, lest we fail to dream of a new heaven and new earth.[6]

We began this chapter with the question "Who am I?" Hopefully, we have begun to appreciate how unique and special each of us is, and how much we have in common. Although our physical, intellectual, and emotional characteristics may vary greatly, nonetheless the common denominators of body, mind, and heart make us one species. There are divergent wants, needs, and tastes among the cultures and peoples of the world, yet all share a common desire for a decent home, sufficient food, and adequate health care. It follows that by acknowledging a sense of our own goodness and creating an identity based upon a personal vision of integrity and service, we will join the ranks of all those committed to a just and peaceful society.

Notes

1   William Shakespeare, *As You Like It*, II, vii.

2   Abraham H. Maslow, *Motivation and Personality* (New York: Harper & Row, 1970), 80–106.

3   Ibid., 91.

4   Erik Erikson, *Identity, Youth and Crisis* (New York: W. W. Norton, 1968), 94.

5   Matthew 11:4–6.

6   Revelation 21:1.

2

Planet Earth

To see the earth as it truly is, small and blue and beautiful in that eternal silence where it floats, is to see ourselves as riders on the earth together, brothers and sisters on that bright loveliness in the eternal cold—brothers and sisters who know now that they are truly one.

Archibald MacLeish[1]

Time/Space/Energy/Life

The Smithsonian Institution in Washington, D.C., houses a giant, twenty-foot ruler representing the length of time from the beginnings of the universe until the present era. Scientists estimate this span of time to be approximately twenty billion years. Back at the dawn of creation, which is often referred to as the "Big Bang," an enormous release of energy occurred, resulting in its partial transformation into matter. It is estimated that within the first three minutes of creation the gross composition of the universe took place.

Since that beginning when the evolutionary process began, the universe has expanded in all directions. About four-fifths of the way down this time-ruler, life began on earth. It started with single-celled animals and plants, then increased in complexity and multiplicity over millions and millions of years, until we see today a planet populated by thousands of species of animal life and millions of species of plants. The presence of human life dates back only a million years and represents less than one-fourth of an inch on the museum's twenty-foot time-ruler. The knowledge that we have gained in recent years about the enormity of time involved in this journey from creation to the present should evoke within us a sense of awe and wonder. Yet time is only one dimension; the size of our universe is equally spectacular.

Recently, *National Geographic* published a map of the universe that visually illustrated this immensity of time and space.[2] Starting with a small cylinder depicting our sun and the near stars, they telescoped the first cylinder into a larger one representing the Milky Way galaxy. Several successive telescopings occurred until one enormous cylinder symbolized the entire universe, about twenty billion light-years in size. In reality, when we look into space, we look back in time. The distant light we see from the stars was emitted years ago; it is only now reaching us. Consequently, to stand looking at the sky on a starlit night and ponder the apparent limitlessness of space is to place oneself within the mystery of creation. How did it begin? What or who caused it to start? Why?

When Neil Armstrong first set foot on the moon on July 20, 1969, millions of people throughout the world witnessed the event via the medium of television. Armstrong and his fellow astronauts were able to see our planet from a moon-perspective. They saw vast oceans, blue sky, billowing clouds, lush forests, endless mountain peaks, and wide rivers. What they were not able to see from space was a planet teeming with life. Animals and plants in abundant profusion literally cover the globe. From the boiling deserts of the Sahara to the frozen tundra of Siberia, life is present not only in the microscopic form of bacteria and plankton, but also in the shape of giant sequoias and huge humpback whales.

It follows that in the understanding of our personal life, we should be aware of this intimate connection to all life. We are obviously a part of the human family, but not so obviously part of a planetary ecological network. Present concerns, however, about the pollution of the oceans and the atmosphere have begun to awaken us to the connectedness of all life. Only when we are conscious of this global life system will we live in harmony with it. From a space-view, the natural boundaries that lead us to divide the earth into nation-states and other political entities appear insignificant. As our view of the planet takes on breadth, we are challenged to rethink the divisions that keep people apart.

Advent of the Human

The world changed radically when Darwin published *On the Origin of the Species by Means of Natural Selection* in 1859. Scientists discovered the linkage among the enormous variety of life forms and proposed a theory of evolutionary process within the plant and animal kingdoms. It became more and more apparent that human origins were linked to this chain of life.

Indeed, less than one hundred years later, Teilhard de Chardin, a renowned French paleontologist, published *The Phenomenon of Man*, which saw evolution as the primary determinant in the formation of the human species. Teilhard's vision of creation was a sweeping declaration that humans are the culmination and high point of a process begun billions of years ago with the explosion of the first atoms. It was as though all creation pointed toward the human. Inchoate matter, from the first moment of creation, was alive with psychic energy. Teilhard described himself as "a pilgrim of the future on the way back from a journey made entirely in the past."[3] For him life began in simplicity and has spiraled ever upward in complexity toward consciousness and love.

In order to appreciate the chronology of human development we might imagine the five-billion-year existence of our planet as divided into large volumes of five hundred pages each. Each page would represent one million years. The story of plants and animals would appear only in the final volume and humans would not emerge until the last few pages.[4] All of the previous volumes would be concerned with the gradual combining of atoms into ever larger composites of molecules. These continued to coalesce into ever more complex and centrally organized structures until megamolecules evolved into microorganisms. Life began!

However, it is crucial to remember that:

> In the world, nothing could ever burst forth as final across the different thresholds successively traversed by evolution . . . which has not already existed in an obscure and primordial way.[5]

Thus, we find a gradual, yet inexorable, movement toward higher, more complex forms of matter, which over eons resulted in a particular species of animal with an ability to reflect upon itself. For Teilhard, this is the true meaning of evolution. His vision of creation was divided into prelife, life, and thought, and offers us a grand overview of the evolution of all life with humans as the natural apex.

In focusing attention on humans as the highest form of creation, Teilhard accepted the similarities between them and other animals, but saw a quantum difference nonetheless.

> The being who is the object of his own reflection, in consequence of that very doubling back upon himself, becomes in a flash able to raise himself into a new sphere.[6]

The activities of the inner life (abstraction, logic, art, creativity, imagination) and our ability to universalize concepts like freedom, justice, truth, goodness, and love are at the heart of our humanness. Furthermore, human cerebral energy has had a cumulative effect throughout history, so that as a species we are making steady progress in our evolutionary development. From observation, of course, this progress is, at best, a mixed blessing. On the one hand, we have created exquisite works of art, built beautiful architectural monuments, and made enormous discoveries about the nature of the world. On the other hand, we have pillaged, plundered, and ravaged the earth and each other. Yet, Teilhard believed that in spite of our present destructive tendency, the future held much promise.

> If we want to understand the specific nature of man and derive his secret, we have no other method than to observe what reflection has already provided and what it announces ahead.[7]

What lay ahead for Teilhard on the evolutionary line of humanity was personalization. By this he meant the ever increasing tendency of human beings to love each other in personal and social ways. He believed that because consciousness had emerged from the space-time continuum of creation it was of a convergent nature, that is, it would fold back upon itself. Individuality was an aberration in the natural order; what will finally emerge is personality.[8]

He noted that the phenomenon that makes humans radically different from other animals is the power of reflection. It is not just a matter of knowing (higher forms of animals also possess a certain ability to know); it is "to know that one knows." This consciousness of the self was something entirely new in the evolutionary chain. It was the beginning of a very slow process whereby the human species gradually took charge of the world. Humans became responsible for the direction of planetary life and moved ever forward to new levels of consciousness. Teilhard postulated that the direction of this evolutionary process moved toward the personal. He foresaw a new state of consciousness drawing the human family together in love.

Ultimate Meaning

What does it all mean? If the universe had a beginning, what caused it? And why? The questions of purpose and meaning are central to our understanding of the universe, in spite of the current tendency (with its empirical data fixation) to shy away from the task of explaining ultimate causes and final effects. Many people fail to ask the important questions about life, much less seek the answers. They are like the guests at a medieval banquet who, having observed a beautiful bird fly in one window and out another, discuss the flight trajectory, wing span, color, and shape of the bird but never ask whence the bird came, or where it is going.

The following quotations offer one answer:

From the standpoint of present evidence, evaluational components such as meaning or purpose are not to be found in the universe as objective aspects of it.[9]

Man is the result of a purposeless and natural process that did not have him in mind. He was not planned.[10]

Taken together, these statements from a philosopher and a biologist represent one side of the argument concerning the meaning of the universe. In a nutshell, both men reject any form of knowledge that cannot be proven scientifically, i.e., by empirical quantitative evidence, and see no meaning to the universe other than that which humans arbitrarily assign it. During the twentieth century, many scientists came to reject all discussions of causes and questions about purpose and meaning for the world.

In the eighteenth century, the Deist philosophers imagined God as a master clock-maker. God wound up the world and it continued to run on its own. By the twentieth century, few in the scientific community bothered to ask about origins or destiny in any ultimate sense. Given the validity of scientific knowledge and methodology, is it not possible to seek truth in other ways? Can we not distinguish between quantity and quality? We do not ask to measure goodness or beauty or laughter or sorrow, yet they are just as real as the randomness of hydrogen atoms. Perhaps there is another path of knowledge alongside scientific reality.

To be human is to ask questions about meaning and purpose. This is not to suppose that complete clarity will occur, but without the questions even tentative answers are impossible. Indeed, even within the scientific community, especially among physicists and biologists who are on the cutting edge of discoveries about the basic constituents of matter and life, a new interest in purpose and meaning has evolved over the past decade. They have begun to realize that:

> . . . if we can know anything at all about the world, it is that everything is related to everything else. Truth cannot be compartmentalized. The implications of this are yet to be felt by a society that insists science and spirituality are separate disciplines to be pursued in separate facilities so that one may not contaminate the other.[11]

When we understand that asking "why" is as important as asking "what" and "how," we will have arrived at the point of integrating the truths of science with the truths of wisdom.

In searching for meaning, we are offered a choice between utter nonsense and a faith that invites us into the regions of the unknown. We can remain indifferent to creation and blind to the immensity of the universe, or we may drink in its wonders. Although nature surrounds us with grandeur, we may stand oblivious before its beauty. On the other hand, we may enter into the realm of mystery, as did Isaac Newton, who discovered the laws of gravity. "I seem to have been like a boy on the seashore diverting myself now and then in finding a smooth pebble or a prettier shell than ordinary while the great ocean of truth lay all undiscovered before me."[12] We begin to discover meaning when we trust that all reality is ultimately purposeful.

This, in the context of religious belief, is known as "seeing with the eyes of faith." In the tenth chapter of Mark's gospel Jesus asks a blind beggar what he most desires. The man responds, "My teacher, let me see again." "Go," Jesus replies, "your faith has made you well." Are we willing to believe that creation is alive with God's presence? Do we trust that our lives have purpose and meaning? To accept the mystery of life is not to throw up one's hands in despair and remain a skeptic. It is rather to admit humbly that we are all seekers of truth called to probe the riches of outer space, the wonders of created nature, and the hidden depths of the heart.

The Problem of Suffering

Judeo-Christian tradition teaches that the world is the creation of a loving and caring God who called the universe into existence as a gift to the human family. This human family is the height of God's creation. "So God created humankind in his image, in the image of God he created them; male and female he created them. . . . 'Be fruitful and multiply, and fill the earth and subdue it.'"[13] But if God is so good and gracious and wants humans to enjoy the fruits of the earth, why are there suffering and pain, why are there disease and sickness, evil and strife? Why did God create a world where children are born deformed and handicapped, where volcanic eruptions and killer typhoons wreak inestimable damage upon innocent people? The questions are as old as Job, the protagonist in an ancient Hebrew folktale, who queried God about his own failed condition. "Why did you bring me forth from the womb? Would that I had died before any eye had seen me."[14] The problems of evil and suffering have puzzled people continually since the advent of thought. Let us examine some of the common answers.

One answer suggests that suffering is the consequence of evil behavior. "As you sow, so shall you reap." This belief that people get what's coming to them has its most recent expression with victims of AIDS. Some people believe that venereal disease and AIDS are punishments for sexual wantonness. The root of this mentality lies within the human psyche. In our hearts we harbor a sense of justification, almost a glee, when someone supposedly gets what's coming to him or her. If the bully who terrorized a neighborhood suddenly "meets his match," we are delighted.

But this answer to the cause of suffering is inherently weak. In his widely acclaimed book, *When Bad Things Happen to Good People,* Rabbi Harold Kushner addresses the punishment solution.

> The idea that God gives people what they deserve, that our misdeeds cause our misfortunes, is a neat and attractive solution to the problem of evil at several levels, but it has a number of serious

limitations. As we have seen, it teaches people to blame themselves. It creates guilt even when there is no basis for guilt. It makes people hate God, even as it makes them hate themselves. And most disturbing of all, it does not even fit the facts.[15]

A second answer to the problem of suffering is couched in the garment of education. Suffering and pain are present in order to build character. Without trials and tribulations we would become indolent and flabby. Just as athletes exercise, pump iron, and eat health foods, so too must people endure suffering if they are to grow spiritually mature. Many people believe that suffering is part of God's plan and is for our own good. Again, this solution is hard to reconcile with our innate sense of fairness, much less with the goodness of a loving God. We are repelled by the notion that God would allow children to be deformed in order that others might learn submission to the will of God. It is nonsense to imagine a God who would send hurricanes to ravage the coastlines of Central America so that people would stand in awe of God's power. Thus, we find that neither punishment nor pedagogy provides a satisfactory answer to human suffering.

Reason and intelligence, however, help us identify much suffering in terms of basic human perversity. Hatred, pride, revenge, war, and attitudes of selfishness and apathy clearly account for much of the suffering we find in the world today. We do not have to look very far to see the suffering inflicted upon the weak by the strong, or on the poor by the rich. But reason and intelligence fail us when we face suffering not caused by human evil.

Only the eyes of faith offer a modicum of comprehension. In the Koran, Allah, speaking rhetorically, asks, "The heaven and the earth and all in between, thinkest thou I made them in jest?" Similarly in the Bible, Yahweh upbraids Job for questioning God's goodness. " 'Where were you when I laid the foundation of the earth?' "[16] Just as we are asked to trust that creation has meaning, so too are we called to believe that suffering has a purpose. If there is a force or power that gives fundamental meaning to the cosmic reality in which we find ourselves, perhaps we should humbly admit that we will never fully understand the source of this reality. We stand dumbstruck before the incomprehensible mystery we name God. There is no doubt that life is filled with suffering. Some say, "There is no God, chaos reigns"; others reply, "I don't understand, Lord, help me to believe."

Seekers of Truth

From the pinnacle of Mount Everest, the world's highest peak at 29,028 feet above sea level, one may view China, Tibet, Nepal, and India. But to ascend that mountain requires preparation, skill, and hard work. The same determination is required in understanding our world. This chapter has discussed the broad physical dimensions of time, space, energy, and life in order to situate us within the context of an evolving universal story. Learning to observe the world around us demands constant attention and a large amount of reflective thinking. Just as mountain climbing offers the reward of spectacular vistas, so also does the pursuit of learning reveal inestimable treasure.

Annie Dillard, an American naturalist, writes, "Seeing is of course very much a matter of verbalization. Unless I call my attention to what passes before my eyes, I simply won't see it."[17] Paying attention involves developing a taste for knowledge. Whenever we delve into the secrets of science, the histories of ancient civilizations, or the current events of our complex human adventure, we find ourselves gaining knowledge and wisdom. Dillard claims that this pursuit of learning adds depth and richness to our personal and social life.

We know instinctively that we cannot know everything. The wise person, however, also knows that the quest for knowledge generates its own rush. Little children badger their mothers with the incessant cry, "Why, Mommy?" Grown-ups cut the umbilical cord, yet retain the question. To question is to seek meaning; to seek meaning gives purpose and direction to one's life. Is that not the reason for the evolutionary thrust of human thought?

As we reject intellectual flabbiness and become truth-seekers, one area of study demands special attention. Self-knowledge is the core of the learning process. Although chapter 1 detailed some of the major characteristics of our identity, we simply wish to reiterate here that lifelong learning should include a continuing search to better understand our motives, intentions, anxieties, hopes, and vision. Peter Maurin, the intellectual and spiritual mentor of Dorothy Day, frequently referred to the need for "clarification of thought."[18] This includes probing the secrets of our heart and paying attention to the yearnings of others.

Our journey through life may resemble a cross-country auto trip. If the trip-plan includes a well-lubricated and dependable vehicle, clearly defined interim stops, road maps, tape deck, air-conditioner, and other refinements, the journey will likely be pleasant. Without preparations and supplies, however, we court disaster. Real life, of course, offers no guarantees. Illness, accidents, and a wide assortment of unforeseen events may transpire to impede our journey. The central task of life involves facing up to adversity.

This all-too-brief reflection on planet Earth and the origins and purpose of evolution were designed to lay the groundwork for the remainder of the text. Most learning involves incremental steps. This way we build to higher levels of sophistication and insight. If we see our planet, our universe, and this evolutionary process as the horizon for the context of human life, we will then be able to understand, if not resolve, many of the conditions and problems within society. History helps us understand the past; a sense of cosmic reality invites us to build the future.

Notes

1   Quoted in Oran W. Nicks, ed., *This Island Earth* (Washington, D.C.: Scientific and Technical Information Division, Office of Technology Utilization, National Aeronautics and Space Administration, 1970), 3.

2   "Universe/Sky Survey Map" *National Geographic* 163 (June 1983): 704a.

3   Hugh McElwain, *Introduction to Teilhard de Chardin* (Chicago: Angus Press, 1967), 11.

4   John F. Haught, *The Cosmic Adventure* (New York: Paulist Press, 1984), 23–24.

5   Teilhard de Chardin, *The Phenomenon of Man* (New York: Harper & Row, 1959), 71.

6   Ibid., 165.

7   Ibid., 190.

8   Ibid., 263.

9   E. D. Klemke, "Living Without Appeal," in *The Meaning of Life*, E. D. Klemke, ed. (New York: Oxford University Press, 1981), 169.

10   George Gaylord Simpson, *The Meaning of Evolution*, rev. ed. (New York: Bantam Books, 1971), 314–15.

11   John C. Polkingham, "Creation and the Structure of the Physical World," *Theology Today*, April 1987, 63.

12   Virginia Stem Owens, *And the Trees Clap Their Hands* (Grand Rapids, Mich.: Wm. Eerdmans Publishing, 1983), 89.

13   Genesis 1:27–28.

14   Job 10:18.

15   Harold A. Kushner, *When Bad Things Happen to Good People* (New York: Avon Books, 1981), 10.

16   Job 38:4.

17   Annie Dillard, *Pilgrim at Tinker Creek* (New York: Bantam Books, 1974), 32.

18   William D. Miller, *All Is Grace* (Garden City, N.Y.: Doubleday, 1987), 23.

3

People

In many ways the saying "know thyself" is not well said. It were more practical to "know other people."

Menander[1]

Variety

Imagine living in a world where everything was exactly the same. Everyone would eat the same food, drink the same refreshments, and think the same thoughts. Boring! Fortunately for our sanity and enjoyment, abundance and variety abound. Even in places where sameness seems the norm, we find a richness of life.

In the southwestern United States, birds of prey hover above the desert floor on the alert for animal life that populates a seemingly barren land. Beyond the Arctic Circle, wildlife roam the snow-covered ice while vast numbers of fish school beneath the surface. In more temperate climates the variety of life forms are so abundant that zoologists and botanists discover new species almost daily. Millions of living creatures, great and small, fill the earth.

At the summit of this cornucopia of life stands the human species. Similar to the variety within plants and animals, humans also come in an assortment of shapes and sizes. We are male and female, young and old, bushy-haired and bald. Within any given family we find look-alikes, but more often than not, physical resemblances are not pronounced. People also change their appearance. Mohawk Indians used to cut off their hair except for an inch-wide swath down the center of their heads. Boy George, the British rock entertainer, did much the same. As a consequence, fans imitated him, even though most people consider "mohawk" hairstyles extraordinary. In general, physical differences characterize humans far more frequently than they do other species.

When we look at the mix of personalities we are astounded. People are abrasive, jolly, energetic, lethargic, moody, humorous, sad, cheerful, pensive, boastful, humble, and all combinations of these under diverse circumstances. Not surprisingly, a bewildering array of theories tries to account for these behaviors. Perforce, one suspects that the last word has not been heard on personality types. Indeed, the more we learn about the behavior patterns of human beings, the more we come to realize how unique each of us truly is. In order to appreciate this uniqueness, let us meet a few companions on life's journey.

Ampero: Not far from the village of Cachipay (catch-e-pie) lives a young woman named Ampero. Cachipay is nestled on the slopes (altitude 5,000 feet) of the Andes Mountains, about fifty miles from Bogotá, Colombia. It is rich coffee country and Ampero's family cultivates a small coffee farm (about ten acres). She is an intelligent woman who smiles easily and is comfortable and friendly with people. While she is about the same age and of equal intelligence as most of the students reading this textbook, her chances for a college education are minimal. She works long hours on the family farm, cultivating the coffee plants and other crops. The climate in Cachipay is continually mild, which results in several harvests throughout the year. Ampero is happy in spite of what might appear to

North Americans as a severely limited life. Her joy seems to come from her openness to others, a sense of her own goodness, and a deep belief in God.

Reino: Reino lives in the town of Ozieri in the north central region of the island of Sardinia in the Tyrrhenian Sea several hundred miles west of Italy. The population of Ozieri is about ten thousand. "Our town is on the side of a hill overlooking a large plain. The sunsets are sensational. Most days after our *la passeggiata* we gather at the edge of town to watch the sun go down," says Reino. "What's *la passeggiata*? It's part of our identity. Your English word means 'stroll.' In the summertime from 7:00 to 10:00 P.M. we walk around the town telling stories and jokes and complaining a lot."

Reino attends the local technical institute, where he is studying to be a teacher. He says it's the only respectable job available. He has a girlfriend but they have no immediate plans for marriage. His big love affair at the moment is with "Julietta," a new model Alfa Romeo! Many North American students can identify with Reino, with the possible exception of his *la passeggiata*. Here again we see similarities and differences in customs and values.

Bobolanga: "My name is Bobolanga. I live near the village of Luhuo in the eastern part of the province of Xizang, China. This land is known to the Western world as Tibet. We are an ancient people proud of our heritage and customs. We like foreigners and we are a friendly people, but do not want them to change our ways of living.

"My family and I live in a mountainous region, where we care for our yak. The yak is an animal like your cow except it has two large horns and is quite woolly. The wool protects it from the winter cold and snow, which are quite fierce.

"We have over two hundred animals in our herd. They provide us with food, milk, and butter, and hides, which we make into tents for shelter. We had some visitors recently who stayed with us for two days. They seemed to cough a lot inside our tent (maybe the smoke from the yak dung fire caused the coughing), and their eyes watered when they drank *potang*, a mixture of yak butter, salt, and boiling tea. They were very polite, however, and did not complain.

"Next year I will take a bride. She is a member of another family in the village of Lhakang. Our families have agreed that we are a good match and should be very happy together. I have great love for my family and know that their decision is a good one."

Ampero, Reino, and Bobolanga represent real people living in cultures different from our own, yet sharing a common heritage on planet Earth. It is important that we develop an understanding of the multiplicity of peoples, customs, norms, and life-styles throughout the world in order that we may deepen our appreciation of other races and nations. Children in France, for example, drink wine with their meals from an early age; Eskimo youngsters, on the other hand, prefer a mixture of animal blood and water. Certain women in Africa frequently place bracelets around their necks in order to stretch them. For them it signifies beauty. Peruvian Indians who have lived for centuries in the highlands of the Andes Mountains "see" things much differently than the jungle island natives of Papua, New Guinea. The food they eat, the games they play, and the clothes they wear are dictated for the most part by their environment.

We should develop a capacity for accepting the diversity of people and rejoice in the endless plurality of humankind. Although local customs and the mores of particular cultures vary, we should learn to respect the ideas and practices of these peoples, and the attitudes, aspirations, hopes, and dreams of each person. Differences in culture and national ideology usually are traceable to economic circumstances, geographical location, climatic conditions, and the historical traditions of a group. Only when we maintain a high regard for the uniqueness of each individual can we expect to show sensitivity toward our common society.

Cultural Context

Archaeological digs provide a glimpse of the past and give us valuable information about the customs and habits of our ancestors. Our friends Ampero, Reino, and Bobolanga have roots not only in family and friends but also with the history, culture, and social life of their respective countries. It is important to understand the context of others' lives. Learning about their surroundings enriches our own life and gives us a more inclusive understanding of our neighbors.

As we contextualize life on our planet during the past fifty years, we see that several major revolutions have occurred. The rapid expansion of technology brought about by the harnessing of light energy and electricity led to the invention of everything from television and the computer to laser weapons and robots. A vast new global communications network has created worldwide enculturation patterns in which indigenous peoples have assimilated the customs and mores of other lands.

Politically speaking, in the United States, we have a two-party system of government with federal, state, and local components. Our electoral process is a winner-take-all contest with no apportionment for minority views. All losers must combine forces if they expect to defeat the incumbent in the next election. Conversely, many European countries operate within a parliamentary system that allows for minority representation. We thus find two different forms of democracy with the preponderance of people content with the system into which they were born. The same is true about the economic systems of capitalism and socialism. Many Americans support democratic capitalism, which believes that the less government the better, while our European neighbors espouse democratic socialism with strong government programs.

Naturally, we are speaking here in relative terms. That is to say, many capitalist features are part of European society, and the United States does, in fact, provide social and economic support for its citizens. Nonetheless, there is a real difference in the thinking of Americans and Europeans about politics and economics. Reino, a European youngster, comes from a different political and economic system than both Ampero and Bobolanga. They may share a common humanity, but the societies in which they live color their outlook on life.

This is nowhere more evident than in the area of religious beliefs. The current revival of Islamic fundamentalism, for example, has played a major role in the ongoing Middle East tensions. While the Arab-Israeli conflict attracts media attention, other currents of bitterness flow relentlessly throughout the area. Within the United States, religious pluralism exerts strong influence primarily because all churches are treated equally before the law and, in general, respect each others' convictions. When church groups, however, begin to take positions on controversial issues like abortion or capital punishment, conflicts inevitably arise and individuals can become quite intolerant of each other. In the final analysis, we need to understand that each individual person is shaped by his or her culture and the social context of his or her life. We are unique, yet communal. Learning to appreciate our own distinctiveness while developing an appreciation for the uniqueness of other peoples and cultures constitutes a major aspect of peace and justice education.

Inequalities

We are born naked into the world. We need constant care, protection, and love in our early years and, indeed, throughout our entire life. We will all die, some in life's prime, others in old age. Birth and death are equalizers, but the in-between years bespeak vast inequalities. In purely physical terms, inequalities may result from natural disasters affecting one place and not another, or from fundamental genetic flaws resulting in illness, diseases, and other functional disorders. A child born with a birth defect or a youngster seriously injured in a skiing accident will remain permanently disadvantaged in the normal pursuit of life. Their lives are still precious and valuable, yet they cannot participate fully in the events of everyday living.

In past ages it was common to blame God for the natural inequalities of life that people suffered. This was due to our ignorance about the causes of many afflictions. Today, medical science has revealed to us a world of genes and microbes that determine much of our fate. Similarly, with a better understanding of the atmospheric conditions of our planet, we are less likely to attribute hurricane and typhoon damage to God's hand. Consequently, we find that many inequalities stand outside the pale of human responsibility. Others do not.

But is it really the luck of the draw when black kids live in slums, get second-rate educations, and are drawn into drugs and crime at an early age? Was it fate that led to the annihilation of millions of Jews in death camps during World War II? When your best friend is run over by a drunken driver, is it just an accident? Much of the inequality that exists today among the human family can be traced to human responsibility or, more accurately, human irresponsibility. For example, a recent legal suit in the state of New Jersey cited the property tax system for funding public education as a major cause of inner-city children scoring lower than their suburban counterparts on statewide examinations. Property-tax assessments for education allow wealthier townships to far outspend urban districts where poor children live. In addition, much of the malnutrition, illiteracy, inadequate housing, joblessness, and limited health care for the needy can be attributed to the selfishness of the haves who refuse to share with the have-nots.

Exploitation of others, of course, has existed throughout history. In order to build the pyramids it is estimated that upwards of one million slaves were employed in the work.

The shameful treatment of Native Americans is well documented. Millions of them were killed or driven from their lands by the greed and racism of our ancestors. In short, examples abound where the powerful have dominated the weak.

The reasons for these humanly created inequalities are many. Excessive pride results in a desire to control the lives of others;

anger, revenge, and violence destroy communal peace; sexual and racial differences have been used to justify unfair relationships among people; greed and gluttony have also played major roles in creating situations of inequality. These evils, sadly enough, have not diminished with time. Sin, although in modern dress, remains a grim reality.

Acceptance/Symphony/Solidarity

We tend to think that everyone else thinks as we do; or that everyone else has the same experiences as we have; or that everyone else has a family background, education, talents, abilities, and opportunities similar to what we have. This tendency to identify others in terms of our own likes and dislikes presents us with a major problem. We universalize our life and project this vision onto others. A first step in accepting the variety of differences among people is to be aware that they think, judge, and act within the context of their particular cultures and experiences. We are guilty of a close-minded, exclusionary attitude if we believe or expect that others should think and act as we do.

The reasons, of course, for the differences among people are, for the most part, obvious. We know that the geography of the land affects the way people do things; the history and cultural patterns of parents and nationalities claim our allegiance; climate, family loyalties, economic conditions, and prevalent ideologies all impact on human behavior. When we add in the genetic package of physical characteristics that gives infinite variety to the human species, the environmental conditioning by structures of society, and the unique individuality of each person, it is not hard to understand our differences. The challenge is to remember and to accept each person's specialness.

If we try to imagine the human family, all the nations of the world, all the variety of cultures and people as one huge symphony orchestra playing "We Are the World,"[2] this image may help us understand each one's abilities to contribute to the whole. Are you a drummer or a cellist? Do you play the oboe or the bassoon? Each contributes in her or his own special way to the making of music. Difficulties arise only when we play out of tune, or don't play at all! The key to appreciating this role in the orchestration of human life is to understand that, although we are each gifted in unique and special ways, there should be a common symphony among all people.

There is an essential solidarity among the peoples of planet Earth. We share basic needs. We seek protection; we want to be accepted and loved by others; we wish to belong to one another by family, by friendship, and usually by identification with a nationality, a religion, or other organizations.

We have fraternities and sororities at our colleges, sport clubs in our cities, national and international institutions that claim our allegiance. In short, we want to belong, we desire solidarity.

In living out this solidarity, the age-old golden rule, "Do unto others as you would have them do unto you," is of supreme importance. We share a common humanity with its multiplicity and distinctiveness; we are called to avoid actions that will violate the basic rights of other humans. Avoidance of harm to others, however, is not enough. Plenty of room exists to reach out beyond ourselves and serve the needs of others. Indeed, we find that our life is enriched by an attitude of care and concern for others.

People are precious. The Bible says that we are made in the image and likeness of God. If that is true, then we should rejoice in our good fortune and appreciate the innate goodness of each human person. In the words of Dom Helder Camara: "Do not be indifferent to anyone's problems. Make the sufferings and humiliations of all of your brothers and sisters your own. Live on a global scale, or better still, take the whole universe."[3]

Notes

[1]   Burton Stevenson, ed., *The Home Book of Quotations* (New York: Dodd, Mead, 1958), 1970.

2 Michael Jackson and Lionel Ritchie, "We Are the World" (New York: Columbia Records, 1985).

3 Dom Helder Camara, *Pax Christi; 1985 Peace Calendar* (Erie, Penn.: Pax Christi, 1985).

4

Human Experience

Clarity and distinctiveness do not necessarily give us reality in its fundamental and concrete aspects. Perhaps we need symbols and myths to put us in touch with reality in its deeper dimensions.

John F. Haught[1]

Communication

Within the past century enormous strides have been made in understanding the psyche. One particularly rich vein of insight is embodied in the work of Eric Berne, a psychiatrist who developed a new method of psychoanalysis, which he called transactional analysis. It enabled people to understand themselves in familiar terms. Berne worked with combat veterans from World War II who experienced psychic disorders caused by the trauma of war. In his observations and conversations with these men, he found that in both body language and verbal communications distinct states of consciousness appeared with consistent regularity.[2]

He followed Sigmund Freud in accepting the Ego, Superego, and Id as the central components of the psyche, but in an attempt to avoid the long and difficult work of exploring the subconscious dimensions of the Superego and Id, he chose instead to concentrate his attention on the Ego. He believed that this conscious state of mind held many answers to human behavior. Berne believed that the outward manifestations of the self had an importance of their own.

According to Berne, the three major Ego states are Parent, Adult, and Child. All three are simultaneously present within us, but only one can operate at any given moment in time. These individual components of the Ego may be likened to a television set that can tune in many stations but only one at a time.

When the Parent is operating, it functions in typically parental ways. In Berne's terms, these are referred to as either the Nurturing Parent or the Critical Parent. "How are you feeling today?" "Can I help you?" and "Oh, I'm sorry to hear that," are common Nurturing Parent remarks. On the other hand, "Stop!" "I told you not to do that," and "You must . . . " characterize the Critical Parent. For the Critical Parent, demanding that someone stop their destructive behavior exhibits a well-developed sense of responsibility; harassing another is unkind. Conversely, for the Nurturing Parent, smothering someone with affection displays a distorted sense of caring; compassion toward the needy is noble.

The Adult ego state acts like a computer. Bereft of emotions, it operates mechanically as we go about the more mundane affairs of life. Solving a crossword puzzle, giving directions to a stranger, calculating a math problem, or sleeping, eating, hiking, and brushing one's teeth are generally done in the Adult ego state. These same actions, if performed with expressions of emotion, may be either Parent or Child actions. Normally, however, we associate work activity with the Adult. Staying in the Adult allows us to look at situations dispassionately.

Finally, the Child ego state, like the Parent, exhibits two predominant modalities. One part, the Natural Child, is carefree and happy; the other part, known as the Adapted Child, is worried, anxious to please, and docile. Berne saw major adaptation characteristics present in all of his patients and concluded that this behavior is learned during childhood and usually associated with disciplines imposed upon young children. He believed that the other dimension, the Natural Child, with its feelings of joy, exuberance, and fun, was meant to exercise a playful and creative role in the psyche.

Maturity, an unending process, consists in gently removing our masks so that others may see us as we truly are and in replacing our game behavior with authentic loving relationships. We can love and be loved in all our ego states, although the Natural Child is the most predisposed of all to give and receive love. The main point, however, of transactional analysis is its ability to understand human communications as the interaction of ego states. Since wholeness characterizes the well-developed personality, various aspects of that wholeness need illumination. Berne offered that.

Levels of Communication

Another contemporary contributor to the discussion on human communication is John Powell. In *Why Am I Afraid to Tell You Who I Am?* he posits four major levels of interaction.[3]

The first one consists of a polite recognition of others by way of such standard greetings as "hello," "O.K.," "thank you," and "good-bye." Here we experience human contact on a generally superficial level.

A higher level of communication combines recognition with information. In exchanging news, in talking about the latest events of one's life, in sharing data and facts, we are beyond the superficial, but are still only scratching the surface of true human interaction.

The third level of communication invites us into the realm of ideas. It is here that people share mutual concerns, listen to the stories of others, and exchange visions and dreams about the future. Conversation with friends concerning our ideas on right and wrong, joy and sadness, fear and hope enable us to tune in to the understanding that others have about life. It allows us, too, to share our stories.

Finally, Powell believes that the deepest level of communication lies in revealing our feelings. Many people conceal their emotions for fear of ridicule or rejection. According to Powell, sharing feelings illumines the true self.

In recalling the two dimensions of our Parent ego state, the nurturing and the critical, we can readily identify several emotions connected with these states. Feelings of concern, compassion, fondness, tenderness, responsibility, and care, summed up in the ideal of a mother/father affection for one's child, capture the emotional aspect of nurturing. Oppositely, feelings of judgment, bossiness, control, and domination reflect our critical nature. For example, when we feel protective of someone, we are experiencing emotions that emanate from the Parent.

Likewise, the Child displays a plethora of emotions. The Natural Child within us wants to show off, to mug and play, to romp and roll, to sing and dance. Thus, feelings of exhilaration, joy, laughter, merriment, and exuberance fill us with delight. We are most happy as natural children. However, just as the cowboy breaks the mustang and the farmer muzzles the ox, so also do parents socialize their children in the interest of family harmony and social order. What emerges is adapted behavior, with emotions of fear, conformity, and duty dominating this part of the personality.

All of this is to say that emotions are central to our identity. The more we are in touch with them, know their triggers and intensities, the more we will come to know ourselves. This level of communication, when we allow others to hear of our deepest feelings and the longings of the heart, forms the basis for true friendship.

It should be noted that feelings, in and of themselves, have no morality attached to them. They are morally neither good nor bad. Frequently, people assume that anger, defensiveness, and the like are wrong. Yet a moment's reflection reminds us of Jesus' anger with the money changers in the temple and our own justifiable indignation when we are used. Furthermore, feelings come and go with the wind. A smile from a friend can often raise us from depression just as a cutting remark can ruin our day. Although feelings do not constitute the totality of our personality, they are the key to our well-being and open the door to honest and loving relationships. The more we learn to communicate our feelings—the joyful, happy, and positive ones as well as the painful, sad, and negative ones—the more we will unfold our real self to others. One result of this honesty lies in the honesty of others toward us.

Thus far we have looked at ourself from the perspective of the Ego states and have stressed the importance of communicating all levels of our personality. In order to seek further clarification about our relationships with our fellow human beings we must now examine the barriers to honest and open dialogue.

Barriers to Experience

Watching a drama unfold in a television story, cheering the performance of athletics in a stadium, attending a concert, an opera, or a play, reading a novel or a magazine, or even thumbing through an album of old family photos are examples of human experience. Our openness to these experiences (whether in furthering our education, making new friends, or traveling abroad) can broaden the horizons of our world and allow us both the pleasure and the challenge of new opportunities. By observing the signs of nature, the changing of the seasons, the ebb and flow of the tides, the life-and-death cycle of plants and animals, we can resonate with the inevitable changes in our own life. In like manner a positive response to the varieties of people and cultures will result in a balanced approach toward all of life. Unfortunately, the demons of ignorance and indifference often interfere.

Too often in schools throughout the country, students take only courses in what they imagine will help them get jobs. Philosophy, literature, and history are "borrrrrring." Ignorance of history, unfortunately, leaves people in midair with little or no appreciation of their roots. For example, the diminishing turnout during elections indicates a lack of knowledge about participatory democracy and the political ideals that brought it into creation. Willful ignorance, a disposition to reject information or ideas that have no cash value, blocks the path toward including others in our world. Its demon brother, indifference, seals the path completely.

The dumping of hospital waste in the waters off the New Jersey beaches raised a storm of protest in the summer of 1988. Hardly anyone mentioned the twenty million people, predominantly women and children, who lived below the poverty line during that same summer. We are selective in our concerns. This is not meant to make light of the toxic waste issue, for, indeed, environmental pollution has increased exponentially over the past decade. The contrasting illustrations were meant simply to indicate our level of indifference to problems that do not impact us personally.

Because of this almost universal apathy toward the plight of the poor here and abroad, millions continue to suffer unnecessarily. Few people today can claim ignorance about the homeless in our land, the lack of medical care for needy children, and the continuing racism and militarism in our nation. Yet only a small minority have engaged these forces of evil. Unquestionably the major social ills of our time are complex and seemingly intractable. Nevertheless, we cannot remain indifferent to the suffering of others while we enjoy the fruits of the land. The barriers of ignorance and indifference must be removed from our minds and hearts in order to communicate the signs of love to which our humanity calls us.

The importance of this truth is evident if we look at the etymologies of the word *peace*. The Chinese understand the term to mean a state of equilibrium between the opposing principles, yin and yang (light and dark, good and evil, joy and sorrow); the ancient Greeks saw peace as a lull between battles, a time to replenish supplies and sharpen their swords; the *Pax Romana* of the Romans was an imposed peace dependent upon the docility of the conquered people; and, finally, the biblical meaning of *peace*, taken from the Hebrew word *shalom*, meant social harmony within the tribes of Israel. What these different meanings of *peace* point to is that unless we understand the language and culture of others we cannot develop true human communication. The study of language in the school systems of the United States, however, is woefully lacking.

Ignorance and indifference eviscerate human solidarity. As we have seen, the translation of a word from one language to another does not always convey its proper meaning. We need to learn the customs and languages of others if we wish to overcome the barriers of communication that arise from these differences.

Listening

The final sections of this chapter deal with the art of open and honest communication. If we aim to build a world of justice and peace, if we desire to open ourselves to the wide variety of neighbors who populate our planet, then we need to develop skills that will help us achieve these goals. At the top of this list stands the skill of listening, and the proper way to begin listening is by hearing the rhythms of our own minds and hearts.

Unfortunately, because of the hectic pace of life and our desire to get all the gusto, we bypass the only true port of call, the Self, where quiet reflection on our past, present, and future can give us the energy to move ahead on our voyage. Why do I boil over at a rebuke? What can I learn from my mistakes? Do I give myself free time to walk in the woods or along the seashore? Why am I fearful? How do I love myself? These, and many similar questions, offer us suggestions in understanding the ways of the heart. Keeping a diary or a journal often proves invaluable insofar as it provides a memory for the unfolding story of our life. Each day is unique: How well do I know the rhythms of my life?

Next, am I good soil for others? The biblical story of the sower and the seed can help us imagine the type of listeners we are.

> A sower went out to sow his seed; and as he sowed, some fell on the path and was trampled on, and the birds of the air ate it up. Some fell on the rock; and as it grew up, it withered for lack of moisture.

Some fell among thorns, and the thorns grew with it and choked it. Some fell into good soil, and when it grew, it produced a hundredfold.[4]

Although this Lukan narrative was intended to illustrate the receptiveness of people to the word of God, we may analogously apply the parable to our ability and willingness to listen to others. If I turn a deaf ear, if I remain indifferent, if I show minimal concern about the needs and hopes of my family members, schoolmates, and others, then I am rocky and thorn-laden soil. On the other hand, the level of my receptivity, my concern and care for others will indicate the quality of rich, fertile soil that I have cultivated in my desire to foster better communication. Oftentimes, the way we allow God's word to penetrate the soil of our heart will condition our sensitivity to others and will be a reflection of our self-love (not self-centeredness). Consequently, the skills for listening include myself, others, and God. By tuning in to the uniqueness of each of these realities, we more fully sense the vibrations of all life.

Furthermore, the adage "One picture is worth a thousand words" suggests the importance of signs and symbols in the process of human communication. We know from an esthetic viewpoint how deeply we can be moved by works of art in painting, sculpture, literature, theater, and film. Similarly, to look into the face of another person or to observe the signals that people convey with their bodies provides us with another avenue of listening. It is both a matter of the ear to hear and the eye to see into the heart of the other.

The roommate or friend who can intuit a change of mood or perceive a shift in attitude will most likely respond with concern if a relationship needs healing. Some married couples write letters to each other daily in order to communicate their thoughts and feelings. When these letters are exchanged they are read twice, once for the head and once for the heart. This is to avoid the possibility of knowing something intellectually without having sensed the inner reality. Everyone exhibits the common external appearances of size, shape, race, and gender, but beneath the surface lies the individually unique mystery of hopes, dreams, anxieties, and fears. What an awesome revelation, to truly know another.

Dialogue

For authentic honest communication to happen, dialogue must occur. When one or the other party in a discussion refuses to hear the "truth" that another brings, i.e., another point of view, the drawbridge goes up and the conversation ends. In order to keep the lines of communication open we need to divest ourselves of the idea that our way is the only way, our truth is the only truth.

Killings have occurred by the millions because people have clashed over what they saw as truth. Naturally, dialogue includes compromise and a willingness to respect the other person even in disagreement. Americans are relatively tolerant of others due to the immigrant nature of our society. Yet in spite of this surface tolerance, the evils of racism, discrimination, and prejudice lurk beneath the surface. A recent wave of attacks upon blacks at several college campuses and the continuing police brutality in some inner cities belies the apparent acceptance of minorities in our country. Dialogue involves an effort not only to find common ground with another person, but, perhaps more importantly, to seek accommodation among the various ethnic groups within society. In spite of barriers that seem insurmountable, racial harmony must continue to be sought through honest and open dialogue.

What is the key element in dialogue? Is there a specific characteristic that indicates sincere dialogue is taking place? While it may be laboring the obvious, it should nevertheless be repeated that good communication cannot happen without a good measure of trust. When we care for and love someone, the trust level is high; when we are suspicious or feel hurt or neglected, trust gives way to hostility and anger. Just as the blood carries oxygen and other nutrients throughout the body in order to nourish it, so too does the amount of trust determine the health of our relationships.

Craftiness, dishonesty, and malice attack the social fabric in much the same way that a cut or wound diverts bodily nourishment. That is to say, if we go through life suspecting the worst of others, if we are constantly thinking of ways to explain and defend ourselves, if we attack the motives of others and blame them for a lack of trust, we had better try pointing the finger in our own direction and begin to assume our share of the responsibility for effective communication.

In order to envision a dialogue among nations, we find that trust is also necessary at the global level. We must learn to distinguish between problems and people. The former need solutions, the latter need love. Granted, at times, humans are their own worst enemies, and even families suffer internal divisions. Yet if we are convinced that God created us for friendship and harmony, then black, white, and yellow people; Russians, Peruvians, and Americans; Jews, Christians, and Muslims; conservatives, moderates, and liberals—indeed, all people—are capable of peace. The importance of accepting and celebrating the tonalities, harmonies, and variations of themes within the human symphony stands as the paramount concern of the third millennium. Honest and caring communications can unlock the door for world peace.

Notes

1   John F. Haught, *The Cosmic Adventure* (New York: Paulist Press, 1984), 6.

2   Eric Berne, *A Layman's Guide to Psychiatry and Psychoanalysis* (New York: Simon & Schuster, 1968).

3   John Powell, S.J., *Why Am I Afraid to Tell You Who I Am?* (Niles, Ill.: Argus Communications, 1969).

4   Luke 8:5–8.

5

Global Cultures

But the cultures of different peoples do affect each other: in the world of the future it looks as if every part of the world would affect every other part.

T. S. Eliot[1]

Many Cultures

The sports played, the food eaten, the pets loved, the holidays celebrated, the myths cherished, and the general attitudes held reflect the culture of a given people. Culture includes customs and norms in education, religion, politics, art, and commerce as well as in the social organization of work, play, and rest. People the world over engage in these activities, but they practice them in bewildering variety.

For example, the following is a list of the favorite foods of people in other lands: Eskimos, blubber; Bataks tribe of Sumatra, dog; Caribbean natives, sea turtle; the French, frog legs and snails; Philippine and Brazilian natives, monkey; the Dutch, raw herring; Polynesian natives, roast pig. In addition, sports and games vary greatly. Indians play pachisi, a dice game; yote, a stone-and-stick game, is played in West Africa;

bocci was invented by the Romans and remains popular among Italians; cockfighting is the national pastime in Indonesia; billoquet is an Eskimo game of skill; shogi, a form of chess, is played in Japan; cards, dice, and other games of chance are popular the world over. Naturally enough, given personal choice, variety also appears within each of the ethnic groups mentioned above.

Other cultural patterns are expressed through rites and rituals. For instance, ceremonies at the Tomb of the Unknown Soldier honor the dead of past wars; playing of the national anthem at sports events celebrates patriotism; praying at meals ritualizes our gratitude to God. Also, celebrating Bastille Day in France, parading elephants in India, and honoring Saint Patrick in Ireland, Saint Lucy in Sweden, Saint Nicholas in Holland, and Saint Joseph in Italy symbolize the collective memory of different countries. In the United States, we observe Independence Day, Labor Day, Thanksgiving, and Memorial Day as part of our tradition. Religious festivals such as Hanukkah and Yom Kippur for Jews, Christmas and Easter for Christians, Kanto Matsuri for Japanese, and pilgrimages to Mecca for Muslims represent different cultural expressions of belief in God and a variety of spiritualities among people of the world.

In addition, art, literature, dance, music, and filmmaking manifest the enduring legacy of a culture. These particular contributions identify and unite people with a cohesive set of ethnic characteristics. This variety presents both a problem and a challenge. How can we celebrate our distinctive cultural heritage, while simultaneously honoring the customs and traditions of other people?

One way of appreciating the diversity of cultures involves a respect for the past. Most of us are aware of the unique contributions made to Western civilization by the ancient societies of the Greeks and Romans. We also have learned that the Middle Ages produced a unique blend of art and faith. Not so well known, however, are the contributions of other ancient civilizations. Recent archaeological discoveries have put us more in touch with the Mayan and Aztec civilizations of Central America and the Incas of Peru. We are gradually learning more about the magnificent cultures of India, China, and Japan, as well as the lesser known yet equally important human advances in Africa. The study of our own past in the United States reveals a melting pot of traditions and customs from the four corners of the globe. This leads to the central issue for this chapter.

The main purpose here is to celebrate the uniqueness and singularity of each person and respect the particularity and specialness of different cultures. We have already indicated how our identity receives its primary definition from our family and our neighborhood. It is important that we also recognize the influence of our national identity and how its cultural characteristics further define us.

Beneath the Surface

The aforementioned examples of cultural practices do not afford much more than a nodding acquaintance with some external and surface characteristics. We need to look more deeply at the character and vision of a people if we are to understand them. The general attitudes and psyche of a society usually express a long history of ingrained habits. Nations live with cultural myths that are as real for them as the cycles of nature.

The British and French, for example, although living in democratic societies, have a rich sense of aristocracy. The royalty of England still receive large sums of money to look and act regal, while the French continue to honor the memory of their monarchical past because it was a time of great splendor and power for them. This cultural proclivity toward the nobility of past ages reflects a nostalgic attachment to the dominant history of both nations.

A recent study of American culture analyzed the attitude of individualism running through much of our history.[2] In spite of strong connections to the motherland, the early colonists developed a new identity around the virtues of self-reliance and independence. The Puritan settlers were, for the most part, breaking away from their European ties. By 1776, our nation's founders had organized the first major revolution from the medieval political order of monarchical Europe. Occurring thirteen years prior to the French Revolution, it paved the way for Western democracy.

As this young nation expanded westward, the strain of individualism grew stronger. Recent scholarship suggests that the frontier experience of conquering new land and subjugating the natives solidified the myth of the rugged individual and even provided the groundwork for the ideology of capitalism and social Darwinism.[3] Stories of the Wild West abound with legends about both good and bad people—Jesse James, Geronimo, Billy the Kid, General Custer, etc. For the most part they stood alone (at least that is the myth) and achieved success or notoriety as individuals. Tonto notwithstanding, the Lone Ranger is the classic example.

Russian history, on the other hand, shows little evidence of expansionism, but a great fear of invasion. The people of Russia have for centuries lived under the rule of powerful kings and despotic lords. The communist revolution, which was supposed to end the oppression, simply replaced the tyranny of a ruler with the tyranny of the state. The Communist party became the apparatus for continued control of the population. Despite recent upheavals, the average Soviet citizen has little sense of free expression or a democratic process as we know it. There is a long tradition of central control by the government.

Conversely, Japan has a long history of customs and habits that gives great weight to the virtues of patience and endurance. Proper forms of respect are also a natural part of their culture. While the Japanese have succeeded in rebuilding a war-torn country since World War II, and have developed the technology and business acumen of an industrial nation, the habits and attitudes that they most cherish as a people have generally remained intact. Businesses, small and large, are run with strong cooperative bonds between workers and managers. Employment is usually for life, and courtesy is always the norm. Other Asian people display a deep spirituality, especially among the Buddhist and Hindu populations of Southeast Asia and the Indian subcontinent.

Thus far we have examined several customs and characteristics of today's societies, and found that these cultural manifestations have a considerable history. But the world is changing rapidly and people are being drawn together as never before. The rapid rise of mass transportation, jet travel, satellite communications, the eye of the television cameras, and the technological revolution in science and industry have created upheavals in the societies of the world. We are aware of the universality of rock music and Western dress, the ubiquity of Coca-Cola and McDonald's, and the transnational reach of global corporations.

Some societies have accepted these changes; others have not. As we move toward the twenty-first century, each society must ask itself to what extent it should reexamine its culture and adapt new forms. We Americans should ask the same question. If the trend is toward global solidarity, how open are we to learning from other cultures? Are we willing to assimilate the values of other people? What are the best cultural values that we have to offer? These and similar questions lead now to a look at our worst and our best.

Cultural Values

Looking good is one of the finer pleasures in life. People have come around to openly believing that looking good is okay.

Bill Blass

Looking good creates an initial seduction of whatever you're after.

Francis Gill (model agent)

The difference between looking good today and being attractive in other times is that more people today think that they can buy good looks.

Perry Ellis (fashion designer)[4]

Let us pause for a moment on this journey through culture to look at the values dealing with outward appearances. The examples used above about looking good illustrate the point quite well, since many people value good looks. "Has it occurred to you that looking good is running our lives more than ever?" asks Kimberly DuRoss, the Henry Ford heiress.[5] Ad agencies, clothiers, decorators, all those in the business of image making foster a climate whereby one must appear at one's best.

But what about the person who's blind or ill or diseased? They clearly are not at their best, according to society's standards. Should they be considered inferior because of their appearance? This raises further questions about who sets the standards for looking good. Do poor people, migrant farm workers, the elderly, or the emotionally disturbed have any say in what constitutes looking good? We shall explore these questions further in the third part of this text. Suffice to say here that we would like to establish cultural value standards based not on one's ability to look good, but on the quality of character and openness to other people that one maintains.

If we assume that love of self is the first and most important place to find an answer to the question "Who's included in my world?" it follows that love of neighbor is the logical extension of that answer. The difficulty, however, rests with translating this theoretical solution into concrete terms. One way of doing that is to say that whatever supports the advancement and welfare of the global community deserves attention, while those things that undermine and destroy that community merit rejection.

In the first instance, global community means a bonding in fellowship with all the nations, races, and religions of the world. It is not an attempt to achieve a naive amorphous likeness for all people; it relies, rather, on an appreciation and respect for the universal individuality of people from many nations, races, and faith convictions.

In the Wild West of the pioneers and wagon trains, the slogan "The only good Indian is a dead one" epitomized the general attitude of the settlers toward the Native Americans.

That chapter in U.S. history has left an indelible blot of criminality on our past. So, too, has our interference in the internal affairs of many countries during the past century. Needless to say, other political and military forces have wreaked havoc on the lives and the economies of other nations. Are we to assume that this behavior is acceptable because it is so commonplace? Do the militarily powerful countries have a right to dictate policy to those who are weaker? Just as we have established that whatever supports global community based on human rights helps the cause of freedom and liberty, it is clear that policies and programs aimed at exploiting others must be eschewed.

In the United States, attitudes toward wealth, military superiority, and sexual freedom have left us with a rich and famous few hoarding their fortunes, to the detriment of homeless and ragged millions eating leftovers; a bloated military-industrial establishment that is resisting conversion to a post–Cold War economy; and a plague of pornography and exploitation; abortion; broken homes; and unmarried mothers; not to mention the painful reality of AIDS and other diseases. These illustrations attempt to alert the reader to the many false cultural values that undermine personal dignity and human solidarity.

Learning from Others

American identity has been forged by the confluence of many races and nations. To be American is to be a part of the great experiment of democratization wherein Irish, Italian, German, Swiss, Swedes, Poles, Jews, Catholics, Protestants, blacks, whites, browns, and yellows cast their lot together with the hope of finding freedom from want and equal justice for all. Waves of immigrants in the nineteenth and twentieth centuries sought relief from the famines and hardships of the "old country." All of their customs, social mores, religious practices, folk music, ethnic dress and food, and family traditions continue to simmer in the melting pot of America. Insofar as our past was created from a multitude of nations, it is imperative that we continue to respect the cultural contributions of these societies.

When America's business community travels to Japan to observe firsthand the employment practices of their counterparts, and when corporate executives and union leaders read essays, articles, and textbooks on Japanese management techniques, you know something revolutionary is happening. The past half-dozen years have seen a new interest on the part of American managers to reassess their policies and practices vis-à-vis their workers. Japanese seem to favor worker/manager harmony rather than the more American-style labor/management confrontation.

This cultural trait of dividedness was illustrated in the early 1950s by David Riesman when he characterized us as a "lonely crowd," people living side by side, but hardly knowing—or caring to know—about each other's hopes, dreams, or aspirations.[6] The Japanese people are only one of many societies where cooperation is more valued than competition; where togetherness is more important than "my space"; where family structure and ordinary gestures of civility count for more than "doing your own thing."

This is not to say that we as a nation are bereft of all forms of cooperation. If we use the term loosely we could well say that the chitchat between the Park Avenue doorman and the wealthy hotel guest is a form of cooperation. In fact, there are thousands of civic, social, and religious organizations throughout the land where many levels of cooperation appear to exist. Yet it is well known that the role of the individual hero, the stand-up guy, the take-charge person, is a more highly valued image in our nation than in other societies. Dirty Harry challenging the bad guy to "make my day" resonates deeply within the American psyche. Perhaps it is time for us to stop and listen to the stories from other cultures.

Another lesson we might learn as we survey the cultures of the world is to respect the history, tradition, and customs of others and to develop more sensitivity to their present historical moment. This is especially true for Third World countries. Many of these nations are only beginning to emerge from centuries of colonial oppression and other forms of domination and exploitation. By including Third World peoples in our world and learning how our life-style often affects them we may begin to develop a new consciousness about the ill effects of valuing competition over compassion.

In addition to replacing fierce competition with creative cooperation and developing a better appreciation and acceptance of the history of other peoples and cultures, we should also attend to our global spiritual heritage. Zen masters, Christian mystics, and humanist monks have contributed greatly to the reflective and meditative part of our humanity. We ignore the spiritual dimension of life at our peril.

Not only do we get caught up in the rat race of work–eat–sleep–work, but we have little inner strength to count on in time of crisis and stress. It is instructive that Japan went into a period of prolonged mourning upon the recent death of Emperor Hirohito and delayed his funeral for several months in order that his memory would not fade too quickly and people might ponder their own mortality. As a nation, we Americans should learn the lessons of patience and contemplation by assimilating the inner spiritual dynamic of both Eastern and Western mysticism.

Sharing Our Best

Abraham Lincoln, in his Gettysburg Address, reaffirmed the principles of equality and freedom as the foundation of American democracy.

> Fourscore and seven years ago our forefathers brought forth on this continent, a new nation, conceived in Liberty, and dedicated to the proposition that all men are created equal.

It is a sad fact of life in our world that few democracies exist. Communist nations are state-controlled, with only limited liberty allowed their people. Many noncommunist countries are controlled by military dictators who in reality are the puppets of a wealthy elite class. We have our failings as a nation, but we also act as a beacon of liberty for millions who yearn to be free.

The United States is the oldest democracy in the world. In our Constitution we have established a system of laws that sets the boundaries and barriers for government. The first ten amendments to the Constitution, the Bill of Rights, guarantee freedom and equality to all citizens. The practice of these rights, of course, has had a checkered history. The Civil War was fought in part to free people from slavery. Women were not accorded voting rights until 1920, and it took the civil rights legislation of the 1960s to remove arbitrary restrictions on the freedom of blacks and other minorities. Notwithstanding the abuses and violations of rights that have marked our history during the past two hundred years, we as Americans can rightly be proud of our heritage of freedom and democracy.

We are also a people of boundless energy and creative spirit. Yankee ingenuity and can-do mentality have been a part of our history since the early colonists founded scores of small towns and villages and pushed west to explore this vast continent. The spirit of Benjamin Franklin—inventor, entrepreneur, statesman—is manifest even today in the technological advances, the productivity, and the standard of living experienced by many Americans.

It is this kind of energy that John F. Kennedy aroused during his presidency. His Alliance for Progress with Latin American countries, his founding of the Peace Corps, and the commitment to explore space are lasting memorials to a man whose vision imagined "new frontiers." Unfortunately, American energy and optimism have led occasionally to bad judgment. The quagmire of Vietnam was due in no small part to a belief in our invincibility as a military power. Nevertheless, our knack of sizing up a problem and tackling it with zest and perseverance can be used both at home and abroad to create a better world.

Today's imperative is to cultivate an awareness of our own cultural traditions, especially those rooted in our sense of equality and liberty. At the same time, we need to learn from people with different histories and cultural values. Will we use our energy and the traditions of freedom and democracy to support movements of liberation, or will our tendencies toward individualism and concern for "things" lead us toward isolation and aloneness? One might hope that as our understanding of peace and justice education increases, we may begin to view more critically our own personal life-style as well as the social culture in which we live. Much in our culture addresses the best within the human heart, and much does not. Developing a discerning spirit is crucial for our education.

Notes

1   T. S. Eliot, *Notes Toward the Definition of Culture* (New York: Harcourt, Brace, 1949), 124.

2   Robert Bellah, Richard Madsen, William M. Sullivan, Ann Swidler, and Steven M. Tipton, *Habits of the Heart* (New York: Harper & Row, 1985), 142–66.

3   Richard Slotkin, *Fatal Environment* (New York: Atheneum, 1987).

4   John Duka, "Looking Good," *New York Times*, "Fashion of the Times" section, Summer 1987.

5   Ibid.

6   David Riesman, *The Lonely Crowd: A Study of the Changing American Character* (New Haven: Yale University Press, 1950).

6

Religions

Render to Caesar the things that are Caesar's, and to God the
things that are God's.

Matthew 22:21[1]

Rationale

Thus far in Part I we have examined our personal and social
identity. We now wish to explore the various expressions of
religion to which people are drawn the world over, to analyze
the general meaning of religion, and to critique its impact
upon the human family. These three tasks are intended to
help the student contextualize religion within the framework
of the overriding question, "Who's included in my world?" The
fact that millions of people throughout the world identify
themselves with one or another of the major religions is sufficient reason to acknowledge the importance of those religions
and to understand them as the embodiment of people's search
for meaning.

Sacred and Profane

Throughout much of human history, dualism and dichotomies have been used to explain the nature of things. Good/bad, true/false, liberal/conservative, and dozens of similar dualities give us a sense of the opposites at play in our world. Although this dualist view of life frequently distorts the integrity and unity of all being, it nonetheless helps to clarify certain distinct realms of reality. Thus, we may distinguish between the sacred and the profane.[2]

Temples, monasteries, synagogues, churches, gentle woods, and peaceful gardens represent a desire to find sacred space. In seeking such space, humans are answering a call to go beyond the immediacy of their everyday life in order to get in touch with the inner desires of the heart and discover the source of life. The rites and rituals, the myths, stories, and legends, the doctrines and the symbols of religion offer a ray of hope in understanding the reality we identify as God.

The real God, whom Karl Rahner, an eminent German theologian, described as "incomprehensible mystery," leaves us awestruck when we consider the duration and complexity of creation. In our grasp of the sacred, therefore, we are invited to acknowledge that

> it is God's life that flows through the arteries of the world, that seeps in the capillaries enclosing each quark, that sustains being at every moment. For what life is there apart from the Creator's?[3]

Conversely, the profane dimension of life encompasses a broad range of activities that include working, playing, eating, and sleeping; and indeed all those human activities that constitute the soil in which the sacred may grow. It is of crucial importance that in acknowledging and honoring the presence of the sacred we do not disparage the profane. If we believe that the human family represents the fullest expression of creation, then we must exult in our body/spirit humanity.[4]

Throughout history the sacred and the profane have mixed inextricably under the rubric of religion. The pharaohs were considered gods; Caesar was venerated; Aztec priests ruled in Mexico; and the medieval courts often were controlled by monks and prelates. Social and cultural life demanded rituals and ceremonies filled with religious significance. Morality plays, church architecture, and Christian art pervaded the Middle Ages, while enormous temples to Buddha and Hindu gods blanketed the Asian continent. All the great religions wove meaning into the cycle of birth and death, fasting and feasting, and human sexuality.

Each of the religions examined below have vast histories dating back thousands of years. The temples of Ellyora near Bombay, India, were hewn from the mountainside by the followers of Buddha and of Muhammad. They stand alongside previously built shrines dedicated to Brahma, Vishnu, and Shiva (the three faces of God, Hindus believe). Their construction spans two thousand years. The tomb of Saint Peter in Rome dates from the first century, and the Wailing Wall in Jerusalem predates Christianity. All of this is to say that religion is both ancient and diverse. Subdivisions abound amidst a profusion of theological interpretations. Religion has greatly influenced history and continues to impact modern society. Whatever one's personal religious convictions, there is a need to understand and remain sensitive to the beliefs and faith-values of other people and cultures. What follows are sketches of the major religions of the world.

Major Religions

Judaism

The first historical moment in Jewish history was recorded in the book of the Exodus (about 1300 B.C.). The Hebrew people, descendants of Abraham and Sarah, were enslaved by the Egyptians. According to the biblical account, God sent Moses to order the Pharaoh, "Let my people go." After much conflict they escaped from Egypt, and Yahweh (the Hebrew deity) entrusted Moses with the Tablets of the Commandments. These laws, if obeyed, were meant to ensure peace for God's Chosen People. During the next three hundred years, the Hebrews gained ascendency in the land of Palestine and finally established a kingdom under the consecutive leadership of Samuel, Saul, David, and Solomon. It soon disintegrated because of internal conflicts. Military domination by the Assyrians and Babylonians followed. Throughout this period of Jewish history, prophets arose from time to time to condemn the false gods of power and greed and call the people back to the worship of the one true God, Yahweh. The Babylonian Captivity (597–38 B.C.), commonly known as the Exile, represents a period of great mourning for the Jews. Finally, in the year A.D. 70 the Romans destroyed the Temple in Jerusalem. The Jews have been dispersed throughout the world for the past two millennia. With the founding of the State of Israel in 1948, a new homeland was established.

The Torah (Law) contains the Commandments, a history of the Jews, and the writings of the prophets. It forms the essential teachings of Judaism. In addition, the Talmud, interpretations of the Torah, provides extensive commentary on daily living. Although a sizable portion of Jews today identify themselves solely on the basis of nationality and peoplehood, the Orthodox, Conservative, and Reform theological schools represent the major constituencies upholding the religious traditions. Finally, the wholesale killing of millions of Jews in the 1930s and early 1940s (the Holocaust) has had an enormous impact on their faith tradition and their identity as a people.

Christianity

Christianity had its beginning in the life, death, and resurrection of Jesus, a Palestinian Jew, who preached repentance from sin and love of God and neighbor as essential for salvation. His early disciples, while mainly Jewish people, broke with their past by proclaiming God's salvation to all people. In spite of suffering persecution for their way of life, the early Christians gradually grew in numbers and Christianity became the state religion of the Roman Empire by the fourth century. For the next several centuries, the Roman Catholic Church dominated Europe while the Greek Orthodox Church held sway in the Near East. From earliest times, codifications of beliefs were formulated by the church authorities in order to avoid doctrinal errors.

Historically, this practice of authoritative teaching and the use of political power to enforce belief resulted in severe conflicts among Christian believers through the centuries. Martin Luther and other sixteenth-century reformers broke with Rome over the issues of ecclesiastical reforms, hierarchical control, and the theological understanding of the Bible. The major Christian groupings today include Orthodox, Roman Catholic, and various Protestant denominations, such as Lutheran, Episcopalian, Presbyterian, Methodist, and Baptist.

All Christians believe that the Bible is the Word of God and that Jesus is God's Son. They believe that Jesus and his Spirit are united with the Father in a Triune Oneness. Most adherents celebrate the Lord's Supper, a Passover memorial meal that Jesus shared with his disciples before he died. It is the central act of Christian worship. Christian tradition has also recognized saints, women and men of past ages who lived exemplary lives.

Within the past half-century an ecumenical movement toward reunion has flourished among the Christian churches. Most are now members of a World Council. The Roman Catholic Church has also undergone a remarkable renewal in its worship, theology, and pastoral practices since the Second Vatican Council of the 1960s.

Hinduism

Dating from prehistoric times, Hinduism is considered to be the oldest religion in the world. Since it contains no particular creedal affirmations, it is better understood as a philosophy of life. Notwithstanding its lack of doctrine, it does acknowledge a source and center of creation (Brahman), has sacred writings (Vedas) with appropriate commentaries (Upanishads), and divides adherents into a system of castes.

Central to the life of Hindus is a process of continual purification by an individual in attaining total freedom of soul.
Hindus believe that human beings move progressively toward
higher stages of life. If you want pleasure, power, wealth, or
fame, you may take them all; however, you will only find true
freedom, the liberation of body and spirit, through the way of
renunciation.[5] This spirit of detachment, Hindus believe, is the
secret to life. All of our desires and wants offer infinite variety
and lead us on an unending pursuit of satisfaction that is
unattainable precisely because there is such unending variety.
Liberation is achieved by turning one's back on desire. The
practice of yoga can help one achieve this perfection.

The caste system practiced within Indian society is in
reality more socioeconomic than religious. Presuming to rely
upon a movement of spiritual growth and the process of reincarnation to higher life, it nonetheless has divided people from
beggars to elites with successive stages in between. Mahatma
Gandhi, the celebrated Hindu politician-mystic of the early
twentieth century, saw this hypocrisy and urged its abolition
among Hindus. In spite of his efforts, many Hindus today perform their religious worship, rites, and ceremonies within the
framework of the caste system.

Buddhism

Gautama Buddha, born in northern India in the sixth century
B.C., searched far and wide for peace of soul and contentment of
spirit. Discovering the "Tree of Enlightenment," he began a life
of meditation under its branches until he eventually achieved a
state of enlightenment. This wisdom led to an understanding of
the problem of suffering. He formulated the "Four Noble
Truths": the reality of suffering, which all must endure; the
origin of suffering in needs and desires; the rejection of suffering by transformation of the mind; and finally, the elimination
of pain through the practice of the "Noble Eightfold Way." This
"way" may be summarized as follows: right views and intuition,
correct speech and action, proper livelihood and effort, and
right concentration and ecstasy. Buddhism, like its Indian sister

Hinduism, is less a religion of belief in a Supreme Being than a way of seeking answers to the secrets of life.

Throughout its long history, Buddhism spread all over Asia and was widely accepted in Tibet, Mongolia, China, Japan, Korea, and Malaysia. Buddhist temples, shrines, and houses of prayer attract followers who practice both simple reflective devotions and more elaborate displays of ritual pomp. In recent years many Western people have been drawn to the Buddhist way of life both for its simplicity and as a rejection of institutionalized Christianity.

Islam

In the year A.D. 612, having withdrawn from the corrupt and contentious environs of Mecca, a desert city in Arabia, Muhammad spent many days in prayer and fasting before being touched by Allah, the One True God. He was sent forth to preach against idolatry and injustice. By persevering in this calling, he began to change the behavior and attitudes of the local people, and within his lifetime saw virtually the entire population of the region give up their evil ways and turn to the worship of Allah.

Muslim is an adjectival form of the word *Islam* that means both "peace" and "surrender." Properly understood it stands for "the perfect peace that comes when one's life is surrendered to God." Muslims worship Allah, the same God as do Jews and Christians. They accept the Hebrew Scriptures as God's revelation and revere Jesus as a prophet of God. Devotion to his mother, Mary, is also part of their tradition. Muhammad, however, is the final prophet, revealing God's will in specific laws given to him, which are compiled in the Koran, the sacred literature of Islam.

There are Five Pillars that constitute the core practices and beliefs of Islam: (1) There is no God but Allah, and Muhammad is His Prophet. This belief is the essence of Islam. (2) Constant prayer in the form of praise and petition mark the worship of Allah. This is done daily at sunrise, noon, mid-afternoon, sunset, and before retiring. (3) Charity is the third pillar, with a strong emphasis on helping the most needy. Those with much, must help those with little. (4) Followers observe Ramadan, a month-long fast from food and drink during daylight hours, in order to teach self-discipline and to reflect upon their dependence upon God. (5) Once during his or her lifetime each Muslim is expected to travel to Mecca, the site of God's revelation, as a sign of devotion and solidarity with other faithful people. At Mecca all are clothed in plain white garments to remind them of their equality before God.

Muslims today number about six hundred million. The countries of the Middle East, large portions of Africa, and several countries in Asia are predominantly Muslim. A revival among Islamic people is taking place partly as a response to the rapid secularization of the world brought about by technological change. The rise to power of Ayatollah Khomeini in Iran was due in no small measure to a rejection of Western cultural values.

This brief glimpse of the major religions of the world highlights the commonality of a fundamental human desire to find meaning in life and to live in an ethical manner. The diversity of ways for achieving this indicates once again the unique charisma of individuals within the history of the human family and the tendency to institutionalize, codify, and ritualize what often began as a movement of human freedom.

Theory and Practice

The early settlers in our country and the waves of immigrants who followed them built thousands of churches across the land. Virtually every city and town has churches, synagogues, and temples that serve as centers not only for worship, but also for community life. These two aspects of religion, namely to provide meaning to life and to offer solidarity and friendship among people, represent religion's most positive influences on society. At their best all religions encourage, support, and affirm personhood and community.

The Hebrew prophets, the saints of Christianity, and Buddhist monks lived faith-centered lives. The example of Jesus, Saint Francis of Assisi, and Saint Catherine of Siena, and the contemporary witness of Gandhi, Martin Luther King, Jr., and Mother Teresa tell a story of truth, justice, liberation, and peace. In its theoretical framework and in the lives of its most sincere followers, religion has dignified the history of the human family. It has brought compassion and love to the forefront of human affairs, and drawn blacks and whites, men and women, old and young, rich and poor, and all nations into bonds of friendship.

Unfortunately, one must also admit that religion has sometimes proved detrimental. When someone questioned Gandhi, who deeply admired and imitated Jesus, why he did not become a Christian, he replied, "Become Christian? Christians not only fail to practice the Sermon on the Mount, most do not even believe it!" Sad to say, there are many people who claim allegiance to a particular religion, but fail to live by its creed. The teachings of Jesus, as Gandhi knew, called for love of enemies, a constant spirit of forgiveness, and a distrust of wealth and power. Thus, the first negative feature of religion, its nonpractice by supposed adherents, represents to outsiders sheer hypocrisy.

Secondly, religion is frequently distorted. "We have corrected your work," said the Grand Inquisitor to Jesus in Dostoevsky's *Brothers Karamazov*, "and have now founded it upon miracles, mystery, and authority. Men rejoice at being led like cattle again, with the terrible gift of freedom that brought them so much suffering removed from them."[6] Authoritarianism such as that of the Inquisitor has been a serious blight on the Western religions of Judaism, Christianity, and Islam. History is replete with instances of power-hungry clerics dominating and manipulating people, from the corruption of the medieval papacy, which Luther opposed, to the hucksterism of modern-day television evangelists who live well on the donations of the emotionally vulnerable.

Finally, we have the criticism of Karl Marx, who saw religion as the "opiate of the people." The elite classes have used religion to narcotize workers and peasants into focusing their hopes and dreams on a world beyond the grave. No need for concern about injustices in this world, when God would reward present suffering with the joys of heaven. Supporting the status quo within a society controlled by the rich and powerful is an ever-present danger to any religion.

We see then both positive and negative aspects of religion. It can give meaning to life and nurture community. It can also mislead, abuse, and corrupt its followers. All religions find their highest expression in the establishment of a unifying philosophy of life and a reflective attitude toward the world.[7] Healthy religion is open to a constant search for truth and meaning. It is a way of pointing the human family, individually and collectively, toward the liberation and freedom for which it yearns.

In conclusion, it appears obvious that because of the tremendous variety of religious beliefs, practices, convictions, truths, moral positions, and forms of worship, we need to develop a degree of flexibility in approaching the subject of religion. Without abandoning one's own faith tradition, it is wise to admit our institutional faults and allow for tolerance in the shortcomings of other religions. In some quite mysterious evolutionary way, God has allowed a religious plurality to develop, which, perhaps, was meant to celebrate the wonderful diversity of the human family. If each of us is created uniquely by God, is it any wonder that we find the Creator in our own unique way?

Notes

[1]   Traditional translation.

[2]   Mircea Eliade, *The Sacred and the Profane* (New York: Harcourt Brace Jovanovich, 1959), 58.

[3]   Virginia Stem Owens, *And the Trees Clap Their Hands* (Grand Rapids, Mich.: Wm. B. Eerdmans Publishing, 1983), 131.

[4]   Teilhard de Chardin, *The Phenomenon of Man* (New York: Harper & Row, 1959).

[5]   Huston Smith, *The Religions of Man* (New York: Harper & Row, 1965), 17–22.

[6]   Fyodor Dostoevsky, *The Brothers Karamazov* (New York: Bantam Books, 1970), 309.

[7]   Gordon Allport, *The Individual and His Religion* (New York: Macmillan, 1959), 60–61.

7

Political Systems

Any human society, if it is to be well ordered and productive, must lay down as a foundation this principle: that every human being is a person; his nature is endowed with intelligence and free will. By virtue of this he has rights and duties of his own, following directly and simultaneously from his very nature, which are therefore universal, inviolable and inalienable.

Pope John XXIII[1]

Polis

To the average person the influence of politics upon daily life appears slight. Yet a moment's reflection about tax laws, sanitary conditions, roads and highway accessibility, police and military protection, and public education, to mention only a few, help us to see that politics represents the horizon of everyday life. Decisions are made constantly about the how, when, where, and why of revenues and expenditures that affect the life of every citizen. We may choose to ignore its importance, or we may learn how to influence public policy.

Who makes the laws and who benefits or suffers from them has changed constantly throughout history. In earliest times, tribal people and clan families were generally governed by the absolute authority of the leader. Gradually, as groups and tribes came together, leaders became more remote from their people and assumed godlike powers. This divine right of the ruler continued well into the Middle Ages. Although attempts were made to govern fairly (most notable was the Code of Hammurabi, under which the Babylonians established the first systematic set of laws about 1900 B.C.), in most instances the political reality was the concentration of power and wealth in the hands of a few with the remainder of the population at their mercy. Slavery, of course, was the accepted norm in these societies. So, too, was the lack of political authority for women. Queens and courtesans had their role, but for the most part it was a secondary influence in a patriarchial system. In short, political systems of rulers and ruled dominated much of the ancient world.

Through the influence of philosophical reflections on the just ordering of society, the Greeks and Romans developed a systematic rule of law designed to govern people justly and fairly. Political rule by the powerful was still the order of the day, but there emerged the beginnings of power sharing, e.g., the Roman senate, where debate and compromise over political issues played a role in the ordering of society.

For a variety of reasons the Roman Empire began a gradual decline at the beginning of Christianity and came to a political end by the fifth century with the onslaught of the barbarian invasions throughout Europe. The breakup of Roman rule led gradually to a medieval political structure, while the spread of Islam brought about a highly religious government in the countries where it prevailed. In the meantime, continents away, Native Americans settled throughout North America, and vast empires of the Aztec and Inca nations dominated the landscape of Central and South America. In China, warlords ruled the villages and towns within their domain, while military shoguns commanded the societies in Japan, and tribal chieftains ruled in Ireland and Africa.

European people were governed by two powerful forces, Church and State. A hierarchical structure had evolved within Christianity with the bishop of Rome, the pope, as the spiritual ruler of all. Kings, lords, and nobles exercised temporal control of the population. Thus, the common people had little or no say in the ordering of society. This medieval political system, known as feudalism, began to crumble with the growth of cities and the development of science and craftsmanship. In the sixteenth century the Protestant reformers rejected the power of the hierarchical Roman Catholic Church and deplored its internal political corruption. Furthermore, nationalism, in the form of exploitation of newly discovered lands, and the consequent conflict over these territories by the countries of Europe grew ever stronger.

By the middle of the eighteenth century new ideas about the governance of society were a major part of the intellectual climate. John Locke and other Enlightenment thinkers were beginning to conceptualize a political system in which the rule of the majority, separation of powers, and fundamental human rights for all citizens were to constitute the central elements of government. The American Revolution was fought to achieve these ends. Democracy, rule by the people, an idea originating with the Greeks two thousand years before, began to play an increasing role in the political makeup of many countries.

This brief review of some historical political structures offers us a sense of the variety of systems that have been operative in the past. Some were better than others at fostering the welfare of society, while many were filled with the injustice of tyrants and despots. As we look now at today's political systems we should keep in mind several questions. Do they protect the rights of all people? Are they supportive of individual freedom? Is the possibility of world government realistic? These and related questions should help us judge the quality and character of different political structures, and remind us of the new possibilities that have opened up in Eastern Europe and throughout the world.

Democracy

The great experiment in democracy began officially with the ratification of the Constitution of the United States in March

1789. Those who founded this nation, the Washingtons, Jeffersons, and Adamses, left us a legacy of balance between individual liberty and constitutional government. By designating a congress to enact legislation, a president to carry out the law, and a judiciary to interpret it, they effectively separated the powers of government. These new democratic principles included equality of treatment before the law, due process, set terms of office, free elections by secret ballot and, most importantly, personal rights. These latter, enshrined in the Bill of Rights, guarantee that the government serves the people. Arbitrary rule by a nobility was coming to an end.

The topography of the land and the attitudes of the American people, however, have put a distinctive brand on their understanding of democracy. It may be called individualist democracy.[2] With millions of square miles of open land, peopled only with red-skinned natives who, for the most part, were thought of as savages, it was not surprising that a frontier, trailblazing, individualistic mentality took hold. De Tocqueville remarked early on that individualism characterized the American people. A capitalist spirit of free enterprise blended well with political freedom, so that by the close of the nineteenth century laissez-faire capitalism was synonymous with democracy in the minds of many Americans.

In addition, the great railroad barons, the financiers of Wall Street, and the wealthy upper classes of Boston, New York, and Philadelphia believed deeply in a government that generally turned a blind eye to the exploitation and greed that was commonplace. Individualist democracy affirmed the right of people to use their freedom however they saw fit. Self-interest and a free market philosophy allowed those with initiative, motivation, and wits (and occasionally larceny and cunning) to acquire enormous wealth and power. In Europe, however, a different form of democracy was emerging.

Brought about as much by the vagaries of history as by a planned philosophy of political order, most European countries, especially following World War II, developed into socialist democracies. Smaller in size than the United States and with indigenous, homogeneous populations, the Western European countries tried to correct for the excesses of a free market system by nationalizing many industries and providing benefits and other welfare subsidies to all citizens in the name of the common good. Social planning, public ownership, restrictions on excessive wealth by progressive taxation, and public works projects that guaranteed employment were the hallmarks of socialist democracy.

In the United States great value is placed on economic freedom, the right of private property, the limits of government, and individualism. Socialist democracies emphasize the need to provide general and specific services from public funds for all of their people. The debate swings back and forth continually. How much should government intervene in the lives of the people? Does a welfare state (socialist tendencies) breed laziness? Does it limit initiative? On the other hand, does individualist democracy, also known as democratic capitalism, ignore the needs of the poor and less gifted and create a fiercely competitive spirit leading ultimately to material decadence? The salient feature of democracies, of course, is that the public debate goes on, and people are free to choose sides on any issue and elect representatives who share their views.

Communism

"Let the ruling classes tremble at a Communistic revolution. The proletarians have nothing to lose but their chains. . . . Working men of all countries, unite!"[3] These words from the *Communist Manifesto* of Marx and Engels, written in 1848, and Marx's subsequent critique of capitalism found in *Das Kapital*, published in 1867, have had a profound impact on twentieth-century political life. Marx believed that economics was the final determinant of the social order. Political power was nothing more or less than the control of wealth. History is filled, said Marx, with the exploitation of the masses by the rich.

We who live in late–twentieth-century America are hard-pressed to appreciate the intolerable conditions of most workers in the early days of the Industrial Revolution. Cynical factory owners demanded fourteen-hour days for minimal wages. There were few safety or health care regulations and no paid vacations or holidays. Children worked in mines and pregnant women baled cotton. In critiquing capitalism, if nothing else, Marx offered an alternative vision for industrial society, one that allowed the workers to control their own destiny.

The theory of communism found a natural ally in the Russian Revolution of 1917. The czar was forced to abdicate; civil war ensued; the Bolsheviks triumphed. These forces, under the leadership of Vladimir Lenin, supported radical social reform and within a few years had established an international Communist party directed and controlled by Moscow. In theory, the Party was the vanguard for a dictatorship of the proletariat. It would henceforth decide—always with the worker's best interest at heart—what was produced.

Communist ideology was unalterably opposed to capitalism, which invariably placed it at odds with capitalist nations. Class struggle, pitting rich against the poor, oppressor against the oppressed, capitalist against communist, was a battle cry for millions of people throughout the world who saw colonialism and economic imperialism as the two greatest evils of the time.

Following World War II, the Soviet Union began to export communism to the newly emerging nations. The United States and Western European countries countered by supporting capitalist and socialist democracies. The East/West conflict was under way. Communist revolutionary governments rose to power—most notably in Cuba under the rule of Fidel Castro, and in China under the leadership of Mao Tse-tung. The Korean War of the early fifties and the Vietnam War pitted, at least in theory, communism against democracy. Although this ideological conflict, often referred to as the Cold War, raged throughout the world, local conflicts among indigenous peoples, religious animosities, and nationalistic jealousies compounded and often confused the issues. In any case, communist influence has dominated the geopolitical landscape for the past half-century and a truce of sorts has emerged only recently.

Today, in China, repression remains the norm although it is not as severe now as it was throughout the heyday of the

Revolutionary Red Guard era of the 1970s. Within the Soviet Union, the winds of reform are blowing strongly throughout the republics and within the corridors of the Kremlin. With the destruction of the Berlin Wall in the autumn of 1989 and the collapse of the Soviet Union's strong central government in the summer of 1991, the entire future of European political life is undergoing realignment.

Furthermore, as Mikhail Gorbachev and Boris Yeltsin move toward the restructuring of Soviet society, not only are the capitalist economic principles of supply and demand taking hold, but new political alignments have surfaced. Gorbachev is talking about further arms reduction in all nations, new alliances with the NATO and Common Market countries, and a rapprochement with the United States. He knows full well that total government control of society saps the creative juices inherent in all people. In his book on Soviet reforms Gorbachev states that "The practice of writing for instructions from above on every matter . . . (makes) people grow unaccustomed to thinking and acting in a responsible and independent way."[4] Communism as a political system in the Soviet Union is in disarray. China, Cuba, and a few other nations have yet to reform.

Other Systems

"Traditional rulers are the foundation of Nigeria and indeed of Africa," said Omowonuola Oyeyode, the Ogiyan of Ejigbo.[5] He reigns as the king of a section of Yoruba Land, a territory a few hundred miles northeast of Lagos, the Nigerian capital. There are literally thousands of local rulers throughout much of Africa who exert far more influence over the material and spiritual lives of their people than the often remote national governments. Unlike former times, however, these local chieftains possess no dictatorial powers. "Chiefs are chiefs of people. If a chief becomes a chief not of the people, the people will throw him out. It's a question of confidence."[6]

In sharp contrast to localized tribal rule, the political system of fascism seeks to exercise total control of the population.

Fascism connotes rule by an elite. The supposition is that only the intelligent, the educated, and the owners of property are capable of ruling a nation. Usually a military strongman who is either part of, or controlled and financed by, the elite leads the country. In fact, fascism is a philosophical cover for dictatorship. The press and media are controlled, civil rights and political liberties are minimized, and dissent is stifled. Labor unions and other forms of worker protection associations are banned for the simple reason that they are the kind of opposition forces that cause trouble for the elite. In modern times the Italian Fascist party, led by Benito Mussolini, and the German Nazi party of Adolf Hitler embodied the political ideology of fascism.

Currently, the new face of fascism appears in the form of military dictatorships throughout the world. In El Salvador, Guatemala, Honduras, and virtually all South American countries, to one degree or another, militarism rules the land. The most virulent forms of military rule have led to torture, mutilation, and the murder of anyone suspected of opposing the military. Although the overthrow of the Marcos regime in the Philippines and the Duvalier and Somoza families in Haiti and Nicaragua, respectively, augurs well for the prospects of democracy in those countries, military dictatorships continue to exert great influence on the lives of millions of people, especially the poor. It is the subjugation of the poor, moreover, that offers a rationale for militarism.

Behind the facade of the military ruler stands the wealthy elite. Military dictators never tire of expressing their concern for law and order as a crusade against communism. Throughout Latin American history, wealthy families built dynasties of power on the backs of the poor. Refusing to share their wealth with the multitude of the people, they instead developed armies and other types of security forces to protect their interests against the demands of the needy. Several United States administrations have supported these efforts of suppression because of business interests. Today, civil war rages in El Salvador primarily because the rich few refuse to share their abundance with the many poor. Justice lies dead under the jackboot of military rule.

Thus, we see several other types of political systems existing alongside democracy and communism. Tribal rulers still claim the allegiance of their followers in much of Africa; Islamic governments comply with the religious traditions of their faith; South Africa continues its false democracy with the exclusion of three-fourths of its people; and military dictatorships flourish at the behest of the wealthy.

In the past, custom and tradition often dictated the form and style of government in countries throughout the world. Today, a new realization is growing that people must cooperate for the survival of the planet and that political systems must respect the rights of all.

Toward the Twenty-first Century

What does the future hold? Orwell saw the future in terms of a Big Brother totalitarian state government dominating every segment of society. Conversely, Aldous Huxley, a prominent British literary critic, saw people so mesmerized by entertainment and consumer goods that they lost all sense of other values. Perhaps these examples are extreme, but do they not offer fair warning as to our possible fate?

In politics as in all human affairs, simplicity, complexity, and failure exist simultaneously. Although the vision of a peaceful world, where human rights are respected and the needy are cared for, holds much promise, it is ultimately utopian. More realistic expectations must focus on building the bridges of cross-cultural understanding through trade relationships and educational and social interchange. Evil in the form of pride, greed, and indifference will always exist alongside gentleness, compassion, and care. If we say No to the oppression of totalitarian governments, No to the mindless materialism in our present age, No to the madness of the arms race, we will have thundered a resounding Yes in our desire to build a better world.

Politics is sometimes thought of as a dirty word. It conjures up images of back-room deals, corruption, and bribery. Occasionally these things do happen. But we also have a long history of men and women who were deeply involved in the political process and whose efforts brought about notable results. The founders of our nation—Washington, Jefferson, Adams,

Franklin—were all politicians. Susan B. Anthony, who led the fight for women's suffrage, and Hattie Caraway, elected as the first woman senator, were immersed in politics. The greatest religious leader of the twentieth century, Mahatma Gandhi, always spoke of himself first and foremost as a politician.

In its best and most democratic sense, politics is concerned with the general well-being of the whole society, rich and poor, male and female, young and old, able-bodied and handicapped. Those who are blessed with health, wealth, and education are responsible for those who are less fortunate. Why? From a spiritual point of view, God calls us to love our neighbor, especially the poor neighbor. But even on a purely secular level, no society will function smoothly when part of its population is marginalized. We are fortunate to live in a free society, but only insofar as we participate actively in its political life for the welfare of all will that society flourish.

In moving toward the twenty-first century we should acknowledge that we are not citizens only of a particular nation, but also of the world. A growing awareness of the damage that has been done to our planet by toxic and nuclear waste, fossil fuel exhaust, and the equally deleterious effects of poverty and hunger for million of our sisters and brothers forces us to take a more global view of life. Granted, the answer to the inclusion question must begin with myself and my family, but it cannot end there. A citizen of the world has global responsibilities.

Notes

1   John XXIII, *Pacem in Terris* (Glen Rock, N.J.: Paulist Press, 1963), 8.

2   Carl Cohen, *Four Systems* (New York: Random House, 1982), 69.

3   Karl Marx and Friedrich Engels, *The Communist Manifesto,* trans. Samuel Moore (New York: Viking Penguin, 1967), 120–21.

4   Mikhail Gorbachev, *Perestroika* (New York: Harper & Row, 1987), 65.

5   Edward Gargan, "King Holds Court in Yoruba Land," *New York Times,* February 13, 1986, 2.

6   Ibid.

8

Economic Systems

Economics is the study of the principles by which society organizes
itself to use scarce resources for the production and distribution of
goods and services.

Walter L. Owensby[1]

Needs/Wants

Huts, tepees, igloos, and high-rise condos provide varying degrees of shelter. Carrots, codfish, and cereal satisfy a variety of
appetites. Throughout the world people fill their basic needs
with a bewildering assortment of food, shelter, and clothing.
Primitive humans hunted game and sought shelter in caves;
ancient tribes gathered in villages and began to grow crops,
herd cattle, and construct their own shelters; medieval life,
while beginning to show signs of urbanization, remained largely
agricultural.

The latter half of the twentieth century has given rise to a
vast array of cities containing complex economic arrangements
designed to provide humans with basic needs. Over the course
of centuries, the creative ingenuity of humans and their pen-
chant for both retaining cultural traditions and changing their

81

tastes, gave rise to enormous complexity in the types and kinds of necessities that people desired. In point of fact once basic needs were satisfied people were quick to move beyond needs to wants.

This distinction between needs and wants has become critical today because, for large numbers of people, the basic needs of food, shelter, clothing, health care, education, and employment go unmet. This contrasts sharply with those who live in affluence. Jesus compared the life-style of the rich man who wore the finest clothing and feasted lavishly each day at his banquet table to that of the beggar, Lazarus, whose sores were licked by dogs. Unfortunately, this situation still exists.

In the United States the gap between the rich and the poor, those who can satisfy their every whim and those who struggle for the bare necessities, grows broader each day.[2] Worldwide, the situation defies description.[3] As we look at past and present economic systems, we should keep in mind several questions. Do needs take priority over wants? Do we have a responsibility to share our goods with others? Is this a question of charity or a cry for justice? Finally, what role does government play in economic matters?

Before looking at the two major economic systems operating today, a few preliminary considerations are in order. First of all, most economists distinguish between positive economics, which predicts market behavior and contains principles and hypotheses about resources and goods, and normative economics, which makes judgments and policy decisions based on values or preferences.[4] The former is concerned with the analysis of supply and demand forces, employment conditions, productivity, consumption, and the like. Normative economics, on the other hand, attempts to analyze the human condition and its economic activity based upon certain values and convictions.

Additionally, the discussion of both positive and normative economies raises four basic questions: (1) Who or what determines what and how much is produced? (2) Who or what determines how it is produced? (3) Who or what determines how the society's output is distributed among the members?

(4) Who or what determines the rate of growth? The *what* in each question emphasizes a deterministic model of economic forces, one which supposedly operates automatically. The *who* focuses attention on the people who are affected by the economy, those individuals who produce and who consume. Although many factors from climate to natural disasters affect economics, the human dimension remains critical. The laws of supply and demand are nothing more than humans making decisions about their wants and needs. Let us look now at the two major systems, which propose different paths to economic well-being.

Free-Market Economies

Adam Smith in *The Wealth of Nations* explained that the common self-interest of all ("an invisible hand")[5] would create new wealth, thereby raising the living standard of all.

This monumental work, first published in 1776, provided the philosophical foundations for capitalism. Economically speaking, the guilds and crafts merchants of the Middle Ages were the forerunners of today's capitalists, but it was not until the ferment of the Enlightenment, with its attention on the freedom and rights of the individual, that a free-market system emerged.

The central tenets of the free-market system, or capitalism, are well known to most Americans. Freedom stands as the fundamental virtue. People are free to produce, purchase, and accumulate whatever they desire. Necessity does not drive the free market; it is driven by want. Since want knows no limits, people continually seek to upgrade their economic condition. If a better mousetrap can be built, or one that is more tasteful, build it. Supply and demand generate the competition.

When operating freely, these two forces determine the price of a product, since people are free to buy and sell at will. Profits fuel the engine of capitalism. The astute and resourceful benefit; the lazy and careless are financially punished. New markets emerge with the invention of better products, and ongoing growth patterns generated from improved technologies and superior skill constantly push the economy toward higher productivity.

These, then, are the major ideas behind capitalism: free enterprise, competition, and profit. Real stories of rags to riches, from poverty to plenty, fill the pages of the capitalist chronology. With a tangible reward system ever operable, the free-market economy has produced more goods for more people than at any other time in history.

For the world as a whole, the third quarter of the twentieth century outshone any epoch in the annals of economic history. As far as growth of total world output was concerned, we had not seen its like before.[6]

Looking back, however, at the human costs of capitalism we see a different picture. For every Rockefeller there were a million Oliver Twists; for every skyscraper built or ton of coal dug, thousands labored, oftentimes in unsafe and unsanitary conditions. The Industrial Revolution created enormous wealth by means of scientific discoveries, inventions, and factory production. It also created untold misery. The writings of Victor Hugo and Charles Dickens in the nineteenth century and Sinclair Lewis and Michael Harrington in the twentieth century tell a story of exploitation and greed. These are the negative consequences of capitalism.

The use of young children in mines, women working long hours in sweatshops, and other abuses of the working class led to serious social upheaval. Capitalism assumed that all people act in their own self-interest. It believed in the private ownership of the means of production (land, factories, money, etc.). It envisioned a market system governed by the price mechanism of supply and demand within the context of free competition. Unfortunately, in its haste for profits, it paid little attention to the rights of the workers. The idea of progress no matter what the cost became the prevailing concept. Capitalism, at its worst, created a dog-eat-dog mentality where self-interest became synonymous with greed, and efficiency and productivity were a cover for a new form of slavery where the worker "owed his soul to the company store."

Planned Economies

The crimes of capitalism gave rise to socialism. Karl Marx's *Das Kapital*, a monumental treatise on the history and theory of the economy, set the stage for the global ideological conflict between socialism and capitalism. During the Middle Ages a feudal system of economic life prevailed throughout Europe. The lords and nobles who owned the land allowed the serfs to farm it and retain a portion of the crop for the benefit of themselves and their families.

With the advent of skilled craftspersons, merchants, and a trading class, society was gradually transformed from a feudal structure into one based on a market economy. Goods were now bought and sold with money. In contrast to earlier times, it became acceptable to charge interest on loans and to make a profit on the exchange of goods. In general, however, much of the society remained agricultural and there was a relative balance within the economic structures.

The rise of capitalism, however, radically shifted this balance. Self-interest became the operable value and the owners of property began to take unfair advantage of the workers.

Marx noted that this exploitation under laissez-faire capitalism would lead inevitably to revolution. As a remedy he proposed a system of socialism in which individuals were not allowed to accumulate vast fortunes and the government would direct and control the economy for the good of all.

In theory, socialism claims a higher moral ground than capitalism. Instead of workers mindlessly producing profits for the factory owners at the lowest possible wages, they share in the profits and have a voice in the management and operation of their work. In addition, the distribution of wealth constitutes a high priority in a socialist society. The government functions as the major conduit for education, welfare, employment, health care, and all social benefits that will assist the most vulnerable and needy.

Socialists claim that cooperation, not competition, brings out the best in people. Thus, the workplace should not operate on principles of coercion and duress, but on the ideals of unity and harmony. Marx believed that "from each according to his abilities, to each according to his needs." This maxim allowed the government to regulate society in a egalitarian manner wherein all were provided with work and all people had their basic needs met.

Communism, the most virulent form of socialism, exposed the worst flaws of this economic system. Control of the economy by the states meant, in effect, control of all society. State planning robbed individuals of their initiative and creativity. What appeared on paper to be a utopia of worker cooperation became an ironclad regime answerable only to itself. The dictatorship of the proletariat became the tyranny of Lenin, Stalin, and Mao. A communist one-party system led to a stagnating economy, bureaucratic lassitude, and scarce, shabby consumer goods. Without the incentive of rewards in the form of better living conditions and quality products, workers lacked motivation and quickly settled into dull and listless automatons.

In their purest forms, both free-market economies and planned economies have serious failings. Capitalism, fueled by greed, ends in exploitation; socialism, idealizing equality, results in conformity. During the past twenty-five years both systems have moved closer to each other. The discussion is no longer about government control of the economy, but rather about how much control it should have. The pendulum swings back and forth from greater to lesser control, depending on the general mood of the country and the political philosophy of the leaders. President Roosevelt in the 1930s brought about sweeping economic reforms by imposing considerable government control over the economy. This was influenced, in part, by the thinking of John Maynard Keynes, a leading economist, who advocated strong government policies to adjust for the uncertainties of recession and depression.

By the 1980s, the Reagan administration had shifted away from government control to a policy of deregulation. The pendulum thus swings between a so-called democratic socialism, with the government setting policies, and a type of democratic capitalism, with the market forces adjusting themselves automatically. No doubt the debate will continue and policy decisions will fluctuate with policymakers.

The Priority of Labor

Fundamental to any economic activity are resources. Resources are things or services used to produce the goods that people want. In broadest terms they may be characterized as land, labor, and capital. *Land* may take on many meanings, from real estate property to natural resources such as minerals, timber, or water supplies. It also includes land used for agriculture, parking lots, and shopping centers. *Capital* generally refers to the buildings, equipment, supplies, and most especially investment monies available for the production of goods and services.

Human labor, of course, constitutes the most precious resource of all, and it is crucial for our understanding of peace and justice education that we emphasize its importance. In the final analysis, it is human effort, both physical and mental, that directs the goals and uses of the land and capital resources. We should not categorize human labor as just another resource. There is a qualitative difference between labor and capital.

This difference is the central issue of the encyclical, *On Human Work*, by Pope John Paul II. He stressed that in the economic affairs of life as, indeed, in all human activity, the dignity and worth of the individual is paramount. "Human work has an ethical value of its own, which clearly and directly remains linked to the fact that the one who carries it out is a person, a conscious and free subject, that is to say, a subject who decides about himself."[7] The pope makes it clear that we can never isolate economic issues from their human considerations. When economists refuse to consider the human dimensions of policy decisions, when employers provide unreasonable or unsafe working conditions for their employees, when government planning attends more to statistical analysis and the ideology of supply and demand than to the real human needs of its citizens, then people are objectified and no longer treated with the dignity they deserve.

The priority of labor over capital challenges both the free-market ideology of maximization of profits and the collectivization philosophy of socialism.

Work, understood in its broadest sense, embraces all human activity that advances and enhances the good of the human family. From migrant farm workers to the stars of stage and screen, from office secretaries to composers and sculptors, from stevedores to scientists—all of these workers improve the quality of life on earth.

By emphasizing the pay differentials among people, a free-market society tends to degrade low-income jobs; by removing the right to private ownership, collectivist economies deny people their creativity. What is most needed, says the pope, is to understand that the "value of human work is not primarily the kind of work being done, but the fact that the one who is doing it is a person."[8] In their quest for ideological justifications, capitalism and collectivism downplay the importance of the human in economic decisions. But are we all not guilty of depersonalization? What's needed are constant reminders that in economics, as in politics, religion, cultural and social life, the dignity of each person has priority over all other considerations.

In attempting to address this question of personal dignity in the economic areas, the pope devotes several sections of the encyclical to the rights of workers. He draws attention to the vast numbers of people who are unemployed or underemployed. He does not hesitate to call for economic planning on the part of business and government to devise suitable means toward full employment.[9] In addition, he stresses the importance of union organizations that allow workers to join in solidarity in order to protect their rights.[10] Moreover, the pope reiterates the Church's long-standing opposition to the class struggle deemed so necessary by Marxism. Unions are meant to build community not only for the workers but also for those who own and manage the means of production.[11]

Recent attempts to involve workers in decision-making policy have vindicated John Paul II's expectations. *On Human Work* gave a new voice to justice in the economic order. Because of the pope's moral leadership, more and more business and government leaders are listening to their employees. Union leaders have been invited to sit on corporate boards, and management has begun to include labor in its long-range planning. The priority of labor over capital is a fundamental principle in all economic decisions, and only when that principle is observed will we find a just society at peace with itself.

The Future

In today's world, unrelenting poverty exists side by side with affluence. A recent United States Bureau of the Census report indicated that 75 percent of the total private wealth, i.e. stocks, bonds, and property, is owned by 20 percent of the population.[12] In contrast to this, more than 35 million people, primarily women and children, live below the poverty line.

The global picture is even more desperate. Half the world's people, nearly two and a half billion, live in countries where the annual per capita income is $400 or less. At least 800 million people in these countries live in absolute poverty, beneath any rational definition of human decency. Despite abundant harvests worldwide, nearly a half-million people go to bed hungry each night. Fifteen out of every hundred children born in these countries die before the age of five, and millions of the survivors are physically or mentally stunted.[13]

Are we not aware that the poor and the needy of the world are our sisters and our brothers? Do we fail to see the connection between the economic decisions we make in our shopping habits and consumption patterns with the plight of others in our world? Are we conspicuous consumers oblivious to the needy, or responsible agents of economic reform?

In recent years church leaders and other voices of compassion have cried aloud for all people to wake up to the reality of world hunger. Hunger is a result of poverty, and poverty is a result of economic disparity. These leaders have attempted to offer insight and guidance from the rich traditions of both

Hebrew and Christian Scriptures. State and federal policies of national and global scope are sorely in need of this moral guidance in order to assist those in need of material support.

Rock concerts like Farm-Aid and Live-Aid can serve a legitimate purpose in awakening us to concern for others, but government and business decisions are monumentally more significant. One example will suffice. In the fiscal 1986 budget the United States allocated 350 billion dollars for defense, and only 100 million for aid to Africa. This means that we spent 3,500 times more money protecting ourselves than we gave to help starving people. Is there something wrong with these priorities? Perhaps we need a collective examination of conscience.

We are all economic actors. Where we work, how productive we are, the amount of taxes we pay, the food we eat, the clothes we wear, the automobiles we drive, and the houses in which we live, not to mention hundreds of other financial decisions and choices we make annually, give each of us an opportunity to play a role in the economic life of the nation and the world. In whatever profession we find ourselves, we can influence economic decisions. Granted we are not all board chairpersons or the chief executive officers of large corporations, but we do make economic choices in our shopping and buying habits, in our entertainment patterns, and in our general lifestyle. We can make a difference.

This chapter began by distinguishing between needs and wants. Should we not close on the same note? Are our desires and wants compatible with the needs of others? Should we share our talents, time, and material blessings more generously with the less fortunate? Are we politically engaged in the economic decisions of our government by calling on public officials to support policies that assist the needy? It is hoped that just as adulthood emerges from adolescence, self-centeredness will give way to a sense of responsibility and compassion. We need to understand that all people are included in our world, and that the least among us deserves an adequate diet, sufficient shelter, and the chance to live a decent human life.

Notes

1   Walter L. Owensby, *Economics for Prophets* (Grand Rapids, Mich.: Wm. B. Eerdsmans Publishing, 1988), xiii.

2   National Conference of Catholic Bishops, *Economic Justice for All* (Washington, D.C.: United States Catholic Conference, 1986), para. 171.

3   Michael Harrington, *The Vast Majority* (New York: Simon & Schuster, 1977), ch. 1.

4   Edwin Mansfield, *Principles of Microeconomics* (New York: W. W. Norton, 1983), 6.

5   Adam Smith, *The Wealth of Nations* (London: Routledge, 1900), 345.

6   Paul Samuelson quoted in Carl Cohen, *Four Systems* (New York: Random House, 1982), 96.

7   John Paul II, *On Human Work* (Washington D.C.: United States Catholic Conference, 1981), 14.

8   Ibid.

9   Ibid., 41.

10   Ibid., 45.

11   Ibid., 46.

12   Owensby, *Economics for Prophets*, 10.

13   National Conference of Catholic Bishops, *Economic Justice for All*, 123.

9

The Reality of Limits

I complained because I had no shoes, until I met a man who had
no feet.

ancient Hindu proverb

Who's Handicapped?

How many of the following people would you consider handicapped: a paraplegic, one who lives in poverty, a child with
Down's syndrome, an elderly person, a well-known author, a
professional athlete, a business executive, an AIDS victim? Perhaps you were quick to identify those people with physical
impairments, while conceding a normal life to those who appear healthy. Had you looked more closely at the real life of any
one of the aforementioned individuals, you would realize that
every person is handicapped in one way or another. Humans
are limited.

We began Part I, Inclusion, by stressing the unique goodness and beauty of each person. We turn now to another important truth, the truth about our limitations. Each of us came into
this life totally dependent upon others for nourishment and
care. Without the help of hundreds of people—parents, family,

neighbors, farmers, builders, and teachers—we would not have grown up and arrived at a point where we could begin to help ourselves. In assessing our response to people who are identifiably handicapped, we should always remember our own limited beginnings and appreciate how much the success and well-being of our own lives was, and is, dependent upon the goodness and support of others. A few examples may help make the point.

Linda is twenty-two years old. She is manic-depressive. Throughout her years in high school she suffered this condition but was never diagnosed. She earned barely enough credits to graduate. For the next three years she drifted in and out of various jobs, finally suffering a nervous breakdown and attempting suicide. During the subsequent hospitalization, doctors diagnosed her manic-depressive condition and prescribed medication to help her. She still hasn't found a job, but she no longer has the drastic mood swings, and there is hope for the future. She is thinking of going to night school and earning a college degree.

Gina is six years old. She suffers from Down's syndrome, a chromosomal disorder that causes mental retardation, heart and respiratory defects, and other physical infirmities. She is a slow learner and has undergone corrective surgery for a heart malfunction. Despite this, her family has always regarded her as a blessing. She has brought much joy into their lives. The extra efforts required by her parents and two sisters seem to have made them happier people. Today, Gina is in school, receives special therapy, and lives a fulfilling life.

Adela is ninety-two years of age. A widow now for fifteen years and the mother of two children who have long since died, she is confined to a wheelchair in a nursing home. She owns a beautiful home in a lovely neighborhood and yearns to return to it. Her diabetic condition and her problem with incontinence, however, make that prospect unlikely. Fortunately, she has many friends who visit her daily at the nursing home and she keeps busy with knitting and other craft activities.

Physical handicaps such as blindness, heart disease, deafness, and paralysis are most apparent. In addition, intellectual and emotional handicaps may include ignorance, retardation, neurosis, psychosis, and a host of phobias. At another level, we may speak of negative and hostile attitudes as a reflection of serious spiritual handicaps. The spiritually dead appear on the surface to function normally, yet within their hearts lie thoughts of revenge, selfishness, and greed. These are handicaps of the heart. People who lack concern, care, and compassion for the needy and who spend most of their time looking after their own interests suffer alienation not only from others, but from their own best self.

Thus, we find a wide variety of handicaps, both external and internal, which represent the limits of human life. Michael Jordan's sky-walk can only go so high; Michael Jackson's energy lasts only so long; the best athletes and superstars of stage and screen eventually peak and begin their decline to normalcy. Presidents and popes must eat and sleep like the rest of humankind. In one way or another, these handicaps represent the limits of life.

Basic Anxiety

Reinhold Niebuhr, a Protestant theologian, argued that "man, being both free and bound, both limited and unlimited, is anxious. Anxiety is the inevitable concomitant of the paradox of freedom and finiteness in which man is involved."[1] The fundamental problem that all humans face is that our human nature pulls us in two different directions. On the one hand, we are a free people longing to achieve a destiny, a hope, a vision, a dream beyond the ordinary and mundane realities of life. Our expectations are limitless. In our minds we think and imagine the wildest, most impossible scenarios. We long to go beyond what we presently are.

In theological terms, we think that we are gods. How often we hear people say, "I can do anything I want!" There lurks within each of us an insatiable desire to get it all. The biblical story of the Fall notes that the fundamental temptation for Adam and Eve, fictional characters who represent the whole human race, presents itself in the guise of this longing for greatness. "...when you eat of it [the forbidden fruit] your eyes will be opened, and you will be like God."[2]

On the other hand, we are limited—not only in the historical moment of time, place, nationality, and culture, but also in thousands of little ways. We get colds, get held up in traffic and cut off on the telephone, and are ignored by some and criticized by others. We scrape our arms, bang our shins, say dumb things, and occasionally sulk. The ultimate limit, of course, is death, but we are faced constantly with the "little deaths" of everyday life. Niebuhr contends that this human paradox of freedom and finitude results in a deep-seated anxiety that all people share and that finds expression in our personal and social life.[3]

This general anxiety caused by the freedom/finitude tension is most obvious in the mental conversations we have with ourselves about handling new and different situations, in our fears about trying something we have not done before, and in the restlessness and drive with which we often push ourselves through life. Many students hit the panic button when asked to stand up in a classroom and present their own particular point of view. Part of this anxiety stems from the fear of exposing one's limitations ("I don't want others to think I'm dumb"), and part of it has to do with an avoidance of responsibility for classroom learning ("only teachers need to talk in class").

Furthermore, this clash between the infinite and the limits of life manifests itself not only in the individual, but also within the group. "We're #1" perfectly expresses this longing for group achievement. Nations historically have fought long and bitter wars to prove to themselves and others that they were the most important and prestigious countries in the world. Powerful corporations expand their horizons constantly in the hope of gaining new markets or crushing the competition. In sports, this competition among professional and collegiate teams reaches epic proportions annually when the play-offs and finals draw near.

Yet the reality of limits is all too evident. All nations, even the most powerful, experience decline. Corporate giants suffer the consequences of inflation, product failure, and stock market anxiety. Only one team wins the World Series in any given year, which means that dozens of other teams must face their failures. Frequently enough, last year's winners do not repeat. On an individual level and within the social context of life, freedom and finitude clash. This foundational human anxiety can drive us to greatness or depravity.

The freedom to which we are drawn, then, and its opposite, the limitations of reality, result in a tension that offers us a radical choice. We may accept our innate restlessness and transform it into the creative energy that gives expression to art, music, work, play, friendship, compassion, and all of the human activities that enhance our world. Or we may resist the limits of life and choose instead to demean the uniqueness of others or perhaps misuse our own gifts. In either case, the choice is ours.

Human Pathology

In choosing to resist limitations we make life more difficult for ourselves. If we are short, we yearn to be tall. If we're fat, we want to be thin. If someone points out a fault, we immediately defend ourselves. It is no easy task to take our own measure, and we frequently resist even the slightest suggestion that we may have faults. When grades are given out to students at the end of a semester, it is not uncommon for teachers to be verbally thrashed for giving a low grade. We should bear in mind that while grades sometimes reflect negligence on the part of the students, they also reflect ability. Trying one's best is important but not everyone has equal talent, which grades usually reflect. Why do many resist this truism?

Limit-resistance also leads to destructive behavior. It is, in fact, the taproot of moral evil. If we look at sin in general terms, we find that all sin ultimately stems from a rejection of the limits of others by either domination or indifference. The neighborhood bully who flaunts his strength by intimidating others in effect manipulates others to do his bidding by threat of force. The classroom teacher who berates and embarrasses students for their ignorance sins against them by refusing to accept the limits of their ability. Similarly, parents who demand perfection from their children or the bosses who cajole and dragoon subordinates fail to allow for the shortcomings and limits of others.

Rebellious pride seeks to dominate others. It accumulates wealth, possessions, and property as proof that more is better (when, indeed, quality and quantity measure different realities). We lie about our weaknesses and shortcomings, and we demand of others what is beyond their limits. We use power, status, and prestige as the marks of a successful human life. All of these are expressions in one way or another of limit-resistance by denial.

Moreover, limit-resistance not only involves domination, but also appears in the form of indifference. There is a tendency to resist limits by actively avoiding the responsibilities of life. By seeking possessions or power rather than entering into loving relationships with other people, we attempt to eliminate the risk and pain of being human. By avoiding contact with those who need us—the entire proposition of humanity is that we need each other—and by behaving indifferently toward others, we avoid situations that would inevitably lead us to see and understand our own limits while accepting the limits of others.

Even suicide, which on the surface seems to be the ultimate in limiting oneself, is, in fact, a running away from the limits of life. A student recently spoke about a friend who was an up-and-coming ballet dancer until she was injured in an auto accident. She subsequently took her life primarily because she refused to face life without her career.

Divorce, too, represents a rejection of limits. Walls of hostility are built up over time. They eventually become insurmountable. Careless and callous attitudes finally result in a rupture of the fabric of marriage with damage to parents, children, and all society. In short, personal limit-resistance surfaces in the forms of domination and indifference. These forms also appear on the global level.

It is less than half a century since a major world war was fought in order to thwart the ideology of a super race. Adolf Hitler espoused the philosophy of Nietzsche, who believed that the "will to power" was, and should be, the prevailing force within society. Furthermore, most rich and powerful nations today are reluctant to share their wealth with poorer countries. Less-developed nations get short shrift because First World nations do not wish to deal with the limits of their poverty by supporting development. Likewise, it seems easier to continue the arms race even after the Cold War has ended, because switching to a peacetime economy may cause short-term political and economic dislocation.

We see, then, that limit-resistance happens on both personal and social levels. It causes destruction of personal relationships through our refusal to accept the limits of human nature and wreaks havoc on the social order by either oppression of or inattention to other people. The way of limit-resistance is the way of moral evil. When we resist our own limits and those of our neighbor we deny the vulnerability that most accurately defines the human condition.

Limit Acceptance

A fundamental truth of Christianity teaches that all creation is good. Throughout history attempts have been made to replace this truth with a dualism that suggested that the spiritual realm was superior to the material world, the soul better than the body. This perennial heresy contradicts the goodness inherent within each person by forcing people to deny the totality and unity of their individual person, both biologically and spiritually.

More specifically, in accepting our finiteness we stop playing God and learn to live with our human nature. The continuum along which we move from limit-resistance to limit-acceptance serves as a reliable measure of our ability to love ourselves and others. This is not to say that we shrink from or stand by passively in the face of limitations. We need to discern constantly between what we can and cannot do.

At times, we may lack the courage to forge ahead in spite of the obstacles, or we may foolishly act beyond the bounds of our talent and ability. In many ways life continually offers us opportunities to test our limits while simultaneously revealing the pathetically limited conditions under which we live. Learning to accept personal limits requires patience, perseverance, and courage. It is a lifelong task.

The ancient maxim, "do unto others as you would have them do unto you," expresses great wisdom insofar as it implicitly recognizes our need for acceptance in spite of our shortcomings, while inviting us to extend the same consideration. If we eschew the temptation to amplify the faults of others and learn the art of forgiveness, life assumes a more harmonious wholeness.

Jesus chastised those who were quick to point out the faults of others, but rarely considered their own misdeeds.[4] "Do not judge, so that you may not be judged"[5] sums up the Christian imperative. How often do I misjudge the motives of others? How frequently do I overlook the human weaknesses of my family, friends, and, perhaps more importantly, my enemies? Many, holding on to the negativity of limit-resistance, conclude that love has no place in the world of business and politics. On the contrary, its absence there has caused irreparable harm. Limit-acceptance begins with the self, but extends itself to all human endeavors.

The chart on page 102 illustrates the human condition into which we are born. It shows how the conflict between our innate longing for the infinite, expressed in our desire for freedom, and the factual reality of our limits in time and space results in an ontological tension that is the soil for both weeds and wheat. Destructive responses to this tension stem from attitudes of limit-resistance, personally and socially, and take the form of avoidance and denial of limits. Morally speaking, we sin by avoiding limits through irresponsible and indifferent behavior, or we sin by denying limits through the excessive accumulation of wealth and the domination of others.

Conversely, we may choose the way of limit-acceptance by loving ourselves and others. In terms of inclusion, we become more open and empathic to those around us and begin to extend our vision of humanity toward different races, nationalities, cultures, and religious, political and economic systems, indeed, the whole human family. We become peacemakers and builders of a just society. Limit-acceptance, then, is the key to understanding peace and justice. Unless we are willing to embrace our limited condition, we will struggle through life resisting one of its central truths.

The Human Condition

We are both

Infinite
- the desire to be "more"
- the desire to be godlike
- "reaching for the stars"

and

Finite
- limitations of reality
- the "now situation"
- time, place, and history

Result is a
Basic Tension
thus we are
Free to Choose

<u>Limit-acceptance</u>	**OR**	<u>Limit-resistance</u>
(Creative Response)		(Destructive Response)

(l) Allowing for Limits
- openness
- tolerance

(1) Avoiding Limits
- irresponsibility
- indifference

(2 Accepting Limits
- care and love
- commitment
- responsibility

(2) Denying Limits
- dominate (power)
- accumulate (wealth)

A Christian Perspective

Keep in mind that the human tendency to reach for the stars is not bad in and of itself. We are created for eternal union with God and quite naturally are drawn in that direction. Augustine prayed, "You have made us for yourself, O God, and our hearts are restless until they rest in you."[6] Striving for success, living life to the fullest, "getting all the gusto," and using our talents and abilities are good. The achievements of the human race are too numerous to mention. They are the result of a never-ending quest for excellence.

Our destructiveness is, however, also there for all to see. The enormous slaughter of life in wars, the hunger and starvation of millions while others look away, pollution of the environment, racism, sexism, the barbarism, and militarism indicate the depths of our destructive death-resistance. Ultimately, all evil results from a failure to acknowledge our limits and accept those of others.

We need to face this fundamental anxiety within our heart. Animals do not have the ability to reflect upon themselves. We do. With this reflective ability comes the choice of accepting or rejecting our creatureliness, our vulnerabilities, our limited condition. In a world that we can only trust was created by a loving and caring God, we are asked to choose life or death. In choosing to accept our limits, we choose life. In rejecting our limits, we choose death. To recognize this truth enables us to love ourselves and others; it enables us to be responsible for our contribution to a society and culture in need of healing; it enables us, finally, to appreciate and respect the rights of even the most severely limited among us.

From a distinctly Christian perspective, the person of Jesus has played a unique role within human history insofar as the fundamental problem of evil is concerned. If our basic pathology, the root cause of evil, lies in limit-resistance, then the healing or cure must be found in limit-acceptance. The expression "Jesus saves" means that he saved us from death-resistance by accepting the final limit of life, death itself.

One interpretation of his death maintains that he died in order to show us that we too must learn to die. In several gospel passages Jesus calls his followers to die to themselves in order to find new life.[7] Whether or not one accepts Jesus as Savior, his profound insight into the fear of death and the other limits of life as central to the mystery of good and evil remains startling. How a Palestinian Jew living in a remote corner of the Roman Empire almost two thousand years ago could offer such wisdom seems to defy human explanation.

Christian believers see the symbol of the cross as the way to new life. There is no crown without the cross; no salvation without suffering; no joy without sorrow. The Christian belief in the Resurrection of Jesus from the dead caused St. Paul to mock death with his famous words, "O death, where is your victory? O death, where is your sting?"[8] For the believer the mystery of the Cross stands as a sign of healing. Death-acceptance paradoxically leads to life.

We began by asking, "Who are the handicapped?" We conclude by saying, "Everyone!" All human beings share in the limits of life; we all experience a variety of handicapping conditions. Yet we are also gifted in many ways. Our talents and abilities, the resources and abundance of the natural wealth on our planet, the creative genius of the human race, the accumulated knowledge, learning, and wisdom of all the ages, our laughter and our love tell a story of goodness, healing, and achievement that continues to unfold. We need to remember that success is measured, not by fame or fortune, but by our ability to realize our potential within the context of our limits.

Notes

[1]   Reinhold Niebuhr, *The Nature and Destiny of Man* (New York: Scribner & Sons, 1941), 185.

[2]   Genesis 3:5.

[3]   Niebuhr, *The Nature and Destiny of Man*, 167.

4   Matthew 7:3.

5   Matthew 7:1.

6   Saint Augustine, *Confessions* (New York: Viking Penguin, 1961), 21.

7   Matthew 16:24–25.

8   1 Corinthians 15:55.

10

Interdependence

No man is an island, entire of itself; every man is a piece of the
continent, a part of the main; . . . Any man's death diminishes me,
because I am involved in Mankinde; And therefore never send to
know for whom the bell tolls; it tolls for thee.

John Donne[1]

Born for Unity

In Part I, Inclusion, we have looked at the wide variety of religions, cultures, economic and political systems, and the social
customs and traditions that comprise our common human heritage. The vast histories of divergent peoples, with their achievements and conflicts, stand as a reminder of the enormous
diversity within the human race. In the present era we are witness to a quantum leap in population. During the past fifty years
it has doubled, so that today more than five billion people
inhabit the earth. This has brought with it new creative energies
in agriculture, industry, education, religion, and the arts and
sciences, but it has also created severe problems in meeting
basic needs and providing opportunities for personal growth.

This level of the personal is of paramount importance to us. We should bear in mind that the fundamental basis for the variety of human experiences and practices can ultimately be traced to the uniqueness of each person. In looking at the larger categories of nations and states, religions and languages, we must resist the temptation to depersonalize the individual.

Along with the uniqueness of each person, moreover, comes an understanding of ourselves as social beings. We were brought into this world by the physical love of two human beings and our bodies will hopefully be lowered into a grave by others who love us. We depend on each other for survival, for understanding and affection, and for recognition. How much less would our lives be without others around to share it? The personal and social dimensions of life are like two sides of the same coin. Heads or tails, they are of equal importance.

The most obvious and natural social side of life is the relationship we share within our own immediate family. Some of us were born into families with brothers and sisters, a mom and dad, and several sets of aunts, uncles, and cousins. Others of us grew up with only one parent, no siblings, and few relatives. Most of us experienced combinations of the above. When we were born we lived in total dependence. We were fed, washed, clothed, and loved by others and relied completely on their support. Gradually we began to do things for ourselves, and, with some urging, began to help with household chores. There was movement from dependence to interdependence.

Our connectedness with those outside our immediate families is apparent enough. We have teachers who help us learn, sanitation workers who collect our waste, police and fire personnel who provide security, and farmers, factory workers, and baseball players to feed, clothe, and entertain us. Some may object that since we pay for these benefits we have a right to them. The point is not how we obtain the services, rather it is simply that we depend on others as they depend on us. A transportation strike in a large city or a shutdown of the electricity or water supply make us realize quickly how dependent we are.

A complex societal structure tends to come apart quickly if vital functions are disrupted.

Furthermore, the autoworker in Detroit is acutely aware that he and his counterpart at the Sagami auto parts plant in Japan have much in common. The New York City garment worker and her counterpart in Seoul, Korea, know that the livelihood of one may hurt the other. Juan, the Brazilian coffee farmer, and the millions of coffee drinkers throughout the world depend on each other for continual production and consumption. Since the advent of large-scale international trade and the shrinking of planet Earth by technological advancements, many people recognize a new and profound global unity within the human family. We are more interdependent as nation-states than at any previous point in history.

Just as with other words, it is crucial to interpret the meaning of *interdependence*. For instance, our own Declaration of Independence officially severed the bonds of colonialism with England, but forged a union of states dependent upon each other for mutual support against the tyranny of the king. The colonists did not wish to live in bondage, but they did not seek isolation either. Indeed, their closing words, "We mutually pledge to each other our lives, our Fortunes, and our sacred Honor," indicate a strong sense of interdependence.

Mutuality connotes a relatedness on a personal level, whereas interdependence seems to fit more properly into a broader social context. In either case, there is a need to disabuse ourselves of the notion that we stand on our own two feet and don't need anyone, or that we got where we are without help from others. Interdependence requires an openness to others, a desire to listen and respect the ideas and vision of different people, a willingness to rely on others for help and to offer support when others are in need. It implies a spirit of compromise, forgiveness, and no small amount of patience, tolerance, and frequent reconciliation of differences. In building a world of peace and justice, human relationships should be characterized by interdependence.

Isolation/Exploitation

We pointed out in the last chapter that all human problems can be traced to a profound inability to accept limits. In the context of Part I, Inclusion, this limit-resistance is expressed through prejudice, ethnocentrism, distrust, paranoia, and parochialism. On a personal level we build walls and barriers around ourselves thinking that others are against us, or that our own group (nationality, church affiliation, club, team, political party, etc.) has the edge on goodness, light, and truth. We make fun of people who are different and reject attempts to include others in our world.

What occurs on a personal level is multiplied on the national and international levels. "Truth" is the first thing to go in any confrontation, so it follows that name-calling and stereotyping become part of the landscape when nations are in disagreement. Terms such as *gringo, kike, jap, spic,* and *gook,* or slogans like "nuke Iran" do little to create harmony. In effect, name-calling and stereotyping exhibit attitudes of self-imposed isolation.

This type of isolation stands in sharp contrast to the solitude of the monk, which is freely chosen, or the aloneness necessary for concentrated study or work. The isolation of which we speak here is an isolation of alienation. The monk loves deeply both God and others. The committed worker is dedicated to excellence and the betterment of the human condition. On the other hand, the isolation of alienation drives one deep within oneself to the point where no room exists for cooperation, friendship, and love. For example, alcoholics and drug addicts have imposed isolation upon themselves by running away from the responsibilities of adulthood.

Frequently enough, this isolation turns into exploitation of others either by demanding excessive attention or committing criminal acts. A wide gulf exists between aloneness and loneliness. In the former case, we seek a place apart for the refreshment of our spirit, while in the latter, we flee from the dialogical encounters with others so necessary for our own well-being and the betterment of society. Personal isolation leads to alienation with oneself as well as one's neighbor.

Within the community of nations similar problems occur. Groups of countries, flying one ideological flag or another, mass resources for their own benefit and often appear unwilling to discuss differences with other states that disagree with them. War, of course, is the ultimate alienation and it has caused the death of millions throughout history. Like personal alienation, barriers of fear, webs of suspicion, and the dark clouds of hostility often impel nations to seek their own interests first even at the expense of global security.

It is plain to see that isolation and exploitation disrupt the patterns of unity for which we were destined. The healthy growth of the person and the nation depends on the support and cooperation of others. Unfortunately, we are prone to forget these simple truths and fall into the old habits of selfishness. Furthermore, even if we do not espouse a position of hostility toward others, we may fail to work for peace by staying in our own cocoon of pleasure. We seek self-satisfaction while others around us yearn for recognition.

Writ globally, this indifference means poverty for the many, affluence for the few. In our schools, homes, offices, and factories, we should practice the skills and techniques of interdependence in order to build relationships of care and concern. Likewise, in our political and economic affairs, we are challenged to use our talents for creating a more equitable and just world order. There can be no peace where children suffer from malnutrition and dictators and greed merchants exploit the poor. The light in our minds and the fire in our hearts challenge us to live and to work in a spirit of interdependence for the good of all.

Peace on Earth

One does not ordinarily conceive of popes as revolutionaries, yet Pope John XXIII was as much a revolutionary as Lenin or

Mao Tse-tung. His predecessor, Pius XII, pope from 1939 to 1958, symbolized a Church dependent upon its tradition for credibility and—after the 1950 publication of the encyclical letter *Humani Generis*—fearful of modern ideas. In visual contrast to the gaunt Pius XII, John XXIII, an overweight, jovial man, believed strongly in the goodness of the human family and embraced people of all faiths. He realized that the Catholic Church needed a thorough housecleaning and convened his fellow bishops (more than 2,500) for four major meetings during the autumns from 1962 through 1965. This is known historically as the Second Vatican Council.

Just as he held a council for the reform and renewal of the Church, so too did he offer a blueprint for peace to the people and nations of the world. This legacy of peace was the encyclical *Peace on Earth.* Published in the spring of 1963, *Peace on Earth* called for the establishment of universal peace based on truth, justice, charity, and freedom. These four values were the natural extension of a social order that recognized each person as a unique individual.

Any human society, if it is to be well ordered and productive, must lay down as a foundation this principle: that every human being is a person; their nature is endowed with intelligence and free will. By virtue of this, they have rights and duties of their own, flowing directly and simultaneously from their very nature, which are therefore universal, inviolable, and inalienable.[2]

John XXIII enumerated such fundamental rights as rights to life and a worthy manner of living; rights concerning cultural and moral values; rights to worship, to choose one's occupation, and to assemble; and, finally, various rights in the political and social order. It is important to note that he placed equal emphasis on the reciprocity of rights, i.e., for each right that a person has, others have a corresponding obligation to acknowledge and respect that right.[3] The pope furthermore insisted that human rights extend to all people, rich and poor, old and young, male and female alike. While cultural norms and economic practices have frequently limited human rights, remedies should be sought to rectify these violations.

Pope John, however, knew full well that governments play a major role in creating a peaceful world order. Far too often antagonisms and hostilities between nations arise because government officials refuse to discuss differences or negotiate mutually acceptable treaties between states. In the first place, he noted that governments are constituted to promote the good of all citizens. "The civil power must not serve the advantage of any one individual, or of some few persons, inasmuch as it was established for the common good of all."[4]

The public order within any state is governed by the basic human rights of each person living within that state. In addition, the relationship between states should promote global harmony. Efforts should be undertaken to promote solidarity among all people, and nations with an abundance of resources ought to assist those who lack adequate economic development.[5] John XXIII was not a minimalist. He made clear that people and nations are responsible for each other.

Efforts must be made to go beyond a self-interested posture that allows people to remain indifferent to others who suffer. The pope challenged the secure, healthy, and affluent to help the oppressed, neglected, and needy. Presupposed in all of his thinking is that all people are created by God and called to love one another.

A quarter-century has passed since John XXIII issued *Peace on Earth*. Are we any closer to living its truths today than we were then? Is it so much wishful thinking to expect an end to violence and war when the human heart remains filled with selfishness and nation-states proclaim power as their guiding light? Since 1963 the United States has engaged in the bloody and protracted Vietnam War, Iran and Iraq have decimated each other's lands, Middle East conflicts between Christians and Muslims in Lebanon and Palestinians and Jews in Israel have continued. The Persian Gulf War in early 1991 simply confirmed that military force still dominates the thinking of political leaders.

In contrast to the violence, however, people have grown more conscious of their responsibility for the environment, world leaders have taken steps to limit the nuclear arms race, and serious peace movements have sprung up worldwide. Perhaps with these and other efforts the world is more conscious of its interdependence today than ever before. The revolution for peace inspired by John XXIII and his encyclical *Peace on Earth* needs continued support.

Building Interdependence

If we feel that we are not valued or that no one will support us; if there is no one to talk to when we are troubled or burdened; if we sense that the world is passing us by and little hope exists for our contribution, then life is a sad and lonely business. Yet, like it or not, we have only ourselves to blame. We can change course, we can take charge of our life and make the choices necessary for our own fulfillment. Isolation provides few answers. The key to true success is love, and this suggests a mutuality of respect and appreciation of others.

Reaching out to others in friendship, trust, and confidence allows others to drop their own barriers of fear and hostility. Students, in particular, have many opportunities to cooperate with their peers in study sessions, off-campus volunteer projects, and student organizations. In addition, the perceptive person will look for ways to identify those among them who appear despondent or left out. The magnanimity of reaching out to someone in need advances the cause of human solidarity beyond measure. This ethical imperative always involves a knowledge of our dependence and the willingness to let others rely upon us.

On the global level, the movement toward interdependence has ebbed and flowed. The United Nations has provided a much-needed forum for international public debate and has acted as mediator between states on numerous occasions. For many years it has sponsored the Law of the Sea conference, which has sought to have the oceans of the world declared "the common heritage of the human family." But the work of the United Nations as a mediator and as a voice for global peace has often fallen on deaf ears. Greater efforts must be made through the U.N. and by direct negotiations in order to lower the hostility levels of nation-states.

Many charitable and church organizations have worked with the needy in developing basic nutrition, health, and education facilities, and governments have provided some help by way of foreign aid programs. Much more needs to be done before these people can claim to possess their share of the world's goods. If we recall that the United States represents only 5 percent of the world population and annually consumes about 40 percent of its energy and food, we get some sense of the unjust distribution of resources. The following story offers us a possible response.

One of the most moving incidents in the gospel narrative concerns the generosity of a man named Zacchaeus. Luke tells us that he was a wealthy man with a lively curiosity about the itinerant preacher and miracle worker, Jesus. When the latter came to town, Zacchaeus, being short of stature, climbed a sycamore tree for a better look. Jesus paused and asked to dine at his house. Zacchaeus was so overcome with joy that he gave away half his fortune to the poor and paid back five times more to those he had cheated.

If only more of us could catch the Zacchaeus fever. It is a spirit of generosity to those who are needy—a willingness to extend ourselves beyond a few token gestures. The key to this generosity lies in a personal awareness of the blessings we have received. Zacchaeus realized immediately that, in the willingness of Jesus to share his table, he was touched by God. This same Jesus continues to share his presence with us in the memorial meal of the Last Supper. Perhaps if we could grasp the profundity of that moment, we might act as Zacchaeus did.

Human problems have human solutions. In learning to say No, we stifle our selfish impulses and check the pride, greed, and indifference from which we all suffer. In learning to say Yes, we develop habits of sharing and caring not just for our immediate family and friends (although love naturally starts with those around us), but also to reach out in an ever widening circle of concern. Ultimately, we are all God's children called to live in peace. As we continue to explore the many facets of peace and social justice, let us work for greater interdependence within the human family.

Notes

1 John Donne, from "Devotions, No. xvii," Burton Stevenson, ed., *The Home Book of Quotations* 10th ed. (New York: Dodd, Mead, 1967), 2298o.

2 John XXIII, *Peace on Earth* (New York: Paulist Press, 1963), 8.

3 Ibid., 14.

4 Ibid., 23.

5 Ibid., 41.

Part II

Perception

How Do We See?

Introduction

At the outset of this text we described peace and justice education as a process that enables students to broaden their appreciation for people of other cultures, to develop a new vision based on humanitarian values, and to participate actively in creating a better world. Having examined in some detail the various dimensions of the inclusion question, we are now in a position to ask the question, "How do I see?" The Perception section begins with the self as both individual and social, then attempts to examine several of the more serious historical societal problems, many of which continue to plague the human family. Finally, we will conclude with a chapter on how we tend to block the future, and how we might open ourselves to a better one.

Let us say at the outset that as a species we have achieved much in the way of intellectual insight and a modicum of civility in our relationships with one another. Erich Fromm, however, in the *Art of Loving*, reminds us that our minds live in the twentieth century, but our hearts still live in the Stone Age. We are not quite so pessimistic, but do believe that unless we are able to grasp the depth of human pathology, personal and social, we are doomed to a repetition of past evils. Only by accepting our weaknesses and failures do we begin to make amends for them.

In another work, *The Heart of Man*, Fromm asks rhetorically whether we are sheep or wolves. He concludes that we are both. More important, it would seem, is what we want to be. If, indeed, we can decide our futures, then we may choose to be neither sheep nor wolves, but men and women of truth, integrity, and goodness. Human evil is the result of human choice. We are not predestined toward destructiveness. If, as previously stated, we can learn to accept our limitations and the limits of others around us, it is possible to have a more just and harmonious society.

In the act of "seeing," we should bear in mind the limits of our point of view. The story of the four blind men describing an elephant comes to mind. The first man, feeling the trunk and tusks of the elephant, described its length and bone structure. The two men on opposite sides agreed on largeness and breadth. The man touching the tail described a long thin rope ending in a knot of bushy hair. All were correct. Their understanding depended on their point of view.

It is hoped that this section on perception will offer us some insight into the need for a variety of viewpoints. We should examine a topic from many points of view before we begin to make judgments and decisions about it. This takes time and effort, but it moves us to a new level of understanding and an appreciation about the complexity of human affairs.

11

How Do I See?

At every moment you choose yourself. But do you choose yourself?
Body and soul contain a thousand possibilities out of which you
can build many I's.

Dag Hammarskjöld[1]

Perceptual Development

If you were to imagine each day of your life as one page in a
book, each month as one chapter, and each year as one
volume, you would probably be surprised at the amount of
material already accumulated in your own personal Book-
of-My-Life. Some pages would abound with drama, others
might appear dull and plodding. Sometimes you might have
experienced fear, anxiety, and danger, while at other times life
for you was serene and happy. In most cases, hindsight can
lead to insight. How do you see yourself? Does looking back
over your infancy, childhood, and adolescence bring a smile to
your face or a tear to your eye? Most likely, the smile or the tear
will depend upon your remembrance of a particular event or
situation.

During infancy our perception of things is extremely limited. Infants are primarily concerned about nourishment and comfort. A baby crying in the middle of the night has expectations only of its mother's breast or a clean diaper. It doesn't take very long, however, for the child to begin looking around. Gradually there is an awareness of teddy bears and other toys, the faces of Mom and Dad, the movements and sounds of other people, and a growing desire to explore and touch everything in sight!

Within a few years the average child has grown enormously aware of his or her surroundings. Brothers and sisters, playmates from school, teachers, television characters, and thousands of "things" are now part of a child's perceptual range. Friendships are beginning to form, likes and dislikes are taking root, basic genetic personality characteristics are appearing, and learning to read and write are increasing the child's knowledge of places and events beyond family and neighborhood.

Adolescence brings with it whole new sets of perception patterns. Erik Erikson, a world-renowned psychoanalyst, contextualized our early years by pointing to the characteristics of autonomy, initiative, and industry as the most salient features of childhood.[2] We became aware of ourselves as individuals, we began to do things on our own, and we developed habits of work. Furthermore, the bodily changes occurring at the onset of puberty brought a sexual component to perception. As teenagers we were smitten with infatuation for each other, at times openly but often privately. Consequently, sexual attraction added a new and exciting dimension to life.

Regional high schools, new friends, broader educational opportunities, travel, and many other experiences continued to impact our minds during these teen years, and the awareness of personal identity took on paramount significance. City kids going away to camp saw a whole new world of rivers, lakes, woods, and wildlife; and many country kids visiting the city for the first time were awed by the hustle and bustle of taxis, buses, and trains, the crowds of people, the bright lights of downtown, and the fast pace and bigness of city life.

Maturity and young adulthood, in terms of perception, necessitate a broadened view of life, a wider range of experiences that open one to a variety of interests, including a knowledge of various personalities and the ability to reflect upon the lessons of history. One's own personal vision of how things ought to be, as opposed to how they are, is also part of adult perception. Human growth, then, is characterized by a movement toward a broader, more comprehensive view of the complexity and variety of the world and a greater tolerance and understanding of one's own limits and those of others.

Perceptual Pathology (Personal)

It is a well-established fact that humans have a variety of psychological mechanisms that affect how they see.[3] Aside from intellectual ignorance and the obvious limits imposed by physical, mental, or emotional handicaps, we all are influenced by our upbringing, by the political, economic, and cultural characteristics of our society, and by an assortment of prejudices, false assumptions, and ideologies that we have accumulated throughout our life. For example, in the Middle Ages most people thought that the earth was flat and that velocity was proportional to force, until Christopher Columbus and Isaac Newton showed them otherwise.

Furthermore, some people are quick to say that the Irish are drunkards, blacks are lazy, Jews are greedy, Germans are warlike, and Chinese are inscrutable. No doubt some in each group fit the description. Yet it is grossly unfair to paint a particular person or group with bad habits found among all people. In any case, people generalize too quickly, rely on outmoded knowledge, allow fears and anxieties to thwart rational thought, and often refuse to change their minds in spite of evidence to the contrary.

It is an obvious though often forgotten truth that our emotions and feelings color our thoughts and moods. When our mood is somber or fretful, as it may be on a wet and rainy day, we are less inclined to be optimistic. In this state of mind it is difficult to see the happy side of life. When the mood is mellow and upbeat, however, with feelings that are similar to strong cool breezes and warm sunshine, we are reluctant to ponder the dark corners of our life or the shadows within our personality. Assessing ourselves is no easy matter, not only because we are changeable in mood and circumstance, but also because our very changeable behavior tends to cloud our perception. This fact has implications for our "seeing" the world around us.

People who suffer from myopia are able to see things reasonably well close up, but need corrective lenses for distance vision. The opposite is true for farsighted people. When the lights are out, because of a power failure or by way of the sun going down, we are in the dark. Lack of light may be compared to lack of knowledge. Our ignorance of people makes us blind to the conditions of their life. On the other hand, astigmatism of the eye may be compared to prejudice in the heart. Something is wrong in either case and we need help.

Blurred vision, literally or figuratively, toward oneself or others, results in a distortion of reality. For example, if I have a negative attitude toward myself it is unlikely that I will think well of others or see the good that they do. If my attitude, however, is one of superiority, I will rarely be found praising the accomplishments of other people. We are also quick to point out the shortcomings of others, while giving little thought to our own failings. Jesus rebuked the faultfinders by reminding them of their own limitations. It is a lesson worthy of reflection.

Alfred Adler, a prominent psychoanalyst, used the term *inferiority complex* to describe a situation common to all people in the early years of life, but one that describes an emotional illness in later years. Unless we grow to a better understanding of ourselves and an appreciation of our self-worth as we grow older, we will go through life with a stunted personality. In recalling Maslow's vision of the healthy personality, a person who is self-actualizing, we see how important it is for us to know ourselves, to accept ourselves with all the talents, abilities, and gifts we possess, and to admit our limitations and our vulnerabilities.

All of these aspects of our life—the positive and negative, the healthy and pathological, the good and bad—need to be acknowledged if we are to grow toward self-fulfillment.

Unfortunately, as Maslow points out, some people stop fulfilling their needs by settling for less than their potential. Many others, because of injustices and violence, are never given the opportunity to develop their potential. In any case, an appreciation of one's own personhood is the basis for an appreciation of the dignity of others.

Perceptual Pathology (Social)

Several years ago tests were conducted among youngsters living in a small town near the Texas-Mexico border. A visual device was used that allowed two different images to be seen with each eye when they were flashed momentarily upon a split screen. One image was that of a bullfighter, the other of a baseball player. While all of the children saw both images, the preponderance of Mexicans identified a bullfighter, whereas the American youths saw a ballplayer. This example highlights the strong environmental and cultural influences that color our perceptions. "We see what we want to see," goes the old adage. Psychologists refer to this problem as one of perceptual screening.

Perceptual screening is a commonly used mechanism for blocking out those portions of reality that make us uncomfortable or threaten to shatter our present mind-set. In the United States our obsessive need for national security has caused a mental blindness to the hunger of others. Billions for security; little for human needs. We help a little, but never to the point of feeling insecure. This fixation for security is now leading us into spending for weapons in space instead of shelters for the homeless, food for the needy, quality education, and adequate medical care for all of our citizens.

Another perceptual problem is that of denial. The classic statue of the three monkeys covering their eyes, ears, and mouth, respectively, comes to mind. Although the artist's intent was to portray the principle of "see no evil, hear no evil, speak no evil," we can also interpret its meaning as a way of refusing to see, hear, or taste the negative side of life. None of us seeks disappointment and sorrow, yet they are part of human experience. Denial of reality may be seen in the aged ballplayer trying to make a comeback or the refusal of a teacher to admit a mistake.

A purely subjective analysis of situations based strictly upon one's own opinions is a third problem of perception. Slogans like "We're #1" and "Why not the best?" tend to exaggerate the importance of a particular group or product. When we are unwilling to listen to the opinions of others or accept sound and reasonable advice, we end up with little more than our own limited subjective outlook on life. Nationalism, a form of group pride, frequently blocks us from an honest assessment of global problems. We tend to see things from our own vantage point. Karl Marx was convinced that much of the culture of a nation is determined by the dominant power structure. While this may not be the whole truth, it is clear that a power position on our part will often blind us to the needs of others.

It is well known that eyewitnesses to an event frequently give conflicting reports on what happened. Not quite so obvious, but equally true, is the variety of story lines from different newspapers and magazines reporting or commenting on the news. The *New York Times* and the *New York Daily News* "see" things differently. The *Times* offers its readers a view of Nicaragua as emerging from a dictatorial past into a society concerned with the basic needs of all, while the *Daily News* portrays that country as oppressive and communist-dominated. Many U.S. citizens who have gone to Nicaragua have a completely different explanation of the situation. In arriving at a judgment on any given topic or situation it is wise to listen and gather information from as many different, and hopefully reliable, sources as possible.

Prejudice is the most common false assumption among people. Prejudice mistakenly assumes that all members of a group share the same qualities. Some people today assume that drugs are recreational, even after the deaths of thousands of drug users. Students often blame their teachers for low grades when in fact they extended little effort in doing class assignments. We should test our own perceptions against those of others. We all carry our own set of assumptions and are predisposed to certain conclusions before the facts are in. We need to avoid hasty judgments and seek a variety of opinions and interpretations. Most social problems are complex and need considerable study before a thorough understanding of them can be reached.

A final perceptual difficulty has to do with inadequate theories. The Copernican revolution changed our understanding of the Earth as the center of the universe to that of only a small planet orbiting the sun. The discovery of radioactivity at the close of the nineteenth century opened up whole new developments in scientific thought. Wider contact with people from different cultures should continue to expand our understanding of people.

Insecurity, fear, pride, greed, selective screening of reality, apathy, indifference, denial, false assumptions, and a whole assortment of factors, internal and external, create an array of obstacles for us in our search for understanding, truth, and meaning. In a real sense the educational task throughout life is to recognize personal self-interest and other blind spots that prevent us from appreciating the broadest possible dimensions of reality. The process of growth is slow and painful (in the sense that we must go through crisis and conflict situations in order to reach new levels of maturity), and yet occasionally we get an insight that helps us reintegrate new facts and events. As is so often the case in other areas of life, the progress that one makes in overcoming the obstacles that distort, or poorly filter, the reality of life around us will be in proportion to the effort expended.

Toward Clarity

Physically speaking, human sight is best when we have 20/20 vision. If our vision is distorted, we use corrective lenses to restore our sight. Analogously, we need to continually seek proper vision when we attempt to understand ourselves, others, and the world around us. What is true? What is good? What is beautiful? How do I find meaning in my life? Are some ways of living better than others? Given the uniqueness of each person, is it possible to develop a generalized moral vision for all people?

These and similar topics are at the heart of the perception question, for we cannot divorce our understanding of particular concerns from the necessary correlative of judgment. As night follows day, judgment follows understanding. If we agree that prejudice, bigotry, ignorance, and fear limit our perception of reality, we must devise methods and strategies for overcoming these impediments to truth and goodness. Truth and goodness, therefore, should constitute the central goals of human life and are the lenses through which we should evaluate reality.

The first task, however, is to see what's happening and to get beyond the surface experience to the meaning behind it. For example, discrimination against women can only be understood in the light of a historical system of patriarchy.

Similarly, the animosity between the United States and the Soviet Union was due in no small measure to the ideological clash between capitalism and communism. These obvious examples establish the necessity of looking beneath the external situation for the roots and causes of our current social ills.

In a real sense we cannot separate social analysis from judgment since they are part of the same mosaic. Consequently, it is only proper to state that our viewpoint will be grounded in the Judeo-Christian humanitarian ethic of love of neighbor. Twenty-twenty moral vision perceives a world of justice and peace. Hopefully, as we explore the major societal problems of our times we will keep this vision before us.

Clear vision, 20/20 insight into the world of today, demands attention to both the past and the future. Formal education implies that educated men and women accept responsibility for building a more humane society. This cannot happen unless one studies the history of the human family and builds the future on past wisdom. The wisdom of the Greeks, our own founding fathers, the philosophers, scientists, saints, and artists offer inestimable insight into human affairs. It follows, therefore, that instead of remaining ignorant of the past—a pathological perceptual condition—we must attempt to study history as a way of seeking truth.

Finally, of significant value in the quest for clear vision is the ability to distance oneself from a situation or problem, which allows for greater objectivity. Most students are familiar with the process of adjusting a microscope in order to properly view the object on the slide. We can use the same process of resolution by developing a view-from-the-moon perspective when it comes to examining the social conditions in our world.

When we observe planet Earth from a distance, we gain a broader, more comprehensive view of things. While it is important to be in touch with the local situations in our life, it is equally important to develop a global consciousness if we ever hope to create a better world. Viewing the world from 240,000 miles away lends perspective to the minutiae of daily life. "Moonview" is not only pleasing to the beholder, but is also a necessary component in grasping the larger reality in the lives of the Earth's population.

We sometimes assume that life is pretty much the same the world over as it is for us. A view-from-the-moon perspective should remind us of our previous observations about the tremendous diversity of language, customs, religions, politics, economic systems, and personalities that exist in our world. It is a point of view that will also help us see the commonality of problems and the global effects that people exert upon each other.

The Eyes of Faith

How does one speak of faith? Faith in what? Faith in whom? First of all, faith is not just a belief in a series of propositions or dogmas. Perhaps it is best understood in relational terms. When I trust another person with my joys and sorrows, knowing that he or she will laugh and cry with me, then I have faith in that person. So, first of all, faith is personal.

In the Hebrew Scriptures we read that Abraham and Sarah put their trust in God even though they were unsure of the direction God was to lead them. In speaking about seeing or perceiving our world through the eyes of faith we are asked to trust in the goodness of creation. Erikson, whom we cited at the beginning of this chapter, posited a psychosocial theory of human development whose first stage was basic trust. A mother's breast, a tender caress, the warmth of a hug ensure the healthy growth of an infant. Without this sustained nourishment children may be scarred for life.

Hope, too, is the natural ally of faith. It emerges as "the basic ingredient of all virtue."[4] Faith, then, is grounded in trust and relies on hope to sustain its strength.

Seeing with the eyes of faith means that we get beyond the shallow values associated with external appearance, popularity, and possessions, to the substantive goodness of friendship, kindness, and compassion.

To see with faith we need to view life from the depth of the heart. The two great pillars of Christian theology are Augustine and Aquinas. In the fourth century the former drew his deepest lessons from the mercy and love of God. The latter, on the other hand, during the thirteenth century saw God's face in knowledge and understanding. This twin revelation by Augustine and Aquinas concerning love and wisdom highlights the mutual compatibility of mind and heart.

Love and wisdom are not opposite ends of the spectrum, but two facets of the same diamond. We all know of instances when matters of the heart must overshadow the logic of a situation. Forgiveness, mercy, and tenderness affect us more deeply than calculated reason; yet our rational faculties remind us of the pitfalls of emotional vulnerability. Many a broken heart has resulted from an inability to use common sense.

In the Book of Kings we read how God appeared to Solomon in a dream to grant him whatever he wished. Instead of asking for long life or riches Solomon said, "Give your servant therefore an understanding mind to govern your people, able to discern between good and evil."[5] God was pleased with his answer and blessed him with a spirit of discernment. The eyes of faith, therefore, allow us to use both mind and heart in seeing what's happening around us.

"If an elephant has his foot on the tail of a mouse and you say that you are neutral, the mouse will not appreciate your neutrality." These words of Archbishop Desmond Tutu, a South African Anglican bishop, confirm the importance of empathy when viewing life. The mouse in question needs help. So do many people in our world.

The hit song "Day by Day" by Stephen Schwarz captures the musical mood of faith perception. "To see thee more clearly, love thee more dearly, follow thee more nearly—day by day"[6] lifts our eyes to a vision once we are attuned to the kingdom of God about which Jesus preached so eloquently. "Blessed are those who hunger and thirst for justice. . . . Blessed are the merciful. . . . Blessed are the peacemakers."[7] Can we take the initiative in bringing the message and insights of faith to bear on the realities of our time? Do the values of compassion, trust, and hope have anything to say about the exploitation of women through pornography, job discrimination, and domestic violence? Should cooperation replace rivalry and coercion? This chapter has argued for the necessity of seeing clearly that the dignity of each person and our responsibility toward all binds us to a 20/20 moral vision.

As we begin to analyze the major social issues of our time, let us seek the truth, not in the surface reality that is frequently no more than smoke and mirrors, but in the meaning of events often hidden beneath the actual experience.

While Madison Avenue programs the package, we must unwrap the covering and discover the contents.

Notes

1   Dag Hammarskjöld, *Markings* (New York: Ballantine Books, 1964), 12.

2   Erik Erikson, *Identity, Youth and Crisis* (New York: W. W. Norton, 1968), 91–128.

3   Richard I. Evans, *Dialogue with Erik Erikson* (New York: E. P. Dutton, 1969), 17.

4   Ibid.

5   1 Kings 3:9.

6   Stephen Schwartz, "Day by Day," from *Godspell* (New York: Herald Square Music & New Cadenza Music, 1971).

7   Matthew 5:5–9.

12

A Fundamental Distortion

A first precondition when trying to unfetter our minds from biases in order to reach a truer perception of reality is to see clearly the opportunistic interests affecting our search for truth and to understand how they operate.

Gunnar Myrdal[1]

Propensity toward Sin

In the last chapter we saw how several factors caused problems in how we see the world. Our emotions and moods tend to cloud our thinking; minimum or poor comprehension about particular issues often leaves us in ignorance; our faulty theories and prejudices and the psychological mechanisms of denial and avoidance also contribute to the lack of clarity with our perceptions. Suggestions were made that we should continue to learn more about world affairs and come to a better understanding of peoples, nations, and cultures. A broader view of the world gives us a more comprehensive view of reality.

In this chapter we intend to move to another level of reflection. Beneath the problems of ignorance and psychological difficulties there lies a more fundamental problem in seeking truth. The issue is moral evil or sin. We should note at the outset that contemporary society tends to avoid the word *sin*. Psychiatrist Karl Menninger, in his perceptive book, *Whatever Became of Sin?* said that a decline in religious faith had given rise to the popularity of psychotherapy, and a new vocabulary designed to avoid guilt had led to the discrediting of sin.[2]

Whether or not we name the reality of moral evil as sin, the abundance of violence, perversity, and crime ought to convince anyone of its pervasiveness. Moral evil is distinguished from the physical evils that nature imposes. Hurricanes, volcanic eruptions, typhoons, and earthquakes wreak havoc upon the earth. But these events are termed natural disasters because we have little control over them. Only when human beings perpetrate harm upon one another can we speak of moral evil. We are responsible for our behavior, and when it hurts another we are guilty of sin. The dispositions of the heart point to the essential nature of sin. In chapter 9 we learned that the tension between our longing for infinity and the limits of our existence created the occasion of sin. Since we are created in the image and likeness of God, we are made for love; yet our reluctance to accept our creatureliness drives us away from love toward selfishness. This reluctance to acknowledge our vulnerability disposes us toward sin.

Insofar as we are created for love—and the first requirement of love is justice—we fail to do justice if we ignore the social ills of our day or contribute to their increase. To live as a just person, to live as a loving person, to live as one concerned about the well-being of others signals the fullness of our humanity. Living destructively is inhumane. Hence, our tendency toward selfishness distorts our sense of truth.

A major criterion for judging right and wrong has always been the basic rights of other people. When rights are violated deliberately, then evil has been done. No one does evil, of course, for its own sake. The mind and heart of humans always seek something good, although we know that many times what appears good for us may harm others. For example, a fixation on my personal security can easily blind me to the insecurity of millions of destitute people for whose welfare I share responsibility.

Freedom of choice stands at the center of the human enterprise. No one expects tigers, tarantulas, or terriers to behave other than by instinct. Humans, however, are judged by their deeds. If we choose to ignore the consequences of our actions, if we live self-centered lives, if we behave irresponsibly toward others because of a distorted view of our own self-importance, then we have sinned.

Furthermore, we should realize that similar to the judgment in a court of law the degree of culpability is determined by the circumstances surrounding a particular deed. Moral responsibility moves along a continuum—from those who, at one end of the spectrum, may be incapable of choice, to those who are fully able to decide. The unemployed father who steals to help his wife and children is much less reprehensible than the public official who extorts payoffs from the business community.

In brief, the distortion of truth results in moral evil. Our selfishness, our inability to deal with vulnerability, and our limit-resistant behavior enmesh us in a web of lies, half-truths, and moral blindness that shuts us off from the love we were meant to give and receive. Let us now look in more detail at several ways in which truth is distorted.

The Seven Deadly Sins

No one would sin if it weren't so appealing. We are nudged toward evil by the natural drives within us when they are not controlled by our will. Centuries ago, theologians identified seven major ways in which we are drawn to sin. Each category represents a variety of attitudes and behavioral patterns that do harm to our own self-worth or to the rights of another. These seven deadly sins kill the spirit of love, kindness, and concern for which we were born.

A fully developed person, one who is spiritually alive, thinks and acts in morally responsible ways. But the seven deadly sins pull us away from human wholeness to fragmentation. Each sin distorts a natural good that ordinarily would contribute to our personal growth. Instead of experiencing spiritual growth we remain entombed in the graveyard of evil. In order to avoid the snares of these deadly sins we should know about their characteristics and understand how they distort our vision of a just and peaceful world.

Pride

Webster's Dictionary defines *pride*, in the context of sinfulness, as inordinate self-esteem. A reasonable appreciation of our self-worth is both necessary and laudable. We are unique individuals with basic human rights who are destined for eternal life. We can be rightly proud of our achievements, our personalities, and our goodness. Pride, however, distorts our sense of the goodness of others, and refuses to acknowledge that ultimately all of life is the gift of God. The temptation of Adam and Eve was to eat from the tree of knowledge of good and evil in order to become like God. They denied their humanity by demanding divinity.

This innate desire to refuse the limitations of our creatureliness leads to vanity, pomp, boasting, and arrogance. Men and women who wantonly deck themselves with expensive jewelry, fine clothing, and fancy accessories are the most obvious examples of distorted self-worth. They value outward appearances more than inner goodness. In the fourth century, Augustine warned that pride lurks even in good works.[3]

Greed

"'Take care! Be on your guard against all kinds of greed; for one's life does not consist in the abundance of possessions.'"[4] After the overthrow of the Marcos regime in the Philippines, it was discovered that first lady Imelda Marcos had two thousand pairs of shoes, five hundred black bras, and several hundred dresses in her wardrobe. This excessive acquisitiveness, especially in light of the grinding poverty among the Filipino people, highlights how greed can distort reality. The sin of greed distorted her perception of life, leaving her blind to the needs of others. Because this disposition of heart is a fundamental problem for each of us, we need to be on guard against our own proclivity for accumulating things. Greed invites me to think only of my needs, my wants, my likes, my desires. Is it possible that the popularization of the 1980s as a "me" decade is telling us something about the greediness of our life-style?

Lust

Those who lust after each other already commit adultery in their hearts, said Jesus in the Sermon on the Mount. Sexual desire comes with the territory. To be human is to be sexual, but indiscriminate sexual desire is subhuman. The most human expression of sexual desire is always focused on one other person in the context of commitment, fidelity, and marriage. When a woman and a man bond themselves in a union of love forever, they witness to the plan of God for the human family.

Subhuman sexuality is impersonal. It may range in scope from the buying and selling of sex through prostitution or erotic display (pornographic magazine models) to the "quickie" on a first date. The voyeur fails to see (note the connection with distorted perception) another person with feelings, hopes, fears, and dreams when he or she craves sexual satisfaction at the expense of the personal. Here again we have a disorientation of a basically wholesome human desire.

Sex outside of marriage and unbridled passion short-circuit the faithful nature of sexuality. Planned by God to foster intimacy, human sexual desire can build deep bonds of love within marriage. Shorn of this mutual commitment, promiscuous sex leads to a fixation on bodily pleasure and an impersonal objectification of others, where no thought is given to tenderness, care, or respect.

Hatred

If we conceive of the opposite of hate to be love, then it becomes apparent how hatred distorts our vision of life. We are made to love, which includes forgiveness, compassion, and acceptance. There is a tragic sadness to witness the unrelenting hatred between some groups of people in Northern Ireland, Lebanon, Spain, Turkey, or wherever. Basque separatists, Irish Provos, and Palestinian guerrillas all bear the mark of Cain. Their hatred eats away at any semblance of humanity that they might have and becomes an all-consuming passion in the pursuit of their cause.

Frequently in our own lives we find it difficult to forgive others who have offended us, and this reluctance may lead to hatred. Hatred is not merely anger, but is a disposition of the heart that seeks revenge. When we find ourselves plotting little strategies about getting even with someone, we are caught up in the web of hatred.

Gluttony

We tend to associate the word *gluttony* with habits of excessive eating or drinking. While this still might apply, especially in the light of the vast numbers of fat farms extant in the land and the enormous amount of alcoholic beverages consumed each day, we might also apply the word *gluttonous* to people who abuse themselves through smoking and drugs. The United States Surgeon General's office has forced manufacturers to label cigarettes as dangerous to one's health, and there is ample evidence to prove the harmful and sometimes lethal effects of drugs. Doping up often leads to dropping out, figuratively and literally.

Obesity creates a fixation of the self, either by continuing the binge or by concentrating on the diet. In both instances, we can see how the sin of gluttony has distorted the perception of the individual insofar as he or she is not capable of much concern for others because of the addiction. This same distortion of reality holds true for drug users. They live in their own little world, which sociologists have labeled a drug culture, where snorting coke, popping pills, or shooting up is far more important than concern for one's neighbor or the betterment of oneself.

Envy

Envy, which may be described as resentment toward another's good fortune with a desire to possess it oneself, has a twin brother, jealousy, which frequently assumes unfaithfulness within personal relationships. Together they create undue anxiety within the heart and cause constant misunderstandings among people. Politicians who lie about their voting records or their efforts on behalf of their constituents in order to gain reelection or college students who put someone down behind his or her back are guilty of these sins. A perception of life in which all share various talents and abilities and where friendship and love are not suspect should be the norm. Envy and jealousy distort that vision.

Apathy

The outpouring of concern and generosity toward the people of Africa during the recent famine is a clear sign of compassion and sensitivity to the needs of others. Millions of dollars were raised by music groups, church organizations, and other associations willing to extend themselves. But how many people remained indifferent? On average, very little assistance was given. In the wealthiest nation on earth, with approximately 250 million people, we donated less than fifty cents per person.

Apathy shows itself in a lack of interest toward others or toward one's responsibility for utilizing one's talents. It may be as small a thing as showing indifference to new students entering school or an unwillingness to help with household chores. In any case, the tendency we have to conveniently forget about each other's needs dulls our minds to the specialness of each person.

Structural Sin

In one sense, all sinful behavior is personal since individuals must ultimately answer to God for their lives. We do know, however, that in legal transactions corporate entities are considered legal persons. Thus, the organization as an institutional structure is given an identity. In a similar manner we can also speak of structural sin.

By way of definition, structural sin is the combination of mores, customs, rules, regulations, and institutional programs and actions in a given society that are detrimental to individuals or the common welfare. These particular, often hidden, characteristics tend to blind the members of society to the harm being done. The whole apparatus of apartheid in South Africa is a case in point. Pass laws, no citizenship status for blacks, the practice of shunning, and other policies are part of the political system in that country. Most whites took the system for granted for many years, just as Western Europeans and Americans accepted slavery in former times. Only recently have people begun to understand how particular structures and ways of thinking that distort our perception of reality can be sinful. Let us look briefly at some examples of structural sin.

Historically, the Roman Empire stands out as a system of government that brought law and order to much of the ancient world. Yet it subjugated local communities and forced them to pay tribute to Caesar. The imperialism of Spain, Portugal, France, and England during the Age of Colonialism is well documented. Maps showing their colonial possessions were used in teaching the geography and history of that period. Little was said, however, about the rights of the indigenous peoples of those conquered lands, nor about how the mother countries exploited the colonies by robbing them of their natural resources.

Totalitarian governments stand as a present-day example of structural sin. For the most part, military dictatorships operate under the cover of protecting people from communism. General Augusto Pinochet overthrew the elected representatives of Chile in September of 1973 with the help of the United States Central Intelligence Agency. The previous regime was bent upon reforms that would have forced the wealthy to share their gains with the needy. Pinochet imposed strict censorship and began a reign of terror to root out all opposition.

In many respects dictatorships resemble communist governments, since it is the state that controls the media, the educational institutions, and the economy. More often than not, the generals and bureaucrats use their power to accumulate wealth and riches for themselves and their friends. The systems of totalitarian government, whether in the guise of military dictatorships or communist states, are structural sin because they do not respect individual liberty and personal rights.

A third form of structural sin embedded within the fabric of Western culture is the cult of consumerism. To accumulate possessions (a house or two, several autos, boats, wardrobes for all occasions, the latest entertainment products from fancy phones to wide-screen television for the playroom) represents the American material success story. The amount of one's paycheck, the size of one's investment portfolio, the neighborhood in which one lives, all indicate whether or not the American Dream has been fulfilled.

This pervasive consumer mentality creates blindness and indifference, if not even sometimes distaste and hatred, toward the poor. Frequently the educational system, churches, entertainment artists, and others appear to support this status quo of things before people. Only when we listen to the Word of God spoken by Jesus about the final judgment, which is based on concern for the needy, will we see the shallowness of consumerism.

These three examples, imperialism, totalitarianism, and consumerism, serve the purpose of demonstrating how sin embeds itself within the structures of society. The institutions of government, the cultural attitudes, and even religious organizations may operate against the dignity of the individual or against the common good of all. Let us conclude this chapter on sin that distorts our search for truth with a short reflection on a healthy spirituality.

A Healthy Spirituality

When we trek off to the local supermarket for a few staples such as milk and bread, our sights are set on basic foods that will nourish our bodies. Once inside the store we are confronted with a blizzard of merchandise whose appeal can quickly distract us from our original mission. Chocolate bars, sodas, doughnuts, chips, and cookies beckon us to a cornucopia of junk food with minimal nutritional value and negative physical benefit. We are tempted.

Analogously, we face similar predicaments in the moral order. We are made for goodness and for love. We are invited to live justly and with compassion toward all. Yet we are frequently distracted. The supermarket of the world calls us to taste the bad fruits of pride, greed, lust, gluttony, envy, hatred, and apathy. Because we tend to spurn the limits of life we succumb to the allurements of power, prestige, and possessions and neglect our responsibility toward others. If we wish to build a healthy spiritual life one of the first steps is to admit our own weakness in the face of temptation and to acknowledge the many times we have sinned against others through domination or exclusion.

"I do not do what I want, but I do the very thing I hate."[5] St. Paul saw his sinfulness within his own heart. It is strange, but true, that the vast majority of saints throughout the ages wept tears at their own failings. One would think that people who lived righteously would pat themselves on the back for their good conduct. But just the opposite was true. Augustine, Francis of Assisi, Thomas Aquinas, and hundreds of other spiritual writers sensed the depth of their own perversity. Even today, Mother Teresa, whose goodness is proclaimed throughout the world, has frequently proclaimed her need for God's mercy and forgiveness.

How, then, are we to proceed? If we are all sinners, what is the point of struggling to create a better world? In the traditional spiritual literature, theologians identified the first stage of growth as the way of purgation. They believed it was necessary to cleanse oneself of selfishness and to avoid the occasions of sin. Without repudiating this ancient wisdom, more modern spiritual writers suggest that spiritual development begins when we are awakened to the cry of the poor in our land. Spirituality demands a communal consciousness. Instead of only looking inward to purge ourselves of sinful disposition, we are also challenged to look up and see the faces of the needy. This opening to the world and its suffering forces us to name the corruptions in society that reflect the evils within our hearts.

In naming social evil we might attend to the voice of Mahatma Gandhi. His tally of the seven deadly sins differed from the traditional list because he wanted to specify the evils of modern society. Contemporary deadly sins include:

wealth without work
pleasure without conscience
knowledge without character
commerce without morality
science without humanity
worship without sacrifice
politics without principle[6]

Gandhi saw the flaw in each of these apparent goods and knew that without a counterbalance any good may be perverted.

In naming the evils of our times, however, we must try to avoid condemning those who do wrong. "Hate the sin, love the sinner," goes the old adage. We cannot direct our hostility at the person of the drug addict, only at his or her behavior. Separating the behavior and the person is no easy task, but if we remember that each person is a unique creation of God we can learn to respect his or her innate goodness while disapproving of immoral behavior. Jesus forgave the woman caught in adultery not because he approved of her wrongdoing but because he knew the weakness of the human heart. "Let anyone among you who is without sin be the first to throw a stone at her."[7]

"Repent, for the kingdom of heaven has come near"[8] was the cry of John the Baptist to the people of his day. The times may have changed but the need for repentance has not. In our examination of the major social ills of the twentieth century, let us keep in mind that we are called to change the world. To tolerate evil involves a complicity of mind and heart. May our vision of a better society strengthen the weary and convince the doubters.

Notes

[1]   Gunnar Myrdal, *The Challenge of World Poverty* (New York: Pantheon Books, 1970), 4.

[2]   Karl Menninger, *Whatever Became of Sin?* (New York: Hawthorn Books, 1973), 10–11.

[3]   Raymond Canning, O.S.A., trans., *The Rule of Saint Augustine* (London: Darton, Longman & Todd, 1984), 12.

[4]   Luke 12:15.

[5]   Romans 7:15.

[6]   Mahatma Gandhi's "Deadly Sins," quoted by President Jimmy Carter at the funeral of Senator Hubert Humphrey, 1978.

[7]   John 8:7.

[8]   Matthew 3:2.

13

Social Analysis

analysis l: separation of a whole into its component parts 2 a: an
examination of a complex, its elements, and their relations

Webster's Ninth New Collegiate Dictionary[1]

Theory of Analysis

Thus far we have seen how prejudice, false assumptions, ignorance, and a proclivity toward selfishness impede our search
for truth. The task now centers on a way or method to ferret
out and understand the global social realities that confront us.
Hopefully, we are now more appreciative of the many peoples
and cultures on planet Earth, which should dispose us to their
concerns as well as our own. In addition, although we will not
address the question of values until Part III of this text, we
should state the major presupposition underlying the social
analysis in use throughout Part II. The starting point for truth
rests upon our own self-worth and the dignity of every person.
We hope to offer substantial evidence for this fundamental
conviction in Part III. Suffice to say, this principle of basic

human rights underlies the entire approach to peace and justice education.

One of the most common practices among human beings is the use of tools. Whether it is a simple can opener, a sewing machine, a ballpoint pen, or a complex computer, tools are designed by the creative genius of their inventor in order to help people do a particular task more efficiently, with greater ease, and often less expensively. Not all tools, however, are material. The Marriage Encounter Movement encourages the use of dialogue between husband and wife as a means to better communication. Dialogue is referred to as a communication tool. This chapter is intended to introduce the student to another tool that can be extremely useful in analyzing social ills. With the help of this particular analytical tool we are able to get behind the surface phenomena of events and begin to understand root causes and the interconnectedness of seemingly separate realities. Several ways of doing social analysis exist today, depending partly on the amount of detail desired and the research time available. More fundamentally, the assumptions and predisposition of those doing the analysis need to be brought to the surface.

For example, Howard Zinn, a critical historian, argues that our understanding of American history, and much of world history as well, has been greatly distorted because it was written by and for the dominant class in society. What appears to be a daring ocean voyage to explore the possibilities of new lands by Christopher Columbus and his small fleet was, from an economic point of view, a journey in search of gold and expensive spices. His second trip to the New World was a much larger expedition. That venture was interested primarily in gold and Indian slaves. Zinn and other historians, as well as many social scientists, have begun to break down the myth of objectivity that has dominated previous social research.

Bernard Lonergan, a Canadian philosopher, believed that there were several dimensions to human understanding.[2] All insight, he said, begins with human experience (what's happening?), then probes beneath the reality to the causes and motivation behind the actions of people. But real insight does not stop with effects and causes. Lonergan understood that ethical questions must also be asked. Unfortunately, many educators balk at a discussion of making judgments about the behavior of others. But if we are to seek a better world we must ask the hard questions about morality, and devise answers that benefit rather than harm people.

In like manner, the task of educating the poor led Paulo Freire, a Latin American educator, to develop a method of teaching known as the circle of praxis.[3] Because of the long history of political and economic oppression suffered by the peasant population of much of Latin America, many of the poor believed that God willed their poverty. Freire and others began to educate them to the fact that wealthy landowners, not God, kept them poor. He, like Lonergan, knew that true education always included questions of conscience.

Consequently there is a circular method of learning, moving through four stages: observation, meaning, judgment, and action. Each stage has its own set of questions. The answers begin to produce a mosaic of reality sometimes much different from the one we thought existed. For example, most social analysts agree that, in spite of claims to the contrary, the high rate of black unemployment is as much a consequence of racism as it is of lack of education. Racism, unfortunately, is alive and well in the United States. In order to grasp the importance of this four-stage learning process, let us examine the stages individually.

Stages of Learning

Color, clarity, cut, and carat characterize the significant elements of a precious gem. Petals, stamen, pistil, and perianth comprise the major parts of a flower. Strings, woodwinds, percussion, and brass denote the instrument groupings for a symphony orchestra. These few examples illustrate the importance of identification as the first stage of learning. Whether we examine our own behavior or the actions of others; whether we observe the movements of the planets or the changes of seasons; whether we study ancient history or current social problems, we must necessarily inspect each piece of the puzzle, in order to fashion a coherent whole.

The first stage, observation, within the context of social analysis, asks questions about "Who are the major players?" "What are the facts involved?" "Have time and place created special circumstances?" Critical observation of human experience identifies the salient features of a situation, since without clear knowledge of a particular social problem little can be done in developing solutions.

The second stage of learning, meaning, goes beyond the facts to ask the key question, "Why?" If we diagnose our own personal behavior, we find layer upon layer of hidden motives for our actions. Some motives address basic biological and emotional needs within ourselves, others hark back to childhood deprivations that continue to affect our behavior. For example, from a psychological perspective, anger is often the result of fear. Likewise, vanity and pride may be traced to feelings of inferiority or related insecurities. In any case, to understand why people act the way they do it is important to get at the meaning behind the behavior.

Having examined the significant dimensions of a particular social problem and unearthed the motivation beneath the surface reality, social analysis next turns to the third stage, judgment. Red lights frequently go on here because our age is prone to relativizing morality. Distinctions between good and bad, truth and falsity are blurred as each one determines her or his own personal code of conduct. While it is true that some aspects of morality have undergone considerable rethinking, notably concerning the importance of circumstances in determining ethical norms, other principles have found renewed strength. Within recent years the worldwide emphasis on human rights has led to an affirmation of the dignity of each person as the pivotal moral imperative. Whatever enhances personal dignity is good and true; whatever besmirches it is bad and false. As we shall see in Part III of the text, the issue of values plays a decisive role in peace and justice education. Indeed, we would argue that values play a crucial role in all learning. We want to examine the criteria for judging social behavior and develop those values that will strengthen the cause of personal dignity for all.

Finally, learning should lead to the fourth stage, action. Recently, Maggie Kuhn, the 84-year-old political activist who founded the Gray Panthers, urged students "to organize, not agonize."[4] Far too often people feel overwhelmed by social problems and refuse to get involved in the betterment of society. Individuals can make a difference whether they are well known or simply private citizens. For example, Terry Rakolta, a Midwest mother, caused panic in the world of sitcom television. Through a series of letters to the sponsors of "Married With Children," a television show that she deemed sleazy and degrading to marriage and family, she persuaded them to cancel their sponsorship of the show. Producers felt the effects of this pressure and began to offer more appropriate fare. Rakolta's example can be multiplied a thousandfold, not only toward television shows but toward the whole gamut of social problems.

Elements of Analysis

According to Joseph Holland and Peter Henriot, the four major elements of analysis are: history, structures, societal divisions, and levels of issues.[5] Each element serves to highlight a particular dimension of a given social issue. By examining each element we begin to get a comprehensive picture of the problem under discussion and are better able to devise solutions. Furthermore, within each of these distinct elements we are able to locate the five primary categories of human activity within which people live. These categories of economic, political, religious, social, and cultural activity help to expand our understanding of the four major elements of analysis. In the following section we will look at the categories of human activity; here we shall examine the elements of social analysis.

History

Central to the understanding of any social issue is the question, "How did things get to be the way they are?" Just as each of us cannot be understood without some knowledge about our parents, family, upbringing, etc., it is equally impossible to isolate a social problem as though it had no past. For example, if we try to compare socialism and capitalism as present-day economic systems without an understanding of their respective histories, we wind up with abstractions. This results in nothing more than an intellectualizing of the pros and cons of each system. In addition, it is impossible to understand the current situation of many developing nations without a knowledge of the colonial dominance of these people for hundreds of years.

For example, in seeking to understand the present-day situation of many black people in the United States, it is necessary to study the effects of slavery during the seventeenth, eighteenth, and nineteenth centuries. Further, we must study how the paternalism and open discrimination practiced in public facilities and educational institutions and present-day racism in the United States marginalize black people. It is only in the light of these historical realities that we can understand the isolation from the mainstream of American society that exists for the majority of blacks.

Structures

Social analysis also helps us explore the institutional or organizational side of a particular issue. For example, the discrimination against women prevalent in much of the world today is embedded in the economic, social, political, and cultural institutions that exercise control over their lives and is sometimes reflected in religious institutions as well. Lack of upward mobility in management positions, lower rates of pay for equal work, minuscule representation in government policy-making decisions, rampant pornography and other sex-object symbols in the media, entertainment, and art institutions have left women with very weak voices when decisions are made that affect their lives.

A recent illustration of this was a front-page picture in the *New York Times* showing Pope John Paul II and several ranking bishops gathered about a conference table. The caption stated that they were discussing the role of women in the Catholic Church. It seemed odd to witness a supposedly high-level discussion about women in the Church with no women present, but the structures of the Catholic Church have yet to allow for women in the governance of its affairs.

Political dictatorships are the most obvious example of a governing structure that seeks to maintain the status quo, i.e., a state of affairs wherein the controlling parties maintain or enhance their authority. This same desire to maintain control exists in all walks of life. Special-interest groups, whether in education, economics, entertainment, etc., always develop bureaucratic structures and policies. Rarely do they share power with opposing forces.

Societal Division

Class division remains a tender issue with many Americans, since we pride ourselves on being an open and democratic society. Yet only a fool would think that no class distinctions exist. *Fortune* magazine annually publishes a list of assets and earnings of the top five hundred corporations. When one notes that virtually every member of the board of directors of these companies is a white male Protestant millionaire, and at least fifty years of age, one is made quickly aware of the selective representation at the top of corporate America. Interestingly enough, many of these men serve on the boards of several corporations, often within the same industry. This fact alone leads one to understand why there is very little real competition in the pricing of so many products.

There have always been divisions and class distinctions within every society. The ancient Egyptians, the dynasties of China and Japan, the Greeks, Romans, Aztecs, Incas, and the medieval societies practiced class discrimination. In modern times, democracy as a political ideal was designed to equalize the political and civil rights of all people. Communism, too, began as an ideal for a classless society. Is it possible to eliminate the distinctions between workers and owners, employers and employees, the governors and the governed? Perhaps in the Kingdom of God all will share the fullness of grace, but in our present world the important question is not so much who has the power, but rather do those who hold power exercise it with fairness and justice?

Levels of Issues

In our own neighborhoods and towns we find people quick to organize a protest and demonstrate for new traffic signals if several accidents occur at a particular intersection. We applaud such initiatives. Not so laudatory are the zoning ordinances in many locales that tend to restrict certain areas for the exclusive use of the wealthy. Recent court rulings have attempted to limit the rights of property owners where exclusionary zoning exists, but the battle is far from won. These local issues of discrimination need scrutiny, because it is at this level of analysis that change can be made most readily.

Global social analysis requires a sensitivity to people and cultures other than our own. Again, the key value is human dignity. Is the arms race a sane solution to the conflicts and tensions in the world? Does it make sense to allow one-half of the world's population to live in poverty? What are the causes of these problems? Global concerns are usually last on our agenda, because they are remote. The hungry Bangladesh child, the poorly clothed Filipino mother, or the unemployed Appalachian miner are not ordinarily on the minds of middle-class college students. We may be inclined to get involved on local issues, but it takes broad vision and a sense of commitment to develop a global conscience. It would seem, nonetheless, that if we are to see a new dawn of peaceful coexistence among the various nations and peoples of the world, we must raise our minds and hearts to a new level of concern.

This brief sketch of the various elements of social analysis should help us to a better understanding of social problems. Institutional structures, the history and traditions of people, the current players, and the divisions within society constitute the essential elements of social analysis. In order to move toward a more just and peaceful world, we must know the forces at work within our world. Some forces are good, some are evil. Since that judgment is not always easy to make, we need to do the hard work of social analysis in order to plan for a future with new hope and promise for all people. If indeed "We Are the World"[6] is to be more than just another song, we are obliged to a lifelong process of reform and renewal.

Categories of Analysis

Under each of the elements of social analysis, there are specific areas of human activity that provide further insight into the meaning of human experience. We shall call these the categories of analysis. Five major categories of human activity are: political, economic, religious, social, and cultural. Understanding each of these will help us grasp the reasons behind particular problems in society. In addition, we will see how the combination of these categories, either in reinforcing an injustice or combining to eliminate one, exerts considerable influence in shaping society.

Political Activity

Political policy and the decisions of governments locally and nationally control everything from the licensing standards for the hospital care rendered in childbirth to the funeral regulations adapted for the burial of a body. From cradle to grave, laws have been established to protect people. Political activity involves the raising and spending of revenues, the establishment of school systems and health care programs, the regulation of commerce, and the adjudication of legal transactions. Although thinkers such as Thoreau advocated limited government, today's complex society demands a multilayered structure of government, including the United Nations, a form of world government, to help facilitate the welfare of all people.

In order to grasp the dimensions of today's social problems, the political nature of these issues demands attention.

Whether we ask questions about an oil spill catastrophe in Alaska[7] or the controversy surrounding the right to own an AK-47 semiautomatic rifle,[8] we are constantly faced with political decision making. Who makes the laws, who interprets them, and who enforces them are crucial questions for social analysis.

Economic Activity

Whether it is the little boy selling lemonade outside his home on a hot summer day or Lucy "the psychiatrist is in" selling advice to the characters in the Peanuts comic strip, they remind us that much human activity is economically oriented. In fact, the German philosopher Georg Hegel, from whom Karl Marx borrowed many of his theoretical ideas about economics, held that economic activity was the prime determinant in human life.[9]

No one doubts that the basic physical needs for food, shelter, and clothing, the broader desire for possessions, and the equally strong drive to build and create new things has energized the human family since time immemorial. This being the case, social analysis must take account of the significant factors at play within the economy. What is the difference between micro- and macroeconomics? Who makes the major economic decisions? Who owns what? How did they acquire it? How do government regulations impact the economy? In order to understand the social realities of our time we need some knowledge about economic policies, the structure of business, the dominant global role of transnational corporations, and the debt crisis in Third World nations.

Religious Activity

The role that religion plays within society may range from a general hostility toward religious practices under communist regimes to a total immersion of religion in the affairs of state as witnessed within many Islamic nations. Religious fundamentalist fervor drives some Jews to demand the expulsion of all Palestinians from Israel; the same ideological fanaticism fans the flames of anti-Semitism among the Arabs. For the most part, religion has had its greatest influence upon the moral and ethical behavior of people. From the Ten Commandments to the papal encyclicals, religion has emphasized the need for good conduct in the affairs of life. At times the message is negative, couched in terms of "shall nots," but the core teaching of all religions has always held up love of neighbor as a guiding principle. In any case, religious teaching and the institutional churches exert considerable influence among people. Thus, it is important to know the prominent religious figures and their appeal.

Cultural Activity

In assessing the impact of culture on a given social problem, we need to explore the many layers of cultural activity. The literature we read, from diet books to romance novels; the music we listen to, from Beethoven to Willie Nelson; the life-styles we live, from affluence to poverty—all suggest enormous permutations within our national culture. Globally, the variety is unlimited.

Nothing has influenced culture in recent times as much as television. Does the affluence of most television actors and actresses create a greater desire for material wealth among viewers? Does the high rate of violence and the patterns of adultery and fornication so popular in films and soaps lead to similar patterns in real life? Do rock lyrics influence the attitudes and behavior of youth? There is little doubt that we are a nation addicted to television. Here we have a recent cultural phenomenon exerting inordinate power on the minds of millions of people, while the level of political involvement and social concern continues to decline.

Social Activity

The patterns of divorce, the incidence of child abuse and teenage pregnancy, the number of abortions, the movement of industrial workers from the rust belt to the sun belt all are indicators of the constant changes within a society. With the present upheaval in Soviet society a major restructuring (*perestroika*) of that country is under way. New opportunities for choice in the electoral system, fresh initiatives in business and finance, and a general openness (*glasnost*) to free speech has created a social revolution. Social customs give clues to the kind of society in which people live. The intensity of "March Madness," Super Bowl Sunday, and the World Series tell us something about the priorities of American society. The billions of dollars spent each year on hunting and fishing, cosmetics and deodorants, not to mention the lavishness of weddings and funerals, speaks volumes about the American way of life. Consequently, in order to better understand many of our social ills we need to be well acquainted with the customs, mores, and social patterns within society.

Methodology

Having gained some insight into the theory and practice of social analysis, and having examined the stages of understanding and the elements and categories of social analysis, let us close with a few remarks about methodology. In the first place we should bear in mind that a bewildering amount of statistical data is available on almost every conceivable human problem. We need to move through the analysis in an intelligent and thorough manner, but not get bogged down in what Martin Luther King, Jr., called the "paralysis of analysis." Sorting out the facts of each situation requires study and patience. However, while it is important to know specific details, we should not forget that the major task of social analysis lies in understanding the primary forces at work within society. If the salient features of a problem are well understood, then we can begin to direct our attention toward the healing of the social illness.

Furthermore, we should be forewarned that we are entering the realm of controversy. In one startling passage from the gospel of Matthew, Jesus states that he has come not to bring peace, but division.[10] Much newspaper, magazine, and television coverage of local, national, and international events reflects a general bias toward the owners and managers of these media. When one begins to question their positions by using the biblical point of reference of social justice or concern for the poor and oppressed, the debate heats up. People are accused of being left wing or right wing, liberal or conservative, depending on the issue and their position. It has been said that to be twenty years old and not liberal is to have no heart; but to be forty years old and not conservative is to have no brain.

Be that as it may, labels are easy to come by, yet are of little help in analyzing social situations.

Americans are known for their pragmatic way of thinking. The quick fix is always sought. Social analysis, however, requires a patient, methodical, and questioning approach to our society and its variety of interlocking systems, many of which are hidden from view. When we eat a bowl of cereal and a sliced banana for breakfast, few of us think about where the grain, fruit, milk, and sugar came from. The Kansas farmer, the banana and sugar cane pickers, and the dairy people, not to mention you, the consumer, have much in common. Analysis will help us see how the economics of breakfast works well for some and poorly for others.

By way of observation we should note that every element of social analysis is ultimately linked to the whole. While we may dissect certain parts of a body or examine particular species of trees in a forest, we cannot forget that there is a unity and wholeness to a body or a woods. Analysis also will lead us to discover things that are not directly visible in society. The exclusion from health care of millions of Americans is generally known only to those excluded. Most people think that everyone is covered by health insurance, but that is far from true. Former President Reagan once asserted that few people in our land were homeless. But many studies have concluded that the problem of homelessness is reaching epidemic proportions. From a middle-class vantage point some problems are invisible. Social analysis hopes to correct that blindness. The facts do not necessarily speak for themselves.

We need to interpret them and try to understand the why, how come, and consequences of events.

During the remaining chapters of Part II, Perception, we will use the method of social analysis to dissect the major social problems of our time. Since *Dignity and Solidarity* is an introductory work, it would be foolish to expect more than a cursory overview of these issues. Our main purpose is to raise questions about the personal values we bring to bear on these concerns. Nevertheless, using the tools of analysis we shall attempt to highlight the significant events and relevant facts around the issues of violence, racism, sexism, militarism, poverty, and environmental damage. Beginning with a look at particular human experiences, then moving through an examination of possible causes, we should gradually arrive at some tentative solutions, or, at the very least, a better understanding of the issues. Education should be aimed at alleviating human misery and building a truly humane society.

Hopefully, social analysis can assist in this twofold task.

Notes

[1]   *Webster's Ninth New Collegiate Dictionary* (Springfield, Mass.: Merriam-Webster, 1989), 82.

2   Bernard J. F. Lonergan, *Insight: A Study of Human Understanding* (New York: Philosophical Library, 1970), 3–6.

3   Paulo Freire, *Pedagogy of the Oppressed* (New York: Seabury Press, 1968), 101–18.

4   Maggie Kuhn, "Women and Poverty" seminar. Villanova University, March 18, 1989.

5   Joseph Holland and Peter Henriot, *Social Analysis: Linking Faith and Justice* (Washington, D.C.: Center of Concern, 1980), 10–15.

6   Michael Jackson and Lionel Ritchie, "We Are the World" (New York: Columbia Records, 1985).

7   *New York Times*, March 31, 1989, 1, 12.

8   *New York Times*, March 20, 1989, 1.

9   Thomas Sowell, *Marxism* (New York: William Morrow, 1985), 51–52.

10   Matthew 10:34–39.

14

Victims of Violence

Whereas recognition of the inherent dignity and of the equal and inalienable rights of all members of the human family is the foundation of freedom, justice, and peace in the world. . . . Now, therefore, the General Assembly proclaims this Universal Declaration of Human Rights as the common standard of achievement for all peoples and all nations. . . .

International Bill of Rights of the United Nations[1]

Definitions and Distinctions

When a massive hurricane storms up along the coast of Florida through the Carolinas and slams ashore across Long Island, New York, spending itself with torrential rains and high winds in Connecticut, Massachusetts, and New Hampshire, or when a similar event occurs in the Gulf of Mexico and destruction takes place in Texas and Louisiana, we generally identify the injured and killed as victims of violence. This type of violence, however, is the result of natural forces. For example, in August 1883, the volcanic island of Krakatau, in the Sunda Strait between Java and Sumatra, blew completely apart, causing colossal tidal waves that killed an estimated 40,000 people. More recently, almost 50,000 people lost their lives in a massive earthquake in Iran (June 1990).

In contrast to those people victimized by natural disasters, we wish to limit our discussion to the victims of violence caused by the malice and ill will of other people. No one is to blame for a natural disaster unless, of course, warnings could have been issued to get people out of harm's way. Human responsibility will set the limits of our presentation on victims of violence. Violence happens when force is used to dehumanize another person or group of people.

The most obvious manifestations of violent behavior may be termed direct violence. During childhood many of us experienced the bullying of an older or physically stronger child. Sibling rivalry occasionally turned violent. These, of course, are minor cases of violence compared with child abuse, incest, beatings, and the like. In the area of criminal behavior, we need only look at the long list of murders, rapes, assaults with deadly weapons, robberies, and muggings to understand that the criminal world thrives on violence. From the hired assassin to the drug-crazed gunman, the perpetrators of physical violence engage in a wide array of violent behavior.

Equally direct, though less damaging physically, are the types of violence done on an emotional level. Many people experience a sense of violation if their house is broken into or if their car is stolen. Likewise, the fear of harm is often as paralyzing as an overt injury. For instance, the K.G.B. (Soviet secret police) until recently exerted an ominous presence throughout the Soviet empire. Millions were afraid to question the authorities for fear of reprisals. This psychological violence asserts itself in much of Latin America and in all countries controlled by dictators.

Violence can also be done in less direct ways. Just as people are called to be responsible for their actions, they may well be judged for their inaction or neglect. The physician who fails to diagnose an illness, the aircraft or auto mechanic who superficially performs an inspection, and the teacher who is insufficiently prepared are guilty of forms of indirect violence. People are hurt, or may be, because of their neglect.

As we examine the many faces of violence throughout this chapter, let us keep in mind that we were born to love. Love begins with the self, extends to others, and includes the world. Sadly enough, as the many victims of violence testify, love often gets short shrift. But it should not be so for us. In educating ourselves for peace and justice, we must work to assist the victims and limit the violence.

National Violence

Guns and Alcohol/Drugs

When Patrick Purdy walked into a schoolyard in Stockton, California, on the morning of January 17, 1989, and opened fire, killing five children and wounding twenty-nine additional youngsters, people wondered how a former mental patient with a criminal record could purchase the semiautomatic AK-47 assault weapon used in the attack. According to statistics compiled by the Hand Gun Control organization of Washington, D.C., more than 11,000 deaths result annually from guns.[2] Thus, Purdy's violence represents only a small portion of the killings in the United States because of easy access to revolvers, shotguns, rifles, and machine guns.

Alcohol kills too! The National Safety Council estimates that more than 22,000 deaths and 320,000 injuries occurred in 1987 as a result of drunken driving.[3] The carnage within the United States attributed to guns and alcohol has reached epic proportions. Only when an aroused citizenry demands a curb on weapons and severe penalties for alcohol abuse while driving will these gun and auto deaths abate.

Abortion

Day one: Today I was conceived. My Daddy's sperm and my Mommy's ovum united and I began my life.

Six weeks: I have a tiny heart, ten toes and ten fingers, and everything's warm and snug here in Mommy's womb.

Eight weeks: Today, my Mommy killed me. She called it an abortion.

Although fetal life is not cognitive, this imaginary diary jolts the reader into a stark recognition of the violence done to an unborn child. When one considers that approximately 1.6 million therapeutic abortions occur yearly in the United States alone,[4] the cumulative horror is numbing.

Following the Supreme Court decision of 1973, Roe vs. Wade, which legalized abortion nationally, various groups began to coalesce into two distinct factions, pro-life and pro-choice. The pro-life advocates, consisting mostly of Roman Catholics and members of other traditional church bodies, believe that abortion is a moral evil in all but cases of ectopic gestation and should be outlawed. Their case rests primarily on the conviction that all life is sacred and God-given, and that consequently abortion is the taking of the life of an innocent and helpless victim. Many pro-life advocates, led by Cardinal Joseph Bernardin of Chicago, have stressed a respect for life from infancy to old age.

The pro-choice advocates, on the other hand, emphasize the right of a woman to decide for herself what is right and wrong. They totally oppose the imposition of law into the realm of what, for them, is a purely private decision to be made in consultation with a doctor. Most feminists believe that denying a woman the right to abortion is one more instance of male domination. "It is insufferable for men whose brothers are responsible for all but the smallest fraction of violent crimes . . . to presume to dictate morality to women,"[5] wrote American feminist Leah Fritz.

The debate, then, moves between morality and law. At the present moment in American history, abortion is legal. Because we live in a pluralistic society it is only by consensus that we can expect moral principles to gain the force of law. If most people were morally convinced of the evilness of abortion, or, in more positive terms, the sanctity of life, the law would change.

"Sexploitation"

A dozen years ago the first Covenant House opened in New York City's Time Square district, well known for its triple-X films, prostitution, drug culture, and other assorted decadence. Since then similar houses have been opened in other cities to help the thousands of youngsters who fall prey annually to the dope pushers, pimps, and others who pander the distorted allurements of the flesh. Many of these children, some only twelve or thirteen years of age, have run away seeking something better than the abusive and dysfunctional situations from which they fled. They often find far worse. It seems obvious that the smut and obscene films that are the general fare in these locations create a situation where exploitation of these youths often occurs.

Apart from the alleged legal rights of those who trade in pornography, from a moral point of view the merchandising of sex with no regard to its interpersonal dimensions of fidelity and commitment is clearly a distortion of its true meaning. The tragic effects of pornography upon the children for whom Covenant House cares consist of both physical and psychological scarring.

A recent voluminous report by the United States Attorney General's office confirms this view.[6] Magazines and films picturing women being branded, beaten, raped, sodomized, and otherwise subjugated by men, together with other publications depicting similar offenses against children, leads to a general deterioration of respect for women and children within society. As such they are patently immoral. The incidence of real rape, rather than that portrayed in movies and adult magazines, is frequently linked to the availability of such prurient material. For example, Ted Bundy, recently executed in Florida for the rape-murders of three women, admitted that pornography fed his appetite for violence to women.

Because of our society's permissive sexual mores there has been an increase in teenage pregnancy, sexually transmitted diseases, and abortion. Sexploitation, while not a new phenomenon within society, has nevertheless grown in proportion to the promiscuous attitudes exhibited in *Playboy*, *Hustler*, and other prurient publications. Is it not possible for men to admire and appreciate the natural attractiveness of women without losing sight of the inner goodness and qualities of humanness possessed by all women?

Domestic Abuse

The dominance of women by men has a long and infamous history. While a later chapter in this text will treat the subject of sexism at more length, it is important here to look at the problem of battered wives and children in the context of victims of violence. This particular kind of sexism is much more severe in its consequences than the role stereotyping of the sexes.

Some sociologists trace the problem of domestic violence to a general macho attitude within the American culture. Others link the problem to the poor self-image of a husband or to the steady diet of violence that has become standard for many television shows and movies. The make-my-day mentality depicted by Clint Eastwood in the role of Dirty Harry, the violence of "Rambo" and "Terminator" films, and the glorification of SWAT teams and "Star Wars" weapons systems tend to create a climate where violence is socially acceptable. Whatever the causes may be, it is becoming more apparent that domestic violence is on the rise.

During the New York City trial of Joel Steinberg in the fall of 1988 on a charge of beating his stepchild to death, his companion, Hedda Nussbaum, testified that she was beaten regularly by him. She, like other women who have been battered, confessed to feelings of inadequacy. Many family crisis support centers support this testimony.[7] Instead of realizing that men are the guilty parties in 99 percent of domestic violence, women blame themselves for provoking their husbands.

How tragic to assume responsibility for the criminal behavior of another!

We have only skimmed the surface of national violence by citing the random deaths caused by drunken drivers, the emotionally disturbed with easy access to guns, the abortionists, the sexploiters, and the perpetrators of domestic violence. Those who exploit women and children in the workplace, who poison the water and air with chemicals and noxious gases, who contribute to the climate of prejudice and racism in our country, and who remain callous and indifferent to the poor contribute to the violence in American society. Let us attend now to the more prevalent forms of global violence.

Global Violence

Death Squads

The term *death squad* came into popular usage during the reign of terror imposed upon the Salvadoran people in the late 1970s. Hired killers, frequently members of the military, tortured and murdered hundreds of men, women, and children in order to stop a growing sentiment for economic justice through the structures of land reform. Death squads are a foreign counterpart to the Ku Klux Klan. The KKK used similar tactics for many years throughout the South to terrorize blacks. Indiscriminate lynchings, the burning of homes, and the bombing of churches occurred often and randomly. People were dragged from their beds under cover of darkness and subjected to brutal beatings simply because their skin was dark. Unfortunately, the Ku Klux Klan still exerts much control in this country.

Torture and murder, of course, have long been the common tactics of the powerful. In medieval times the iron maiden and the rack were part and parcel of the castle dungeon. Princes, barons, and kings subjugated their enemies with the same fearful stratagems in use today. The torture-murder of Steve Biko in a South African jail, the slaying of Chico Mendos, a Brazilian rubber tapper who opposed the slash-and-burn exploitation of the Amazon forests, and the martyrdom of Archbishop Romero and four American churchwomen in El Salvador amply testify to the never-ending violence by those who refuse to share the goods of the earth and respect the right of personal dignity for all.

Genocide

These examples of local and individual violence are dwarfed by the genocidal realities of the twentieth century. In a later chapter we will study the Holocaust of World War II. Here let us simply note some other mass executions. Turkish forces massacred hundreds of thousands of Armenians from 1907 to 1915; Idi Amin, the despotic ruler of Uganda, slaughtered several thousands of his countrymen during the late 1970s until his overthrow by General Milton Obote. Sadly enough, Obote proved to be Amin's equal. By 1984, the human rights organization Amnesty International reported human rights abuses in Uganda "among the worst in the world."[8] In Southeast Asia, the Khmer Rouge troops of Pol Pot killed an estimated four million Cambodians between 1975 and 1979.[9] The slave camps operated by Stalin, the mass execution of Mayan Indians in Guatemala, and the recent carnage among noncombatants in the Lebanese civil war remind us that mayhem didn't end with Attila the Hun or Genghis Khan.

Terrorism

Pan Am flight 103 was blown to bits in the night sky over Lockerbie, Scotland, on December 21, 1988. It took several days to recover the 258 bodies and to prove that a terrorist bomb had caused the explosion. Not far away in Northern Ireland, sectarian killings by the Irish Republican Army and the Ulster Defense Forces continue to terrorize the population. Reportedly Muammar Qaddafi, the Libyan leader, has funded and trained terrorist guerrillas from all parts of the world.

Global terrorism finds its roots in the political ideology of national independence movements and the equally insidious fundamentalism of those unwilling to accommodate the aspirations of others. Terrorists generally abhor compromise by holding firm to the conviction that only violence will achieve their ends. But is it possible to justify the killing of air travelers or the slaying of tourists on cruise ships (as in the hijacking of the Italian liner *Achille Lauro* in October 1985) or the random bombing of restaurants and cafes for the most noble cause?

Does the end justify the means? Are we permitted to kill and maim others in the name of righteousness? We shall see in Part III, Values, that respect for human rights is the ultimate value and is an inviolable right. We must always aim to defend the innocent and halt the activities of terrorists of both the left and the right.

Refugees

One final addition to the portrait of global violence can be found in the 13 million political and economic refugees who roam the world. In our own country the plight of the homeless has reached epic proportions. There are 44,000 persons on the public housing waiting list in Chicago; 60,000 in Miami: 200,000 in New York City; 23,000 in Philadelphia; and 13,000 in Washington, D.C.[10] Rural homelessness has also increased to the point where comparisons are now made with the vast migrations of poor farmers during the Great Depression of the 1930s.

More than a quarter of a million Salvadorans have fled their homeland because of political oppression. Almost the entire population of Palestine (about 3 million people) suffer displacement as a result of Israeli occupation. In the Asian countries of Vietnam, Laos, and Cambodia, millions of people have crossed borders seeking political asylum.[11] Haitian and Cuban boat people and Mexican laborers consistently dodge U.S. immigration officers in attempting to find a better life for themselves and their families.

The issues of immigration and the assistance due political and economic refugees have many complications, yet to deny the violence done to people who are uprooted and homeless flies in the face of overwhelming evidence. We thus find a bleak picture of domestic and global violence. Let us examine some of the reasons behind these problems.

Causes of Violence

No doubt the underlying causes of violence are attributable to the various dimensions of sinfulness found within human behavior. Having explored these capital sins in chapter 12, we need to search for more concrete reasons to the violence we see in the world. We shall attempt to use the four elements of social analysis, namely, history, structure, levels of issues, and societal division in conjunction with the political, economic, religious, social, and cultural categories of analysis in order to delineate the more immediate causes of violence.

For example, one major reason for the tolerance of guns within the United States is attributed to our historical glamorization of the old Wild West. Davy Crockett, Jim Bowie, Jesse James, Wyatt Earp, Billy the Kid, and dozens of other American folk heroes exemplified the myth of the rugged individual ingrained in our communal psyche. Likewise, the traditional Muslim reverence for the Jihad, or Holy War, exerts considerable influence on today's Arab terrorists. They believe that they are doing God's work. In addition, America's love of the automobile, combined with the socially acceptable cocktail hour, allow for much tolerance toward drunken drivers. Other countries impose far more stringent penalties for the same offenses, but because historically we have invested heavily in mobility and pleasure we are reluctant to restrict the freedom to drink and drive.

In terms of the structural causes of violence, we need only be reminded that organized crime families control the drug trade and gambling rackets; that the tobacco, pharmaceutical, and alcohol industries encourage drug use; and that sexually provocative magazines and films reap enormous profits for Hollywood and Madison Avenue. What do the Mafia, Phillip Morris, Anheuser-Busch, Dow Chemical, and United Artists have in common? To one degree or another they represent a vested interest in achieving profits at the expense of drug and alcohol addiction, toxic air, and prurience.

In analyzing the local, national, and global levels of particular issues of violence we can frequently see the interconnectedness of causes. For example, who caused the death of a ten-year-old boy who was accidentally shot to death on a street corner in South Philadelphia? Was it the members of two rival gangs warring over the drug trade in the neighborhood? Was it the drug merchants of Medellín, Colombia, who supply the cocaine products? Perhaps the taxpayers are to blame for cutting the budget on police protection?

Almost every large-scale societal problem has an array of causes that can be diagnosed on both a large and a small scale. Frequently enough, the solution to one problem may well create others. Instance the recent increase in prison terms brought about by stricter sentencing procedures. While the theory of deterrent punishment may prove publicly appealing, the resultant overcrowding of jails has led to inmate violence and a substantial rise in recidivism. Thus violence has many causes on many levels, and solutions to one set of problems may create new problems elsewhere.

Finally, it is important to recall the comments on structural sin made in chapter 12. Structural sin results in institutionalized violence. Segregation laws, curtailment of political and civil rights under the pretext of national security, and the justification of poverty in the name of free-market forces illustrate the pervasiveness of structural violence. When basic human rights are denied because of various policies, programs, and legal or codified regulations, then the economic, political, and religious institutions responsible are engaged in the practice of structural violence.

New Directions

The emergence of human rights as the central concern of the human family in the last quarter of the twentieth century highlights the revulsion most people instinctively feel when they witness violence. We were not created in violence. Clearly, God's plan ordained that each human life would begin with an act of love, and it is God's will that we live in love. Violence is not the norm; it is an aberration. As such, we need to work against the violence within ourselves and society.

This chapter has presented a rather gloomy picture of the world we live in and has reminded the reader that violence is not only a matter of direct harm to others, but also includes an indifference to those who claim basic needs. We are called to set our sights on higher things—the things that will deepen our respect for human rights and create a longing in our hearts for an end to violence. Naturally the place to begin is with ourselves. Unless we have a profound sense of our goodness and are willing to work at the task of exorcising our demons and energizing our spirits, we will do violence to ourselves by wallowing in our own selfishness. A few suggestions are in order.

In the first place, we ought to acknowledge the violence within our own hearts. Is there a person alive who has not harbored some resentment or hostility toward others? Hardly a day goes by without some confrontation or apparent injustice done to us. We may feel overcharged for a purchase, cut off by someone in traffic, or ignored by friends. These negative signals tend to accumulate and may cause us to attack others by way of retribution. It is important, therefore, to get in touch with the attitudes, beliefs, and behavior that we exhibit as a result of an injury done to us. Only when we know our own dispositions toward violence, will we be in a position to change our values.

One oft-repeated rule of thumb suggests that we distinguish between the person and the behavior. At times we all behave badly, yet that does not make us evil. We should break the habit of making blanket judgments about others when, in fact, only a portion of their behavior may be repugnant. Far too often the blame extends beyond reasonable limits. To ferret out the lingering grudges, to surface the hidden anger, to sublimate hostility to hospitality calls for our best efforts. We need to search for new directions in overcoming the latent potential for violence that lurks within each of us.

Secondly, we should begin to align ourselves with groups and organizations that are committed to limiting the violence in our world. MADD (Mothers Against Drunk Driving) was founded by the relatives and friends of people who were killed or injured by drunken drivers. Members have attempted to educate the public about the enormous violence of alcohol-related auto accidents and to push for increased penalties for violators. Amnesty International has received worldwide recognition for its unrelenting work in revealing the incarceration and torture of political prisoners in many countries throughout the world. Several hundred crisis support centers throughout the country offer assistance to battered women and children, while urging police and courts to restrain violent husbands. Finally, along with turning our backs on the violence in our hearts and joining organizations that support nonviolence, we should develop daily habits that lend themselves to nonviolent values. For example, in the gospel stories Jesus urged people to turn the other cheek and go the extra mile with those who attack them.[12] While our level of tolerance at times seems stretched beyond limits, the practice of forgiveness of our enemies will reap immeasurable benefits toward peace of mind. Lugging around the bricks of resentment will cause our heads to bend and our eyes to see dirt. That is not a very good position for people called to a new vision. Ultimately, the fullness of peace will only be realized in God's kingdom. A journey of personal nonviolence will contribute to its building.

Notes

[1] *International Bill of Rights,* General Assembly of the United Nations, 1948.

[2] Gerard A. Vanderhaar and Mary Lou Kownacki, O.S.B., eds. *Way of Peace: A Guide to Nonviolence* (Erie, Penn.: Pax Christi USA, 1987), 24.

3   *Accident Facts,* 1988 (Chicago: National Safety Council), 52.

4   Spencer Rich, "Abortion Fight Batters Family Planning Efforts," *Washington Post,* September 3, 1987, 14–21.

5   Leah Fritz, "Abortion: A Woman's Right to Live," in *Reweaving the Web of Life,* ed. Pam McAllister (Philadelphia: New Society Publishers, 1982), 395.

6   United States Attorney General's Commission on Pornography (Washington, D.C.: U.S. Government Printing Office, 1986).

7   N.A., "Violence in Her Own home: A Survivor's Story," *House Hearth* 2 (September 1988).

8   *Information Please Almanac 1988* (Boston: Houghton Mifflin), 272.

9   Ibid., 164.

10 *Homelessness and Housing: A Human Tragedy, A Moral Challenge* (Washington, D.C.: United States Catholic Conference, 1988), 4.

11 "World Refugee Crisis: Winning the Game," in *FACTS for Action* (Boston: Oxfam America, 1982), 4–5.

12 Matthew 5:38–42.

15

Sexism

If one recognizes that patriarchy divided our society by sex, class, and race, then all these forms of exploitation converge concretely in triple exploitation of poor women of color. Thus, the vision of liberation from patriarchy, if it is to be about the liberation of all women and not just about white, middle-class women, must look at the whole system of patriarchy from the vantage point of the women of color.

Rosemary Radford Ruether[1]

The Many Faces of Sexism

A student writes:

When I was eight I was told that I couldn't be G.I. Joe. I had to be the nurse. . . . In Catholic high school the boys who were seniors had a smoking room. The girls were not allowed to smoke because it was not "ladylike." . . . In one restaurant where I worked I was told not to carry heavy trays since that was a man's job; and in another place the owner freaked out when I questioned him about my paycheck. "Don't ever try to embarrass me," he said. "I can get a million other 'obedient' girls to do the same job."

Maria's experiences are not unlike those of women the world over. Although the circumstances and conditions may differ, the ugly face of sexism appears in many guises, as Rosemary Ruether reminds us in the introductory quotation. Amazingly enough, the word *sexism*, defined as a "prejudice or discrimination based on sex," was not recorded in a dictionary until 1970. At that time, with the heightened aspirations of minorities and people of Third World nations, women began to name the age-old sexual victimization from which they suffered. This chapter will attempt to identify the major patterns of sexism, analyze the meaning behind them, and, finally, offer some possible remedies for healing the wounds caused by sexist behavior.

Rape unquestionably represents one of the worst fears of women. Historically, soldiers saw rape and pillage as the just spoils of victory. When King David spied Bathsheba bathing he sent for her, "and he lay with her,"[2] in spite of the fact she was married to another man. The king had his way. The physical violation of women stretches back to the stereotypical caveman dragging his mate around by the hair.

Although camp followers and prostitutes have sold their bodies "voluntarily" for centuries, most of these women were forced economically to resort to this, the "oldest profession." Prostitution illustrates the sadness of sexuality gone awry. Recall how Aldonza, the "battered one," from the Broadway musical *Man of La Mancha*, hated herself for a life of prostitution.

It is fair to say that unless human sexuality is expressed within the context of love, sexual exploitation is present. Forced sex violates the body; uncommitted sex cheapens commitment and fidelity.

One might expect that religion would provide a place where women could find comfort from their wounds and opportunities for their abilities. Alas, organized religion stands as a bastion of male prerogative. From the mosque at Mecca to St. Peter's in Rome, women find the same sexist attitudes that prevail in secular society. Only since Vatican II have women been permitted to enter churches with uncovered heads, to read the Word of God from the pulpits, and assist with communion.

Within much of Islamic society the role of women is severely restricted with regard to dress, mobility, education, and employment. Concubinage and the male pleasures of the harem for Saudi princes belie a surface modernity.

Meanwhile many Christian religions, in particular Roman Catholicism, discriminate openly against women by excluding them from ordination. From pope to parish priest, maleness stands as the sine qua non for entrance into the clerical ranks. In spite of the many gospel instances where Jesus openly enlisted women in his ministry, institutional Christianity historically has followed the same patterns of sexist behavior as its political and economic counterparts.

Work/Home/Politics

Thus far we have seen the effects of sexism manifested in religious discrimination and physical and emotional abuse. Let us turn our attention now to the economic, social, and political dimensions of the problem. Beginning with our own country, a few statistics reveal the fate of women in the workplace:

- In America less than 7 percent of women hold managerial positions, and only 10 percent earn more than $20,000 a year.
- Women earn, on the average, about 60 cents for every dollar a man earns; for minority women the figure is only 54 cents per dollar.
- About 35 to 40 percent of the disparity in average earnings is due to sexual segregation, which results in lower paying "women's work."
- Black mothers who work full-time, year-round have a poverty rate of 13 percent, the same rate as white men who do not work at all.[3]

These and similar facts amply testify to the discriminatory practices against women in the labor force. At the management level, few or no adjustments are made for women who wish to raise a family as well as pursue a career. Efforts toward a new "Mommy Track" have emerged recently, but most companies are unwilling to offer corporate women flexibility for maternal needs.[4] Male cronyism on the golf course, at the chamber of commerce, and in the many "male only" clubs effectively excludes women from the camaraderie necessary for career advancement.

Women in less-developed countries suffer even more degradation. Modernity, with its assumptions about technological development and the "steady march of progress" view, has eroded the values of rural subsistence living and forced women into menial, low-wage jobs.[5] A new phrase that has come into recent usage is *feminization of poverty*. Although it was popularized by Hilda Scott, in reference to single-parent families headed by women in the United States,[6] the phrase came from the pen of Valentina Borreman, a Latin American educator. She highlighted the negative effects upon Third World people who developed First World economic models. For example, not only did a mixed labor force (men and women competing for the same jobs) deprive women of their traditional gender-specific tasks, but also "the economically measurable benefits of growth have accrued disproportionately to men, and have been produced disproportionately by women's unpaid work."[7] If we remember that "work" in preindustrial societies was primarily determined by gender, we can see how industrialization forced women into unfair competition with men, since it is men who control the industries. In short, economic exploitation falls most heavily upon women's shoulders.

Within the political sphere of life, there has been vast improvement in recent times. Western and Asian democracies can point with pride to the many statutes and policies that guarantee political and civil rights for all women. Furthermore, most communist- and socialist-inspired governments have eliminated sexually biased discrimination from their ideological considerations. Sadly enough, the same cannot be said for most military dictatorships and the more fundamentalist Islamic nations. Even within the countries that respect women's political rights, custom and culture continue to play a strong role in determining the political power of women. The facts speak for themselves:

- Margaret Thatcher's Conservative Party chose 23 men to fill 23 cabinet positions in the 1987 election in Great Britain.
- Less than 5 percent of the United States Congress are women.
- Only 3 governors of the 50 states are women.
- Of the 47 standing committees of the House and Senate of the Commonwealth of Pennsylvania, only one committee is chaired by a woman.

It is evident that women are vastly underrepresented by their numbers within the halls of legislative, executive, and judicial power. No one argues that some political power is better that none at all, but until the United States and other countries begin to approach a more balanced male-female membership in both elected and appointed government positions, charges of sexual discrimination will continue to be made.

Behind the Curtain

In keeping with our method for social analysis, we have observed thus far several examples of sexism, ranging from the physical and social through the economic and political. Let us now peek backstage at the reasons and rationale for the existence of sexist beliefs, attitudes, and behavior. What brought about these conditions of servitude and exploitation? Does the problem have several interrelated causes? Are there fundamental tensions that indicate no resolution to this male-female conflict? In seeking answers to these questions, we will look at the historical and structural elements as well as the political, economic, religious, cultural, and social categories that particularize the causes of sexism.

Physical strength and a biological determinant appear as the most obvious reasons for sexism. It is no secret that within the animal kingdom, where size and strength play a decisive role in the control and dominance of the group, the largest male is the boss. How much of this distinctly animal behavior remains buried within the unconscious dimensions of the human mind is anyone's guess, but history and most personal experience testify that men have dominated women more by physical strength than by wits. Indeed, this latter quality has helped to right the balance in untold situations of conflict.

The biological determinant refers to the sex drive, which for men is generally an aggressive, forceful, almost frenetic drive to satisfy a biological need. Since, physically speaking, the female receives the male, it is not surprising that men envision themselves in a dominant position not only sexually but also in many other roles. Historically, menstruation has also been seen as a debilitating condition, further enhancing the idea of male superiority. This combination of male strength and sexual aggressiveness reveals the two most tenacious roots of sexism. Because women are generally physically weaker, nature seems to provide a basis for male dominance.

Physical prowess has led to attitudinal conditioning among men. For example, the Spanish word for male, *macho,* has taken on a distinctly exaggerated sense of masculinity. *Machismo* describes an attitude of mind that sees power and control, especially over women, as a natural right for men. Furthermore, social patterns among ancient people amply testify to rampant discrimination against women. Aside from providing sexual pleasure and the care and nurturing of children, most especially the male children, women had no political rights and few legal ones because the social customs and cultural mores, determined by men, dictated a second-class status for women. Even Mahatma Gandhi, for all his sensitivity to the truth of nonviolence, was not the most loving of husbands. Indian society left little doubt about who was the master of the house.

Finally, from an ideological referent, the historical role of patriarch looms as the giant oak in the forest of sexism. Ruether's observation in the chapter epigraph stresses the triple exploitation of patriarchy by sex, class, and race. Further, she finds the roots of patriarchy in the Hebrew stories of creation and the societal conditions of these ancient tribal peoples. "Then the

LORD God said, 'It is not good that the man should be alone; I will make him a helper as his partner.'"[8] This and similar references throughout the book of Genesis were interpreted to mean that men were God's primary creation and women were created, not as equals, but as helpers.

Paul the Apostle, while stressing the importance of love and reverence between husbands and wives, nevertheless suggested a patriarchal role for men. "Wives, be subject to your husbands as you are to the Lord. For the husband is the head of the wife. . . . Just as the church is subject to Christ, so also wives ought to be, in everything, to their husbands."[9] Most scriptural scholars today attribute these admonitions not to the will of God, but rather to an identification with local familial customs. In any case, patriarchal structures have greatly influenced Western civilization up to the twentieth century. The rise of democracy, the ideological significance of human right, and a strong feminist theology have shredded the credibility of patriarchy. Although it still exists, it is receiving serious criticism.

Other Causes

We have already noted the negative effects of the Industrial Revolution. Long hours in factories, poor working conditions, and lack of health care and other benefits were the lot of workers who had no land and thus had to sell their laboring skills in order to survive. The preeminence of industrial capitalism in the nineteenth century, created, albeit indirectly, an entirely new situation for women. In an agricultural society gender tasks were readily discernable. Men did the work of planting and harvest while women tended the home. As industrialization increased people were drawn to the urban industrial centers in the hope of bettering themselves.

But the elimination of gender-defined tasks and the creation of a common work force, within which men and women compete, has always hurt women. Although this process gives a special opportunity to a few women, it degrades the majority, and brings those two groups into conflict with one another.[10]

Industrial capitalism has brought an abundance of products to the marketplace, and modernity has seen new opportunities for women in medicine, law, education, and other professions. Borreman's point, however, is that a downside also exists. The benefits of industrialization are now juxtaposed against massive environmental pollution, vast poverty and destitution, and the possibility of planetary annihilation by nuclear war. Have women improved their lot during the past two centuries of development? Unquestionably, some have. But at the expense of how many deprived sisters?

Another cause of sexism, a sort of modern-day version of patriarchy, is referred to as the "old-boy network." While specifically aimed at providing favors for one's own friends, it sharply constricts the opportunities for women to advance in the business world or in politics. Granted there are exceptions, such as Geraldine Ferraro's nomination for vice president in 1984, but the exception proves the rule. Cronyism has raised its ugly head from the steps of the Roman Senate to the salons of Paris, from the courts of the Medici to the corridors of Congress. All of this poses special problems for women. How does one break the pattern of male bonding rituals that exclude women? In recent years court rulings have forced private clubs and associations to open their doors to women. Perhaps real change will only come about as women demand a more active role in business and political decision making. Power is rarely relinquished voluntarily. Sexism will wither away only when women commit themselves to full participation in the political affairs of the world and in seeking a just economic order.

The Kinsey Reports[11] on male and female sexual behavior helped to usher in an era of presumed sexual enlightenment. With the rise of sexually transmitted diseases, the increase of teenage pregnancy, the burgeoning rate of divorce, and a general laissez-faire attitude to sex, one might question the benefits of the Sexual Revolution. Surely if one believes in the sanctity of marriage, modern pagan attitudes toward fornication, adultery, and pornography have distorted the meaning of fidelity and commitment. Sexism deals in exploitation; pagan sexual morality promotes manipulation and the empty joys of the one-night stand.

In addition to the personal sexism we have examined, we should be mindful of the structural sexism that prevails in the institutions of society. We have already noted that some Christian churches discriminate against women, especially with regard to clerical status. Many Islamic states also limit the rights of women by proscribing access to jobs, education, and political power. These institutional policies and practices constitute a structural prejudice against women in much the same way as the apartheid system of government restricts the political and civil rights of blacks in South Africa. Thus, personal and structural sin spin a web of sexist anti-values that continue to impede harmony between men and women.

The Liberation of Women

"Feminism is primarily a revolution of consciousness, having countless forms of political expression and action."[12] Although women of courage and conviction have always existed, it has only been in the twentieth century that they have rallied to demand the same rights guaranteed to men. In contrast to the extremes of female passivity, in which women assume a totally dependent role, and radical feminism, where total independence reigns supreme, a balanced feminism seeks to maintain the natural complementarity between the sexes. It is not sexist to endorse the idea that men and women are different and to rejoice in that reality.

Unquestionably, men have become much more sensitive to the aspirations of women, particularly with regard to their political and economic rights. Within marriage, many men have moved toward a better understanding of shared responsibility for child-rearing and housekeeping. Today's good marriage relies more on dialogue and equality than the previous generation's insistence on division of labor and role stereotyping. Furthermore, women engineers, doctors, lawyers, and business executives are no longer a dream but a reality. It is important to applaud this new consciousness and continue to root out the vestiges of male superiority.

Even within some Third World countries, the idea of women's liberation has begun to strike a responsive chord. The proverbial machismo of the Latin male must now withstand the global cry for human rights and the particularity of female emancipation. The Nicaraguan revolution of the late 1970s found women in many positions of authority, including military command. In its earliest years of reform, the Sandinista government guaranteed the rights of women and insisted on the protection of wives from abusive and negligent husbands.

Socialists, as well as democratic societies, have continued to support the rights of women and to foster an essential equality with men. Yet much more needs to be done. Women must assert their prerogatives in the political order by running for public office and assuming the mantle of leadership in public life. They must demand equal pay for comparable work in the marketplace and a voice in the boardrooms of corporate America. The time is past when women were expected to play the role of obedient wife and long-suffering mother, while men decided the fate of the world and the direction of the economy.

On February 11, 1989, in Boston, Massachusetts, thousands of people gathered to witness the consecration of Barbara Harris, a black woman, as the first Episcopal woman bishop. The Episcopal Church has permitted women's ordination to the priesthood since 1976 and, in spite of continuing controversy, saw fit to raise up a woman to its highest clerical office.

In the final analysis, each of us must find the right way to express our love for one another. There are certain androgynous qualities to which all humans should aspire. Care, respect, compassion, love, sensitivity, responsibility, trust, patience, and honesty are required of everyone. Freedom, too, is indivisible. While my sister suffers from sexist behavior, I cannot consider myself a free man. On a personal level men and women must find fresh and creative ways in which to relate. When men fail to recognize the distinct individuality of each woman and continue to treat women as objects of sexual satisfaction, or when women play a similar game, both sexes have fallen prey to their instincts. If the dance of life requires a smoothness and harmony of motion with female and male partners moving in an affectionate embrace, then we should play the music of mutual respect and concern, not the cacophony of selfishness and abuse.

Notes

1 Rosemary Radford Ruether, "Feminists Seek Structural Change," *National Catholic Reporter*, April 13, 1984, 6.

2 2 Samuel 11:4.

3 Vicki Kemper, "Poor and Getting Poorer," *Sojourners*, March 1986, 17.

4 Felice N. Schwartz, "Management Women and the New Facts of Life," *Harvard Business Review*, January–February 1989.

5 Valentina Borreman, "Technique and Women's Toil," *Crosscurrents* 32 (Winter 1982–83): 422.

6 Hilda Scott, *Working Your Way to the Bottom* (Boston: Pandora Press, 1985).

7 Borreman, "Technique and Women's Toil," 424.

8 Genesis 2:18.

9 Ephesians 5:22–24.

10 Borreman, "Technique and Women's Toil," 423.

11 Alfred C. Kinsey, *Sexual Behavior in the Human Male*; *Sexual Behavior in the Human Female* (Philadelphia: W. B. Saunders, 1948, 1953, respectively).

12 Nancy F. W. Passmore, "A Consciousness Manifesto," *The Politics of Women's Spirituality*, ed. Charlene Spretnak (Garden City, N.Y.: Anchor Press/Doubleday, 1982), 169.

16

Racism

Racism is an evil which endures in our society and in our church. Despite apparent advances and even significant changes in the past two decades, the reality of racism remains. In large part it is only the appearances which have changed.

National Conference of Catholic Bishops[1]

A Sordid Past

The concept of race found initial acceptance in the works of Comte Georges de Buffon, the renowned French naturalist, during the eighteenth century. Since that time anthropologists have attempted to develop criteria for differentiating among the six major geographical groups that he established.[2] Presently, skin color and other physical and cultural differences define race. Interestingly enough, the differences between individuals of a given race are far greater than the differences among all races. Nevertheless, in spite of the similarities among races with respect to intelligence, emotions, aspirations, compassion, and love, the poison of racism still flows through the human community.

Racism consists in a belief that the different physical and cultural characteristics produce an inherent superiority of one race over another. Adolf Hitler carried this conviction to extremes by his genocidal assault upon the Jews. Because of its particular impact upon the twentieth century, we will explore the Holocaust in more depth in the following chapter. Suffice to say that although the general notion of racial superiority has been discredited, the effects of its evil touch the lives of millions. In this chapter, we shall look briefly at some past and present examples of racism, offer some reasons for its existence, and conclude with a reflection on how to fight against its destructiveness of human relationships.

The slaughter of the Guarani Indians by Spanish soldiers, depicted in Robert Bolt's film *The Mission,* captured on screen one tiny segment of a vast human conflagration that destroyed indigenous cultures throughout Latin America over the past four centuries. Collusion between Spanish and Portuguese governments wrested land and slaves from native tribes, even while they were ostensibly protected by church authorities. Hernando Cortés led his troops across Mexico in the early sixteenth century, destroying the entire Aztec civilization within a few short years. It is hard to imagine the havoc and destitution that millions of Native Americans, both north and south of the equator, suffered. To the conquistadors the natives were subhuman. Because these people were unlettered, wore animal skins for clothing, and lived what were considered primitive lives, they were cavalierly dismissed as an ignorant and inferior species of humanity. Having no sophisticated weapons with which to defend themselves, the Indian nations fell to the explorers' desire to claim new territory for their European monarchs.

One of the most abominable examples of racism was the African slave trade. Slavery had existed since ancient times but it was only with the advent of colonialism that it began to play a dominant role in the economy. This was particularly true in the British colonies of Virginia, the Carolinas, and Georgia. Seamen plied their nefarious trade along the western coast of Africa, capturing Africans by, among other methods, randomly invading villages and kidnapping the occupants. It is estimated that about nine million Africans were shipped to the New World prior to the abolition of slavery in 1863.[3]

But our American ancestors were not finished with racism at the conclusion of the Civil War. Another pernicious chapter was just beginning.

> They made us many promises more than I can remember, they never kept but one; they promised to take our land, and they took it.[4]

Although the early colonists had systematically taken Indian lands and wiped out entire populations up and down the Atlantic seaboard throughout the seventeenth and eighteenth centuries, nothing compares to the three decades following the Civil War for the mayhem, greed, and destruction visited upon the American Indians.[5] The myth of the frontiersmen cutting trees for log cabins, fording rivers in search of land to farm and raise cattle was only part of the story. The pioneering spirit that energized people to "go West," as the quintessentially American journalist Horace Greeley urged, resulted in obliterating the homelands and destroying the culture of hundreds of native tribes.

Prior to the Civil War the Cherokees, Choctaws, Chickasaws, Creeks, and Seminoles had been packed off to the West. Now it was time to dislodge the Plains Indians from their lands. The Mohaves, Modocs, Yumas, and Paiutes lost their homes to the gold-rush prospectors in California. The most powerful nation of Indians, the Sioux, were separated into several subdivisions from the Dakotas to the Teton Mountains. By deception, broken treaties, and outright thievery they were subjugated between 1870 and 1880. Finally, in the arid Southwest, the Comanches and Apaches suffered virtual annihilation after gallantly standing off an onslaught by homesteaders, ranchers, and the army. The symbolic end of Indian freedom came with the deaths of Sitting Bull and Big Foot in December 1890. Dee Brown's tragic account of this genocide, when whites believed that "the only good Indian is a dead Indian," is chronicled in *Bury My Heart at Wounded Knee.* This book exposed the past racism of Americans toward the indigenous people of this land.

An Ugly Present

Perhaps nowhere else in the world today does the evilness of racism appear so glaring as in South Africa. In a country of 39 million people, only 18 percent of that number, the white minority, completely controls the institutions of government and industry and has systematically disenfranchised the native black population of their economic and political rights. *Apartheid* is the name given to this system of discriminatory regulations. It both restricts the freedom of blacks and limits their opportunity for economic advancement. In many instances the white government arbitrarily relocates blacks into ethnic homelands and invariably provides inferior education and inadequate health care. Whites who have spoken out against these racist policies are banned from public discourse and shunned, i.e., limited to conversations with no more than a few people.

Nobel Peace Prize-winner Archbishop Desmond Tutu, a black church leader, has joined with many others in decrying apartheid. Concurrently, most nations throughout the world have publicly called for an end to apartheid. Yet, paradoxically, they have contributed willingly to its prolongation by continuing to permit trade with transnational corporations in South Africa. Several transnationals have severed ties with South Africa; others are reluctant to end all trade for fear of doing further harm to blacks. Although some compromises have been reached between black leaders and the white government, the massive power of a modern police state apparatus will make political and social change a long, slow process. The imprisonments, beatings, and discrimination will continue until blacks obtain a voice in their future.

The roots of oppression began in the sixteenth century with colonialism, and have grown steadily into a worldwide array of discriminatory practices based primarily on color and cultural differences. Most racist behavior finds expression in economic exploitation, although racial prejudice ranges from the poor taste of ethnic humor to the full-blown hatred of the Ku Klux Klan.

We have already noted the existence of slavery in the British colonies prior to the American Revolution. Yet only about 500,000 slaves were in North America by 1790. By 1861, at the beginning of the Civil War, the number had risen to four million. Why? The expansion of slavery coincided with the invention of the cotton gin. The consequent expansion of the plantation system developed in order to accommodate this new technology, which increased production a hundredfold.

Following the abolition of slavery, a hundred years of false freedom settled upon the black minority in the United States. In spite of the fact that they enjoyed the status of citizenship, few were actually permitted to cast ballots in public elections and fewer had the temerity to run for public office. Throughout the South, where most of the black population was concentrated following the Civil War, racism was rampant. The emergence of the Ku Klux Klan, a secret society dedicated to the continued suppression of blacks, led to constant fear and intimidation by means of whipping, branding, tarring and feathering, mutilating, and lynching.[6] Rarely were whites punished for harming or killing blacks.

In the present scheme of things, racism continues unabated. A recent Klan Watch report (February 1989) by the Southern Poverty Law Center cited hundreds of crimes throughout the United States during the previous year that were racist inspired.[7] The latest wave of hatred has been led by skinhead gangs who espouse a particularly virulent form of racist behavior. In Portland, Oregon, where several skinhead gangs operate, assaults and beatings of racial minorities are commonplace. As David Simpson, a spokesperson for the Portland Police Department, said, "They really believe in their cause and they will die for it. These people deal in hate."[8]

The integration of neighborhoods, schools, and management positions in business remains an elusive goal for the vast majority of blacks. Asians and Hispanics suffer proportionately.

By all accounts, blatant and continuous discrimination abounds. If there is any hope of lessening the effects of this cancer within the human family, we should look beyond the racist attitudes and behavior in order to discover the causes of this disease. In the following sections we shall attempt to discover the motives behind racism.

Wealth/Land/Labor

A thorough analysis of racism would include a study of the origins and social conditions of its various manifestations throughout history and a careful delineation of the political, economic, religious, social, and cultural dimensions of the problem. Since we are limited to an examination of racism within the larger context of peace and justice education, we must restrict the scope of our study to a general overview of those causes that appear most likely to have sustained prejudice and discrimination.

Certainly close to the top of the list would be the pursuit of wealth. Columbus's search for gold led him to the New World, no less than bankers' desires for higher profits lead to the present redlining of neighborhoods. Greed in all its forms reigns supreme—from the use of black athletes to provide colleges with nationally recognized sports programs that fatten endowments, to the apartheid policies of white South Africans who enrich themselves by keeping blacks out of the economic loop. Marx believed that all behavior was ultimately traceable to economic considerations. While this may not be the entire truth, it certainly plays an important role in the discrimination of one group against another. Hitler used this very argument against the Jews of Germany. Since Jews had accumulated wealth through trickery, so the Nazis taught, they must pay for their perfidy by being deprived of their ill-gotten possessions. This phony racist argument was used to steal from the Jews.

Land appropriation, another form of greed, has also been behind the racially motivated ill treatment afforded Native Americans. Certainly the numerous broken treaties between the Native American Indians and the United States government were caused in no small part by the desire to expropriate land previously granted to the Indians in perpetuity. The murder of Sitting Bull, one of the last great Sioux chiefs, on the morning of December 15, 1890, originated in the corridors of Congress.

The land-grab attempt did not come until the following year, when a commission arrived from Washington with a proposal to carve the Great Sioux Reservation into six smaller reservations, leaving nine million acres open for settlement. The commissioners offered the Indians fifty cents an acre for this land. Sitting Bull immediately went to work to convince the commissioners that the Sioux would not stand for such a swindle.[9]

Millions of acres of rich tropical lands were either stolen outright or taken by connivance from native peoples and converted into coffee, banana, and rubber plantations throughout Central America. The constant government promises to redistribute the land testify to the widespread abuses that have caused the present unrest. Many inner-city minorities are currently experiencing an urban version of the land grab. With the implicit cooperation of city governments that allow whole neighborhoods to disintegrate, real estate developers buy up cheap properties and replace them with condos. This so-called gentrification process has dispossessed thousands of poor people. The present national crisis of homelessness has strong roots in land appropriation.

The need for cheap labor also looms high among the greed causes of racism. When the philosophers of capitalism and the captains of industry relegated labor to a quantitative resource, rather than a qualitative person, exploitation followed. We have already mentioned the enormous numbers of slaves toiling in the United States prior to the Civil War. In response to a query about ending slavery, James Hammond, a supporter of slavery, replied:

> . . . do you imagine you could prevail on us to give up a thousand millions of dollars in the value of our slaves, and a thousand millions of dollars more in the depreciation of our lands . . . ?[10]

Slavery ceased to exist in its crudest forms, yet it continues in the modern guise of poverty. It is no secret that blacks are last hired and first fired in many companies. The unemployment rate among black teenagers has approached 50 percent in recent years. The resulting drug addiction and violent crime rates represent the highest forms of slavery in modern society. "People get into crime as a way of making it in American society," said former Representative William H. Gray III recently to a gathering of delegates from the Urban League.[11] As long as our society continues to undervalue the person of whatever color, sex, or nationality and overvalue possessions and power, discrimination and racial hostility will remain.

Pride and Insecurity

Nationalism ranks 11 on a scale of 1 to 10 in identifying one of the longest and most perduring "isms" in human history. Although it was not until the rise of the modern nation-state system that it received complete recognition, an inchoate sense of closeness with one's kind has always existed. Its reciprocal, mistrust of the stranger, has also found perennial favor. The evil of ethnic superiority, which is rooted in a false pride of one's tribe or nation, has created untold misery throughout the centuries. Since the dawn of recorded history, commanders have exhorted the troops with speeches filled with inflammatory language about their enemies. Believing that the enemy was inferior bolstered the courage of soldiers marching into battle. Psychologically, racist and ethnic humor often mask a need to reinforce one's own self-worth at the expense of another.

Pride in one's self, one's family, and one's country does not constitute racism, nor are we expected to renounce all forms of celebration surrounding gender, race, and nation. But we need to remember that respect and sensitivity toward all things human, both personal and social, mark the civilized person. Unfortunately, excessive nationalism still blocks many from the solidarity and unity that should flourish among people.

The ancient worldview that society was naturally divided into rulers and the ruled translated in medieval times into a ready deference and obedience owed to higher-ups in the ordered culture that Christianity was. Externally, the centuries-long defense of Christianity against the Muslim threat by land and sea not only enforced the harsh disciplines of survival. It generated a settled attitude of anger and contempt for the religion of the enemy as well—and a toleration for violence—aided in some part by the triumphalism of Catholic theology. By Reformation times, both the evangelical ideal and religious intolerance—on both sides—accounted for religious wars on the continent. In Spanish America, the same forces soon saw to the high-handed conversion of native peoples in the New World, with small respect for the native culture and ways.

One major aim of peace and justice education propounded throughout Part I of this text is to develop a sense of inclusion about other people and cultures. By comparison with the minuscule percentage of people actively involved in working for justice, a vast majority remains indifferent to the racial hatred and bigotry still extant in our land. Not working to alleviate a social problem makes one an accomplice by default.

Recently, Morris Dees, director of the Southern Poverty Law Center, noted the "shocking increase during 1988 of racial violence."[12] In spite of this, many remain indifferent because they are not directly affected by the violence. The sin of apathy leads us to shirk responsibilities that are imposed upon us by the very nature of our humanity. If indeed we are one human family, then an injustice to one concerns all. Racial hatred and its many variants remain a major injustice in the world. Only when people of different races unite to combat the mutual enemy will we see its demise. "All that is needed for evil to conquer is for good people to remain silent," said Edmund Burke, the eighteenth-century British statesman. It is as true today as it was in his time.

Convictions

Underlying the call to love one's neighbor and to care for the stranger in our midst is a belief in the common fellowship of all under God. Unless this basic conviction lies at the center of our value system, little can be expected of us in building a world of peace and social justice. In subsequent chapters we will try to justify and offer additional evidence for the solidarity that should exist among all people. Suffice to say here that without a belief in the solidarity of the human family no hope exists for an end to racism.

People will always tend to identify, first and foremost, with their immediate family and friends. No one can be expected to relinquish or deny the roots of their humanness. Nevertheless, if we stop to observe planet Earth from a few thousand miles up in space, it is plain to see the commonality of the human species. Perhaps in the distant past, tribal and national loyalties helped to sustain a sense of unity among different clans. However, with today's appreciation of our unique place in the universe and the interdependence necessary for planetary survival, we can no longer afford the luxury of isolated complacency. Going it alone deserves no praise. We need to believe and live out the conviction that all people are our sisters and brothers.

This is the stance that the American Catholic bishops urged in their pastoral letter of 1987, *Brothers and Sisters to Us*.[13] They urged people not only to affirm a solidarity with others regardless of race and color, but also to take positive steps toward achieving racial harmony. For example, Jim and Sally, who were childless, decided to adopt two orphan children of another race. Jeannie and Bob adopted a Native American child. Ed and Sue went through months of red tape in order to adopt two Honduran sisters. Thousands of parents like them have opted for multiracial adoption so that they may show their love for children of other races. Children, perhaps more than adults, help us realize our common bond. Their dependence, their smiles and tears, their innocent trust cuts across all races, creeds, genders, and classes.

At an adult level, the General Assembly of the United Nations also testifies to the wonderful variety of races and cultures. African leaders mingle with Asian diplomats; Irish representatives confer with their Peruvian counterparts. In spite of the sometimes serious ideological differences, the women and men of the United Nations struggle to maintain global peace. Many a cross-cultural friendship has averted conflict and led to greater respect for racially different people. Bridge building can take place in many ways. The central point lies in a commitment to that goal.

The interdependence of people has never been more apparent than at the end of the twentieth century. Nations are taking collective action in order to combat the dangers of global suicide. Deforestation, damage to the ozone layer surrounding the planet, chemical and oil pollution of rivers and seas, and massive poverty have challenged us as never before to stand in solidarity as one planetary people. We are personally called to examine our attitudes and behavior toward each other and our shared environment.

In like manner, we need to acknowledge the essential unity of people of all races. Black, brown, white, yellow, and red skin cover the body. Beneath each surface lies a unique individual with hopes and dreams, fears and joys. We share a common humanity in spite of the superficial difference of skin pigment. Granted, culture and ideological differences may find us at odds, but even here accommodation and peace can be found when we approach each other in good faith. We must be convinced that in the eyes of God all are created equal. All are entitled to the necessities of life; we are our brother's and sister's keeper. Ultimately, the solidarity of the human family demands nothing less than the observance of the Golden Rule: love your neighbor as yourself.

Notes

1   National Conference of Catholic Bishops, *Brothers and Sisters to Us* (Washington, D.C.: United States Catholic Conference, 1979), 1.

2   Ashley Montagu, "The Concept of Race in the Human Species in the Light of Genetics," in *The Concept of Race*, ed. Ashley Montagu (London: Macmillan, 1969).

3   *Collier's Encyclopedia*, Vol. 21 (New York: P. F. Collier, 1983), 74.

4   Quote from Chief Red Cloud in Dee Brown, *Bury My Heart at Wounded Knee* (New York: Washington Square Press, 1970), 449.

5   Howard Zinn, *A People's History of the United States* (New York: Harper & Row, 1980), 167.

6   *Collier's Encyclopedia*, Vol. 14, 193.

7   *Klan Watch Intelligence Report #42* (Montgomery, Ala.: Southern Poverty Law Center, 1989), 10–11.

8   Ibid., 3.

9   Brown, *Bury My Heart at Wounded Knee*, 428.

10 Zinn, *A People's History of the United States*, 170.

11 William H. Gray III, "Address to Urban League Delegates," *Philadelphia Inquirer*, April 23, 1989.

12 *Klan Watch Intelligence Report #42*, 9–11.

13 National Conference of Catholic Bishops, *Brothers and Sisters to Us*, 13–14.

17

The Holocaust

Exterminations: Chelmno, December 8, 1941–January 18, 1942: 360,000 Jews; 5,000 Gypsies from Lod Ghetto. Auschwitz, January 1942–November 1944: 2.5 to 4 million Jews. Belzek, March 1942–December 1944: 600,000 Jews. Maidenek, April 1942–July 22, 1944: 500,000 Jews. Sobibor, May 1942–November 1943: 250,000 Jews. Treblinka, July 23, 1942–November 1943: 700,000 Jews, of these 300,000 from Warsaw.[1]

The Camps

The word *exterminations* at the beginning of this list is crucial. It establishes the context for what might first appear to be little more than statistical data about events that happened in the distant past. If there is one event in the twentieth century that grounds the present generation in the reality of human evil, it is the Holocaust. The mind is left numb by the millions of people murdered simply because they were Jews!

Each of the statistics in the list represents a man or a woman, a boy or a girl; almost one million of the estimated six million Jews who were "exterminated" were children. These innocent victims were no different from members of one's own family, next-door neighbors, or fellow workers. Yet in the course of a decade (1935–1945) they were herded off to death camps (the above-mentioned ones were the largest—the total list numbers nineteen) by the German secret police, the Gestapo, where they were systematically exterminated in gas chambers and then incinerated in crematoria. All because they were Jews! At the end of World War II the Allied armies found some survivors, gaunt and half starved skeletons in prison uniforms with tattooed numbers for names. Near Tel Aviv in present-day Israel stands a bronze statue of a large broken Torah, depicting the desecration of the Jews. It is completely covered with identification numbers to memorialize the victims of the Holocaust.

Prescinding momentarily from the reasons why this event occurred, we need to assimilate not only the enormity of the crime, but also its deliberate ruthlessness. For example, the camps were built to particular specifications. Civil and mechanical engineers were required to design buildings, roadways, and kitchen and sanitary facilities, and to plan all the necessary structural facilities for these camps. Special rooms for gassing hundreds of people simultaneously were needed. So too was it necessary to produce, package, and ship the Zyklon B, a cyanide gas used at the camps. The crematoria required bold, innovative construction techniques in order to burn bodies at a faster and faster rate. Nothing was left to chance. Documents were found explaining in exquisite detail the amount of wood required to incinerate a specific number of bodies and how long the process would take. All of the camps had factories attached to them. Men and women were forced to march several miles back and forth to work each day with little regard for their health or welfare.

If they escaped the initial sorting out upon arrival at the camps—some were immediately consigned to death at the whim of the Gestapo officer on duty—they joined a work battalion for job assignments. Since this Jewish slave labor was found in abundance throughout much of Europe, there was no need to take care of the prisoners. Death from exposure during the wintertime, dysentery, and malnourishment raged throughout the camps. Because the newly enacted laws of the Third Reich had declared Jews to be without rights, they were reduced to the status of nonpersons. This enabled the local authorities to confiscate their property, ransack their homes, and deport them to the camps.

One particular camp, Auschwitz, symbolized the total evil that unfolded each day. Following a meal of watery soup, hundreds of men and women marched off to the factory for a day of work without pay. In another part of this camp, doctors and nurses were preparing for their unusual medical experiments: victims were submerged in vats of ice water to measure how long it took them to die; limbs were amputated to see how victims would cope with handicaps; testes were removed in order to observe the behavior of eunuchs. Meanwhile, another trainload of Jews arrived and the selection process began again. Within a few hours the sorting was complete. One can only wonder if those condemned to death in the Auschwitz gas chambers were not better off than those assigned to the work crews. Moments after the gas fumes were vented from the death chambers, other inmates and guards would enter the room and methodically remove gold fillings from teeth and the women's hair. The bodies were then carted to the crematoria. During the peak of the slaughter 3,000 people were murdered each day at Auschwitz. American soldiers who took part in the liberation of these death camps were physically sick when they saw the evidence of the wholesale destruction of fellow human beings.

Eyewitness Accounts

"Anne loves Peter" might have read the logo scratched on walls inside the building on the Prinsengracht Canal. For it was surely true that her first teenage romance affected her deeply. Unfortunately, it was her only romance. Anne Frank, together with her parents and sister; the Van Daan family, of whom Peter was the only son; and an elderly dentist, Albert Dussel, were sequestered for twenty-five months in a hidden apartment attached to a warehouse in Amsterdam, Holland, during the Nazi occupation of that country in the early 1940s. She and her family, like thousands of Jews, were trapped when the occupation began. They went into hiding rather than risk arrest and deportation to a concentration camp. In her diary Anne tells us about the secret annex where she lived from July 9, 1942, until August 4, 1944. Although not a concentration camp in a formal sense, it nonetheless served as her prison. She spoke of tensions that built up among the eight people who shared the close quarters, about the poor food, the inadequate clothing, and the rundown conditions of their quarters. Fear of detection pervaded the atmosphere daily.

> This evening . . . there was a long, loud, penetrating ring at the door. I turned white at once, got a tummy-ache and heart palpitations, all from fear. At night when I'm in bed, I see myself alone in a dungeon . . . or our "Secret Annex" is on fire, or they come and take us away at night.[2]

In fact, the Nazis finally did come. Betrayed by an informer for less than ten dollars, Anne and her companions were arrested and sent to Auschwitz in August 1944. She died of malnutrition in February 1945, simply because she was a Jew.

But the little camp of the "Secret Annex" was dwarfed by the real thing.

> Not far from us, flames were leaping up from a ditch, gigantic flames. They were burning something. A lorry drew up at the pit and delivered its load—little children. Babies! Yes, I saw it—saw it with my own eyes . . . those children in the flames. (Is it surprising that I could not sleep after that? Sleep had fled from my eyes.) So this was where we were going. A little further on was another and larger ditch for adults. I pinched my face. Was I still alive? Was I awake? I could not believe it. No, none of this could be true. It was a nightmare. . . .[3]

For Elie Wiesel, the author of *Night*, from which the above passage was excerpted, this was his first day at the Auschwitz concentration camp. It is hard to imagine the fear and anxiety that confronted this fifteen-year-old boy just moments after he was separated from his mother and sisters. With his father and other male victims, he was marched past the incinerators into a caldron of living hell. It had been only two days since all the Jews in his village of Sighet had been rounded up and loaded on trains for deportation. No one expected that the Jews in that Hungarian village would feel the wrath of the Nazis. Yet during the early 1940s trains from villages and towns all over Europe continued daily to carry their victims to the death camps. Wiesel and others survived to tell their awful story, with a hope that future generations would never allow it to happen again.

Viktor Frankl writes of a similar fate in his book, *Man's Search for Meaning*. He was a practicing psychiatrist before his imprisonment and was thus able to bring the insights of his profession to the stresses of the concentration camps. He noted that phase one for prisoners consisted of developing survival skills, retaining a sense of loss for the things of the past, enduring the ugliness of the surroundings, and acquiring a kind of gallows humor as a defense against the constant fear.

In the second phase the inmates succumbed to apathy. This indifference or resignation was caused not only by the harsh labor, little sleep, and poor food, but also by the prisoners' mental defenses against the constant threat of death.[4] For example, the capos, many of whom were common criminals, were directly in charge of the prisoners and beat them at the slightest provocation. Since this fear hung over the entire camp from morning until night, only a mindset of feigned indifference could get one through each day.

Frankl said that he survived through a series of fortunate circumstances. In fact, just prior to the Allied armies' liberation of Auschwitz, he missed a truck that carried several fellow prisoners to their deaths.[5] Subsequent to his release, Frankl developed a new theory of psychotherapy, which we will examine in chapter 22. Suffice to say here, the horrors of the concentration camps taught him many lessons about human depravity.

Finally, Yankel Wiernik, who escaped from the Treblinka death camp, vividly describes the horrors of the gas chamber.

Into the chamber of twenty-five square meters 450 to 500 people were jammed. The congestion was unbelievable. The victims carried in the children, somehow hoping to save them from death. On their way to die they were beaten and driven by truncheons and pipes. Dogs were set upon them.... Everyone, eager to escape the blows and the dogs, rushed screaming into the lethal chamber. The stronger pushed the weaker.... The doors closed with a clang on the packed chamber. The motor was connected with the input apparatus and switched on. In twenty-five minutes ... all lay dead. But they did not really lie, for they had no room to fall. They died standing, their legs and arms entangled. There were no more screams. Mothers and children were clasped in death's embrace. There was no friend or foe, no envy. No one was more beautiful or ugly—all were suffocated, yellowed by gas. No rich, no poor—all were alike.[6]

Wiernik's graphic observations of the circumstances and final moments in the lives of the victims only hint at the terror they must have felt. Imagine the inner fear and disbelief that gripped the minds of literally millions of Jews as they were brutally shoved toward death. How many bites did they get from Doberman pinschers on the way? How much blood was spilled? What kind of madness could have allowed this incredible inhumanity to continue day in and day out for almost a dozen years? That, of course, brings us to the central question: Why did it happen?

Why Did It Happen?

When Christians emerged from the catacombs following the victory of Constantine in the early fourth century, they gradually developed a religious structure, which, over the centuries, wedded itself to the power of the state and was virtually synonymous with Western society. In the background, however, over all those times lay a shameful and cruel practice, namely, the widespread persecution of the Jewish people—ostensibly as an aftermath of their rejection of Jesus as chronicled in the Gospels. In modern times, this history of often treating European Jews as second-class citizens worthy of complicit and open abuse and discrimination (and the mentality appropriate to this treatment) played a role in the premier scandal of the twentieth century—the genocide of 6,000,000 Jews in the Hitler era. And the Christian churches, Catholic and Protestant, did not necessarily escape with unstained hands. Paul Hilberg, for example, in his book, *The Destruction of the European Jews*, finds grounds for comparison between the canonical laws of the Catholic Church and the legal decrees of the Nazis as setting the stage, in part, for the Holocaust.[7]

The charge against the Jews, from medieval times on, led them to be maligned, beaten, confined to their homes on major Christian feast days, and forced to live in ghettos and even suffer exile. Martin Luther, for one, vehemently condemned Jews as a "plague, pestilence, and pure misfortune,"[8] who, additionally, desired to rule the world and eliminate Christianity. Thus, when Hitler looked for a scapegoat for the disorder and economic chaos of post–World War I Germany, he had the precedent of this long-term animosity to justify the savage decrees set in motion in 1937 and after.

Likewise, some of the secular philosophers of the nineteenth century played a theoretical role, principally Nietzsche. His philosophy of cultural determinism and his exaltation of the Aryan folk hero were made to order for Hitler's move to champion racial purity by segregating and ultimately trying to eliminate the Jewish people.[9] Nietzsche attacked Christianity for its themes of compassion and love and attacked Greek philosophy as well for its belief in universal truth and goodness. For him, tenderness was weakness, and individual human rights were a myth.

Hitler thus concluded that the white Aryan nation must not be defiled by mixing with inferior blood. To his mind, it was the Semitic blood-line of the Jews, not their rejection of Jesus nor their economic prowess, that endangered German society. Equally, he saw the themes of human solidarity and the dignity of the individual as egregious lies designed to dilute the natural superiority of the Nordic peoples. Against non-Aryans, Hitler hailed blond hair and blue eyes as marking the interior strength of the German nation. Altogether, long-enduring anti-Semitism joined forces with Nietzschean determinism and Aryan pride to make a case for the separation of the Jews from the body of the German people. Hitler's single-minded rage did the rest.

One additional factor that played a decisive role in the Holocaust was the ascendency of the National Socialist German Workers Party. This Nazi Party, founded in 1920, precluded Jews from membership and made it plain that Jews should not be considered as citizens of Germany.[10] The conclusion of World War I saw Germany prostrate. Not only did it lose the war but the Allies—Britain, France, Russia, and the United States—demanded significant reparation. Germany stumbled through the 1920s living in economic hardship. The worldwide collapse of the economy during the Great Depression, which began in 1929, further debilitated the German people. They were groping for direction and leadership, as were many nations. The global depression brought with it high rates of unemployment, breadlines for the poor and destitute, loss of productivity, and, above all, a general malaise for millions of people. Could nothing be done? Was there anyone who could offer hope to the downtrodden? In the United States, the people chose Franklin Delano Roosevelt; in Germany, the fateful choice was Adolf Hitler.

Envisioning himself as a messianic figure, he believed that he was destined to lead the Aryan race to new heights of grandeur. In the wake of the many problems that beset Germany, it was not surprising that people would turn to a strong authority figure who promised not only to restore their pride and dignity, but also to show the world the true greatness of the Germanic nation. Since his anti-Semitic views were well established before he gained political power, it would be unfair to exonerate the German population from responsibility for the Holocaust. They knew that Jewish persecution was one of his political aims. Like many people, unfortunately, they did not believe he would go to the extremes of a "final solution."

The Judgment of History

In the early years following World War II the names of Martin Bormann, Hermann Goering, Rudolf Hess, Alfred Jodl, Joachim Von Ribbentrop, and Albert Speer were well known. All had been senior officials in the Nazi high command. All were put on trial for "crimes against humanity" at Nuremberg, Germany, in 1946. After months of detailed testimony depicting the extent and gruesomeness of the concentration camps, these men and several other lesser-known figures were found guilty.

All admitted to their respective roles in the atrocities of the Holocaust, yet each denied responsibility.

How does one justify evil deeds? They were not responsible, they claimed, because they were simply obeying orders.

The judgment of history, however, says that individuals are responsible for their actions. The capos, the SS (Schutzstaffeln), so-called storm troopers, the manufacturers of Zyklon B, and the designers and railroad officials who abetted in the logistics of the deportations were all responsible for the roles they played in the extermination of the Jews. Those who stood by and did nothing were equally guilty.

One of the many lessons of the Holocaust is that people can say No to evil, if they are willing to judge right from wrong and have the courage to live that conviction fully.

Subsequent to the Nuremberg trials, other Nazis were gradually tracked down throughout Europe, Latin America, and the United States. As recently as 1986, the United States extradited an 86-year-old Croatian, Andrija Artukovic, to Yugoslavia for his role in killing 200,000 people while he served as Minister of Justice in the Nazi-occupied territory of Croatia.[11]

Perhaps the most celebrated Nazi criminal was Adolf Eichmann. Captured in May 1960 by the Israeli secret service, he was abducted from Argentina and brought to Jerusalem to stand trial for war crimes. According to testimony at his trial, he was privy to Hitler's plans for a final solution to the Jewish question. Although not serving in the front echelon of the Nazi party, he ranked sufficiently high up to have received direct orders from Reinhardt Heydrich, Hitler's deputy of state, that "the Fuhrer has ordered the physical extermination of the Jews."[12] He, too, played the broken record, "I'm not responsible, I just followed orders."

Hannah Arendt, who chronicled the Eichmann trial for the *New Yorker,* discovered the "banality of evil" in the events of the Holocaust. The modern bureaucrat obediently follows the orders coming from his superiors. Eichmann was not a policymaker, but a functionary who faithfully did what he was told. Such was the sickness of the German military and political structure that no one asked if the orders were moral or immoral!

What will be the judgment of history on our society? Can we learn from the past? Does a study of the Holocaust teach us something about the evilness of power and the ease with which people can be duped into following a demagogue? Surely the trials at Nuremberg showed the world that supposedly cultured men, who could sip fine cognac and listen rhapsodically to Beethoven's Fifth Symphony, were capable of the most inhumane treatment of their fellow humans. They also helped to show us the difference between right and wrong. Not infrequently, we hear that we are not to judge others for their behavior or attitudes. In some areas of life this is clearly good advice. The food I eat, the job I hold, and my personal likes and dislikes are of little consequence to others. But if I am anti-Semitic, if I harbor hostility toward people of different races or religions, if I propagate my hatred, should I be encouraged because I am doing my own thing? The Holocaust has declared definitively that evil must be resisted. No one can sit by idly while other humans suffer injustice. This is the first and most important lesson of the Holocaust. There are others.

The Commanding Voice of Auschwitz

If the victims of the Holocaust could speak from the grave, what would they say? Emil Fackenheim, in his work *God's Presence in History*, believes that the "Voice of Auschwitz" commands four actions: (1) Jews must remember and remind the world of the six million victims of the Holocaust. (2) Jewish survival is a sacred duty. After the concentration camps, Jews must never allow them to exist again. (3) Jews must not turn their backs on the world. They must continue to enlighten it with an ethical concern for all that is good and holy. (4) Jews must not despair of God. God's apparent absence at Auschwitz cannot allow Jews to forsake their Mosaic inheritance. While wrestling with the mysterious ways of God, they must not lose faith.[13] Jews have known oppression before. In fact, the foundational experience of God's concern for the Jews was the Exodus. The Hebrew people suffered oppression under the Egyptians, until God led them to freedom.[14] Not until the Holocaust, however, had such cataclysmic horror been imposed upon them. Thus, the "Voice of Auschwitz" must not be silenced. It must speak clearly about the crimes against humanity. Henceforth, every generation must be taught about what happened not only to Jews, but to everyone. If there is any hope of not repeating the Holocaust, it will only come from remembering its evilness, says Fackenheim.

"Never again," swear Israeli soldiers during their induction into military service. All able-bodied men and women must serve in the defense of their country, and the oath reminds them about their past and present. In A.D. 70, Roman armies stormed the city of Jerusalem and destroyed the Temple. They then laid seige to the town of Masada, atop a mesa overlooking the Dead Sea. Nine hundred sixty members of the Zealot party committed suicide rather than surrender to the Romans. Jews today know they cannot let the tragedy of Masada nor the criminality of Auschwitz ever happen again.

The lessons of the Holocaust demand the same witness from all who are concerned with peace and justice. People of good will must stand together in condemning racism in all its forms. Passivity reflects cowardice, resistance shows courage.

> We, the members of the Christian Community of the Greater Philadelphia area, join with you, our Jewish brothers and sisters in this solemn remembrance of and reflection on the Holocaust. . . .
> In honor of the six million martyrs whom we remember this day, and the other millions more, we covenant with you by the power of God to strive to rid our troubled world of such genocidal deeds

for all time to come. Together we share the ideal of the eternal worth of the human person.

This solemn pledge was offered at the annual memorial service for the victims of the Holocaust on April 16, 1978. A similar tribute is repeated yearly in many places throughout the world. Christians have begun to admit their historic guilt for the anti-Semitism that led to the Holocaust. Several official documents have been issued by the Vatican condemning racism and acknowledging implicit Catholic acquiescence in the persecution of Jews.[15] It is fair to say, however, that today virtually all Christian churches have repudiated anti-Semitism.

In concluding this chapter, a caveat is in order. While the State of Israel represents the aspirations of many Jews today, other Jews are embarrassed about the way Israel has dealt with its Palestinian population. Although many Jews would like to resolve this issue by establishing a Palestinian homeland on the West Bank and Gaza, others would drive the Arabs out of Palestine. A rabidly fanatic Zionist minority has shaken the credibility of a traditional Jewish respect for the stranger. In her critique of present-day Judaism, *The Fate of the Jews,* Roberta Feuerlicht reminds her Jewish brethren that their moral behavior is the true determinant of their Jewishness.[16] In short, while we must identify with past Jewish suffering, we cannot condone present Jewish injustice. The human rights of all people must be respected regardless of race, gender, or creed.

Notes

1   Thomas A. Idinopulos, "Art and the Inhuman: A Reflection on the Holocaust," *Christian Century,* October, 16, 1974, 954.

2   Anne Frank, *The Diary of a Young Girl* (Garden City, N.Y.: Doubleday, 1967), 130.

3   Elie Wiesel, *Night* (New York: Bantam Books, 1960), 30.

4   Viktor E. Frankl, *Man's Search for Meaning* (New York: Washington Square Press, 1967), 13–33.

5 Ibid., 96–97.

6 Idinopulos, "Art and the Inhuman," 954.

7 Paul Hilberg, *The Destruction of the European Jews* (New York: Holmes & Meier, 1985), 11–15.

8 Ibid., 17.

9 Allan Bloom, *The Closing of the American Mind* (New York: Simon & Schuster, 1987), 307.

10 Hilberg, *The Destruction of the European Jews*, 32.

11 Robert Pear, "U.S. Extradites Croat to Yugoslavia," *The New York Times,* February 12, 1986, 22.

12 Hannah Arendt, *Eichmann in Jerusalem* (New York: Viking Press, 1963), 78.

13 Emil Fackenheim, *God's Presence in History* (New York: Harper & Row, 1970), 84–88.

14 Exodus 6:2–9.

15 Edward H. Flannery, *The Anguish of the Jews* (New York: Paulist Press, 1985), 265.

16 Roberta S. Feuerlicht, *The Fate of the Jews* (New York: Time Books, 1983), 5.

18

Militarism

The arms race is one of the greatest curses on the human race; it is to be condemned as a danger, an act of aggression against the poor, and a folly which does not provide the security it promises.

National Conference of Catholic Bishops[1]

Warfare and Weapons

We love to smell flowers, swim in a lake, or dive into an ocean wave; we love to climb trees and tell funny stories; we love to watch the moon and stars at night, to embrace, to create, to enjoy the company of our friends and the peacefulness of quiet moments. We also seem to love war!

The first weapons of war were "sticks and stones to break men's bones." This was followed by bow and arrow, gunpowder, and the use of musket and pistol. Swords, spears, and cannons escalated the amount of harm soldiers could inflict upon their enemies. Much creative genius went into developing the art of warfare. With each passing century, the crudeness of primitive technologies gave way to more scientific pursuit of warfare.

In quick succession came the repeating rifle and automatic weapons. The invention of the airplane quickly led to the development of bombs that rained terror from the skies. Then, finally, with the discovery of nuclear fission and fusion came the ultimate weapon, the nuclear bomb.

The kill ratio of weapons has grown at an exponential rate. An arrow kills one person; a gun may kill several; bombs will destroy hundreds; atomic weapons annihilate millions. We have gone from wars fought between armies on designated battlefields to the massive destruction of civilian populations. Past eras saw wars fought between armed combatants; today, in war, the death of children and the aged, the sick and the disabled is a foregone conclusion. The atomic bombs that the United States dropped on Hiroshima and Nagasaki killed more than one-half million people, most of whom were civilians.

In ancient times, the kings of Egypt and the Middle East fought to impose control over people and territory. Alexander the Great conquered much of Europe and as far east as India in the fourth century B.C. The Roman empire stands above them all, having dominated Europe and the Mediterranean for almost five centuries. Roman legions were stationed from the British Isles to the hills of Galilee and woe betide any insurrectionists who confronted them. For example, because Jews demanded political freedom, Rome lay waste the city of Jerusalem in A.D. 70, forever altering Jewish history. The exploits of tribal chieftains in Ireland, Viking warriors from Scandinavia, hordes of barbarians from northern Europe and Asia, and warlords in China and Japan remind us of the constant battles and military escapades throughout the ancient world.

The Middle Ages found knighthood in bloom. The warrior became a man of character and virtue. The rules of chivalry forbade taking advantage of the weak and honored those who upheld the rights of others. The rules of war allowed for days off, replenishment of foodstuffs, and a sense of camaraderie with the enemy. Surrenders were cordial, and soldiering took on a professional cast. Wars continued to be fought, but there was a sense of limit to the destruction allowed.

This gradually began to change with the coming of the modern era. In the battle of Gettysburg (1863), General Robert E. Lee lost 20,000 troops in a three-day fight with the Union forces. In the Battle of the Somme (1916), the British general, Sir Douglas Haig, lost 60,000 men in one day against the Germans. This latter battle raged on for almost six months during World War I with no appreciable gain for either side. The losses, however, were staggering: 190,000 French, 500,000 Germans, and 410,000 British lay dead.[2] The twentieth century has witnessed mass killing on an unprecedented scale. The Turks slaughtered one million Armenian peasants during World War I; Stalin executed millions of Russians who resisted collectivization during the 1930s; the total numbers of people killed during World War I surpassed thirty million while that figure almost doubled during World War II.[3] The Germans used mustard gas at the beginning of the century; today many nations possess arsenals of highly potent chemical and biological weapons. Will it never cease?

Today's Reality

One need only read the newspapers closely for a week or two or view a monthly world news roundup on public television to know that many serious conflicts rage throughout the globe. El Salvador continues to suffer a prolonged civil war that has cost almost 75,000 lives. Until recently, Shiite Moslems battled Christian Phalangists in the streets of Beirut with the Syrian army and the radical Hizballah (Party of God) fueling the hatred. The people killed to date number 125,000. A protracted conflict between government forces and communist guerrillas has cost 100,000 lives in the Philippines during the past twenty years. An on-again, off-again tribal struggle has resulted in a half-million deaths in Uganda since 1970. The Israeli-Palestinian conflict continues; Protestant-Catholic hatred smolders in Northern Ireland; Peru is terrorized by Maoist Shining Path guerrillas; in Sri Lanka Hindu Tamils are fighting Sinhalese Buddhists; and

Afghan rebels struggle to overthrow the government. Indeed, it is virtually impossible to find a place in the world where weapons and military presence do not play a dominant role in the affairs of people.

Nor should we forget the nuclear arms race that has flourished for the past forty years. Following the fission bomb of 1945 came an avalanche of related weaponry. Intercontinental bombers, intercontinental ballistic missiles (ICBMs), early-warning radar, satellite tracking systems, submarine-launched ballistic missiles, multiple warheads, independently targeted warheads, a neutron bomb (kills people, but will not destroy property), a new mobile ICBM, and a Stealth bomber. Conventional weapons, too, grew in sophistication and numbers. Assault rifles, napalm bombs, antipersonnel mines, surface-to-air missiles, B-1 bombers, jet fighter aircraft, combat helicopters, Trident submarines, and a host of exotic and expensive weaponry poured off the production lines in the United States and the Soviet Union in the name of defense. A triad system of defense emerged in which nuclear submarines at sea, bombers in the air, and missiles in land-based silos could withstand any attack and retaliate immediately. This was aptly named Mutually Assured Destruction (MAD).

Thus, the arms race, which began as mutual deterrence, has risen to the point where both sides possess 10,000 more nuclear weapons than they need. We should note in passing that the power of one of today's nuclear weapons can destroy a territory 60 times larger than Hiroshima, where 200,000 died. The United States and the Soviet Union possess about 25,000 nuclear weapons.

During the early years of the arms race former Army General Dwight D. Eisenhower, in 1953, poignantly expressed his personal anguish over weapons spending.

> Every gun that is made, every warship that is launched, every rocket fired signifies, in the final sense, a theft from those who hunger and are not fed, those who are cold and are not clothed. This world in arms is not spending money alone. It is spending the sweat of its laborers, the genius of its scientists, the hopes of

its children.... Under the cloud of threatening war, it is humanity hanging from a cross of iron.[4]

Eisenhower clearly saw the connection between guns and butter. If we spend enormous amounts of money on military procurements, then education, health care, job training, and many other human needs languish at the bottom of the priority list. In conclusion, we face today empires of military power fueled by conflicting ideologies, antagonistic nation-states, and greedy arms merchants. Military dictators control well over half the countries in the world and military expenditures absorb more than half of the government budget for most nations. Why is this so? Let us examine briefly some of the reasons for this incredible outlay of resources for military needs.

Fear/Greed/Revenge

Since the end of World War II, the United States and other Western European countries, acting under the umbrella of the North Atlantic Treaty Organization (NATO), have confronted the Soviet Union and the Soviet bloc nations (Warsaw Pact) in what was known as the Cold War. Communism vs. democracy was the ideological basis for this hostility, resulting in forty-five years of antagonism, mistrust, and fear of attack. These suspicions dominated the thinking of these adversarial forces and led to reliance on military power for protection.

What developed from this ideological impasse was a new entity called the "national security state." Because we were at war with communism, both national and foreign policy considerations focused on the question of fighting the socialist enemy. Third World countries that sought land reform and other social changes were suspect and subject to overthrow. The United States helped to topple reform governments in Guatemala in 1954, in the Dominican Republic in 1965, and in Chile in 1973. Even today the U.S. government continues to support the privileged classes in El Salvador. Internally, voices of dissent are subject to harassment and investigation. Granted the courts have upheld the right of free speech, but the executive branch, in the name of national security, went from the witch-hunt days of the McCarthy era in the 1950s to spying on citizens who help Latin American political refugees in the 1980s.

The excessive reliance on military power to resolve conflicts found support among the arms manufacturers and the generals and admirals who procured the weapons. As long ago as 1961, President Eisenhower, in his Farewell Address to Congress, warned of the coming problem.

> In the councils of government we must guard against the acquisition of unwarranted influences, whether sought or unsought, by the military-industrial complex. The potential for the disastrous rise of misplaced power exists and will persist. We must never let the weight of this combination endanger our liberties or democratic processes.[5]

The military-industrial complex that Eisenhower warned of has grown exponentially since then. Aircraft, munitions, and electronic corporations have spun a web of interlocking companies throughout the U.S. that resist demilitarization. From Silicon Valley, California, to the Route 128 high-tech complex outside Boston, Massachusetts, hundreds of thousands of people owe their livelihood to the arms race. Knowing this, it is not surprising that government officials and many Americans have acted coolly toward Gorbachev's overtures for peace. Attempts to get companies to convert to peacetime manufacturing have often met with hostility. The arms race is ultimately attributable to both the legitimate need for reasonable defense and the unquenchable desire to build the most expensive and sophisticated weapons imaginable. Military commanders want the best; contractors compete for the business.

Thus, we find a variety of reasons for weaponry. They give a sense of national security and assuage our collective fears of external enemies, real or imagined. They keep Latin American dictators and repressive governments in power.

They also allow guerillas to challenge repressive governments. In the final analysis, weapons can be put to good or bad uses. Militarism, on the other hand, uses weaponry to foster a dependence upon the use of force as the only solution to conflict situations. Military solutions rule out nonviolent approaches and result in enormous cost to all nations. Let us look for a moment at these costs.

Human Costs

Lives in all nations are warped by the arms race. The United States and the Soviet Union together spend about $1.5 billion a day on military defense. Yet the United States ranks eighteenth among all nations in infant mortality, the U.S.S.R. forty-sixth.[6]

Since 1975 Ruth Leger Sivard has published an annual edition of *World Military and Social Expenditures.* Her concern highlights the economic underdevelopment that results from the arms race. In the first instance, the growing gap between rich and poor during the past several decades owes its existence to an emphasis on technological progress at the expense of human needs. Capital invested in high-tech companies is unavailable to help the poor in bettering their lives. For example, it was not a coincidence that the large increase in United States military spending in the 1980s was accompanied by a rise in homelessness and malnutrition among poor children. Furthermore, global unemployment has risen because military expenditures create fewer jobs than investments in housing, road construction, hospitals, and schools. In addition, military products are useless. Money spent on missile launchers and rockets contributes nothing to the economy; washing machines and soap powder at least will keep us clean!

Sivard further cites neglect in the areas of education, health care, and nutrition as a major consequence of militarism. In the United States most schools within major cities suffer the effects of classroom overcrowding, inadequate maintenance, and poorly funded school activities. This is a result of taxes spent on defense rather than education. One might imagine the impact on national education if the current plan to put missiles on railroad cars was canceled (estimated cost $10 billion) and allocated to the most needy school districts in the country. Needs such as prenatal care, vaccinations, and health support for the elderly and infirm often go unmet because priorities are misplaced.

Government budgets for health care in many Third World countries average about one-quarter of their military spending.[7] Malnutrition, hunger-related illness, and outright starvation are often the result of warfare. The civil wars in Chad and Ethiopia during the past dozen years have cost thousands of lives through starvation simply because the warring factions denied international relief agencies permission to enter disputed territories. Sadly enough, illiteracy, unemployment, malnutrition, and inadequate health care can be directly traced to militarism.

When we add in the cost of political repression, we begin to measure not only the physical problems created by militarism, but also the damage done to liberty and freedom. Because our military is controlled by elected officials and our Constitution is respected, we have been spared the worst effects of dictatorship in the United States. The same is not true elsewhere. Virtually every Latin American country has suffered the effects of military rule in the past quarter-century. Duvalier in Haiti, Somoza in Nicaragua, Pinochet in Chile, and Castro in Cuba all have exercised total control of their governments. Throughout the world, the names of Idi Amin, who slaughtered thousands of his people in Uganda, and Pol Pot, who killed millions in the name of revolution in Cambodia, symbolize the evilness of warfare and the violence that comes from seeking military answers to social problems. All too often repression is the first response from a militarized government to those who seek reform.

Militarism is an excessive reliance on force to solve social problems and the accumulation of unnecessary weapons beyond the rational norms of self-defense. A permanent war mentality erodes the humanitarian instincts of people. Instead of working toward affordable housing, quality education, and medical care for all, we have accepted instead a national security state that has lowered its social expectations in order to use its resources on military-related programs. In many parts of the United States, highways and bridges have fallen into disrepair, water and sewer systems are overtaxed, drug addiction programs and assistance for the blind, disabled, and mentally retarded go begging. Ironically, it costs $21,000 per flying hour to operate the new B-1 bomber,[8] while José, Michael, Rachel, and Sally eat bologna sandwiches at the school lunch table. It is time for a change.

The Future

The first and most important step in solving any social problem is to acknowledge its existence. Until Americans realize the extent of our dependency on the military-industrial complex and the propaganda they spew forth in order to continue the arms race, little will happen in the way of changing priorities. Also needed is a deep horror of nuclear war. Should one Soviet SS-N-8 missile explode over the White House, everything within a two-mile radius would be incinerated. The Lincoln and Jefferson Memorials would be ruined; the Capitol destroyed; the Smithsonian, National Archives, and National Museum of Art would be leveled; and hundreds of thousands of people would be wiped out. All this from one nuclear bomb! In a later chapter we will deal with the moral question of targeting cities; for the moment we need to develop a profound fear of the annihilation this planet faces if the nuclear buttons are pushed. Militarism will only relinquish its grasp when people wake up to the horror of war and decide to find nonviolent ways to solve conflict.

One serious attempt at bringing a moral and humanitarian dimension to the spiraling militarism of the world was the pastoral letter on peace, *The Challenge of Peace: God's Promise and Our Response*, issued by the American Catholic Bishops in 1983. Using the teachings of the Hebrew and Christian scriptures as points of reference, they carefully delineated several principles that they deem essential in the making of nuclear policy decisions. Primary among these is the absolute immorality of the "indiscriminate destruction of whole cities or vast areas with their populations."[9] While they admit to a justification of the current policy of deterrence, they insist that this cannot be an end in itself. Every effort must be made to work for arms control. The bishops repeat the words of Pope John XXIII's encyclical *Peace on Earth,* which "demanded that the arms race should cease; that the stockpiles which exist in various countries should be reduced equally and simultaneously by the parties concerned; that nuclear weapons should be banned; and that a general agreement should be eventually reached about progressive disarmament and an effective method of control."[10]

Several treaties have been signed between the United States and the Soviet Union, limiting the use of nuclear weapons. The Intermediate-range Nuclear Forces (INF) treaty of 1987 and the Strategic Arms Reduction Treaty (START) of 1991 have begun this process. With the end of the Cold War, the time appears ripe for continuing weapons reductions. Perhaps the last decade of the twentieth century may usher in an era of peace among the nuclear powers. But much more needs to be done. When we begin to address the needs of the poor, when we stop supporting military dictators abroad, when we say Yes to human needs and No to militarism, only then will we give our children a bright tomorrow.

There is admittedly a certain utopian vision expressed in the moral witness of religious leaders and others who protest the ever-increasing use of force to solve human conflicts. It seems important, however, that each of us examine the questions surrounding the arms race and judge the issue in the light of the human values that were enunciated in the preceding chapter. We share one planet with people of different races, religions, and nationalities. We must learn to work together in building a better world. If, indeed, we have a responsibility to future generations as well as to those living in subhuman conditions today, one can only conclude that the arms race is "one of the greatest curses of the human race."[11]

Notes

1   National Conference of Catholic Bishops, *Challenge of Peace: God's Promise and Our Response* (Washington, D.C.: United States Catholic Conference, 1983), 3.

2   Richard L. Rubenstein, *The Cunning of History* (New York: Harper & Row, 1975), 9.

3   Ruth Leger Sivard, *World Military and Social Expenditures, 1987–88* (Washington, D.C.: World Priorities, 1987), 29–31.

4   Dwight D. Eisenhower, "The Chance for Peace," address to American Society of Newspaper Editors, April 16, 1953.

5   Dwight D. Eisenhower, "Farewell Address to Congress." *Annals of America, Volume 18, 1961–68* (Encyclopædia Britannica, 1968), 1–5.

6   Jean Mayer, foreword to Sivard, *World Military and Social Expenditures.*

7   Ibid., 24.

8   Ibid., 15.

9   National Conference of Catholic Bishops, *Challenge of Peace: God's Promise and Our Response,* 3.

10   Pope John XXIII, *Peace on Earth* (New York: Paulist Press, 1963), 39.

11   See note 1.

19

Poverty and Hunger

Poverty is a strange and elusive thing. I have tried to write about it,
its joys and its sorrows, for twenty years now.... I condemn poverty
and I advocate it; poverty is simple and complex at once; it is a
social phenomena and a personal matter. It is a paradox.

Dorothy Day[1]

Faces of the Needy (National)

If we could talk to the dozens of people who stand in line daily
outside of Saint John's Hospice in Center City, Philadelphia; if
we could meet the hundreds who eat at Mother Teresa's soup
kitchen in the Bronx each day; if we could experience the
plight of the thousands upon thousands who eat one meal a day
at the Catholic Worker houses, Salvation Army centers, and
church-related soup kitchens throughout this country, we might
begin to understand the depth of poverty and malnutrition
across this land. A few, no doubt, are deadbeats, derelicts, bums,
if you would, who possibly could change things for themselves.
Most, however, are uneducated, illiterate, slow of mind, and

generally lacking in the kinds of talent and skills so necessary to survive in today's economy.

Mary sleeps nightly at St. Rita's Shelter. She was born out of wedlock fifty years ago and was shunted back and forth through several foster homes, resulting in a disorientation toward life. She finally experienced an emotional collapse. She was placed in a state hospital where she lived peacefully for fifteen years, but overcrowding, underfunding, and a woefully misplaced judgment about her need for freedom put her on the street with little means of support. She has great survival instincts, but little else.

Gloria Walker is a forty-year-old woman whose husband was killed in an auto accident. She works at three jobs: part-time cook in a rectory, school-crossing guard, and janitor in a cafeteria. All of these jobs pay minimum wage. In addition to herself, she must feed, clothe, and shelter her six children on $8,000 per year. She, too, is a survivor.

To rise above the poverty level for a family of seven, a full-time worker would have to earn about $7.00 an hour, almost twice Mrs. Walker's current hourly pay.

The specter of homelessness has begun to haunt the United States as adequate housing at affordable prices becomes harder to find. In the newspapers, stories abound about families living in their automobiles or doubling up with relatives for long periods of time. With a precipitous falloff of jobs in the steel industry and other manufacturing areas, many blue-collar workers have been forced into poverty. When mortgages come due, foreclosure is inevitable.

Even people who can afford shelter suffer in other ways. Malnutrition among infants and children, brought about by cuts in federal programs, has risen dramatically in the past few years.[2] In America it is estimated that more than 20 million people, including 12 million children, experience the effects of hunger during a portion of each month.[3] People living in impoverished neighborhoods lack proper police protection, decent schooling for their children, and adequate health care facilities. In New York City alone, the percentage of children living in poverty rose from 25 percent in 1975 to almost 40 percent by 1987. Most are black or Hispanic.[4] The commissioner for human resources, William J. Grinker, estimates that one-third of New York's children on public assistance are "living in isolated pockets of such intense poverty that they are cut off from the world of work and independence."[5]

The psychological effects of poverty in the United States create additional burdens. Because our society stresses the importance of work and emphasizes the benefits of material success, the loss of a job exacts a severe toll on most people. Loss of self-worth caused by unemployment often leads to bouts of depression, alcoholism, and domestic abuse. The lack of work in many inner cities also gives rise to selling narcotics as a means of livelihood. When youngsters see an older teenager driving a sports car and wearing gold jewelry, they find it difficult not to desire that life-style. In spite of the astronomical death rate among teenagers from drug-related crimes, the lure of the fast buck is hard to resist. This is especially true where little hope exists for breaking the cycle of poverty.

Much of the history of this country was predicated on the upward mobility of its citizens. Each generation did better than the previous one; the children of immigrants sought and achieved middle-class status. Unfortunately, this is no longer true. According to a recent study by the House Ways and Means Committee of the United States Congress, income polarization has taken a dangerous turn. From 1973 to 1987 income for the poorest fifth of Americans fell by 11.8 percent, while the wealthiest fifth of the population enjoyed a 24.1 percent increase.[6] Twenty years ago most Americans expected to better their situation; today many feel caught on a treadmill where both parents must work just to stay even. This uneven distribution of wealth puts to rest the imagined equality in our society. A recent Federal Reserve Board report stated that the top 10 percent of families in the United States owns 57 percent of the net wealth.[7]

Statistics, however, give us only the hard numbers associated with poverty. It is vastly more important to keep before our minds the faces of poverty. The malnourished child, the widow without a pension, the teenage dropout who has lost hope, the divorced mother struggling to support her children—these are the faces of the poor.

Faces of the Needy (Global)

The picture is much bleaker elsewhere. Listen to the testimony of Michael Harrington in *The Vast Majority:*

> Who are the wretched of the earth? Some of them are people in countries where one child in two dies before reaching age five. They are the overwhelming bulk of the 70 percent of the world's population without safe water. Four hundred and fifty million of them are afflicted by schistosomiasis and filariasis, the leading cause of blindness. They are the more than two billion human beings—54 percent of mankind—who live in countries where the per capita Gross National Product in 1973 was under $200. The poorest among them, 30 percent of the world's population, have 3 percent of its income. And they are the impoverished citizens of nations which are statistically "well off," like the 50 percent of the Brazilians who have been excluded from, and even injured by, an economic "miracle."[8]

Silvinio is a ten-year-old boy living in an orphanage on the outskirts of Bogotá, Colombia. He was not always so fortunate. At about five years of age he was abandoned by his mother and left with a street gang of teenagers. He learned to ride the buses, begging his way down the aisles at first, then later was taught by the older boys how to pick pockets while continuing to beg. During the evenings the gang would roam the downtown area, looking for lone victims to attack and rob. Before his mother left him with the street kids, he had lived in a hillside barrio on the slopes of Monserrate on the eastern edge of the city. His house, like the others in the barrio, was made of wooden slats and corrugated tin with no windows and a cloth drape for a door. Electricity was lacking, the floors were dirt, and a common outhouse was shared by several families.

Haiti ranks as the poorest country in the Western Hemisphere. It has a per capita yearly income of $360 compared with $2,629 for Venezuela, its next-door neighbor, and $16,444 for the United States, the colossus to the north. Life expectancy is only fifty years of age, the infant mortality rate measures 100 deaths per thousand births, and only a third of the population can read and write.[9] Haitians have been long subjected to both internal and external exploitation. Historically, it was a French colony, but during much of the twentieth century the United States has dominated its economic and political life. Dictators and military juntas have systematically suppressed all attempts at reform. Occasionally a bright light will shine in the darkness. Lawrence Bohnen, a Belgian priest, has spent much of his life in Haiti trying to feed and educate the children who live in the slums of Port-au-Prince. "Empty stomachs," he says, "have no ears." Beginning in the mid-1970s, he has constructed dozens of local schools and feeding huts where 12,000 children daily receive nourishment for mind and body.[10] Sadly, thousands more in Haiti and millions more throughout the world go hungry and uneducated.

To leaf through the pages of *Forced Out,*[11] a pictorial journey with the refugees of the world, is to experience waves of sadness and anger simultaneously. From the pictures of ragged Ethiopians trekking into the Bati aid station by the thousands, to the photographs of the bodies of Haitian boat refugees washed ashore at Deerfield Beach, Florida, a scant few miles south of the opulent Palm Beach resort area, the book visualizes a story of human deprivation and death. Afghan villagers, fleeing from war, living amid the squalor of refugee camps set up across the border in Pakistan. Thousands of Cambodian women and children, also victims of civil war, are seen baking in the sun at Site 2 camp in Thailand. We witness frightened peasant women being intimidated by soldiers in a Guatemalan village. There are pictures of bodies lying twisted in death following an army sweep through a Salvadoran village in search of guerrillas. A Somalian father supports the limp head of his starving son in another scene.

Tragically, malnutrition is the primary killer in refugee camps throughout the world.[12] In a world where two pounds of grain for every person on earth is harvested daily, millions go hungry because they are poor. We must now look into the reasons for the evilness of hunger and poverty in order to understand that it is a human problem requiring human solutions. Perhaps in previous ages we might blame it on an "act of God." Today, that statement smacks of blasphemy.

Causes of Poverty (United States)

The reason people are hungry is that they are poor. Without money one cannot buy bread. The reasons for poverty, however, are complex. Although children, the elderly, the disabled, and the ill cannot work and consequently must depend on others for their material needs, critics frequently blame poverty on the poor themselves. "If only they would stop drinking and loafing around they'd amount to something," say many.

Others, with a more historical perspective, realize that much of the poverty in the United States has its roots in racism, especially the slavery of the past and the discrimination of the present. In support of this thesis, William Wilson, an American social scientist, argues that inner-city poverty among blacks and Hispanics results from a "ghetto culture" brought about by physical isolation and economic distress. They are not in the same job loop that most whites enjoy. Wilson rejects the term *culture of poverty*, believing that it implies moral indolence. The crime-ridden drug culture of the ghettos sprang from a refusal on the part of the larger white society to integrate its black and brown neighbors.[13] In any case, social and cultural factors play a large part in the reality of poverty.

A 1980 Appalachian Land Ownership Study surveyed that region in order to determine the economic reasons for poverty. More than one million acres of land with mineral and forest rights are owned by outside investors, so it is not surprising to find that it is the poorest area in the country. Fifteen years ago (1975) the Catholic bishops in the Appalachian region spoke with one voice, decrying the exploitation of land and people by the coal and steel industries.[14] Not much has changed since then. New technologies in mining replaced thousands of workers. This was accompanied in other parts of the U.S. by the closing of factories in order to relocate in countries with a cheap labor force.

Furthermore, poverty in the United States is also a result of the boom-and-bust cycles that are allowed to flow in a free-market system. Capitalism seeks to maximize profits and minimize wages. This law is inexorable if one wishes to idolize free enterprise. Unquestionably, the profit motive has served to better the lives of millions, but has cost others dearly. Is it not possible to find ways that will benefit all people rather than just a few? Unfortunately, the major shareholders of most corporations care little about laid-off workers. The economic system demands an excess labor pool and the highest return on one's investment. Thus, unemployment ranks as a major cause of poverty.

In addition to the cultural and economic roots of poverty, government policy plays a central role. We have already referred to the vast expenditures on military programs that have come at the expense of human needs. Tax dollars that might have gone toward job retraining for the unemployed have been spent on new and ever-more-sophisticated weapons systems. Not all of the tax dollar, however, goes to the military. Agricultural subsidies, commerce and transportation expenses, health care and educational benefits, as well as general government costs demand attention. Most of these expenditures are aimed at the middle class. Tax breaks for the wealthy have become a stock joke, but it is no joke for a person who cannot afford higher education and is trying desperately to support a family on a minimum wage. The political power of the poor is negligible and so are the benefits they receive.

Finally, we cannot overlook the moral reasons behind the debilitating and horrific poverty that exists here and abroad. Violence in the hearts of dictators continues to create havoc for the downtrodden masses. Streets flow with blood when the poor raise their voices seeking justice. Greed, in all its forms, lurks in the hearts of those who bend to the task of enriching themselves while caring little for those in need. Few who have earned their money the old-fashioned way, by inheriting it, share their good fortune with the poor. Discrimination, blatant racism, and hatred of those who are different exact a heavy toll on the less fortunate members of society.

Perhaps, worst of all, apathy, or as Michael Harrington suggests, a "cruel innocence,"[15] looms over this land of plenty. Lukewarmness and inertia—unconcern by whatever name— dull the mind and heart. The natural feelings of compassion and concern for the poor shrivel up and die when chilled by icy blasts of indifference. If we allow ourselves to remain blind to the plight of the poor, we pass severe judgment upon ourselves for having lost our true humanity.

Causes of Poverty (Global)

Poverty in Third World countries today has its roots in colonialism. The Age of Discovery found the European powers staking claim to newly discovered lands. Native populations were considered backward and inferior. Thus began, in the fifteenth century, a systematic exploitation that has lasted almost five hundred years.

Following World War II many of the countries throughout Africa and Asia gained political independence, but an economic stranglehold continued. Under the guise of such theories as "comparative advantage," in which each country supposedly specializes in one or two products, for example, bananas and coffee, the rich Western nations continue to allow poverty and hunger to mount in the underdeveloped nations. The real advantage lies with countries who develop a diversified economy, agricultural and industrial. Ultimately, profits gained from bananas go to the plantation owners, not the poor. The wealthy landowners, those oligarchies that control the political as well as the economic systems, exploit their own people more directly than outside forces.

Population growth has also contributed to poverty. In less than fifty years the population of the world has more than doubled, going from 2 billion in 1930 to 4 billion people by 1975 and to almost 6 billion by 1990. Although population increase may rightly be called an explosion, it is misleading to attribute all hunger and poverty to this growth. Food production rates have easily surpassed this population increase. The panic concerning food and overpopulation among some theoreticians during the 1970s became so intense that they offered grim scenarios that would allow millions to die while others remained well fed. Little thought was given to sharing the crumbs from the affluent tables of America with the beggars of Bangladesh or Ethiopia.

The fact is that consumption patterns and economic and political policies play a far greater role in hunger than does overpopulation. In the former case, beef and other livestock consume vast amounts of grain that might otherwise feed hungry people. Cattle must eat eight pounds of grain to generate one pound of meat. With Western society's emphasis on meat consumption, it is no wonder that animals are fed better than many humans.

Greed, too, plays its role.

> . . . every nation has the capacity to feed itself, but is prevented from doing so by an economic elite in the poor and rich nations and by a few powerful multinational corporations that control agricultural production for the purpose of producing profit rather than for meeting the basic food needs of all people.[16]

While millions of humans suffer from malnutrition in northern Africa, hundreds of thousands of acres in the same region are used to grow peanuts, which are processed for cooking oil for sale to Europeans. In Brazil, peasants go hungry amid huge tracts of unused land. It is estimated that five thousand individuals (about one-thousandth of the population) control half of Brazil's arable land.[17] In the Central American nations, cotton, coffee, sugar cane, bananas, and tobacco crops dominate the landscapes. Before the eyes of malnourished peasants, cattle are fattened for the fast-food chains of North America.

One further question remains. How does the political order contribute to poverty and hunger? When the Agricultural Trade Development and Assistance Act was enacted into law on July 10, 1954, it was intended to assist American farmers in finding new markets for their products and to offer foodstuffs to hungry people in other lands. Although this legislation, commonly known as PL (Public Law) 480, has been amended several times during the past three decades, its basic thrust has not changed. On the one hand, it provides government support to American farmers in the way of subsidies, but it undercuts local farmers in other lands by supplying excess food to their markets. In addition, PL 480 encouraged high-tech farming methods in foreign countries, thus eroding labor-intensive methods that employ far more workers. The International Monetary Fund has further exacerbated the problems of Third World nations by demanding austere social programs, which have hurt the poor, in exchange for credits and capital to develop these societies. Debt repayment has exacted far more than a pound of flesh from the needy, yet it too finds little forgiveness.

We see, then, that hunger and poverty are the result of many factors. Social, political, and economic determinants wreak havoc on the world's poor. Only when patient and caring people make an option for the poor will the picture begin to change. Including the poor in our world calls for courage and compassion.

Responses

The Hebrew prophets cried out incessantly about the exploitation of the poor by the rich. They spoke about the "widows and orphans" who suffered injustice.[18] Jesus warned about the dangers of wealth, primarily because it distracts people from human relationships by focusing on "things." We are keenly aware of the profit motive, the so-called bottom line, which drives the engine of capitalism, yet we often lack the compassion necessary to feed the hungry.

When we give it sufficient thought we are often embarrassed by our own relatively sumptuous life-style in comparison to many who do not have even the necessities of life. We worry endlessly about how the new English fabric will match the Oriental rug while the face of a hungry child stares at us from the cover of a magazine. Couples spend thousands of dollars on wedding receptions and honeymoons with hardly a thought about the "widows and orphans" of the world. These comments are not meant to traumatize us with guilt, but simply to highlight the pervasive cultural sickness that envelops a society that places such high value on personal satisfaction at the expense of sisters and brothers in need. It would indeed be a cultural revolution to put care of the poor ahead of personal gain.

A Latin American priest once remarked, "When I helped the poor, I was called a saint; when I asked why they were poor, I was called a communist." Much of the unrest in today's world can be traced to the inequities that exist among people. If we ask questions, as did the priest, about the reasons for local, regional, and global poverty we are likely to become embroiled in controversy. Systems of government, economic philosophies, personal aggrandizement, and social mores all play a part in the evil of poverty. When these powers are identified and named as perpetrators, they strike back at their accusers. Not infrequently, the victims are blamed for their own misfortune, and those who point the finger at the forces of greed are depicted as radicals and revolutionaries. One must be willing to face ridicule and rebuff in standing up to those who exploit the poor or are indifferent to their plight. The hard tasks of this age, perhaps every age, revolve around human rights, not the least of which are the rights to food, shelter, and clothing.

The following illustration may serve to distinguish between those who share the blessings of heaven over against those who suffer the ravages of hell. In both heaven and hell people are seated at a lavish banquet table filled with meats, wines, and fruits. All are provided with long spoons to enjoy the meal. Because the spoons are so long the residents of hell can't manage to feed themselves, thus they suffer eternal frustration. In heaven, however, spoon length is an asset. The people of heaven simply reach across the table and feed each other. It is this attitude of sharing that we need to acquire if we want eternal life.

No immediate quick-fix solutions to hunger and poverty exist, and, because of human perversity, exploitation will always remain; nevertheless we can take measures to limit the effects of these twin evils. If we are generous with our time and money toward the needy, we will have expressed in a tangible way that they are included in our world. If we use our political influence to demand better programs for the poor of our country and increased assistance for Third World nations, we will have exercised our citizenship in a morally sound manner. If we join with others in turning swords into plowshares and missile silos into grain silos, we will have contributed greatly to the cause of peace.

One concluding note addresses the paradox of poverty. Unquestionably, the debilitating effects of poverty and the barbarous situation of inadequate food, medical care, education, and housing must be deplored. Every thoughtful person realizes that the plague of dehumanizing poverty demands rectification. But poverty, or perhaps more appropriately, simple living, contains much beauty. The great saints of the past, Augustine, Aquinas, Francis, Clare, and Catherine, embraced poverty as a pathway to God. The sages of history—Buddha, Confucius, Jesus, Muhammad—witnessed to poverty as a way of life.

In our own day, religious communities of women and men profess vows of poverty in order to serve the needs of others by divesting themselves of worldly goods. For example, Mother Teresa of Calcutta and her Missionaries of Charity eloquently express an ideal of simplicity of life in the service of the poor. Consequently, we ought to both loathe poverty and embrace it. It is at once a curse and a blessing. In the opening quotation of this chapter, Dorothy Day, a modern American saint who spent her life among the poor, summed up the paradox of poverty. To love the poor, one becomes like them. In fasting, we feel their hunger; in stripping ourselves, we know their nakedness; in experiencing their want, we stand in solidarity with them.

Notes

1   Dorothy Day, *Loaves and Fishes* (San Francisco: Harper & Row, 1965), 67.

2   Bard Shollenberger and Barbara Howell, "Underfunded and Underfed: Food Programs and Hunger in America," in *Bread for the World Policy Paper, No. 75* (Washington, D.C.: Bread for the World, 1984), 1–6.

3   *World Hunger 1988: A Review* (Washington, D.C.: Bread for the World, 1988), 1–2.

4   John Barbanel, "How Despair is Engulfing a Generation in New York," *New York Times*, April 2, 1989, 6.

5   Ibid.

6   James Lardner, "Rich, Richer: Poor, Poorer," *New York Times*, April 19, 1989, op. ed. page.

7   National Conference of Catholic Bishops, *Economic Justice for All* (Washington, D.C.: United States Catholic Conference, 1986), 90.

8   Michael Harrington, *The Vast Majority* (New York: Simon & Schuster, 1977), 15.

9   *The World Almanac, 1991* (New York: Scripps Howard, 1991), 716.

10 M. Basil Pennington, "Beans for Father Beans," *America*, June 18, 1983, 480.

11 Carole Kismaric, *Forced Out* (New York: Random House, 1989).

12 Ibid., 111.

13 William Julius Wilson, *The Truly Disadvantaged: The Inner City, the Underclass, and Public Policy* (Chicago: University of Chicago Press, 1988).

14 Catholic Committee of Appalachia, *This Land is Home to Me* (Whitesburg, Ky.: Catholic Committee of Appalachia, 1975).

15 Harrington, *The Vast Majority*, 13.

16 Suzanne C. Toton, *World Hunger* (Maryknoll, N.Y.: Orbis Books, 1982), 12.

17 Arthur Powers, "Land and Violence in Brazil," *America*, April 18, 1987, 324.

18 Isaiah 1:23.

20

Environment

Never before has man had such capacity to control his own environment, to end thirst and hunger, to conquer poverty and disease, to banish illiteracy and massive human misery. We have the
power to make this the best generation of mankind in the history
of the world—or make it the last.

John F. Kennedy[1]

We began our journey through Perception by asking how we
viewed the world. Having first looked at the many ways we
tend to distort reality, we then turned our attention to several
major social problems confronting the human family at the
dawn of the third millennium. Few doubt that the twentieth
century has been a watershed in history, productively and destructively. The population has tripled, wealth has increased a
thousandfold, longevity, health care, and literacy have all shown
marked improvement. The downside, however, is that millions
have been killed in war, vast poverty and malnutrition cover the
planet, and the threat of nuclear annihilation hangs like the
sword of Damocles over the entire world. If things were not bad
enough because of the racism, sexism, militarism, and classism
that plague us, we must also face the prospect of environmental

destruction. This concluding chapter offers overwhelming evidence that we must change our ways.

Poisons and Pollutants

At 12:40 A.M. on December 3, 1984, a worker at the Union Carbide plant in Bhopal, India, went to investigate a leak in the storage tanks of methyl isocyanate (a substance mixed with other chemicals for use as a pesticide). Suddenly the earth around the tanks began to tremble and a large crack appeared in the cylinder. Almost instantaneously the tall ventilation stack poured out a cloud of white gaseous vapors that began drifting toward the nearby neighborhood. The leak went out of control and caused the worst industrial accident in history, killing at least 8,000 people and injuring 300,000 others.[2]

That this tragedy occurred is of little surprise. In the United States most people know that a large array of exotic chemicals, which were produced originally to help us, have resulted in untold damage to individuals and the environment.

Buried chemical waste at Love Canal in upper New York resulted in cancer-related illnesses for people who unwittingly built homes on the landfill. The fishing and crabbing industries along the East Coast, especially in the Chesapeake Bay area, have virtually come to a halt because of pollution in rivers and inlets along the seacoast.

On March 28, 1979, the worst nuclear accident in the United States occurred at the Three Mile Island reactor in Middletown, Pennsylvania. Although the health and environmental damage was minimal, the plant came within an hour of a catastrophic meltdown. The citizens of Chernobyl in the Soviet Union were not so fortunate. In late April 1986, the cooling system of a local nuclear power plant failed. This caused the uranium fuel rods to melt. Operators compounded the error by flooding the reactor with water. This water, on contact with the burning uranium, instantly became superheated steam, which, in turn, reacted with the graphite and zirconium to produce flammable hydrogen, methane, and carbon monoxide. A nuclear cloud spread radiation poison throughout much of Europe and caused panic among Western governments.

It goes without saying that nuclear war would dwarf a power plant accident.

> Nuclear war is the greatest environmental threat we face. . . . The nuclear winter effect refers to sunlight obscuration and corresponding reductions in air temperatures at the Earth's surface brought about by the endemic influence of dust injected into the atmosphere by nuclear weapons and wildland fires resulting from nuclear war.[3]

Carl Sagan spoke recently of a nuclear winter that would ensue from a war between the Soviet Union and the United States. Together they possess more than 50,000 nuclear weapons, or a combined total of 15,000 megatons (15 billion tons of TNT). With 2,500 cities worldwide containing in excess of 100,000 people, one billion humans would die in the initial exchange of missiles. Sagan points out, however, as did President Kennedy thirty years ago, that they would be the lucky ones. The smoke, soot, dust, and radioactive debris would cause massive worldwide destruction for the entire planet's environment. The atmosphere would be so contaminated that the global ecosystem would be destroyed. "We have, by slow and imperceptible steps, been constructing a Doomsday Machine."[4]

In 1962, Rachel Carson's *Silent Spring* was of enormous help in waking people up to the damage being done to the environment in the name of progress. As a professional biologist she was able to show with facts and reams of data compiled by scientists and government agencies throughout the country that the air, water, and soil that we had long taken for granted was becoming dangerously toxic. Her efforts banned the use of DDT as a pesticide and people awoke to the need for a clean and safe environment.

Although cancer did not begin in the twentieth century, it is the only disease that has increased dramatically during the twentieth century. In 1900 cancer accounted for 3 percent of the death rate; by 1975 it caused 20 percent of the annual deaths in the United States; the last fifteen years have seen further increases. Experts believe that the rise of cancer-related deaths is directly attributable to the introduction of new chemical products into the environment since World War II.[5] For example, the United Farm Workers have been fighting an uphill battle with the agricultural industry in California over the use of pesticides on crops. Kern County and the state health departments are investigating the abnormal rise in low-weight births, miscarriages, and fetal deaths among the residents of the town of McFarland in the San Joaquin Valley. Water contaminated by agricultural pesticides is the likely suspect.[6]

Although not obvious to North Americans, deforestation looms as yet another destructive force upon the environment. It is estimated that tropical rain forests are being destroyed faster than any other natural resource. If the "slash and burn" programs continue at their present rate, virtually all the world's rain forests will be gone by the year 2032.[7]

Most scientists today discount the effects that rain forests have on the world's supply of oxygen. Although they were previously thought to be the "lungs" of the planet, few now accept the credibility of the theory.[8] All, however, agree that preserving the forests is crucial because their destruction adds considerable carbon dioxide to the atmosphere. Scientists studying atmospheric conditions believe that the destruction of tropical rain forests would change the world's climate, resulting in the destabilization of the polar ice caps. A few degrees difference would result in the melting of millions of tons of ice, swelling the oceans and playing havoc with present shorelines.

Damage and Destruction

Perhaps no two issues have gotten more global attention than those of ozone depletion and global warming. In 1975, Professors Rowland and Molina of the Department of Chemistry of the University of California startled the scientific community by reporting on the damage occurring to the upper atmosphere by the release of chlorofluorocarbons (CFCs).[9] These chemicals were used as coolants and insulation in aerosol sprays, cushions, and packaging. After some initial attempts to limit the use of CFCs, the problem seemed to disappear until the British Antarctic Survey team in 1985 published reports of an ozone hole over the Antarctic that was larger than the United States and taller than Mount Everest. Substantial increases have continued into the 1990s.[10]

Unfortunately, because the manufacture and use of CFCs represents a multibillion-dollar business, little substantial progress has been made in addressing this problem. Yet, together with the carbon dioxide pollution from auto and factory emissions, CFCs are slowly creating a greenhouse effect about the planet.[11] These artificial chemical gases have accumulated at an enormous rate in recent years, gradually producing a global warming effect that will seriously affect the climate in the years ahead. Worst-case scenarios predict massive flooding along the coastlines of the oceans within thirty years and deserts sweeping across wide areas of the world.[12]

If things were not bad enough in the atmosphere, we can always weep over the pollution to our rivers, lakes, and streams. A veritable witch's brew of chemicals continue to ruin the nation's water and forests. Environmental Protection Agency (EPA) researchers estimate that almost one-half of the open water in the Upper Midwest and nearly 75 percent of the lakes in the East will shortly be devoid of aquatic life because of acid rain. The figures are staggering. "In 1987 industry routinely released 2.4 billion pounds of toxic substances into the air. . . . It includes 253 million pounds of carcinogens such as benzene and formaldehyde, and 527 million pounds of neurotoxins."[13] According to EPA studies, gaseous chemicals cause more than two thousand cases of cancer yearly.[14] Acid rain from the factories throughout the Midwest has created tensions not only with New Englanders whose trees are dying and whose fish are almost inedible, but has created hostility with our neighbor to the north. Canadians have demanded action on the part of the United States government to halt the spread of acid rain because it has damaged many of the lakes and forests of Canada.

Solid waste pollution further exacerbates the problem of environmental cleanliness. Americans average about three tons of garbage annually for a family of four, in addition to 160 million tons of waste from industry and 2.5 billion tons from mining and agriculture.[15] All this waste must find a dump. Sadly enough, the needles and syringes washing up on New Jersey beaches in the summer of 1988 gave us only a view of the surface. In many coastal harbors and bays "scuba divers talk of swimming through clouds of toilet paper and half-dissolved feces, of bay bottoms covered by a foul and toxic combination of sediment, sewage, and petrochemical waste appropriately known as 'black mayonnaise.'"[16]

Each year the National Wildlife Federation issues a report card on the environment for the United States. They sample the air, water, and soil; assess the impact on wildlife and forests; and measure energy conservation. In most cases, the trend during the past decade has been dismal. On a global scale, the Worldwatch Institute issues an annual *State of the World* report in which food prospects, land degradation, atmospheric pollution, and other international environmental problems are analyzed. Here too the outlook is pessimistic.

In spite of well-intentioned politicians, businesspeople, and other civic-minded groups, planet Earth continues to suffer stress at the hands of humans. We have seen how human error caused the death of thousands in Bhopal, India, and irradiated much of Europe as a result of a nuclear explosion at Chernobyl. Attempts at controlling the infestation of pests by chemical agents has led to the poisoning of groundwater, the near extinction of some animal species, and the increase of cancer among humans. What has brought us to this unhappy state of affairs? Why has the human family created so much havoc on this beautiful planet? Are there too many of us, or do we live out of sync with nature? Let us look now at the reasons for our environmental woes.

Roots of the Problems

In the early hours of March 24, 1989, the supertanker, *Exxon Valdez*, ran aground near Valdez, Alaska, discharging more than 10 million gallons of crude oil into the pristine waters of Prince William Sound. The oil had been pumped from under Prudhoe Bay 800 miles north and transported along the Trans-Alaskan pipeline. Its destination was the oil refineries near Seattle, Washington. It was the worst environmental disaster to a natural area in United States history. Within days, thousands of birds and marine animals perished. This one incident symbolized the totality of environmental destruction brought about by the industrialization of the planet.

It would be futile to argue that technological progress has not brought vast improvements to the lives of millions of people. But we must also admit that the cost has been enormous. The revolution in motorized transportation, the mechanization of farming, the invention of engines, turbines, and generators have contributed greatly to improved living standards. The rise of a capitalist society, in which each succeeding generation must increase the quantity of its products, has allowed the captains of industry to call the tune on factory outputs with little or no restraint on environmental damage. After a century and a half of smokestacks and several decades of automobiles, the time has come to pay the piper.

Industrialization, however, is fueled by the real culprit, over-consumption.

> Homo sapiens is consuming its "capital," a one-time bonanza of nonrenewable fossil fuels and other mineral resources that formed over eons are now being destroyed and disbursed in decades . . . resource consumption in rich nations threatens earth's capacity to sustain us all.[17]

In a comparative study of the consumption patterns of families throughout the world, Paul and Anne Ehrlich, demographers at Stanford University, showed how the disproportionate life-styles of different peoples reflect the problem of environmental harm. For instance, a citizen of Kenya or India will use, on average, the energy equivalent of only one-half barrel of oil per year. In the United States, Japan, and Western Europe we consume the energy equivalent of 45 barrels per person per year.[18]

Imagine the net effect of carbon dioxide gases on the atmosphere if everyone on Earth drove an automobile, or the ozone damage caused by the CFCs in refrigerators and air conditioners if every family on Earth owned one of each, or the planetary suicide that is slowly occurring as a result of nuclear waste pollution. We have been sold a bill of goods, that more is better. The planet cannot sustain itself in terms of clean air, water, and soil if more and more people develop the life-style of the "rich and famous" First World. "Rich and famous," of course, is often just a euphemism for "greedy and vain."

Underlying the industrialization and the frenzied consumption marking modern times is one of the dynamic ideas of Western culture—progress. Heeding the biblical admonition to "fill the earth and subdue it; and have dominion over the fish of the sea and over the birds of the air and over every living thing that moves upon the earth,"[19] and spurred by Darwin's discovery of evolution, Western thought has served progress in a distinctive way. Eastern philosophy, with its emphasis on karma and reincarnation, has generally rejected a linear history of human progress, although the modern global impact of Western culture has recently influenced the Asian nations. To put it simply: quantity took precedence over quality; the masculine dominated the feminine; scientific data outranked intuition and the spiritual dimensions of life; more was better than less. In this insatiable quest to subdue the Earth, Western philosophy failed to foresee the consequences. We are only now beginning to assess the damage of our relentless pursuit of progress.

Can We Keep Going?

In the 24th Psalm we read that "the earth is the LORD's and all that is in it."[20] One of the major reasons for the environmental

damage happening to the planet can be traced to the secularization of Western society. Without an acknowledgment of God as
creator and sovereign of the world, humans are free to grab
what they can for themselves and disregard any sense of responsibility for the rest of the Earth.

Perhaps the question is somewhat naive, yet we must ask,
"Whose environment is it, anyway?" Even those who refuse to
recognize a transcendent power as the rightful master of the
universe would concede that the air and the oceans are the
common heritage of all. Private property rights were unheard
of among Native Americans and caused enormous grief and
bloodshed for them when the Europeans invaded their shores.
Historically, under capitalism, land was bought, sold, divided,
plundered, and ravished. Today, throughout the world a major
struggle exists over the right to explore public lands for oil
and minerals and to harvest the timber. Too often government
policies condone environmental abuse. As more and more
people realize that the air, water, and soil are a common responsibility, we may yet redeem the environment.

Even if most agreed that clean air and water are the common property of all people, there would still remain the crooks
and cheats who would refuse to cooperate. We have already
pointed out that resistance to the inherent limits of life gives
rise to selfish behavior. In any given percentage of the population, there are those who break the law or act against the common interest of all. The driver of the chemical truck who deliberately opens the spigot on the rear of his truck in order to
discharge waste on the highway cares little about his responsibility toward society. The corporate executives who bribe civic
officials in order to prevent an examination of their chemical
inventories see only the bottom line as significant.

During the past several years the business community has
begun to address the issues of corporate responsibility. Prod-
ded by environmental groups, shareholders interested in good
citizenship, and management concerned about its image, many
transnational companies have begun to act as good neighbors.
Whistle-blowers inside government have also contributed to
the public knowledge about environmental mismanagement.
Recently, Federal Bureau of Investigation (FBI) agents raided

the headquarters of the Rockwell International Company at Rocky Flats, Colorado, searching for evidence of collusion between Department of Energy officials and plant managers in the dumping of toxic wastes.[21]

This and similar actions highlight the concerted efforts being made to police the polluters and toughen the laws against environmental damage. Amendments to the Clean Air Act of 1970 are currently under review.[22] If enacted, nitrogen oxides, sulphur, carbon monoxide, and other industrial pollutants would be reduced considerably. Sustaining the growth rate of the post–World War II era, measured in terms of environmental damage, can no longer be tolerated. Currently, people from all walks of life are joining forces with government and business leaders to reverse the effects of pollution. Clean air and pure water do not represent a luxury. They must be seen as a fundamental right and responsibility for all.

The key to change lies in the educational and consciousness-raising efforts that must take place. It must become socially unacceptable to damage the environment. The campaign by C. Everett Koop, the former United States Surgeon General, against smoking is a case in point. During the past decade, millions of smokers have quit: not only because of health worries, but also due to peer pressure. Changing attitudes toward the environment constitutes one of the greatest challenges of our time. To give up smoking pales in comparison to switching from autos to public transportation. As Americans, we are addicted to speed. From speedboats to swift cars, we enjoy action in the fast lane. Unfortunately, the fast lane spews excess pollutants into the atmosphere. Faster and bigger spells harm and damage. *Small Is Beautiful,* by E. F. Schumacher, was published in 1973, yet its message is only beginning to be heard. Economics of scale, labor-intensive productivity, and economic planning[23] must begin to impact our consciousness before we can hope to offer our children a clean Earth.

A Time for Decision

A major landmark in the journey of self-discovery comes with a recognition of responsibility for future generations. When a married couple holds a first child in their arms, they experience powerful feelings for ensuring its survival. What needs doing, at the close of the twentieth century, is to transfer that sense of personal bonding to the social order. The natural instinct for preserving life on an individual level must be transformed into energy for global survival. The question "What will our children inherit?" should establish the agenda in the years ahead.

With a concern for future generations as our guide, we can personally begin to develop environmentally sound habits in our attitudes and actions. Past practices that created problems must give way to new approaches. For example, under pressure from environmentalists, schools across the country have discontinued the colorful spectacle of balloon launches at graduation and other functions. Although the displays were a visual delight, the latex products released played havoc on the digestive tracts of small animals and fish. Similarly, recycling paper products, aluminum cans, plastic bottles, and the like can prove inconvenient and troublesome, yet it is the price we must pay personally if we are to begin repairing the damage done to our natural environment.

At the political level, governments are responding to the cries of their citizens to halt the pollution. In a recent interview with the editors of *National Geographic*,[24] French President François Mitterrand indicated that the European community of nations plans to mount an assault on the problem of environmental damage. In conjunction with the bicentennial celebration of the French Revolution, which proclaimed liberty, equality, and fraternity, Mitterrand feared another massive uprising of the poor, who are denied basic needs, as a result of the wealthy's overconsumption and pollution of the land. He also called for the creation of a supranational authority to monitor the protection of the environment.

In the United States, local, state, and federal officials have begun to take environmental issues more seriously.

No longer are environmentalists regarded as sentimental tree huggers. Because much of the legislative action in this country arises from the sustained concern of the majority, it is imperative that people exercise their citizenship responsibly by electing public officials who are determined to curb pollution in all its forms. Several cities across the country have begun campaigns to halt smog and clean up chemical dumps. As always, political willpower follows people power. If we are to undo past damage to the environment, only a concerned, alert citizenry will provide the impetus.

"If you're not part of the solution, you're part of the problem" goes the popular slogan. Unless we join others in the struggle to clean up our act with regard to waste and pollution, we invite ecological disaster. "With added billions of people struggling to survive, poverty and starvation inevitably will provoke massive political unrest and violence. Faced with an environmental apocalypse, we must and will change our destructive patterns. But when?"[25]

Let us conclude this chapter on the environment with the reflections of an American Indian. Few letters in American literature can compare with the one Chief Seattle, the leader of the Suquami Indians of the Northwest Territory, wrote to Millard Fillmore, President of the United States, in 1852. The occasion was a U.S. request to purchase Indian lands.

The President in Washington sends word that he wishes to buy our land. But how can you buy or sell the sky? The land? The idea is strange to us. If we do not own the freshness of the air and the sparkle of the water, how can you buy them? Every part of the earth is sacred to my people. Every shining pine needle, every sandy shore, every mist in the dark woods, every meadow, every humming insect. All are holy in the memory and experience of my people. . . . This we know: the earth does not belong to man, man belongs to the earth. All things are connected like the blood that unites us all. Man did not weave the web of life, he is merely a strand in it. Whatever he does to the web, he does to himself. . . .

We love this earth as a newborn loves its mother's heartbeat. So, if we sell you our land, love it as we have loved it. Care for it as we have cared for it. Hold in your mind the memory of the land as it is when you receive it. Preserve the land for all children and love it, as God loves us all. As we are part of the land, you too are part of the land. This earth is precious to us. One thing we know: there is only one God. No man, be he Red Man or White Man, can be apart. We are brothers after all.[26]

Notes

1   John F. Kennedy, "Address before the General Assembly of the United Nations, September 20, 1963," in *Respectfully Quoted* (Washington, D.C.: Library of Congress, 1989), 107.

2   Dan Kurzman, *A Killing Wind* (New York: McGraw-Hill, 1987), ix.

3   Herbert D. Grover, "The Climatic and Biological Consequences of Nuclear War," *Environment* 26 (May 1984): 6–13.

4   Carl Sagan, "Nuclear War and Climatic Catastrophe: Some Policy Implications," *Foreign Affairs*, Winter 1983–84.

5   D. Stanley Eitzen, *Social Structure and Social Problems in America* (Boston: Allyn and Bacon, 1983), 330.

6   "McFarland: Too Much Cancer," *Food and Justice*, May 1986: 7.

7   *Rainforest Destruction: An International Tragedy* (New York: Environmental Defense Fund, 1987).

8   Catherine Caufield, "The Rain Forests," *New Yorker*, January 14, 1985, 62.

9   Paul Brodeur, "In the Face of Doubt," *New Yorker*, June 9, 1986, 70.

10   Susan Solomon, "Progress toward a Quantitative Understanding of Antarctic Ozone Depletion," *Nature*, September 27, 1990, 347–54.

11   Cynthia Pollock Shea, "Protecting Life on Earth: Steps to Save the Ozone Layer," *Worldwatch Paper 87*, December 1988, 6.

12   Philip Shabecoff, "The Heat is On," *New York Times*, June 26, 1988, 1.

13   Sharon Begley, "Is Breathing Hazardous to Your Health?" *Newsweek*, April 3, 1989, 25.

14   Ibid., 25.

15   Eitzen, *Social Structure and Social Problems in America*, 330.

16   Ted Morgenthau, "Don't Go Near the Water," *Newsweek*, August 1, 1988, 43.

17   Paul R. Ehrlich and Anne H. Ehrlich, "Population, Plenty, and Poverty," *National Geographic*, December 1988, 916–17.

18   Ibid., 942–43.

19   Genesis 1:28.

20   Psalm 24:1.

21   David Johnston, "Weapons Plant Dumped Chemical into Drinking Water, FBI Says," *New York Times*, June 10, 1989, 1.

22   Philip Shabecoff, "President Urges Steps to Tighten Law on Clean Air," *New York Times*, June 13, 1989, 1.

23   E. F. Schumacher, *Small Is Beautiful* (New York: Harper & Row, 1973), 59–60, 161–79.

24   Wilbur E. Garrett, "Mitterrand Interview," *National Geographic*, July 1989, 4–5.

25   Wilbur E. Garrett, "Editorial Comments," *National Geographic*, December 1988, 764.

26   Letter of Chief Seattle, in Joseph Campbell, *The Power of Myth* (New York: Doubleday, 1988), 34–35.

Part III

Values

What Are My Values?

Introduction

We must now address the value questions. What is a value? Are some values more important than others? Says who? Are some ways of solving value conflicts better than others? Why are they better? Perhaps the most important question to ask is "What are my values?" In many respects, Part III, Values, is the centerpiece of peace and justice education. Knowledge about social issues, and even techniques for change, will be helpful only to the degree to which they relate to human values. Laws, codes, customs, habits, attitudes, beliefs, and, most importantly, personal behavior reflect the values of individuals and their societies. In a world of conflicting interests we need to distinguish between good and bad values, supporting the former and rejecting the latter.

In this section of the text we shall argue that among the key values in life are personal dignity and human solidarity. Do I see myself as unique and worthy of respect? Do I treat others as I would have them treat me? Am I my sister and brother's keeper? While the exploitation and oppression of people are hardly new phenomena, their overwhelming dimensions in our century demand that we develop personal attitudes as well as political, economic, and cultural values that will lessen violence and lead to peace and harmony. Personal dignity and human solidarity are the essential elements of a new social order.

Furthermore, we shall see that other human values flow from the inner cohesiveness of dignity and solidarity. The values of justice, truth, peace, freedom, liberation, and love are extensions of the core values. Each of these will be explained in some detail in order to present the reader with a developed sense of their importance and their connectedness to personal dignity and human solidarity. These discussions should offer us a standard by which to measure the distance we have to travel toward a more humane society. By now we have been sensitized to the richness and diversity of the human family and have come to see more clearly the extent of our social ills. By testing and realizing our moral values, we can participate more effectively in reform and renewal.

21

What Is a Value?

Old men with advice for youth are like traffic signals blinking
their greens, reds and yellows after midnight, in the rain, at empty
streets.

Michael Niflis[1]

Value Free

In *Webster's Dictionary* there are seventeen different meanings
for the word *value*. These range from the relative worth or
importance of something to an understanding of the intrinsic
qualities that humans possess. In our discussion of values we
shall include the totality of beliefs, attitudes, and behavioral
patterns of people. The way I live my life, the prejudices I hold,
the manner in which I spend my time and money, the people
I admire, the goals I have, the hopes and dreams I possess are
all indications of my values. Thus we can say that every person
possesses a system of values that may be judged on its own
merits. My life is a reflection of my values. What I consider
valuable will be reflected in the attitudes I hold and the choices
I make.

One of the major trends of the modern era has been the pursuit of objectivity. In the search for scientific facts and empirical data, many educators sought to develop a value-free system of learning. No one wished to impose his or her values on anyone else, and so it was reasoned that only facts should be taught. This value-free model was a product of the Age of Enlightenment, the emergence of which was partly due to people's disgust with the religious wars of the sixteenth and seventeenth centuries. Since Christians fought among themselves about their beliefs and values, the new secularists used reason alone to seek the truth. This led to the secularization of all issues. Unfortunately, in their attempt to find objectivity they tended to disregard spiritual and moral insights.[2]

The ultimate irony in all of this, of course, is that if one chooses to make education value-free, that in itself has become a value! Whatever choices we make in life, be they scientific or humanitarian, they reflect our values. For example, a researcher's values influence all aspects of the research. What to study, which design and methods to use, and how to interpret the data are value questions. We are, one way or another, living out our lives as an expression of our values.

Our patterns of eating, sleeping, studying, playing, and communicating indicate the relative importance we attach to these activities. People act in different ways. These differences are evidence of their particular values.

A second trend quite prevalent in our time is moral relativism. If we push individual subjectivity too far we make a god of each person, and we begin to think that all must "do their own thing" even if it means being a racist or a sexist. How absurd to equate the values of Gandhi or Mother Teresa with those of Adolf Hitler or the Mayflower Madame (convicted for running a high-class prostitution ring in New York City from 1981 to 1985). The unavoidable conclusion is that education must be concerned about truth, goodness, beauty, and virtue. Consequently if our beliefs, attitudes, and behavior reflect our values, then it is proper to ask if these patterns are good or bad. Let us examine now some of the characteristics of values.

Clarification of Values

"Show me your checkbook and calendar, and I'll tell you what your values are." While this statement may serve the purpose of checking out the values of money and time, both of which are interesting value indicators, it nonetheless fails to do justice to the wider variety of our interests and values. These include concerns about family, friends, relatives, associates at work, classmates, and, in general, all our relationships with other people. Although many of our values were garnered from parents, teachers, or religious educators, at some point in life we began to take responsibility for our own values. In this regard the work of Simon, Howe, and Kirschenbaum[3] has been especially helpful in clarifying the values that people hold. They leave aside the question of value-worth, or content, in order to clarify the nature of a value. Prizing, choosing, and acting on one's convictions are at the heart of value clarification.

When I prize someone or something, I take on an attitude of ownership. It may be a possessive or dominating type of concern, or it may be an ownership more akin to the notion of stewardship. I become responsible for the care, protection, or well-being of the person or object. Cherishing, of course, has certain degrees of intensity. We may liken our value concerns to a baseball with stitched horsehide over a twine-covered center of cork. The cork represents our core values, those for which we might die; the twine represents values that we hold with some conviction, but are not essential; the outer covering represents attitudes or beliefs that are of little consequence in our life. My choice of toothpaste is hardly as important as my concern for my family. Prizing, according to Simon, may well include a public affirmation of those values that I cherish. It is not simply a question of telling myself that I cherish or prize someone or something; it is also a question of expressing these convictions.

Choosing one's beliefs and behavioral patterns is the second criterion for assessing values. True value choices are those that are affirmed after having considered alternatives and examined the consequences of our choice. Human choice is frequently affected by fear, desire, coercion, ignorance, or anger. All of these diminish our ability to choose freely and in many instances block responsible behavior. Frequently enough, we are quite capable of making choices. Indeed, the courts generally hold people responsible for their actions. In developing a morally mature personality, we need to consider the alternatives to the values that we received as children lest we fail to make those learned values part of our own responsibility.

Finally, our living out the values that we profess represents the third criterion for personal ownership. How we spend our money and where we spend our time have been pointed out at the beginning of this section as two indicators of our value system. Do I spend quality time with my family and friends, or are they simply an afterthought once I have accomplished a particular task? One of the frequently mentioned causes of divorce is the workaholic routine of many men. Are my behavioral patterns growing in nonrelational ways? Is work more important than play? Do I spend my money on myself, or do I share generously with those who are in need? We obviously could go on at length about how our actions are a reliable measure of our values. Suffice to say, as we continue to examine the question of values, we should take stock of our own beliefs, attitudes, and behavior and ask if these patterns are worthy of our best self.

Moral Development

The expression "You can't put an old head on young shoulders" captures the essence of human development. Just as we mature biologically, intellectually, and emotionally, there is development in the sphere of our moral life as well.

As adults this development is often linked to our spiritual vision, but in the early formative years of life, it is based primarily on parental admonitions and peer pressures. Answers about right and wrong are learned very early. The child whose hand is slapped for trying to touch a hot stove, or who is bribed with a cookie to go to bed on time, learns quickly that pain is bad and pleasure is good.

Jean Piaget, a world-renowned child psychologist, analyzed the thinking and behavior of children toward issues of right and wrong. He concluded that "All morality consists in a system of rules, and the essence of all morality is to be sought for in the respect that the individual acquires for those rules."[4] Children make moral judgments based upon the rules of conduct set by parents and teachers. They also judge good and bad behavior by conformity to game rules learned from older children. Around the age of eleven or twelve a cognitive reorganization occurs in which abstract reasoning begins to play an increasing role in the thought processes of the preadolescent. All of the previous moral judgments remain, but reason now asserts itself in the development process.

At this juncture the studies of Lawrence Kohlberg, a professor of social psychology at Harvard University, bear mention. Leaving aside the way people actually behaved, he attempted to probe the moral reasoning people used to justify their behavior. If a thirty-year-old man states that he doesn't steal because "My mother said not to," we instinctively know that we are dealing with arrested moral thinking.

Kohlberg categorized moral reasoning into three broad groupings. Stage one, preconventional moral reasoning, was typical of childhood, i.e., pleasure/pain and reward/punishment were seen as the most significant factors in judging good and bad. The dominance of the Parent-Child relationship and the authority figures of other adults cause the child to view morality from a top-down obedience-to-commands framework.

The second stage, conventional moral reasoning, is attributable to group consensus. In the larger society people agree to a wide variety of laws to govern behavior. Cultural norms dictated, or at least acquiesced to, by the majority of the population set the standard for good conduct. Kohlberg found that most people associate their moral decisions with this conventional wisdom.

Beyond this, however, a postconvention moral reasoning process exists. In this third stage people base their moral judgments on a higher law. While Kohlberg, a secular humanist, avoided religion in his studies, he saw evidence that a universal ethical orientation existed in which principles of justice, respect for life, and equality among all people played a decisive role in the moral thinking of some people.[5]

Before concluding these remarks on moral development, we should note the studies by Carol Gilligan, a social science educator and colleague of Kohlberg at Harvard, that suggest that the voices of women have yet to be heard. Freud believed that "for women the level of what is ethically normal is different from what it is in men."[6] This pejorative thinking about women's ability for moral reasoning was a result of sexist attitudes so common in the past. Today, in appreciating the uniqueness of women's moral reasoning, based primarily on the subjective relationship with other people, we add additional color to the portrait of morality. Gilligan states that "since masculinity is defined through separation and femininity is defined through attachment, male gender identity is threatened by intimacy, while female gender identity is threatened by separation."[7] A woman's sense of right and wrong is more attuned to the personal relationship she has with others, as opposed to her male counterpart, who is generally more interested in knowing the rules of the game.

The study of moral development, from both a cognitive masculine viewpoint and a female relational frame of reference, helps us see the linkage between our moral thinking and our values. Indeed, in mathematical terms they are dependent functions undergoing constant change throughout our lives. Yet in spite of these changes, it is important to ask if there is not a deeper foundational basis for differentiating good and evil. Let us look at some possible answers.

Foundations of Morality

The rich tradition of the ancient Greek philosophers, particularly Plato and Aristotle, spawned what became known as natural law. Christian philosophers added to this ordered view of nature a foundation nothing less than the eternal will of God. The Ten Commandments were seen as a moral code carved in stone and handed down by God to be obeyed by all people. Just as there was a natural order for the motion of the planets and the movement of the stars, so too was it accepted that universal standards of good and evil existed in a permanent and irrevocable way. God, so it was thought, had decreed it thus! The Founding Fathers of our country believed in a natural timeless order of nature. "We hold these truths to be self evident ... " states the Declaration of Independence. This traditional thinking was predicated on a static world view, and thus it was not surprising that when Darwin's evolutionary theories burst upon the nineteenth and twentieth centuries the natural law foundations for morality began to crumble.

With the knowledge that we live in a dynamic and ever-evolving universe, with the expanding concepts of matter, time, and energy and with a revolutionary understanding of the human species evolving from primate ancestors, morality came to be understood in relative terms. Gone were the granitelike principles. These were replaced by a variety of theories, all of which depend upon evolution in one way or another. Ayn Rand, a popular American novelist and proponent of survivalism, took Darwin's lead by portraying morality as the survival of the fittest. A code of ethics for her was designed only to assure one's safety.[8] Hitler, too, espoused this Nietzschean form of power morality by calling for the extermination of the Jews, who were thought to dilute the virility of the super race.

In a more amorphous way, many people today have little or no sense of moral foundations. They are fearful of judging others by any standards. They tend to shy away from making judgments about right and wrong, good and evil. This is most unfortunate since there is an almost worldwide intellectual acceptance of a foundational principle for morality that combines biblical and natural law standards with the new relativism. In a word, the fundamental dignity of each person stands as the foundation for morality, and the International Bill of Human Rights spells out in great detail the respect and dignity due to each person. Let us look for a moment at some implications of this truth.

Morality may be understood to contain both public and private values. How we care for ourselves, our family, and our friends; how we treat our neighbors; how we work, play, and associate with others; and how we relate to God are generally issues of an individual nature. Presumably, if we think of ourselves as worthy of respect, we will live according to personal norms that respect others.

Unfortunately, in the public arena many have settled for a legal code as a kind of minimal societal morality. They believe that law determines right and wrong. Granted that many laws do protect the rights of individuals, the fact remains that law plays a limited role in determining morality. Legal codes do not demand that we love one another. Therefore, whether on a personal or a social level, or in the private or public domain, the basic human rights of each person remain the standard for morality. We can judge good and evil or right and wrong by how we treat ourselves and others.

Truth/Goodness

"What is truth?" asked Pilate.[9] This age-old question is more daunting than ever. We hear people on the right and left of the political, economic, and religious spectra proclaiming their truths for all to hear. Jimmy Swaggart, the morally stained and censured televangelist, says that millions will go to hell unless he continues his media ministry.

Ultraconservative politicians decry any serious negotiation with the Soviets as a betrayal of our country. At the same time, economists, apparently blind to the cry of the poor, manipulate and interpret statistics in order to determine economic truth.

So what is truth, and how does it relate to goodness? Gandhi once said that the real test of truth is what is good for life. As a Hindu he believed strongly in the holiness of all life and saw truth as an expression of respect for life. This means that attitudes and actions that betray life are false. If we believe that truth and goodness are central to human dignity, we can distinguish between noble and base values. On one end of the spectrum we find Nazism with its value system of white supremacy, male preeminence, military dictatorship, and suppression of the weak and handicapped. On the other end, we find a value system taught by Jesus where the last are first, and forgiveness, gentleness, and mercy have priority. Truth and goodness, then, are in sharp contrast to falsity and evil.

Thus, goodness and truth are intimately tied to the human person. When we think of the millions of people who lack decent housing, clean water, and proper nutrition—all those who live in conditions of poverty and need—we see evil in our midst. Consider their opposite number: the so-called decadent rich who, instead of using their wealth to help others, hoard, conspicuously consume, and blame the needy for their own misfortune.[10] The falseness of these wasted lives is readily apparent. If the adage "do good, avoid evil" possesses any validity today, it might well call us to have a reverence toward our own person and a willingness to confront the evils of our world.

Is all of this too idealistic? Is it possible to address the ME generation with an agenda for social change? Who knows? Who cares? say the voices of indifference. A generation ago the youngest American president ever elected said, "Ask not what your country can do for you; ask what you can do for your country."[11] John F. Kennedy tried to call forth the best efforts of a nation. Can we not raise the clarion call again? Is it not appropriate to ask, as we move through the value section of the text, if we are giving our best? Although idealism is often a particular attribute of the young, it is more a state of mind than a condition of age.

Our vision of life—about what might be—will determine our values. If the twentieth century has been cast as an age of Holocaust, in which millions were slaughtered in war and millions more died of hunger and neglect, is it not possible to write history in a new way for the twenty-first century? The students of today are the women and men of the twenty-first century. Will historians one hundred years from now look back and name their century an Age of Concern? Is it not possible that the next generation of Americans and, indeed, all their young global companions will put the values of compassion and concern for the poor ahead of self-interest and material success? The challenge for building a better world has never been more opportune!

We began Part III by asking the question, "What are my values?" It has become evident that our values are a compendium of our attitudes, beliefs, and behavior. Perhaps it is time for an inventory. What are the major concerns in my life? How do I express my gratitude to those who have cared for and nourished me? How do I use my time? On what do I spend my money? Do the poor have a place in my heart? The things I cherish, what I freely choose to do, and my words and deeds all reflect my personal values. As we begin to understand the connections between the general ideas of truth and goodness, we need to assess our own particular truths and the goodness of our lives.

Notes

[1] Michael Niflis, "Signals," *Commonweal*, March 26, 1976, 211.

[2] Abraham H. Maslow, *Religions, Values, and Peak-Experiences* (New York: Viking Press, 1971), 11–12, 51–52.

[3] Sidney B. Simon, Leland W. Howe, and Howard Kirschenbaum, *Values Clarification* (New York: Hart Publishing, 1972).

[4] Ronald Duska and Mariellen Whelan, *Moral Development* (New York: Paulist Press, 1975), 8.

[5] Ibid., 47.

[6] Carol Gilligan, *In a Different Voice* (Cambridge, Mass.: Harvard University Press, 1982), 7.

[7] Ibid., 8.

8 Daniel Maguire, *The Moral Choice* (Minneapolis: Winston Press, 1979), 63.

9 John 18:38.

10 John Paul II, *Sollicitudo Rei Socialis* (Washington, D.C.: United States Catholic Conference, 1987), para. 37.

11 Inaugural address of John F. Kennedy, January 1961.

22

Search for Meaning

As he was setting out on a journey, a man ran up and knelt before him, and asked him, "Good Teacher, what must I do to inherit eternal life?" . . . "Go, sell what you own, and give the money to the poor, and you will have treasure in heaven; then come, follow me."

Mark 10:17–21

Truth and Meaning

If a teacher were to write a sentence on the blackboard in a strange language, and then turn to the students and ask if it were true, the teacher would, no doubt, get many blank stares. Eventually someone would suggest that the class must know what something means before it can judge if it is true. This simple example contains much wisdom since it begins to help us see the connection between truth and meaning. More importantly, however, it reveals that meaning points the way to truth.

We know that truth deals with reality. Is there evidence to affirm or deny something? Does a statement square with the facts? Is it provable? Meaning, on the other hand, is concerned with purpose. Its favorite question is "Why?" If we say this or that person is good, we are generally asked to flesh out the statement by giving reasons for this assertion.

This process enables us to get to the meaning of the statement. It is similar to peeling away layers of paper to get at the contents of a package. Meaning often lies beneath the surface of reality.

Michael Polanyi, a professor of chemistry and a social scientist at the University of Manchester, England, in his insightful book, *Meaning,* describes two kinds of knowledge, factual and tacit. The former we gain through our senses, the latter by reflection. Polanyi argues that much of the present turmoil in our world can be traced to the loss of balance between these two ways of knowing. If we stress scientific facts and experimental data, we are distracted from seeking any meaning beyond these facts. This has led to an almost blind faith in technology as the answer for all human problems. Conversely, if the person is the only source of truth, values simply arise from our own choices. "We do not choose because we see the value of something. We see the value of something because we have chosen it."[1] If the individual is the sole arbiter of what is of value, the higher, or spiritual, truths of justice, freedom, and human dignity become meaningless.

Yet, paradoxically, we find within the individual the basis for seeking these higher truths. Erik Erikson (whom we discussed in chapter 11) categorized the development of human personality into eight basic stages of growth from infancy to old age. Here we are reminded of the importance he placed upon the maturation level of each stage being dependent upon a well-developed prior stage. Each stage of maturity builds upon its predecessor. Personal growth occurs when we respond affirmatively to the challenges presented to us for further maturity. Erikson contends that this growth is inevitable, given the essential makeup of humans.

At the heart of his theory of personality development rests the epigenetic principle, which says that humans contain within themselves a ground plan designed to reach full potential. The meaning of maturity for Erikson has to do with fulfilling a destiny to which each of us is called. Juxtaposing Polanyi's desire to ground truth in a balance between the external world of material reality and the inner world of personal reflection and Erikson's discovery of a ground plan for individual human growth, we may conclude that the central developmental principle within each person is to appreciate his or her own truth and goodness within the greater context of all reality.

In ancient times when people were beginning to raise serious questions about the meaning of life, many of the unexplained phenomena were attributed to the gods. It was believed that they controlled human lives and were the immediate cause of blessings and curses. Gradually, at least in Western society, monotheism became the accepted belief. It became one God who caused famines, plagues, and earthquakes as punishment for sin, and wealth, happiness, and joy as the reward for a good life. It was God who gave meaning to natural events—or so most people believed.

With the advancement of scientific thought we are less likely to attribute to God the ravages of nature. We now know that disease is caused by viruses and bacteria; hurricanes are due to low-pressure atmospheric conditions; earthquakes result from the sliding motion of different layers of the earth's crust; and so on. We have new meanings to explain events, so old truths lose their relevance or are adjusted to include new data. As we learn more about the workings of our universe and discover new truths about our humanness, we are forced to seek new meaning for our lives. We may speak of God as the foundational cause of all creation, but far more immediate interventions also offer meaning to life.

Frankl

In the early part of this century, Sigmund Freud, the father of psychoanalysis, broke new intellectual ground with his studies about the inner dynamic of personality. He saw evidence that the strongest drive within the individual was a will to pleasure. Our appetites for food, shelter, companionship, and sex arose from a desire to avoid pain and to seek satisfaction and pleasure. This was at odds with the nineteenth-century German philosopher, Friedrich Nietzsche. He professed that the will to power, a self-assertive drive to attain power, was a fundamental attribute of humans. Not convinced that Nietzsche or Freud had fully understood human nature, Abraham Maslow, the noted American humanist psychologist, drew attention to a hierarchical order that he saw existing among various human needs. In chapter 1 of this text Maslow's categories of needs were explained briefly.[2] We wish here only to note that the highest needs of humans according to Maslow were of a transcendent nature. Because we long for meaning, our real needs exceed the biological and social dimensions of life.

All of this is by way of introduction to a man who, although less well known than the above-mentioned seminal thinkers, has contributed greatly to an understanding of the person. Viktor Frankl, a Jewish psychotherapist who spent several years in Nazi concentration camps, developed a new school of psychiatric medicine known as logotherapy. In the process of healing through meaning, Frankl believed that true north lay in the will to meaning. If we are able to find and give meaning to our lives, we have discovered the essential ingredient that can satisfy our deepest longing to live in a worthy manner. Frankl built on the work of Maslow by exploring the dimensions of our highest need.

At one of his many lecture engagements, Frankl was asked to give a brief description of logotherapy. He asked the questioner to briefly describe psychoanalysis. "That is when," came the reply, "one lies down on a couch and reveals some unpleasant truths about oneself." Frankl retorted by describing logotherapy as a time when "one sits down in a chair and hears some unpleasant things about oneself."[3] Frankl broke with his psychoanalytic predecessors in several ways, the two most important of which were (1) his willingness to offer direction and advice to his patients, and (2) his constant challenge to them to ferret out the meaning of their lives. He believed there are some basic truths in life that are important to learn and that because each person is unique, there is a unique meaning to each life.

The organic, or animal, dimension to our humanness is demonstrable. We are flesh and blood, we procreate, and we have all the quantitative characteristics of the other primates. But we are more. There is a psychological dimension to our life. We are able to reflect on ourselves, to know who we are. We can think, understand, choose, and love. Finally there is a spiritual, or transcendent, dimension to human life, says Frankl. At its center lies our search for meaning. These three dimensions, the biological, psychological, and spiritual, constitute our humanity. To the degree that we grow more humane, we are able to control the organic dimensions of life and allow the psychological and spiritual qualities to predominate. We choose for ourselves the direction our lives will take.

But how can this be if, as sometimes happens, we have no control over events or circumstances? Frankl's years in the concentration camps led him to understand the importance of inner strength. It is here, with Frankl's help, that we are able to make the connection between values and meaning. We observed in the last chapter that everything we do in life points to a personal system of values. The work we do, the place we live, the efforts we make, the sins we commit, and the good and bad we seek or reject all indicate what is, or is not, of value to us. These values act as reference points for the meaning we give to our lives. When we experience a change of heart or offer a helping hand, we redirect ourselves toward a more worthwhile life. Our values, therefore, are an expression of the meaning we give to our lives even in the worst of circumstances.

Creative and Experiential Values

Every human person constitutes something unique; each situation in life occurs only once. The concrete task of any person is relative to this uniqueness and singularity. Thus, every person at any given moment can have only one single task.[4]

Given that the individuality and specialness of each person are the starting points for the particular meaning that he or she assigns to his or her life, Frankl saw that certain categories of values provided the context for meaning. In the first instance, a person is called to respond to the demands of the tasks that life offers. What one is doing is not nearly as important as how one does it.

This category of work-related values is called creative values. We are able to find meaning in the creativity that we bring to the job at hand. Since our work takes on fresh meaning, each day new opportunities present themselves and different challenges arise. Although we honor a talented musician, a gifted artist, or a skilled craftsperson for his or her creative ability, it is also true that a creative spirit can be brought to the more mundane tasks of life. A bus driver who announces with gusto each stop on the route and helps the elderly on and off the bus surely has found creative value in his or her work.

It is much the same with the duties assigned to us in life. Students who have a sense of responsibility about their studies and bring a positive, creative spirit into the classroom find a much greater level of satisfaction in their education than those students who exert little effort. Not only is the grade-point average boosted by a zest for learning, but, more importantly, the individual, wholeheartedly engaged in the task at hand, finds meaning in life by doing what he or she ought to do. This holds true for all the duties that life places in our path. Parents who nurture and care for their children, women and men who approach their jobs with interest and responsibility, or anyone who responds affirmatively to the daily task of life has discovered that happiness is not found by pursuing it directly, but comes in proportion to the energy we expend on the task at hand.

In addition to the meaning we get from the creative values of work, Frankl also saw an abundance of meaning in experiential values. By this he meant the values realized in openness and receptivity to the experience of life. Whether we set the agenda for new experiences by traveling to distant lands or taking a quiet walk in the woods, we are frequently able to decide for ourselves what experiences will come our way. Of course, many unavoidable things happen too. We are placed in situations not of our choosing, or we are forced to deal with people we might have otherwise avoided. In either instance, what we experience in life can provide a richness of new meaning each day.

This is nowhere more evident than in the experience of love. For Frankl, "love is living the experience of another person in all his uniqueness and singularity."[5] On the level of friendship most of us have had experiences of closeness to other people. Growing up is generally associated with playmates who laughed and sometimes cried with us; with siblings or other relatives who cared for us in ways that were different from parental care; and with an occasional teacher, minister, or significant adult who made us feel good about ourselves. Most commonly, however, we think of love in terms of the bonding between men and women. While "falling in love" represents, at best, infatuation, it is nonetheless an experience that elicits strong emotional responses. Ultimately, genuine love is characterized by tenderness, respect, sensitivity, and a real desire to know and understand the other. To be loved this way, or to offer this fullness of love, is clearly of great value, perhaps the highest value of all! It is in loving relationships as human beings that we find life to be filled with meaning.

Attitudinal Values

What are we to do when few or no opportunities exist to bring creativity to the task of life? How do we respond if there are no opportunities to experience the beauty of a sunset on a lake or a moment of tenderness with a friend? When creative and experiential values are severely limited, as was the case for Frankl during the darkest days of his incarceration in the death camps of the Nazis, he believes that we are still able to give life meaning. He found this meaning in attitudinal values.

We know that our attitudes toward life are conditioned by the type of personality we have. By nature people are introverted and extroverted, quiet and boisterous, morose and happy. Various combinations of these and other personality traits abound. Some people grumble when given lemons; others make lemonade. Frankl, however, was not interested in the surface attitudes we carry around with us. What is significant, he says, is a person's attitude in dealing with an unalterable fate.[6] The limiting factors of life pose the core challenges. In chapter 9 we dealt extensively with the problem of human limitations and their personal and social effects from a philosophical and theological frame of reference. Here, from a psychological vantage point, we see the importance of our attitude toward limits as offering meaning to life.

If we have ever been in a situation that posed a threat of death, we know how reluctant the mind is to deal with that reality. Recent studies, moreover, on the process of dying have shown clearly that denial is the first reaction by a patient to the evidence of a fatal ailment. There is such a finality to death that we are hard-pressed to see its meaning. Frankl contends, however, that death too has meaning because it brings closure to a unique and singular life. "In time and in finiteness man must finish something—that is, take finiteness upon himself and consciously accept an end as part of the bargain."[7]

We argued earlier (chapter 9) that all human anxiety is rooted in the tension between our infinite desires and our finite reality. This results in a resistance to limits, especially the ultimate limit of death. Yet resistance to death does not rob it of meaning. Indeed, the more meaningful a life one has led will add a richness to death. Thus, a healthy attitude toward the inevitability of death and the daily limits of life that we cannot change allows us to accept more gracefully life's inescapable conflicts and frees us from a morbid anxiety about things we cannot control.

We wish to stress again that the search for meaning is most personal. Each one must find his or her own meaning to life. This arises from the uniqueness and singularity of each human being. Frankl offers insight into the search for meaning by indicating the way to meaning through the actualization of values.

The creative values are what we do; the experiential ones are what we enjoy; the attitudinal values are tested in the crucible of life's limits.

Having looked at the reality of death, let us conclude with some remarks on suffering. "To live is to suffer, to survive is to find meaning in the suffering."[8] With this simple statement, Frankl revealed a central tenet of human life.

He decries those who couch fulfillment in terms of success. Most humans fail constantly, and it is in failure that we are tested for our true worth. Because of the strong influences of a materialistic culture to measure success in terms of power and wealth, we tend to think negatively about failure. Yet from the attitudinal values we bring to suffering and failure, we can derive new meaning. Illness may be viewed as an opportunity to step back from the rush of life and count our blessings; a failure in a course may lead to more responsible study habits; a broken relationship may cause us not to take friendships for granted. Consequently, we are able to find meaning in all the situations of life when we realize that it is our responsibility to search for that meaning.

Christian Meaning

Has God spoken about the meaning of life? Does Christianity have anything worthwhile to say about living out our daily lives? We know that for many people these are not even real questions. Since the catastrophic breakup of Christianity in the sixteenth century, there has been a steady erosion of the influence of religious faith by the winds of secularism. The sacred and the profane have been neatly separated into a private and public order. In the United States it is estimated that over half the adult population is not connected with a religious body. In many respects the Christian churches brought this upon themselves. Their internecine warfare over doctrines and faith practices resulted in a kind of fortress mentality. Lost was any sense of fraternal love. In its place was a demand to defend the ancient traditions (depending on how one interpreted them!).

Fortunately, the past half-century has seen a gradual thaw in the relationship among Christian denominations, especially among the larger institutional churches. There has been a return to a common belief that the central meaning of God's revelation through the Hebrew people, and especially the person of Jesus, is more important than the differences that divided Christians. What then, is the central meaning of God's revelation?

In the beginning, the Bible tells us, darkness and gloom hovered over the land. God spoke and the chaos disappeared, and the earth was filled with abundance. This creation myth in the book of Genesis, while not scientifically factual, provides us with an interpretation of the wonders of the created universe that came into being about twenty billion years ago. The stories of God found in Sacred Scripture were not written as journalistic reporting might be today. Instead, they are faith interpretations of the mystery we call God. The Hebrew people praised this God of creation, the God of Abraham, Isaac, and Jacob, who freed them from the slavery of the Egyptian pharaoh and led them to the Promised Land.

Their history is interpreted as a process of salvation. Thus, the meaning attached to their lives as the people of God is understood in cycles of dying and rising. The people sin and are punished; they repent and are saved. Throughout the millennium before Christ, the Hebrew prophets spoke on behalf of God about the injustice of not caring for the widows and orphans (the poor), and of the idolatry surrounding wealth and power. The meaning that they gave to God had much to do with the value of helping the needy and avoiding the pitfalls of pride and greed.

The Christian interpretation about the meaning of life finds its fullest expression in Jesus Christ. "I am the way, and the truth, and the life,"[9] says Jesus in response to a question by Thomas. This declaration, has both direction and substance. In its succinctness it sums up the meaning of Jesus' life. He will lead his followers along the path of rightness; he speaks the truth about how we are to live; and he reveals to us that eternal life is our final destiny.

The Sermon on the Mount speaks volumes about the values Jesus calls all to live by. "Blessed are those who hunger and thirst for righteousness ... blessed are the merciful ... blessed are the peacemakers."[10] Of course, the dominant reality in Jesus' life was the cross. Although Jesus was crucified by the Romans for incurring the wrath of the Jewish leaders by attacking their hypocrisy, his death has always been interpreted as the saving action by God's Son for all people in all times and places. The cross of Jesus stands as a sign of hope to those who acknowledge their sinfulness. The suffering of Jesus in his capture, trial, and crucifixion offers unlimited meaning to the suffering we all must endure. The mystery of his death on the cross is related to suffering, just as his resurrection is related to eternal life. Even though death and resurrection appear as polar opposites, nonetheless they constitute the apex of Christian meaning.

The early Christians attempted to live in the Spirit. This involved them in preaching the message of Jesus to their fellow Jews and to Gentiles as well. It was a message of God's love and faithfulness to humanity. They gathered in community to share, to pray, and to support one another. They believed that service was a way of life. Centuries later, having weathered its own institutional sickness, the atheistic assaults of communism, and the greed of capitalism, Christianity is again proving that it offers value-laden meaning for all people. "As the Father loves me," Jesus says, "so I love you. Live on in my love." The proliferation of Christian-based communities in Third World countries and the renewal of social awareness by the churches has made the message of God's love more relevant than ever.

Notes

1   Michael Polanyi, *Meaning* (Chicago: University of Chicago Press, 1975), 4.

2   Abraham H. Maslow, *Motivation and Personality* (New York: Harper & Row, 1970), 38.

3   Viktor Frankl, *Man's Search for Meaning* (New York: Washington Square Press, 1967), 152.

[4] Viktor Frankl, *The Doctor and the Soul* (New York: Bantam Books, 1969), 34.

[5] Ibid., 106.

[6] Ibid., 35.

[7] Ibid., 54.

[8] Frankl, *Man's Search for Meaning*, xii.

[9] John 14:6.

[10] Matthew 5:7–10.

23

Personal Dignity

To dare stammer and stutter without pretension, pointing without
expecting adulation for the pointing finger, but inviting disdain of
the experts whose skill consists in being objective about that which
is not objective, to stammer without any other defense than: this is
my experience, this is my vision, this is how words and concepts
once irreconcilable, clashing in my brain, echo in my heart and
fuse easily.

Frederick Franck[1]

Self-Worth

The quotation cited above from the work of Frederick Franck,
noted poet and world traveler, captures both the humility and
power of one's own personal insights that need no defense
other than to say "They are mine!" I am who I am. We have
already seen in the previous chapter on meaning that Victor
Frankl based his practice of logotherapy on the uniqueness of
each individual person. This simple yet profound truth is at the
heart of values education. Never before in the history of the
world, not today with a global population of five billion people,

and never again in the possible millennia to come will there be another you.

If you would, imagine a young child standing on a sun-drenched beach with her arms outstretched and the waves roaring approval: "I am a Child of the Universe," she proclaims. We need to appreciate fully the depth of our singularity, our specialness in the plan of creation. We need to rejoice each day of our lives because each person is unique. Our hopes, dreams, and expectations may seem similar, but in the final analysis, we are free to choose for ourselves the direction of our lives. We need to begin with our own self-worth if we are to live with purpose, truth, and goodness.

In speaking to the men of his time, the Apostle Paul asserted that husbands "should love their wives as they do their own bodies."[2] This proposal assumes that one will naturally care for one's own body. Unfortunately, such is not the case in modern American society. In spite of the diet centers, fat farms, and zillions of fitness programs, many people continue to overindulge their bodies with rich foods, alcohol, tobacco, and drugs. This results in everything from heart disease and lung cancer to neurotic behavior and death.

Care of the body is an acknowledgment of self-worth. The ancient Greeks taught that having a sound mind in a sound body is the proper way to live. When we care for our bodies through good eating habits, exercise, and sufficient rest, we find that our minds are alert and our stamina levels are high. It goes without saying, however, that general care of the body is not to be confused with a fixation on the flesh. Pampering the body with lotions, creams, and endless combinations of cosmetics or clothing the body with garments and accessories beyond reasonable need is decadent and morally barren. In reality, this type of behavior confuses external appearance with inner self-worth. Real self-worth begins with caring for our bodies without making them an end in themselves.

Care of the mind is of higher importance than care of the body. Although the two are not totally separate entities, for the sake of clarity we generally speak of the intellectual and reflective sides of our personalities as centered in our minds. In the first instance, how we think of ourselves is of utmost importance since all psychologists agree that we act the way we think. Alfred Adler, a colleague of Freud, coined the term "inferiority complex," by which he recognized certain levels of subservient behavior in all people. Because all humans begin life in a parent-child relationship, these dependent feelings often carry into later life. We need to constantly improve our self-image through an appreciation of our own talents and abilities.

Furthermore, care of the mind requires feeding it healthy food. Junk in means junk out. Thus, a steady diet of soaps, cops-and-robbers stories, trashy novels, banal banter about sports, or the latest gossip item does little to improve the mind. Admittedly, we all need an occasional distraction from the realities of life, but the mind that does not put a high priority on seeking new insights and refuses to think creatively about fresh possibilities soon falls into disuse. In the final analysis, care of the body and the mind contribute to a richer sense of self-worth.

Lastly, it is of utmost importance that we include care of the heart in our quest for self-worth. It is here that we ought to work most diligently. If a sound mind and body are important, how much more so is a sound heart! The heart refers, of course, to that part of us that lives out of a spirit of courage and generosity. Care of the heart means that we develop habits of love, trust, kindness, compassion, forgiveness, etc. These attributes that speak of service and selflessness are "heartfelt." All too often we neglect the heart and it grows cold and hard. We build barriers around ourselves that often blind us to the needs of others and isolate us from the love and affection that others offer. Scrooge, the famous character created by Charles Dickens, was a hard man not given to sentimentality and gentleness. Do we at times imitate his conduct? Yet Scrooge had a change of heart and therein lies a central truth. We are all basically good though our actions sometimes belie that goodness. If we care for the heart, as well as the body and the mind, we can learn the ways of love. Our self-worth is predicated on the healthy development of all three dimensions of our being.

Human Rights

If we look around at the world today with its system of apartheid in South Africa, its exploitation of peasants in Latin America, civil war in Lebanon, terrorism in Northern Ireland, and the awful specter of a nuclear holocaust hanging over the planet, one can only attempt to whisper or, as Franck suggests, to stammer about the goodness and worth of each person. Life seems to be very cheap on the streets of Belfast, in the rubble of Beirut, or in the slums of Calcutta. Here and there we see a Mother Teresa or are reminded of an Albert Schweitzer, but for the most part the newspaper headlines and the television evening news programs remind us constantly of the rapes, muggings, and murders that seem to be a part of everyday life.

In spite of this, the past few decades have witnessed a universal cry for human rights. Personal rights that exclude the accidents of birth—sex, color, ethnicity, class, and religion—have taken center stage in the thinking of the human family. Even with the horrendous abuses, we are more conscious than ever that every person has basic fundamental rights to which he or she is entitled. Personal dignity belongs to everyone in all times, places, and circumstances.

Although awareness of human rights predates our own American Bill of Rights, it was not until recently that it has received such worldwide attention. Beginning with the Universal Declaration of Human Rights signed by the United Nations in 1948 and continuing through the International Covenants on political, economic, social, and cultural rights ratified in the mid-1970s, virtually every country in the world at least acknowledges in theory that "All human beings are born free and equal in dignity and rights. They are endowed with reason and conscience and should act toward one another in a spirit of brotherhood."[3]

In the American Declaration of Independence, the phrase "life, liberty and the pursuit of happiness" characterizes the essence of rights, but it took the addition of ten amendments to the Constitution almost twenty years later to spell out the particulars of that phrase. In recent years the phrase *right to life* has been used to identify the essential feature of human dignity. More particularly, the right-to-life principle implies that all people should be afforded dignity from the beginning of human life in the womb until its termination in death. Advocates of abortion argue that until birth a mother has an exclusive right to terminate the life of her fetus if she so desires. Proponents of euthanasia believe that a quality-of-life criterion should be applied. Lacking quality, they say, life has no meaning. In both cases, judgments are made about what constitutes the right to life, and someone other than the one whose life is in jeopardy makes that determination. However, in moral terms, our first responsibility is to do no harm. Could we not apply the same rule of thumb to the question of the right to life?

Another important characteristic of human rights is equality. In ancient times we know that rulers held complete sway over their subjects. It was commonly held that slaves had no rights. In many societies women were only a step or two above the slaves. Even the seriousness of an offense was determined by the importance of the one offended. Although Adam and Eve were mere humans, their sin was seen as an infinite offense because it was viewed as disobedience to an infinite deity. Much of this thinking continued throughout the Middle Ages when kings ruled supreme. It may be said that the most noble gift of the Age of Enlightenment was democracy. All people are equal before the law and are endowed with basic rights because of their individual uniqueness.

But have we really lived out this principle of equality? Today, the right clothing, the best zip code, the "in" crowd, or the total look have replaced slavery with a new inequality. The determinants are power and wealth. Are the rich better than the poor? Does the bank president have more rights and privileges than the pauper? Sadly enough, the inequalities between the affluent and the needy of our world are so great that a global change of heart is needed. In the words of John Paul II, "Those who are more influential, because they have a greater share of goods and common services, should feel responsible for the weaker and be ready to share with them all they possess."[4]

Other Essential Human Rights

In the last section we briefly examined the universality of rights, their origins in the dignity of life, their applicability for all and the right of free choice as central to all rights. We now wish to look at some particular rights deserving special consideration. At the top of the list stand political rights and civil liberties. These hold the key to an understanding of social freedom. Political rights involve participation in the enactment of laws, the election of government officials, and the general governance of society, whereas civil liberties relate to freedom of speech, the press, and associations of one's choosing.

Every schoolchild knows that the American Revolution was fought to obtain liberty from a tyrant. To read the detailed grievances over British abuse in the Declaration of Independence is to understand why the colonies rebelled. "The history of the present King of Great Britain is a history of repeated injuries and usurpations. . . . He has . . . dissolved Representative Houses . . . made judges dependent on his will alone . . . kept among us standing armies . . . [imposed] taxes without our consent . . . [suspended] our legislatures . . . plundered our seas, ravaged our coasts, burnt our towns, and destroyed the lives of our people."[5] Political and civil freedom are essential for democracy. It should go without saying that participation in the political process helps to guarantee good government.

The Communist Manifesto, issued by Marx and Engels in 1848, was a reaction to the economic exploitation of workers throughout Europe. Writing in the midst of the Industrial Revolution, when parents and children worked in mines and factories six days a week for twelve hours a day, they decried the tyranny of the factory owners as much as the founding fathers of our country condemned King George III. Liberal capitalism with its eye on profit has equated economic rights with the right of business to be free of governmental restraint. Marxist collectivism, on the other hand, suppresses free enterprise and political choice in favor of guaranteeing its citizens food, shelter, and clothing.

Thus, trying to find a balance in which people are free to engage in productive activity and enjoy its rewards and the equally important freedoms to obtain decent housing, sufficient nourishment, and other basic economic necessities challenges all people of good will. How far should a government go in regulating economic life? How much incentive is needed to keep people productive? In light of global poverty, what level of taxation of the wealthy is just? Clearly there is a long way to go in achieving economic rights for many, yet we cannot lose sight of the fact that these rights are basic to human dignity.

Another group of rights that are a part of our common heritage are social and cultural rights. These include everything from educational opportunities with clean classrooms and quality teaching to an openness for a broad range of creativity in the arts and literature. The recent policy of *glasnost,* i.e., openness to new ideas, in the Soviet Union (ushered in by Mikhail Gorbachev), has allowed artists and writers to express themselves with a candor previously unheard of in a communist society. One can only hope that it will continue.

Cultural rights include the preservation of family and national traditions. The customs, folkways, and other practices that connect a people with their past are basic human rights. When we consider how many of our forebears uprooted and killed many Native Americans and enslaved African blacks, or how the Chinese communist Cultural Revolution of the 1970s destroyed art treasures and tore families apart, we get some idea of the abuse of social and cultural rights. At its best, culture links us to and explains our past. Respect for social rights helps us to be civil with each other and work together for the common good. Let us conclude this section with a brief reflection on this idea of commonality.

We may understand the common good as the totality "of social conditions which make possible, for groups and for individuals, the full and timely attainment of their own perfection."[6] This definition addresses the need for a society to be organized in such a manner that both individuals and groups have ample opportunity to develop their talents and abilities to the fullest extent possible. We have seen how the biblical concept of peace emphasized harmony within the community. Promotion of this common good is the responsibility of all the members of a society.

Foundation of Human Rights

From a purely humanistic point of view, it would not be difficult to construct an argument for the foundation of rights to reside within our primary needs. The survival needs of food, shelter, and clothing; our need for self-worth, acceptance, and love; and the need for meaning or transcendence justify the protection of all the human rights we have enumerated in the previous two sections. All humans have a right to satisfy their basic needs.

The faith traditions of most major religions, however, go beyond a purely human foundation and ground human rights in God. " 'Let us make humankind in our image, according to our likeness.' . . . So God created humankind in his image . . . male and female he created them."[7] The biblical story of creation, which empowered the human family to create and multiply and to have dominion over the earth, stands as the foundation for human rights. It is God who has endowed us with our rights and has commanded us to respect the rights of each other. God called Moses to confront the Egyptians for enslaving the Hebrews and to liberate them from servitude. This root experience of the Jews, this passing over from bondage to freedom, acts as a paradigm for all people. We are called to freedom.

The early Christians, taking their lead from Jesus, did not place much emphasis on their own needs. Their highest priority was to announce the Good News about Jesus, the Messiah. In a sense, they were willing to die—and many did—for their right of religious freedom in proclaiming Jesus as the light of the world, but they did not see political, economic, or cultural rights as very important. In addition, they believed that the building-up of the Christian community for Jew and Gentile and an attitude of loving service to each other were far more important than challenging the political order of Rome. In point of fact, some persecution of Christians during the early centuries was a result of the Roman emperors' search for scapegoats for their own ineptitude.

In our own day the picture has changed entirely. Martin Luther King, Jr., epitomized the present Christian concern for following Christ when he organized against the unjust laws of segregation. Many Christians today tend to read the Bible within the framework of justice and peace. As such, they are more likely to be in the forefront of human rights advocacy than were their sisters and brothers of the past.

For Muslims, the Koran is the sacred book. "Take not life, which God has made sacred . . . we honor every human being. . . . Observe your duty to Allah . . . be staunch in justice."[8] Although there has been a long-standing dispute among Islamic scholars whether or not the Koran outlawed the practice of slavery, in practice it continued for many centuries within both Christianity and Islam in spite of the Bible or the Koran. So much for following the will of God!

It is to the enduring credit of the philosophers of the seventeenth and eighteenth centuries that we owe our present appreciation of human rights. In his second treatise on government, John Locke wrote that all human beings are originally in

> . . . a state of perfect freedom to order their actions, and dispose of their possessions and persons as they think fit within the bounds of the Law of Nature, without asking leave, or depending upon the Will of any other man.[9]

This initial state of freedom into which people are born is the natural foundation for our rights. With Protestants and Catholics warring among themselves, a new generation of thinkers arose who argued that each person was free to determine his or her own destiny. This dawning of modernity, where democracy gradually replaced the sovereignty of the king and the churches were disestablished, asserted the dignity of each person and brought about the emergence of political and social freedoms. In our own day, the Christian churches have made peace among themselves and have supported the structures of democracy. Thus, we find the third millennium beginning with a global consciousness concerning human rights with both secular and religious support.

Responsibilities

Duty is a four-letter word. It generally conjures up ideas about cleaning the house, doing one's laundry, or putting the cat out each night. On the other hand, the notion of responsibility is usually greeted with nods of approval. Why is this? Perhaps the question of duty somehow implies an obedience to a task, while responsibility connotes a willingness to respond to the needs of another person. In any case, duty or responsibility constitutes the other side of the coin of human rights. As the pundit said, "Your rights end at my nose!"

For most people this reciprocity of rights is granted in theory, however difficult it is to live it out in daily life.

Most quarrels, arguments, and litigation are the result of people's rights clashing with each other. Smokers want their rights protected even if it kills them. Many nonsmokers would ban tobacco completely. We have literally thousands of laws regarding right-of-ways for traffic and statutes regulating commerce, education, and sports. In the final analysis, all law is concerned with establishing the parameter of legal rights. But legal obligations and responsibilities are limited by common consent. We need to ask if there is a further agenda to human responsibility than the letter of the law.

In asking the question "Who is my neighbor?"[10] the teacher of the Jewish Law opened himself up to an entirely new message from Jesus. The story of the Good Samaritan that followed this question was to show God's concern for all people, both Jew and Samaritan. Not only does Jesus point out that the true neighbor is the one who binds up the wounds of those who are injured, but he also reminds his own people that anyone who helps another is doing God's will. Our responsibility for another is not predicated solely on the basis of public law. At a much more fundamental level we are called by way of moral obligation to be concerned about the welfare of everyone.

Naturally enough, these responsibilities begin with those who are closest to us. "Honor your father and mother" has always been interpreted to include not only parents, but also other family members and by extension all those who serve in the place of parents. Further along, we usually include the neighbor next door or people we know from work, school, or other associations. Jesus pushed for much more. We ought to be able to answer the question "Who is my neighbor?" with the principle of inclusion that was developed in Part I of the text. There is need in our time for an ever-expanding sense of neighbor.

Every human being has a right to adequate food, shelter, clothing, and the other previously enumerated rights. We in our turn have a responsibility to guarantee those rights. We are sometimes disheartened when we witness the global violations of human rights and feel powerless to respond. If we begin to think of ourselves as citizens of the world responsible for its future, we will take heart and realize that we can make a difference even in small ways. I know that the young teenager living in an orphanage in Bogotá, Colombia is helped by my check each month, and that the generosity of millions of people like me has helped millions of the poor. This spirit of generosity, this sense of responsibility, can change the world.

We began this chapter by stating that personal dignity represents the highest human value. The argument began by asking the student to step back for a moment and appreciate his or her own uniqueness as a person. The importance of caring for oneself in body, mind, and heart was stressed. We attempted to delineate the various categories of human rights, their universality, and the central task of social life to promote the common good. The basis for these rights from a psychological, biblical, and secular viewpoint was indicated, and we concluded the chapter by noting that for every right there is a responsibility.

In the next chapter we want to demonstrate that human solidarity is the companion value to personal dignity. Together these values constitute the heart of peace and justice education.

In a sense, all of the previous chapters in this book led up to these chapters on dignity and solidarity, and the remaining chapters will draw out the richness of these complementary values. As we continue to seek peace in our works of justice, let us be motivated by a sense of all people's dignity and our solidarity with them.

Notes

1   Frederick Franck, *Pilgrimage to Now/Here* (Maryknoll, N.Y.: Orbis Books, 1974), 9.

2   Ephesians 5:28.

3   *International Bill of Human Rights*, General Assembly of the United Nations, 1948, Article No. 1.

4   John Paul II, *Sollicitudo Rei Socialis* (Washington D.C.: United States Catholic Conference, 1987), para. 39.

5   Declaration of Independence.

6   *Propositions on the Dignity and Rights of the Human Person*, International Theological Commission (Washington, D.C.: United States Catholic Conference, 1986), 2.

7   Genesis 1:26–27.

8   Riffat Hassan, "On Human Rights and the Qur'anic Perspective," in *Human Rights in Religious Tradition*, ed. Arlene Awidler (New York: Pilgrim Press, 1982), 58.

9   *Encyclopedia of Philosophy*, Vols. 3–4, essay on John Locke by James Clapp (New York: Macmillan, 1967), 487.

10 Luke 10:29.

24

Unity of the Human Family

I am a Christian, and a Hindu, and a Moslem, and a Jew.

Mahatma Gandhi[1]

Signs of Unity

From the moment of bonding between egg and sperm, we were destined to be in relationship with others. The nourishment we received in the womb sustained our fragile life, and we continued to grow and develop in total dependence upon our mother. When we left a world of fluid and warmth, we emerged into a world of brightness, sound, and activity. Yet we remained completely helpless and in need of support from our parents. The sexual attraction and subsequent love of a man and woman, our parents, led to our birth. Their bonding together in marriage, their willingness to be open to the possibility of children, and their constant protection, nourishment, care, and love were the foundational gifts of life they gave us.

In establishing a case for our solidarity as one people, one human family, it is important to remind ourselves that every human person starts from the same essential biological determinant. We are bonded from birth to death. Just as the hands of an obstetrician or midwife brought us forth from the womb, so, too, will other hands lower us into a tomb. From the cradle to the grave we depend on others.

Whatever the nationality—be it Italian, Russian, Japanese, or Argentinian—the family unit represents the core of society. All races and colors of people, various religious traditions, and disparate cultures respect this sacredness. Love of children knows no boundaries among the human family. Tragically enough, there are instances of child abuse, but all realize that this is wrong and contrary to the love that most families show toward the young. The bonding that begins at birth continues through childhood.

By the time we are old enough for school, friendships have begun to form through the interaction of our families and neighbors and our own desires for belonging and recognition. As we grow older, we take on a sense of identity with our neighborhood or town. This is as true for remote Indian villages as it is for an inner-city area like the Bronx. Likewise, as people attend school, they take on further identification with these institutions. Sometimes it happens that these schools have such popularity (generally because of an outstanding sports program) that people will identify with them even without attending them. Probably the most outstanding example of this is the University of Notre Dame, which receives donations annually from its "subway alumni" throughout the country. Although the Notre Dame football team's excellence is the external symbol of the university's identity, beneath the surface, the subway alumni are mostly immigrant Catholics bonding with a public symbol of their faith. Celtic mania in Boston, Flyer fever in Philadelphia, or Mets madness in New York attest to the fact that people desire to bond together not only at the level of family and neighborhood, but also in the larger world of schools, teams, and churches.

Probably the strongest single binding energy among humans over the past one thousand years has been nationalism. Since the Middle Ages, loyalty and devotion to one's country have exerted greater force on people's consciousness than gender, race, color, and even religion. In fact, many of the religious wars were far more nationalist than religious. Within our own country we need think only of the parades and celebrations on Independence Day, the commemoration of Memorial Day, Veterans Day, Armed Forces Day, Flag Day, and the birthdays of Washington, Lincoln, and, most recently, Martin Luther King, Jr., to sense the bonding we experience as Americans. Bruce Springsteen's "Born in the U.S.A." was more than a hit tune.[2] It touched American pride and made us feel good about ourselves, in spite of its satirical analysis of the culture. Sylvester Stallone's characters, Rocky and Rambo, while caricatures of real people, represent the cultural traits of independence and individualism characteristic of many Americans. Throughout the world, in Eastern Europe, divided Ireland or Korea, in socialist Spain and Sweden, in Latin American dictatorships or capitalist Germany and Japan, the forces of nationalism still dominate the world. People everywhere identify strongly with their country. It is another sign of human bonding.

Degrees of Unity

One of the more interesting phenomena of human experience is its cyclical nature. This holds true for both personal individual lives and for the stories of nations and cultures. Life begins in total dependence, gradually moves toward a harmony of independence and interdependence, and finally winds down as we return to dependency. Shakespeare remarked that we are born and we die without teeth, without hair, and without understanding. The empires of Alexander the Great and the Caesars of Rome rose and fell. Recent history also testifies to the rapid demise of once-mighty nations. Witness the deterioration of the British Empire during the past fifty years. In a similar fashion, we should note the functional elasticity in relationships. The need to belong, to identify with a person, group, team, or cause, is satisfied when a mutuality of support is experienced. Healthy bonding occurs when the give-and-take between parties allows for individuality and creativity. When divisiveness and friction begin to dominate a relationship between individuals, families, groups, or nations, the unity is ruptured and isolation follows.

One of the major dangers present today is the unity based upon the false premise of blind loyalty. The totalitarian dictatorships of Hitler and Mussolini and the communist-dominated governments of one-party rule are perhaps the worst examples of the individual being forced to bond with the group. They are not, however, the only examples of this desire for uniformity.

Many fundamentalist churches demand complete and uncompromising loyalty from their followers. Different interpretations or understandings about faith are neither encouraged nor tolerated. Political parties expect loyalty toward the party platform and support for the candidates who are running for office. Frequently enough, blind loyalty to a particular group carries with it a rejection of other groups who view things differently. The Iran-Contra hearing of 1987 revealed strong ideological convictions on the part of several defendants who went to the point of breaking the law to support their worldview. On many campuses, sororities and fraternities, which were meant to provide friendship and cooperation within the university community, have lost all sense of their original purpose by becoming exclusive and cliquish. There is a real difference between bonding that respects individuality and that which expects blind obedience.

Recently, the influence of Japanese management style and a lessening of hostility between owners and workers have led to more cooperation between these former enemies. When workers can share in the profits of a company, help plan certain aspects of production, and not feel constant job stress, they are generally far more productive. We see again that respect for the dignity of each person creates natural bonds between people. Ideological ties and forced relationships are ultimately self-defeating.

In addition, our relationships with other people often take on the appearance of concentric circles. At the inner core are those relationships that mean the most to us, usually family and perhaps a close friend or two. Moving outward from the center, we experience a diminishing sense of unity with distant relatives and people with whom we have only a casual acquaintance. At any given moment, however, because of some circumstance or another, we may find ourselves strongly linked to another person or group. A neighbor who has suffered an illness or injury may for a time need a great deal of our support. Farther out from the center, we usually have little sense of connectedness on a personal level, but, in fact, may have strong ties because of faith or nationality.

If this is a true picture of relationships, is it expecting too much to ask that we become more inclusive toward the needy? Are we genetically condemned to live out the maxim "Out of sight, out of mind"? Is it true that students only call home when they need money? Consciousness raising, which is an aim of values education, challenges us to broaden the horizon of our lives. We are limited in time, space, talent, and abilities. We have responsibilities that start at home. But as the last chapter reminded us, we have a common Creator and share a common destiny.

The Problem of Disunity

When Adam blamed Eve and she in turn blamed the serpent, we saw the first classic example of "passing the buck." This is a mythological and, admittedly, minor example of disunity in ancient biblical literature. A few chapters later in the Genesis narrative we find the first murder. In a jealous rage Cain killed his brother Abel. Thus began a journey of alienation and disunity without apparent end.

History, from ancient times to the present, is littered with examples of fratricide, patricide, matricide, and sororicide in all ages, shapes, and forms. From petty fights and arguments to full-blown murder plots, the disunity, brokenness, and hatred among people is heavily documented. How many times each day do we feel some hostility toward another person? In driving to work, shopping, eating out (and frequently enough at home!), waiting in line for a movie, or just hanging out, the habits, idiosyncrasies, attitudes, beliefs, actions, looks, and behavior of others can cause us to feel everything from minor irritation to deep-seated resentment. How are we able to talk about the unity of the human family with any seriousness in the face of such evidence to the contrary?

If the situation were not bad enough on the personal level, we need only turn to the social milieu to find things infinitely worse. The writing of history, by and large, has been a chronicle of wars among tribes and nations. The major cities of ancient Greece, Athens and Sparta, were constantly at war. Rome, as we know, conquered everything in sight to build an empire from Africa to the Barents Sea and from Asia Minor to the British Isles. The colonial empires of the past few centuries thought very little about the exploitation and annihilation of native people from the jungles and plains of Africa to the mountains and valleys of Latin America. Spain, England, and Portugal outdid each other in their cruelty to blacks and Indians alike.

In our own country, a civil war was fought that cost more than a half-million injuries and deaths. The wars of the twentieth century have claimed almost one hundred million casualties.[3] Near the close of World War II, two nuclear weapons killed a half-million Japanese people, including thousands of children and other noncombatants. It was a final slaughter of the innocent in a war that killed more than fifty million noncombatants! Again, we ask how we can claim any degree of unity for the human family in the face of history. Pogroms, genocide, terrorism, wars, and poverty clearly seem to have the upper hand. Is there any hope left?

If we reflect upon our own personal lives, we find ourselves in a rhythmical pattern. Research into the biological patterns of our bodies offers some chemical evidence to what we observe in our mood shifts. In the case of a psychotic personality, these swings are extremely pronounced, while in normal individuals they ebb and flow within a relatively limited range. The point here is that we are quite changeable. We have all experienced times when we were content within ourselves and things were going well. Suddenly, without warning, we were thrown into turmoil.

Aside from the major causes of upset, such as an accident or bodily injury to ourselves or those close to us, even minor mishaps generate headaches. Crack your elbow, crick your neck, bump your shin, or be ignored, put down, or slighted in any way and you can be sure that your mood and feelings will change. Analogously, groups in society, and even whole nations, behave in similar ways. Italians, Irish, Poles, Germans, and virtually all ethnic groups who immigrated to the United States clung together for protection in what they found to be a hostile environment upon their arrival. It took several generations before these nationalities were accepted and assimilated. Thus, both personally and socially, we find that patterns of harmony and peace can change quickly into attitudes of suspicion and hostility. Humans, alone and in groups, generally live on an even keel, but the rough waters of life and other boats cruising by can often rock the most stable ship.

In a recent statement, Pope John Paul II reminded his listeners that they must have confidence in the human race.[4] Admittedly, we are both saints and sinners. Within each of us there is a wolf ready to devour whatever comes its way and ready to kill in protecting itself. But there is also a lamb. Our gentleness, warmth, and hospitality are evident in the way we care for our young and often try to avoid conflict. We are capable of evil as well as good. Although a Hobbesian view suggests a wolflike existence for humans, the present Pope thinks otherwise. He is not naive or blind to the suffering and pain that people inflict on one another. Nor does he dwell in a world of false optimism, assuming that the problems of today will go away by themselves. As a realist he knows that unity and disunity reside in every human heart. He calls people to reject their selfish side and live for others.

An Essential Human Bond

When Neil Armstrong set foot on the moon in the summer of 1969, he uttered those memorable words, "One small step for a man, one giant step for mankind." Space exploration at the end of the twentieth century is more than a milestone in the human adventure. For the first time in history we can leave our planet and look back at its beauty and unity. It was not by chance that Armstrong and fellow astronauts named their moon base "Tranquility," for they could actually see the tranquility of planet Earth before their very eyes. Back home, on television sets and radios, almost every person alive witnessed that event.

In life, as in space, we need to take the long view. The nineteenth-century gift to the human family was the discovery of our evolutionary past. Darwin opened the way for those who followed him to unearth the fossil remains of our prehistoric ancestors dating back hundreds of thousands of years. We have come a long way as human beings, and perhaps space exploration is inviting us to continue the journey. The science of paleontology and the study of anthropology leave little doubt about the unity of our species. Whatever our name, nationality, color of skin, size, or shape we are sisters and brothers. We can see our unity from space and we can understand it in the story of our past.

On a more personal level, we know that we are one family in time of trouble. Whether the tragedy be an earthquake, a serious accident, a volcanic eruption, a landslide, or disaster of whatever sort, it brings out the best in the human heart. There is unity in adversity. We all know of instances in our own lives when we lent a helping hand to someone who needed us. Many students spend long hours in the privacy of their rooms in the campus resident halls where they listen to the disillusionment and pain of their peers and offer them support and comfort. Even in the midst of evil we find untold goodness. Many concentration camp survivors testified to this. Stories of sharing a bit of food or a cigarette were not uncommon. All of these examples lend validity to humanity's fundamental unity, but let us add two additional reflections.

After many years of hostility and surrogate wars, the confrontation between the superpowers has begun to lessen. Will it pave the way for a new era of peace among the people of the world? Who would have imagined a U.S. president calling the Soviets an "evil empire" in 1984 and then signing a nuclear arms treaty with them in 1988? While there are many issues unsolved in the treaty ratification, there is a new willingness by the Soviets and Americans to work for reduction of nuclear arms. Historical movements are hard to assess, especially if one is happening before our eyes, but there is little doubt that many people in the world today are hard at work trying to prevent war and develop peaceful means for conflict resolution. Although efforts have failed to reduce global poverty, malnutrition, and environmental pollution, and several internecine conflicts remain, there are the beginnings of a global consciousness about life on planet Earth. It is much too early to project what the world will be like when the present generation of college students reaches old age, but it appears that the twenty-first century may truly be an age of peace.

The confluence of East and West is also evident in the area of religion. At a recent major religious conference in the town of Assisi, where St. Francis, a model of gentleness and humility since the twelfth century, spent much of his life, the heads of every major religion in the world convened to pray for peace. With new lines of communication now open among most church groups, the Catholic pope stood beside the Dalai Lama from Tibet, Shinto priests from Japan, and others representing their own faith persuasions. Without compromising what they believe to be the central truth of God's revelation, they nonetheless are able to give witness to their common bonds as a human family. People have different histories and experiences that give rise to different beliefs and value systems. Nations, as well as individuals, are in different stages of growth. Some have learned to work together and to respect individual differences. Others, like adolescents, struggle with questions of identity, or like children, still depend on parental authority figures to govern them. Whatever the stage of development, all religions teach that love of neighbor is the highest priority. If we learn that lesson, we are truly educated.

Building Solidarity

Human solidarity builds on a willingness to change those attitudes, beliefs, and actions that are contrary to love of self and others. It means exchanging one set of values for better ones. We acknowledge that change may be slow and difficult, and we realize that some people must make radical decisions because they are far off the mark; nonetheless, dignity for each person and solidarity with all are life's chief tasks.

The Meditation Room of the United Nations building in New York City is empty. This was done purposely, in order to avoid offending the major world religions by excluding any of their faith symbols. Somehow, no symbols implied total acceptance. At first blush, it seems to make sense, but the emptiness of the room may well epitomize the central problem of our time. We fail to celebrate particularity. Although we are aware of the enormous variety in language, customs, styles, art, etc., throughout the world, we fail to appreciate our difference. Celebrating our own particularity and acknowledging that of others leads to a sense of solidarity. Solidarity on the local level affirms the uniqueness of each person.

Globally, it "includes all faiths and cultures without obliterating them; . . . [and] is the *cure* for the core of our greatest contemporary trouble."[5] To think that solidarity consists of McDonald's in Peking and Moscow is to miss the idea of particularity completely. We need to celebrate, not subjugate, our differences. When I admire, accept, and love you in all your humanness, and you accept me, we are living in solidarity.

The term *solidarity*, important as it may be, implies a steady state situation. *Community*, while conveying a similar togetherness, is much more dynamic. We might say that community is solidarity in action. Scott Peck, the noted author-physician, writes that "the capacity for transformation is the most essential characteristic of human nature."[6] When we think of ourselves as possessing this power of transformation, this ability to change, to grow, to bring something new to each day, we are less likely to get trapped in a boring routine. For example, marriage is often characterized as going through the stages of romance, disillusionment, and joy.

After the initial glow wears off, couples wake up to the reality of living with someone who has different tastes, temperaments, habits, and values. Divorce is the result of people being unable or unwilling to transform themselves. Only when transformation occurs for the sake of love do couples find joy in marriage.

Community building goes through much of the same process. Small groups attempting to experience community inevitably find that after the initial rush of enthusiasm, personality clashes begin to appear. Unless the individuals in the group are willing to transform themselves, no growth will take place. Globally, we find similar situations. The current process of restructuring or *perestroika*, which the Soviet Union is undergoing, is a response to the bureaucratic malaise that had gripped the country for the past several decades. In short, if relationships are to remain growing, active, and alive, they must be dynamic. They need to be constantly transformed and renewed. Living in solidarity and building community, similar to our own personal development, provides us with a daily challenge.

In the following chapters of Part III, we shall examine the extensions and implications of our core values, personal dignity, and human solidarity. By recalling that all of our beliefs, attitudes, and actions constitute our value system, and that these values give meaning to our lives, we have now a standard by which to measure ourselves. If the truest and richest meaning to life can only be realized within the context of dignity and solidarity, our search for meaning has a clear direction. We shall see that this direction leads us to justice, truth, freedom, peace, nonviolence, and, ultimately, to love, the richest and most precious value of all.

Notes

1   Louis Fisher, *Gandhi* (New York: Mentor Books, 1954), 130.

2   Bruce Springsteen, "Born in the U.S.A.," (New York: Columbia Records, 1984).

3   *Information Please Almanac* (Boston: Houghton Mifflin, 1988), 313.

4   John Paul II, *Sollicitudo Rei Socialis* (Washington D.C.: United States Catholic Conference, 1987), para. 47.

5   M. Scott Peck, *Different Drum* (New York: Simon & Schuster, 1987), 20.

6   Ibid., 178.

25

Satyagraha/Justice

To be true to one's self, to trust that the world is good and that others are not evil, although at times their behavior is wrong, is at the center of human life. This inner energy of spirit is necessary for each person to develop within themselves, if they are to control their own destiny and direct the political, economic and cultural life of the world toward the truth.

Mahatma Gandhi[1]

A Singular Life

From his birth on October 2, 1869, in the seacoast village of Porbandar, India, until his death seventy-nine years later at the hands of an assassin, few people have ever impacted the world as did Mohandas K. Gandhi. When the news of his death was received, the United Nations flag was lowered to half-mast; world leaders mourned his loss; millions wept openly.

As a boy he was shy and did not do well at school. However, since his family was financially secure, he was sent abroad to England and eventually received a law degree. Returning to India, he experienced the humiliation of British rule in a legal hearing and decided to go to South Africa, where he remained for almost twenty-one years.

When he finally went back to India in 1914, he brought with him the lessons he had learned about facing up to injustice. He organized an ambulance corps to help the British during World War I, but following the war he began the long struggle against them for a free India. *Mahatma,* the title by which he gradually came to be known, signifies someone who is held in the highest esteem because of his goodness and wisdom. There is no more fitting way to continue our exploration of personal dignity and human solidarity than by reflecting on the life of Gandhi.

The major turning point in his life was an incident on a train ride in South Africa shortly after his arrival. He had purchased a first-class ticket but was told by a white man, moments after taking his seat, that he would have to give it up. Brown skin in South Africa was as unacceptable as black. When he protested, he was thrown bodily from the train by the police. Although he could have found seating in the third-class section, he choose to spend a chilly night in the train station at Maritzburg, not far from Pretoria, the capital of South Africa. The incident gave him a new sense of direction for his life. He determined that while he might be physically weak, he could be morally strong.[2] Gandhi began to champion the rights of minorities by standing against the unjust laws that discriminated against minority groups.

His fame grew and upon his return to India, he protested the many injustices that the native populations had to endure there. In his famous March-to-the-Sea during the spring of 1930, he walked 241 miles in 24 days, an action that riveted the attention of all India. When he arrived, he picked up some salt left by the waves. This broke the British law, since the Salt Tax Act made it a crime to use salt not purchased from the government. Gandhi was arrested and shortly thereafter hundreds of his followers were beaten senseless when they tried to breach the Dharsana Salt Works 150 miles north of Bombay.[3] The Oscar award–winning film *Gandhi,* by Richard Attenborough, graphically depicts the brutality of the British in responding to Gandhi's militant, yet nonviolent, resistance. Gandhi was a pragmatist who only attempted what he thought he could achieve. His willingness to continue the struggle against injustice came from an inner strength and a life-style that gave witness to simplicity.

The Sanskrit proverb "Forgiveness is the ornament of the brave" characterizes one of the dominant features of Gandhi's personality. In all of his dealings with government officials, he never sought to gain the upper hand or to see them as the enemy. This forgiveness of spirit grew out of a simple way of living that emerged for Gandhi during his lifetime. The famous picture of his final possessions: a bowl and a spoon, a pair of sandals, his glasses, a book of songs, and his watch pay tribute to the austerity in which he came to believe wholeheartedly. It was as if the simplicity of life allowed him the freedom to live without fear of others. This in turn prevented him from seeing those who opposed him as enemies.

Gandhi's contribution to the human race was to break the cycle of violent revolution and offer an alternative. One did not have to choose between passivity and violence. There was a better way. He learned from the writings of Henry David Thoreau, the nineteenth-century American naturalist, and the Russian novelist, Count Leo Tolstoy, that nonviolent civil disobedience was a far more humane way to find freedom than with a gun. He chose the path of nonviolence because he knew that *truth* was an elusive term. How can I be so sure of my truth that I would kill you for it? Nonviolence was the result of desire to seek truth, but in a way that another's truth might be respected.

Satyagraha

Various English terms have been used to characterize the dynamic word, *satyagraha*. It is a term coined by Gandhi in his native Indian Gujarati dialect to describe the active energy needed to resist injustice. His mind and heart were already living out of a conviction that injustice must be resisted, but the phrase *passive resistance*, which many people used, implied weakness. Amusing as it may seem, he ran a contest in the newspaper *Indian Opinion*, which he edited, in order to find a new term for this inner strength. The winning entry combined the Indian words, *sat* (truth) and *agraha* (firmness), and thus was born, *satyagraha.*[4] The commonly accepted English words in use today are *truth-force* or *soul-force,* both of which describe that power or inner quality possessed by a practitioner of satyagraha. Gandhi said that:

> A satyagrahi bids goodbye to fear. He is, therefore, never afraid to trust the opponent. Even if the opponent plays him false twenty times, the satyagrahi is ready to trust him the twenty-first time, for the implicit trust in human nature is the very core of his creed.[5]

Satyagraha excludes the use of violence. Because people are never able to know the whole truth, how can one be absolutely sure of one's cause? Is there not truth on both sides of an argument? Gandhi was a seeker of truth, not the sole possessor. "I am but a seeker after truth . . . but I admit I have not found it. To find truth completely is to realize oneself and one's destiny, that is, to become perfect. I am painfully conscious of my imperfections."[6]

Seeking after truth, however, is not to imply that there is total uncertainty about moral issues. We may recall from chapter 21 that truth is connected to a respect for life. Child abuse, torture, nuclear war, and concentration camps are realities that have happened and can happen again. Their falseness, or evilness, lies in their total disregard for personal dignity. For example, a centuries-old problem that Gandhi tried to address was the caste system among the Hindus. The four castes in order of importance were: the Brahmans, or priests; the Kshatriyas, or rulers and warriors; the Vaisyas, or craftsmen and land owners; and the Sudras, or laborers. Below these, not even considered Hindus, were the millions of the poor outcast untouchables.

Although in his early life he accepted the traditional system of caste, he gradually came to realize how debilitating this system was to those at the bottom, and how well it continued to serve the interests of those at the top. In similar fashion, the prejudice against blacks in the United States was taken for granted until white people began to realize the hypocrisy of discrimination and prejudice in a country professing equality.

Thus, we see that each age has its own truths to seek. Am I antagonistic toward minorities or different religions? Do I make fun of homosexuals? On a scale of one to ten, how do I rate myself in terms of honesty and truthfulness? It is important to remember that truth is tested in the specific, concrete situations of daily life.

Another aspect of satyagraha concerns the idea of freedom. For Gandhi and the people of his country, freedom meant economic independence and home rule. From the early sixteenth century the European empires had dominated native populations throughout the world. Although by the end of the nineteenth century the British were supposedly enlightened rulers, they nonetheless controlled the economy for their own benefit. For example, huge amounts of cotton grown in India were shipped to England for processing into clothing, which in turn was shipped back to India for people to buy. Gandhi saw this situation as one of economic dependence for India and urged people to spin their own fabric.

Likewise, the struggle for home rule was a struggle for political independence. *Swaraj* was an ancient Indian word that Gandhi and others began to use for economic freedom and political independence.[7] While *satyagraha* represented the energy and willpower to oppose evil, *swaraj* meant the goal or destination toward which one was drawn. The long journey upon which India was embarked during Gandhi's lifetime led to freedom. He believed that only by using the fuel of truthforce that, by definition, was truly potent but not volatile, would true freedom be achieved.

Justice

A blindfolded woman holding a balance scale in her hand is the personification of justice. We are immediately drawn by the twin symbols of objectivity and equality. On the one hand, justice implies that decisions about right and wrong necessitate a disposition of impartiality. The priest in the confessional, the judge in a law court, and the labor arbiter are expected to be disinterested observers, simply trying to judge evidence on the merits and facts of the case before them, not on the basis of favoritism. On the other hand, the balance scale represents a fundamental fairness in weighing evidence, allowing the scales to tip in whatever direction the evidence determines. Objectivity and equality, then, are essential ingredients of justice.

In *The Moral Choice*, Daniel Maguire, professor of ethics at Marquette University, argues that justice is "the minimal manifestation of the foundational moral experience and the minimal manifestation of other-love."[8] Maguire asserts that the foundational moral experience is a universal concern for the person, or, as we have indicated elsewhere, the value of personal dignity. Furthermore, the ancient Greek philosophers and the Christian thinkers who inherited their tradition saw justice as the obligation "to render to each what is due to them." All of these different dimensions of justice—objectivity, equality, a minimal concern for another, and a responsibility to meet the needs of others—are categorized under the headings of: (1) commutative, (2) legal, and (3) distributive justice. Let us examine each of them more closely.

We all know that in spite of our best efforts there are people we do not like. Also, even in the best of relationships, there are times when either one or the other party is out of sorts, or an argument arises where both people seem to have an honest difference of opinion. Democrats may argue with their Republican counterparts on the floor of the Senate, conservatives and liberals may engage in a heated television debate, and girlfriend-boyfriend relationships have been known for occasional disagreements. Throughout all of this, justice is done if respect for the opponent is retained. In a sense, we may say that commutative justice is a five-dollar expression for common courtesy.

In the second case, legal justice characterizes the relationship between an individual and the political order. All nations have laws that its citizens must obey under penalty of punishment. In democracies, because the people make the laws themselves they are generally evenhanded and fair. At least in theory all are equal before the law. Rules for voting, trial by jury, right to counsel, and protection against arbitrary arrest are regulations that signify fairness for all citizens. Rule by military dictatorship or a one-party system, as is the case in most communist countries, frequently evidence little respect for the individual.

This brings us to the third major category, which is known as distributive justice. In his *Theory of Justice,* John Rawls, a Harvard philosopher, suggests that, all things being equal (he postulates a situation in which everyone in a given group knows nothing about the others' abilities), people will choose equality over preference.[9] The phrase "all things being equal," however, belies the natural inequalities that exist in terms of talent, ability, education, age, etc. Some people are more energetic, productive, and responsible than others and have a right to the benefits of their labor. But because we are one human family and are called to live in solidarity, those who are blessed with a larger share of the world's bounty are obligated to share with the less fortunate.

Thus far, we have seen how the concept of justice as a philosophical principle has had a long and multidimensional history. For the most part, our reflections have dealt with a secular understanding of justice. Let us attend now to biblical justice.

Biblical Justice

"I am the LORD; I act with steadfast love, justice, and righteousness in the earth, for in these things I delight, says the LORD."[10] Perhaps no passage in the Bible sums up the disposition of God as does this one. For the most part, as we have seen from our discussion of secular justice, there are no thoughts of love, mercy, and kindness in the world's viewpoint of justice. With God it is different, since God's justice is always concerned with the whole person—physical, psychological, and spiritual. In order to understand God's justice, we must first concede that God is constrained to act always from love.

When the apostle John says that "God is love,"[11] he identifies the creative goodness, the saving mercy, and the comforting spirit that we find in a Trinitarian God. Punishment for an

offense against the law in secular society is primarily used for
deterrence and retribution. With God, punishment for sin is
always associated with the hope of changing the sinner's heart,
bringing one to conversion. While the Ten Commandments
are couched in negative terms (thou shalt nots), in reality, they
are positive directions. The first three call us to love God; the
remaining seven tell us to love our neighbor. We see that justice
for God involves far more than the letter of the law.

Nowhere in the Bible do we find more instances of God's
justice mentioned than in the writings of the prophets.

> Wash yourselves; make yourselves clean;
> remove the evil of your doings
> from before my eyes;
> cease to do evil,
> learn to do good;
> seek justice,
> rescue the oppressed,
> defend the orphan,
> plead for the widow.[12]

To seek justice was to relieve the suffering of the oppressed
within society. The prophetic tradition began as a reaction against
the excesses of the rulers of the people. Following the establishment of the Hebrew kingdom by David about 1000 B.C.,
abuses immediately began to appear. In the words of the prophet
Amos:

> Alas for those who lie on beds of ivory,
> and lounge on their couches,
> and eat lambs from the flock . . .
> but are not grieved over the ruin of [others].[13]

God's justice is not simply a matter of staying out of harm's
way; rather it is walking the way of righteousness. The prophets
kept calling the people to walk on a pathway of justice where
concern for the widows and orphans was the sign of God's
plan. The pathway of God's justice was an attitude of mind that

enabled a faithful Jew to live a just life by joining reverence to God with concern for the neighbor.

The Hebrew words *misphat* and *sedagah* are most closely associated with God's justice. *Misphat* was used to mean both the suit before a judge and the verdict as well.[14] At other times, it referred to God as Judge and even to the punishment inflicted on those who were guilty of injustice. *Sedagah*, however, was more an attitude of mind or path of righteousness. These words taken together convey a sense that God's justice is all-encompassing and inclusive. All creation stands under the judgment of God.

In our own day, society, which because of its size and population is vastly more complex than ancient Israel, must find other ways to care for its widows and orphans. There is always a need among charitable organizations for volunteer help. Hospital volunteers, Big Brother and Big Sister programs, and adopt-a-child groups need support to continue their good works. What most of us do not realize is that these are works not only of charity, but also of justice. Because we see justice in secular legal terms, we forget our biblical roots that merge justice and love. In God's eyes, we are obligated to help others. We cannot be indifferent. Furthermore, that part of the crop left for the needy among the rural Israeli people may be seen today as welfare programs that assist the poor.

Particularity

We began this chapter by looking briefly at the life of Mahatma Gandhi, a man who claimed not to be a mystic, but a politician. By profession, he was a lawyer; by conviction, he was fully human. We saw how his distaste for the injustices, discrimination, and prejudice heaped upon blacks and Indians alike led him to satyagraha, truth-force, a power to resist opponents, but always with the hope of winning them over. Are not satyagraha and God's misphat strikingly similar? Because Gandhi, born and raised as a Hindu, was drawn naturally to a life of detachment, it took a great deal of inner strength for him to stand against injustice. His exposure to Christianity, most notably to the gospel stories of Jesus confronting the hypocritical leaders of his own time, offered him the example of others who stood against evil.

However, no matter how many models we have, no matter how much we theorize about satyagraha and misphat, the justice of God and the force of truth are meaningless if we do not place them in the context of particularity. It is always in the concrete that life is lived. This was true for Jesus in his troubles with the Pharisees; it was true for Gandhi in confronting the British; and it will be true for us in confronting whatever injustice appears.

Particularity on a personal level means examining our own attitudes and behavior, our values, from the perspective of a satyagrahi, one who lives with God's justice in mind. We all know of situations and circumstances where a particular person is shunned by the group or made fun of because of some mannerism or personality trait. Do we find ourselves joining in the ridicule, perhaps adding fuel to the fire by our own caustic remarks? Do we come to the defense of someone who is mocked? Do we find in another's weakness something to be taken advantage of or an opportunity to help? Most college students know friends who are incipient alcoholics or drug abusers. If I am an alcoholic, do I have the inner strength to admit my problem and seek help? If a friend suffers from alcoholism, do I have the courage to confront him or her and offer a way out?

Gandhi constantly called upon his Indian sisters and brothers to straighten their backs and stand against the British oppressors. Can we not call each other, especially those we call friends, to stand tall against the current personal evils in our culture, e.g., drug and alcohol abuse, wealth and power as the measure of success, indifference toward the poor, sexual promiscuity, and loss of faith in the justice of God? As Gandhi said, "A satyagrahi bids goodbye to fear." More than ever, we need young adults to measure their lives in terms of moral courage.

The particularity of biblical justice and truth-force come together in the political arena. Our citizenship not only offers us rights, it also demands responsibility. On a recent class trip to Washington, D.C., where students visited the offices of their congressional representatives, the majority were impressed by the accessibility to Congress and the enormous importance of the work being done. The United States federal government plans to raise and spend over one trillion dollars each year during the 1990s. Do we care how it's raised, or where it goes? Current taxes for the wealthiest 20 percent of the population have dropped markedly in the past decade. The tax burden was shifted to the middle class. Furthermore, the military budget doubled from 1980 to 1988, while school-lunch programs, child-care subsidies and aid to women and dependent children were cut by 30 percent.[15] Homelessness in America is at an all-time high, due in part to a policy of cutting funds for federal low-income housing programs. What is involved here is not a question of partisan politics; it is not a matter of liberal vs. conservative thinking. At stake is a decent place to live, an adequate, nutritionally sound diet, clean air and water, and educational and employment opportunities; in short, fairness and justice for all of our citizens. Beyond that, we must continue to extend a hand to our sisters and brothers in the global human family.

Living out a vision where truth-force energizes us to work for a just society is by no means an easy task. Indeed, it is the work of a lifetime. What is important to realize, however, is that it can be done. The specialness of being human is the ability to choose. If we cherish the values of human worth and social solidarity; if we build character by meeting the challenges and conflicts of life with the firm conviction that justice is right; if we decide to hold this vision before ourselves each day, then we will find an inner peace in the knowledge that we are living a truly human life.

Notes

1 Louis Fisher, *Gandhi* (New York: Mentor Books, 1954), 40.

2 Ibid., 22.

3 Ibid., 100.

4   Mohandas K. Gandhi, *An Autobiography* (Boston: Beacon Press, 1957), 318–19.

5   Fisher, *Gandhi*, 36.

6   Gerard A. Vanderhaar and Mary Lou Kownacki, OSB, eds., *Way of Peace: A Guide to Nonviolence* (Erie, Penn.: Pax Christi USA, 1987), 41.

7   Ignatius Jesudasan, S.J., *A Gandhian Theology of Liberation* (Maryknoll, N.Y.: Orbis Books, 1984), 47.

8   Daniel Maguire, *The Moral Choice* (Minneapolis: Winston Press, 1979), 95.

9   John Rawls, *A Theory of Justice* (Cambridge: Harvard University Press, 1971).

10   Jeremiah 9:24.

11   1 John 4:8.

12   Isaiah 1:16–17.

13   Amos 6:4–6.

14   Eliezer Berkovits, "The Meaning of Biblical Justice," in *Man and God: Studies in Biblical Theology* (Detroit: Wayne State University Press, 1969), 189.

15   Barbara Howell, *U.S. Hunger: The Problem Grows* (Washington, D.C.: Bread for the World, 1988), 2.

26

Liberation/Peace

They shall beat their swords into plowshares,
and their spears into pruning hooks;
nation shall not lift up sword against nation,
neither shall they learn war any more.

Isaiah 2:4

Interior Freedom

The search for freedom, as for truth, occurs within the self. We
have already seen how human development is a gradual process
physically, psychologically, and intellectually. Since our moral
development is contingent upon our freedom of choice, we
might say that we can grow morally only insofar as we develop
our capacity for freedom. In the early years of life, we act to
satisfy our instinctual needs. As we grow older we begin to assert
our autonomy and seek to rely upon our own resources. The
verbal battles between parents and teenagers reflect this growing need for freedom.

Freedom, in its true sense, does not mean that we can do
anything we want. Many of the passions and appetites of the

317

body could easily lead us to hurt ourselves. True freedom means that we have learned to control our biological drives and have also learned to respect the freedom of others. The person who knows how to say no after a few drinks, the one who is able to put aside a pet project in order to listen to the pain of another, and the parents who can let go of parenting as their children mature are people who live in freedom. There is an inner sense that one is not controlled by either internal or external forces.

American psychiatrist Erich Fromm wrote that "an individual has no choice but to unite himself with the world in the spontaneity of love and productive work, or else to seek a kind of security by such ties to the world as destroy his freedom and the integrity of his individual self."[1] Our most instinctual drive is toward self-preservation. This leads us in time of danger either to attack what confronts us or to acquiesce to its power. Fromm realized that many people relinquish their freedom because they are threatened by the internal demons of anxiety and fear or the external forces of authority and power.

Adolescents and young adults, in particular, are frequently inhibited in their behavior because they fear the disapproval of their peers. This is true both in avoiding goodness (fear of being laughed at or of being called a "goodie") and in doing harm (playing chicken in an auto race or chug-a-lugging beer). We all have our own internal demons—from the minor fear of trying something new to the major difficulties of anxiety, depression, and addiction. Many students break out in a cold sweat when they are called upon in class, while others are embarrassed or shy when relating to the opposite sex. Only insofar as we are able to break down the barriers of our ignorance and fear do we grow in freedom.

In many respects, this is the primary task of life.

The consequences of escaping from freedom are many and varied. One of the most poignant stories in the gospels tells of the rich young man who was asked to give up his possessions and follow Jesus. "When the young man heard this word, he went away grieving, for he had many possessions."[2] How many of us become attached to wealth, rank, or other status symbols that serve as chains to keep us from a freer life?

Another consequence of avoiding freedom is intellectual stagnation. One of the saddest results of playing the success game in the United States is the narrowing of educational horizons for many college students. Instead of using higher education to open their minds to new and challenging ideas, many choose easy courses in order to ensure a high grade-point average, or they choose areas of study that are narrow and limiting. The better schools, of course, demand a core curriculum that ensures some breadth of learning for their students, but many do not. Ultimately, whether through fear, attachments, laziness, or a poor self-image, we rob ourselves of new possibilities for life when we avoid freedom. In the final analysis, however, the most important consequence of inner freedom is the satisfaction of knowing that we have made our own choices. To reject the fears and addictions to which all of us are prone and accept the freedom for which we were created calls forth our best efforts. It is a worthy calling.

External Freedom

The Statue of Liberty at the foot of New York harbor embodies the spirit of political freedom that has been the hallmark of our country since its beginning over two hundred years ago. The millions of immigrants who saw the Lady holding high the torch of liberty knew that this was a land of freedom and opportunity. Granted that full freedom has not come for women, blacks, and other minorities and that our government has had its fair share of corruption and venality; nevertheless, the civil and political freedom in the United States ranks among the highest in the world.

In general, external freedom means the right for people to control their own affairs; it does not mean escape from social obligations. External freedom is realized more fully in the areas of political rights and civil liberties, though in recent years there have been efforts to include the concept of economic rights in the discussion of freedom. Civil liberties, such as freedom of the press, the right to associate freely, and guarantees to worship without interference, protect the rights of minorities. Majority rights are preserved by the political processes of free elections, representative democracy, and separation of powers. In the ideal order of things, all people in our world should live free from the coercion of others.

There has always been a high price paid for freedom, because those in power are reluctant to share it. History has recorded many instances of slave uprisings, but few successful ones. Indeed, it has only been during the past half-century that the average person might expect to live in freedom. Most of the battles and wars during the Middle Ages were for control of lands by one king or another, not for the freedom of the individual. As we have previously mentioned, it was the Enlightenment philosophers, notably Locke and Montesquieu, who laid the foundations for political liberty. The French Revolution in 1789 followed on the heels of our own. Their cry of "liberty, equality, fraternity" marked the beginning of the end for the reign of kings and queens.

Today we find the struggle for freedom still raging throughout the world. It has many different faces and a complexity of circumstances, but it still centers on the right of individuals to self-determination. The majority black population of South Africa has fought against the injustices of apartheid for generations. The killing and torture of thousands of blacks has raised the cry of moral outrage from democratic societies. In our country, the debate continues over economic sanctions, some believing that a total embargo will force the white rulers to capitulate, others seeing that policy as detrimental to the blacks. Elsewhere, the Palestinians are engaged with the Israelis for a homeland; the Irish fight to oust British soldiers from their native soil; and guerrilla terrorists, or freedom fighters, depending upon one's political allegiance, fight wars of independence from Angola to the Philippines and from Peru to El Salvador.

Since 1973, Freedom House, an organization designed to measure the respective freedom in the countries of the world, has published the results of an annual survey on each state or territory based on the relative freedom that exists there. On a scale of 1 to 7, they range from "free" to "not free." This judgment is made by examining the political rights and civil liberties within each country. Political rights guarantee a fully competitive electoral process and rule by elected officials. Civil liberties are judged upon guarantees to publish opinions with an intent to influence the political process. The freest countries are those that possess the highest degree of political rights and civil liberties. The following is a sampling of countries chosen to illustrate the information available from the survey for the year 1991.

Argentina
economy: capitalist/statist
polity: multiparty
population: 32,300,000

political rights: 1
civil liberties: 3
status: free

El Salvador
economy: capitalist-statist
polity: multiparty (military influence)
population: 5,300,000

political rights: 3
civil liberties: 4
status: partly free

Israel
economy: mixed capitalist
polity: parliamentary democracy
population: 4,600,000

political rights: 2
civil liberties: 2
status: free

Kenya
economy: capitalist
polity: one party
population: 24,600,000

political rights: 6
civil liberties: 6
status: partly free

Philippines
economy: capitalist-statist
polity: presidential democracy
population: 56,800,000

political rights: 3
civil liberties: 3
status: partly free

Poland
economy: mixed statist
polity: democracy
population: 37,800,000

political rights: 2
civil liberties: 2
status: partly free[3]

In conclusion, this section on external freedom, measured in terms of freely elected governments, gives us some sense of the continuous struggle to achieve and maintain freedom throughout the world where political and civil rights are denied to many. Those of us who have maintained our freedoms should cherish them, participate actively in the political process, and choose representatives who are committed to dignity, solidarity, and freedom for all.

Liberation Theology

In the past two decades, Latin America has experienced a cry for liberation. It was a cry from the voices of the poor, most of whom were Roman Catholic. The Catholic Church had experienced a reform and renewal of its rites, practices, and its beliefs in the early 1960s, and, as a consequence, a new way of thinking began. Theological reflection, instead of starting with questions about God as it traditionally did, decided to start with questions about human experience. It was called an anthropological shift and was, in many respects, as profound as the Copernican shift of the Renaissance.

Classical theology made distinctions between beginners and those in more advanced stages of spirituality. This advanced stage was monastic in character and confined primarily to clerics and religious. In many ways, it was removed from worldly concerns and was essentially an intellectual discipline combining faith and reason.[4] The renewal of the Catholic Church emphasized a return to the roots of its life in the gospel of Jesus Christ and a willingness to engage its faith tradition in the context of the modern world. Thus began a liberation of theology, which in the words of Gustavo Gutiérrez, a Peruvian priest who pioneered its acceptance, "offers a new way to do theology. Theology as critical reflection on historical praxis is a liberating theology. . . . It is a theology that is open—in the protest against trampled human dignity, in the struggle against the plunder of the vast majority of people, in liberating love, and in the building of a new, just, and fraternal society."[5]

When the Latin American bishops began to do theology in this new way, their immediate attention was drawn to the squalor and misery in which the vast majority lived and to the oppressive governmental systems that supported this societal order. Marxism, as a philosophy for analyzing society, had made inroads into much of Latin America, and so it was not surprising that some of the Marxist critique began to play a role in theological reflection. The economic connections between the capitalist centers of Europe and the United States and the wealthy elites of Rio de Janeiro, Bogotá, and Buenos Aires were more than obvious.

Whereas in previous centuries the Church had been aligned with the rich and powerful, it now began to take the side of the poor. The biblical renewal within the Church helped it to see that Jesus' mission was "to bring good news to the poor . . . to proclaim release to the captives, and recovery of sight to the blind, to let the oppressed go free, to proclaim the year of the Lord's favor."[6] Yet everywhere the Church looked in Latin America, it saw the same signs of the times: lack of health care and education and the general conditions of poverty and tyranny. It appeared that one primary cause was a capitalist system of exploitation, greed, and control. The teachings of Jesus and the voice of God in other biblical sources condemned oppression and spoke for liberation.

A great deal has been written about liberation theology during the past decade and it is beyond the scope of this text to do little more than outline its major themes. It has been both praised and criticized by the Vatican: in the first instance, for its deep concern for the needy of the world, and, in the second instance, for its admiration of Marxism.

Leonardo Boff, a Brazilian Franciscan theologian, was severely rebuked by Joseph Cardinal Ratzinger, prefect of the Sacred Congregation for the Doctrine of the Faith, for his indictment of the Catholic Church in his book *Church: Charism and Power.*[7] As a liberation theologian, Boff lamented the conservative atmosphere of the Church and called for more democratic structures. In another work, Boff noted several key themes in liberation theology. Among them are: (1) a living faith includes the practice of liberation; (2) the living God sides with the oppressed; (3) faith should energize politics and economics; (4) Jesus took on oppression to set us free; and (5) the Church is a sign and instrument of liberation.[8] Because of its particularity to place and time, however, it is not easy to generalize its content. Theological reflections on liberation have sprung up in Asia, Africa, India, and almost every Third World country with a sizeable Christian population. How would it fit for the Catholic Church in North America?

Is it possible to begin a consciousness-raising process about the spiritual poverty so prevalent in our own society? The poor have the advantage of knowing their poverty; the wealthy do not. Or, at least, it is not so obvious. If one begins to look at the divorce rate, alcohol and drug addiction statistics, the disdain for the homeless and needy, the pitiful decay of many inner cities, the vast numbers of people who find solace in empty television programs, amoral literature, and tabloid sleaze, we can sense the malaise afoot in our country.

Peace

Peace is a word with many meanings. The glory days of the Roman Empire have frequently been referred to as the Pax Romana, the peace of Rome. It was surely a time of peace in the Roman sense, that is, where the empire imposed its will on the tribes and other nations it had conquered. This idea about peace as the imposition of order has carried down to the present day. Within many family units, it is not uncommon to see a father demand obedience from both his wife and his children. On the job, there are innumerable situations where bosses impose their wills on employees for the sake of peace. Many classrooms in our nation's schools are controlled by mini-dictators who berate and coerce their students into submissive behavior in the name of peace.

The foreign policies of the major powers throughout history have always placed a high priority on maintaining the peace. Essentially, this has meant that militarily weaker countries must submit to the will of the more powerful ones. The Soviet Union and the United States continue to play out this theme of imposed peace in their respective spheres of influence, most notably Eastern Europe and Central America. All this means, of course, that one way to define peace is as the imposition of order. It implies that anyone who disagrees with the agent of control, whether it be boss, husband, teacher, or government, will be expelled, fired, or bludgeoned into obedience.

Another type of peace presupposes that the nature of the universe consists of energies and forces in constant tension. This is represented by the Chinese cosmological principles of yin and yang, a duality in nature between active and passive, hot and cold, darkness and light, male and female, etc. Peace is achieved when a balance, or equilibrium, exists between these forces. State leaders and political scientists commonly refer to this as the theory of balance of power between nations, which, it is supposed, will maintain peace in the world.

This principle is at the heart of the Mutually Assured Destruction (MAD) policy of the nuclear powers. We are strong enough to destroy each other; therefore, we are at peace. A typical slogan that represents this type of thinking is "Walk softly, but carry a big stick," attributed to Teddy Roosevelt, a turn-of-the-century U.S. president noted for his macho image and bullying tactics toward the Caribbean nations. Today, it is almost anathema to suggest a foreign policy other than one based on a strong military presence. Nuclear weapons are named "peacemakers," and large armies are needed to maintain peace. This balance of power theory is founded on a deep mistrust of other nations. If we are well-armed no one can harm us.

We come now to a third way, the way of biblical peace. The Hebrew word *shalom* does not mean peace imposed by the strongest power, nor does it mean a balance of forces that keep each other in check. *Shalom* is a biblical word that describes a situation of harmony, tranquility, and mutual love among people. The Hebrew people, following their movement into Palestine, the Promised Land, were tribal. The twelve tribes of Israel sought peace within their own ranks by living out the Ten Commandments, the Law that God had given them on Mt. Sinai. Anyone minimally acquainted with the Hebrew Scriptures, however, is familiar with the bloodshed, battles, and constant hostility between the Hebrews and the neighboring tribes and nations. Shalom did not exist in time of war.

With the coming of Christ, a new dimension was added. God's peace was tied to the following of Jesus. Paul wrote "For he is our peace; in his flesh he has made both groups one and has broken down the dividing wall, that is, the hostility between us."[9] He refers here to Jesus' mission not only to the Jews, but to all people. No longer can those who accept Jesus live with hostility toward anyone. Since God is called Father, all the children of God are sisters and brothers. In the home, this calls for mutual respect; in the workplace, for cooperation and common purpose; in the classroom, for a reciprocal search for truth; and among nation-states, for new and creative ways to help the less economically developed countries attain a fair share of the basic human necessities.

Where do we stand today as humans? Will the slaughter and mayhem of the twentieth century continue unabated until we incinerate the planet? Or is it time to put away the weapons of war, to let down our guard, to reach out with a helping hand, to listen to the reasons behind the hostility that exists? Jesus gave the human race the example of his life. Are we called to follow that example?

Peace as Development

In 1967, Pope Paul VI established a Pontifical Justice and Peace Commission in order to:

> bring to the whole of God's people the full knowledge of the part expected of them at the present time, so as to further the progress of poorer peoples, to encourage social justice among the nations, to offer to less developed nations the means whereby they can further their own progress.[10]

Shortly thereafter, he wrote his famous encyclical letter *On the Development of Peoples*. In it, he identified himself with the growing aspirations of all people in seeking a decent standard of living. He noted that many nations were just emerging from the burden of colonialism, which in some instances had been imposed for centuries. He saw that the work of the Church was to help lighten the burden of poverty and oppression for the poor. A new integration of faith with economics and politics began with the reforms of Vatican II.

Pope Paul stressed that nations must take on "the duty of human solidarity—the aid that rich nations must give to developing countries; the duty of social justice—the rectification of inequitable trade relations between powerful nations and weak nations." He pleaded for a world "where freedom is not an empty word and where the poor man Lazarus can sit down at the same table with the rich man." In his concluding remarks, he said that, "development is the new name for peace,"[11] and urged all people to face up to their responsibility to help the needy. It was a time of great hope. The United States had recently begun the Peace Corps and created an Alliance for Progress with its Latin neighbors. An enthusiasm for building a better world was in the air.

In marking the twentieth anniversary of Paul VI's peace as development theme, John Paul II issued a letter entitled *On Social Concerns*. Gone was the tone of optimism. In its place was a somber voice almost pleading for an attentive audience. "One cannot deny that the present situation in the world, from the point of view of development, offers a rather negative impression."[12] He noted a widening gap between rich and poor, the global effects of a housing crisis, unemployment, and underemployment, and the international debt crisis. He laid most of the blame for these crises on the geopolitical struggle between the East and the West.

Furthermore, "if arms production is a serious disorder in the present world with regard to true human needs, the arms trade is equally to blame." With anger, he noted that at times capital lent for development has gone to buy weapons. In addition, while there has been a growing consciousness about human rights, interdependence, and ecological issues, the conflict between communism and capitalism has overshadowed them. He saw the all-consuming desire for profit and the thirst for power as the greatest evils of our time. Interestingly, the new influences of liberation theology from Latin America and the Solidarity labor movement in Poland are apparent. In his closing remarks he argued that solidarity and the works of justice produce peace, and that the desire for liberation is the first principle of action. "Thus the process of development and liberation takes concrete shape in the exercise of solidarity, that is to say, in the love and service of neighbor, especially the poorest."[13]

All of these lofty ideals are no more than verbiage unless we know how, and are willing, to put them into practice. What does it mean to be in solidarity with our families, or to seek liberation for our roommates who use drugs? How do we relate to the poor when we never see them? Or being aware of them, do we learn how to walk with them? We began this chapter with a reminder about the need to take responsibility for our own lives. The same is true about integrating the values of liberation and peace into our lives. We will not support either of these values in the social order unless they are part of our personal lives.

We need to trust that our efforts for liberation and freedom will bear fruit. The June 1988 celebration of Nelson Mandela's seventieth birthday is a case in point. Mandela, a black South African leader, imprisoned for over twenty-seven years for his opposition to apartheid, was honored at Wembley Stadium, London, with a ten-hour rock concert. This Freedomfest, broadcast worldwide to an estimated one billion people, featured hundreds of Artists Against Apartheid. After singing "We just called to say we love you"[14] for Mandela, Stevie Wonder said, "Until you are free, no one is free; the oppression of anyone is the oppression of everyone." Only when we identify with the Nelson Mandelas of the world will we be walking the path of liberation and peace.

Notes

1   Erich Fromm, *Escape from Freedom* (New York: Holt, Rinehart & Winston, 1941), 23.

2   Matthew 19:22.

3   R. Bruce McColm, *Freedom in the World, 1990–1991* (New York: Freedom House, 1991), 69, 153, 212, 226, 300, 304.

4   Gustavo Gutiérrez, *A Theology of Liberation* (Maryknoll, N.Y.: Orbis Books, 1975), 4–5.

5   Ibid., 15.

6   Luke 4:18–19.

7   Leonardo Boff, *Church: Charism and Power* (New York: Crossroads, 1985).

8   Leonardo Boff and Clodovis Boff, *Introducing Liberation Theology* (Maryknoll, N.Y.: Orbis Books, 1986), 49–59.

9   Ephesians 2:14.

10   Paul VI, *Development of Peoples* (Boston: Daughters of St. Paul, 1967), 4.

11   Ibid., 27, 29, 45.

12   John Paul II, *Sollicitudo Rei Socialis* (Washington, D.C.: United States Catholic Conference, 1987), 20, 33–34.

13   Ibid., 39, 71, 93.

14   Stevie Wonder, "I Just Called to Say I Love You" (Motown Records, 1984).

27

Nonviolence

Three main mechanisms by which nonviolent action may produce victory are . . . conversion (the rarest), accommodation, and nonviolent coercion. Massive noncooperation may paralyze and disintegrate even an oppressive system.

Gene Sharp[1]

Just War Theory

We have seen thus far how important it is to measure our personal values, i.e., our beliefs, attitudes, and behavior, against the standards of human dignity and solidarity. We observed how these two central values provide the foundation for an authentic meaning to human life and for an understanding of truth as life-giving and justice as fairness. The concepts of liberation and peace were solidified and united in the twin objectives of supporting freedom for each person and the human development of all. But how do we approach this task? Is it possible to do injustice while attempting to achieve justice? Does a good end justify any means? A classic jungle warfare example is burning down the village to make it safe for the villagers!

331

Both the Hebrew and Christian traditions are filled with examples of violent behavior. The Jews called upon their God, Yahweh, to smite their enemies as they made their way into the Promised Land. Yahweh led their armies into battle and strengthened Saul and David as they established the Kingdom. Following hard on the heels of acceptance by the civil authority in the fourth century, Christian writers began to ally faith with public order. Virtues hitherto ignored, such as patriotism and fidelity to one's country, received widespread prominence. Less than one hundred years later, under the influence of Saint Augustine, Christians began to justify war. Augustine's voluminous writings, especially the *City of God,* played a decisive role in the subsequent thought of philosophers and theologians with regard to military combat.

Augustine, of course, was no warmonger. It was the sad consequence of sin that drove good people to use violence in order to constrain evil. "War and conquest are a sad necessity in the eyes of people of principle, yet it would be still more unfortunate if wrongdoers should dominate just people."[2] The presumption for all Christians is to do no harm to your neighbor and to love your enemies. When we act in a belligerent manner toward other people, whether it is physical or verbal abuse, we sin against them. Hostility, returning tit for tat, is antithetical to Christian belief. It is only in self-defense or to protect an innocent party that we can justify the use of force. In Augustine's view war was not only the result of sin, but also the tragic remedy for sin in the political order.[3]

Two categories of principles apply to the just-war theory. The first category involves the reasons for going to war; the second is concerned with the justice to be maintained in fighting a war. Going to war can be justified if:

1. *The cause is just.* There is a real need to protect the innocent, preserve personal dignity, and secure human rights.

2. *Competent authority is maintained.* This principle sets the context for the issue of guerrilla terrorists vs. freedom fighters. Who declares war is a vital question.

3. *Comparative justice is assessed.* Is the harm being done enough to justify the violence, suffering, and death that accompany war?

4. *It is a last resort and has reasonable hope of success.* Peaceful methods of resolving the conflict have been exhausted and there is some probability of rectifying the injustices.

Two other principles apply and involve both the reasons for going to war and its engagement:

1. *Proportionality.* Nothing can justify taking innocent lives, be they hostages or noncombatants, to further the war effort. Restraint is always implied in justifying war.

2. *Discrimination.* Massive retaliation against children, the ill, and the elderly is never right. The use of any chemical and biological weapons and nuclear weapons targeted at cities is immoral.[4]

These principles place severe restrictions on the use of force for war to be justified. In the present Nuclear Age, they make the use of warfare as a means of settling disputes justly a highly unlikely proposition. As a result more and more Christians are returning to the way of nonviolence.

Nonviolence as Strategy

Nonviolence as a strategy or tactic is based on the assumption that "the exercise of power depends on the consent of the ruled who, by withdrawing that consent, can control and even destroy the power of their opponent."[5] In *The Politics of Nonviolent Action*, Gene Sharp, an American scientist associated with the Center for International Affairs at Harvard University, refuses to discuss nonviolence on philosophical grounds. He believes that it is always a better strategy than violence since it accomplishes the same end, that is, to redistribute political power. Although he avoids arguing that bodily harm and property damage are minimized by nonviolent action, he implies as much.

His main concern is behavior modification. No matter what the end result, good or evil, nonviolence is a better method for achieving it. "The violent actions and the nonviolent are different methods of trying to make it unrewarding to do other things."[6] For Sharp, it is always a question of who has the power. Do we allow ourselves to be coerced? Can we coerce others more efficiently by nonviolence than by violence? In limiting his argument to techniques and strategies, Sharp mistakenly believes that actions in themselves have no right or wrong. On the contrary, we have stressed that all behavior is value-laden and that motivation is a central question. Nevertheless, Sharp does offer an exhaustive list of nonviolent tactics that are noteworthy.

In general, people think of nonviolent action as reserved for a Jesus, a Gandhi, or a Martin Luther King, Jr. Precisely the opposite is true. Most people, on most occasions, behave nonviolently. Oftentimes, when we disagree with someone, we either walk away or search for a compromise. In public life, we endure abuse and frequently tolerate mistreatment. Only when we are seriously threatened do we tend to act violently.

One of the most commonly used methods of nonviolent action is the boycott. In the early 1970s, millions of people throughout the United States supported César Chavez, the president of the United Farm Workers, when he called for a boycott of California grapes and lettuce. This nonviolent tactic was used to pressure growers into improving the working conditions and wages of migrant farm workers. With the negative action of not buying a product, consumers stood beside the workers in their protest against agribusiness.

Similarly during World War II, many of the citizens in Norway and Sweden refused to cooperate with the Nazis in identifying and imprisoning Jews. Blacks in Montgomery, Alabama, successfully boycotted the city buses in 1955 and brought about legislation giving them the right to sit where they wished. Rent boycotts, slowdowns by municipal employees, withdrawal of deposits, and embargoes on trade all constitute forms of negative nonviolent action that are intended to change the behavior of the person or the group who wields authority.

Thus, we see that a wide variety of nonviolent strategies have been used in changing the arrangement of power within society. Yet it would seem that if we do not address the deeper question of why we should practice nonviolence, we are left with no rationale for its use other than its effectiveness. As we have already seen, Gandhi's nonviolence was more a way of life than a tactic. He reasoned that no one, least of all himself, could know the complete truth about anything. Therefore, not being totally sure, he must give the adversary some room in which to move. Furthermore, Martin Luther King, Jr., in studying and applying Gandhi's thinking to his own situation, realized that his fellow blacks and their white supporters would need more than some knowledge about strategy if they were to persevere in the face of police dogs, lynch mobs, and racial hatred.

There is no question that timing, strategy, organization, and planning are of vital importance in discussing the question of nonviolent action. But is it merely a distribution of power that we fight for? In the context of peace and justice, because we are dealing with human rights and personal dignity, because we believe that some values are better than others and that some people oppress their neighbors while others try to empower them, we think it of vital importance to see nonviolence not so much as a strategy, but as a way of life. What better place to continue this reflection than with the person of Jesus?

Jesus

The Roman Empire was the dominant political force in the time of Jesus. In their own ways, the Pharisees and the Sadducees made their accommodations with it, accepting the status quo and concerning themselves with temple worship and the minutiae of Jewish law. One of the major reasons for their hatred of Jesus was that he named their hypocrisy. Another group of Jews, the Essenes, chose to exclude themselves from contact with Roman rule by living an austere and isolated life in small communities outside of Jerusalem. Finally, the Zealots, as their name implies, were the revolutionaries. They were deeply resentful of the Roman presence and were awaiting the long-sought-after Messiah who, in the tradition of Moses and David, would free them from a foreign ruler and restore the Kingdom. For them, the Messiah would be a political leader sent by God. With the sword and lance, he would drive out the Romans and reign as their King. How different was the person of Jesus!

> Come to me all, all you that are weary and are carrying heavy burdens, and I will give you rest. Take my yoke upon you, and learn from me; for I am gentle and humble in heart, and you will find rest for your souls. For my yoke is easy, and my burden is light.[7]

He spoke of himself as light for the world; as the way, the truth, and the life; as a good shepherd; and as the anointed one of God. Yet there are few passages in the gospels that offer as much comfort and support as do those verses that identify him as gentle and lowly. He rejected the idea that the Messiah should be a political ruler. He opted instead for a rule of love. "My kingdom is not from this world,"[8] he told Pilate, then went on to add that legions of angels would come to his aid if he wanted them.

The gentleness of his personality, his disposition for non-violence arose from his intimacy with a creative and caring God. By the various teachings and actions of his life, it is clear that his values did not include coercive power, but rather a kind of persuasive power that encouraged people to get beyond their own needs and live in service to others. Jesus was unquestionably a leader, a ruler, even a king, if you wish, but not one who would destroy, injure, or do violence to the dignity of any person. The God of love sent Jesus to teach the human family how it ought to live. Jesus was killed for being faithful to the way of nonviolent action.

Scripture scholars tell us that the gospel narratives were compiled from word-of-mouth stories passed down through at least a few generations of early Christians. They were woven into a cohesive whole for the sake of clarity and to respond to the needs of different communities. That being the case, it is not surprising to see the central teachings of Jesus summed up in the Sermon on the Mount,[9] even though these lessons were probably taught separately in several locations. The first part of the Sermon addresses that which brings happiness. Among other things, Jesus says, "Blessed are the meek . . . , blessed are those who hunger and thirst for righteousness . . . , blessed are the merciful . . . , blessed are the peacemakers . . . , blessed are those who are persecuted for righteousness' sake."[10]

Jesus establishes the foundation for true happiness in these simple nonviolent values. When we seek to control, manipulate, and dominate others, we will be unhappy. When we seek after possessions and places of honor instead of God's justice and mercy, we will find disillusionment. The danger for people today is that the materialistic culture and the world's insistence on self-satisfaction have blurred the vision of Jesus' teaching. Power politics was not part of his plan. He came not to be served, but to serve. [11]

Unlike the Zealots, he did not espouse political revolution; unlike the Pharisees and Sadducees, he had little time for external appearances. What did concern Jesus most of all was a conversion of heart. He knew all too well of the evil desires and inclinations to which humans are prone. In reading the minds of the chief priests, he saw that their jealousy of him led to hatred and would eventually result in his execution. Yet he pressed on in speaking about the Kingdom of God.

> "You have heard that it was said, 'An eye for an eye, and a tooth for a tooth.' But I say to you, do not resist an evildoer. But if anyone strikes you on the right cheek, turn the other also." [12]

This is a difficult saying even if we do not take it literally. The meaning is clear that Jesus invites his followers into a way of nonviolence. Although his own anger flared at times, most notably his righteous indignation at the money lenders in the Temple,[13] he did no physical harm to anyone. Unfortunately, centuries have encrusted his truth about nonviolence with the rest of the same institutionalized religion that he condemned. Only recently, due to a renewed interest in biblical studies, do we find Christians supporting this way of Jesus. Let us look at the essential ingredients of his nonviolence.

Way of Jesus

"You have heard that it was said, 'You shall love your neighbor and hate your enemy.' But I say to you, Love your enemies and pray for those who persecute you."[14]

There is little doubt that this particular teaching of Jesus has been ignored by most Christians throughout the centuries. Since it is found in the Sermon on the Mount, it led Gandhi to once remark that Christians not only failed to practice the Sermon on the Mount, few even believed it. In dealing with enemies, the classic choice is flight or fight. How often do we find one partner in marriage stomp out of the room during the heat of an argument, rather than try to settle the issue with further discussion? Furthermore, there is the macho mentality of "stepping outside" to settle things. Whether it is a domestic quarrel or a barroom brawl, the willingness of people to settle their differences in violent ways is evident.

How then am I to love my enemy? And why should I? In the first instance, we are called to recognize every person, even those who injure us, as a child of God. If we believe this truth, if we are convinced of the basic dignity of every person in spite of bad behavior, we are at least beginning to understand why Jesus called for love of enemies. In addition, if we understand that conflict results from unmet needs, we might try to listen to the needs of the enemy and share our own. Stonewalling impedes respect, which is the vehicle for reconciliation.

It is this reconciliation, or forgiveness, that is the second essential characteristic of Jesus' way of nonviolence. Again, we find this truth expressed in the Sermon on the Mount: "For if you forgive others their trespasses, your heavenly Father will also forgive you."[15] Jesus also told parables about the kind of openness and generosity of spirit needed for forgiveness. Nowhere is this better illustrated than in the story of the Prodigal Son.

The Lord's Prayer adds a further dimension. Forgiveness of our sins is conditioned on our forgiveness of others. Together these biblical truths challenge us to heal the wounds of division and seek peace with our enemies. Sadly enough, the ways of the world often urge us to get even with those who hurt us. We are encouraged to punish wrongdoers, to teach them a lesson, or to instill fear in them. Consequently, forgiveness and love of enemies are often seen as a sign of weakness.

Even more foolish in the eyes of the world is the way of the cross. This is the third and final characteristic of nonviolence taught by Jesus.

> "If any want to become my followers, let them deny themselves and take up their cross and follow me. For those who want to save their life will lose it, and those who lose their life for my sake, and for the sake of the gospel, will save it."[16]

In the context of nonviolent action, taking up the cross means to take on the violence of the opponent without retaliation of any sort. This behavior can be quite disarming to the enemy. During the recent downfall of the Marcos regime in the Philippines, thousands of unarmed civilians stood in the path of soldiers and tanks. They were willing to die in order to bring down an unjust regime. This nonviolent action touched the hearts of the soldiers, who were unable to kill innocent people. The paradox of nonviolence is that in losing, we win.

These three teachings of Jesus, love of enemy, reconciliation, and the way of the cross are the foundation principles of Christianity. Yet honest and sincere Christians still disagree on their interpretation and implementation. We have already acknowledged the right of self-defense, and we have examined the principles used in deciding if war is justified. We also know that Jesus cured the centurion's servant, and one of the first well-known Gentile converts was Cornelius, a captain in the Roman army. So it would appear that Jesus did not rule out the police or the military from his Kingdom, nor did he ask them to resign from their jobs.

In trying to reconcile these apparent contradictions, we should acknowledge the difference between the ideal order of things and the real world. Sin and evil are realities we find within our own hearts and in the hearts of all humans. While I may willingly turn the other cheek to my adversary, do I not have an obligation to prevent him from slapping someone else's cheek? Evil, too, has a way of being cumulative in society. Structural sin infects governments, businesses, churches, and all human organizations. We are not so naive as to think that others will not take advantage of us should we choose the way of complete nonviolence. What we need to do is to see non-violence as a choice. Countering injustice with force should not be a first alternative. It is only a last resort and one utilized with reluctance.

Options

In 1980, handguns were connected to the deaths of 77 people in Japan, 8 in Great Britain, 24 in Switzerland, 8 in Canada, 23 in Israel, 18 in Sweden, 4 in Australia, and 11,522 in the United States.[17] Add to those horrific statistics the further fact that we have spent more than two trillion dollars on the military budget since 1981, an amount that averages to $21,000 per U.S. family per year and you begin to get an idea of how violent a society we live in.

All reform must begin in our own heart. Have I lately inventoried the violence that lies within myself? Who are my enemies? How well do I know them? Have I tried to walk in their shoes, or to get beyond the surface behavior to the motivations, anxieties, fears, etc., that generate their actions? We need to examine our own beliefs, attitudes, and behavior for signs of violence and begin to take on new forms of gentleness and nonviolence. It is a change in one's values. Biting our tongue or counting to ten, before responding to a perceived hurt is still good advice. Recently, Pax Christi, a Catholic peace group, urged fellow Christians to adopt a nonviolent life-style:

1. by striving for peace within myself and seeking to be a peacemaker in my daily life;
2. by accepting suffering rather than inflicting it;
3. by refusing to retaliate in the face of provocation and violence;
4. by persevering in nonviolence of tongue and heart;
5. by living conscientiously and simply so that I do not deprive others of the means to live;
6. by actively resisting evil and working nonviolently to abolish war and the causes of war from my own heart and from the face of the earth.[18]

Some argue that this is unrealistic in light of the violence that surrounds us. However, if we move into the eye of the hurricane, a place of calm and peace, perhaps we can begin to enlarge that center by joining others who are committed to nonviolence. Gradually, with more and more people adding their presence, the storm of violence may begin to subside.

> In the nonviolent army, there is room for everyone who wants to sign up. There is no color distinction. . . . Nonviolent soldiers are called upon to examine and burnish their greatest weapons— their heart, their conscience, their courage, and their sense of justice.[19]

This call to arms by Martin Luther King, Jr., poses both a challenge and an invitation. If we accept the challenge, we have joined King's army. In this army there is no need for spears and swords or the more sophisticated missiles and bombers. There is also no need for disinformation campaigns to deceive the enemy, or tactics and maneuvers that ridicule and confuse the opposition. The army of nonviolence marches to a different beat. It is the beat of patience; always willing to listen to another explain his or her situation. It is the beat of compassion, always ready to reach out and lend a helping hand to those in need. It is the beat of God's heart spilling over with love for every human person: old and young, rich and poor, man and woman, black, white, yellow, and red. When our hearts are in sync with that beat, we shall know the fullness of our humanity.

Notes

[1] Gene Sharp, *The Politics of Nonviolent Action* (Boston: Porter Sargent Publishers, 1973), i.

[2] National Conference of Catholic Bishops, *The Challenge of Peace: God's Promise and Our Response* (Washington, D.C.: United States Catholic Conference, 1983), 27.

[3] Ibid., 26.

[4] Ibid., 26–34.

[5] Sharp, *The Politics of Nonviolent Action*, 4.

[6] Ibid., xx.

[7] Matthew 11:28–30.

[8] John 18:36.

[9] Matthew 5:7.

[10] Matthew 5:3–10.

[11] Matthew 20:28.

[12] Matthew 5:38–39.

[13] Mark 11:15–16.

[14] Matthew 5:43–44.

15 Matthew 6:14.

16 Mark 8:34–35.

17 Gerard A. Vanderhaar and Mary Lou Kownacki, OSB, eds., *Way of Peace: A Guide to Nonviolence* (Erie, Penn.: Pax Christi USA, 1987), 24.

18 *Pax Christi USA*, Spring 1988, 15.

19 Quote from speech by Martin Luther King, Jr., *Pax Christi USA*, Winter 1987, 1.

28

Love

Strive for the greater gifts. And I will show you a still more excellent way.

1 Corinthians 12:31

The Many Meanings of Love

We have now arrived at the lodestone of all values, that which strongly attracts everyone, yet can be the most disillusioning. A songwriter once wrote that "love is a many-splendored thing" and a novelist stated that "love means never having to say you're sorry." On the other hand, the gospel says that "the greatest love is to lay down one's life for a friend." Well, which is it? Are these ideas compatible or mutually exclusive? It would be fair to say that the word *love* has such a variety of meanings that it is virtually impossible to define. We are better off describing the various features that range across the emotional landscape, while including several cerebral components as well. Needless to say, almost everyone knows something about love, its complexity, and its simplicity. Let us begin with some distinctions in order to clarify our understanding of love.

In ancient times, the Greek god Eros symbolized sexual love. Today, the Playboy bunny fills a similar role. In either case, sexual attraction between men and women has dominated the human race. There is a beautiful magic about falling in love. As a boy and girl reach the age of puberty, bodily and hormonal changes create strong desires that move them out of childhood into an adolescent stage of sexual awakening. In times past, marriages would be arranged by families for these youngsters, but today, in most cultures, marriage is by the common consent of the individuals and usually occurs several years after puberty.

The term *making love* has become equated with sexual intercourse, whether or not a marriage exists. This makes for much confusion when a one-night stand can be equated with conjugal fidelity. In addition, the sexual revolution of the 1960s, during which sexual intercourse was shorn from the moorings of marriage, tended to remove the human qualities of fidelity and commitment from the sex act. Promiscuity became commonplace. Be that as it may, the word *love* has enough sexual connotations to force us to ask in what context the word is being used.

A fuller meaning for the word *love* derives from the Greek word *philos*. A philanthropist is one who loves human beings. Philadelphia is the city of brotherly (and sisterly) love. Love in this sense is much richer and broader than sexual love. Friendship, camaraderie, and community imply a getting along with others. Mutual respect is the common denominator. Thus, the disparity between love as eros and love as philos is apparent, since the former can be totally bereft of any humanness while the latter is its essence.

In the early days of Christianity, the Greek word *agape* was used to denote the coming together of the followers of Jesus in order to share his presence in the eucharistic meal. This so-called love feast was in reality a sharing of the common bond of faith in God, in and through the person of Christ. In a sense, this expresses the deepest kind of love, that which finds its center and its power in the love of God. If one acknowledges that God is the ground of all existence and the energy that sustains creation, then it follows that a God-source for love would touch at the heart of human dignity and solidarity. A community of faith gathered in the name of God should be a sign of love. If it is filled with rancor, bitterness, and strife, it does not reflect God's love and is as much a false sign as an umpire betting on a game.

Thus, we have found many meanings for *love*. It involves our sexuality, our friendships, and our community. It is a many-splendored thing. Let us glimpse some of its treasures.

Art of Loving

In *The Art of Loving*, Erich Fromm, an eminent psychoanalyst, states that our awareness of aloneness and separation creates a desire for union and belonging. In trying to overcome loneliness, some people find refuge in drugs or alcohol; others seek to conform to the norms and customs of society and find their identity in a crowd; still others plunge into a workaholic frenzy in order to allay the anxieties of separation.

For Fromm, the only authentic way to overcome aloneness is through union or relationships with other people. This, however, has problems too, since several fallacies exist about the relationship of love. The first misconception is that people confuse loving with being loved. For example, men may strive to be successful, to make a lot of money, and to present a good appearance so that they might be loved. Or again, women may dress well, use the right cosmetics and lotions, and cultivate sexual appeal so that they too might be lovable. The second error about love is that modern society has objectified humans to the point where they are expendable. Just as cars, clothing, or other material possessions wear out their usefulness, so do people. A final false assumption, according to Fromm, equates romance or infatuation with love.[1] Falling in love becomes the norm. Staying in love is a drag. The high rate of divorce today tends to confirm the premise that permanency is not a highly regarded value in relationships.

In order to counter these errors that distort the value of real love, Fromm argues that the essential meaning of love lies in the notion of giving. "Giving is the highest expression of potency. In the very act of giving, I experience my strength, my wealth, my power. . . . Giving is more joyous than receiving, not because it is a deprivation, but because in the act of giving lives the expression of my aliveness."[2] I do not passively wait for someone to love me, or spend my time and energy preparing myself to be the object of love. Because I know that love involves reaching out, I take charge of my life by gearing it toward the concerns of others rather than toward the dead-end of self-concern.

Although ostentation and compulsive buying have stereotyped the celebration of Christmas into an extravaganza of gifts and glitter, it still retains some semblance of its original meaning, i.e., God's gift of Jesus to the human family. The feast of the Incarnation, in which divinity gifted humanity, became the paradigm for giving. We know too from our own personal experience how we feel loved when someone gives us a gift that is not expected, but is purely gratuitous. Giving, then, is the primary ingredient in understanding love. But Fromm also includes four other elements that are always found in love. Let us examine each of these briefly.

Just as length, breadth, and height constitute the dimensions of space, likewise do care, responsibility, respect, and knowledge establish the parameters of love. Care is seen in the love a mother shows to her child. The constant daily tasks of feeding, washing, and carrying a baby demand much patience and gentleness. Infants are completely vulnerable. Without love they would die. Parental love testifies to the caring dimension that is so necessary in a loving relationship.

Secondly, responsibility is a characteristic of love that requires one to pay attention to the needs of the other and to respond to those needs as appropriately as possible. The responsible friend, the one who really loves, acts as the designated driver at a party or the peacemaker in a conflict situation.

Respect is the third element in a loving relationship. It has nothing to do with awe or fear, but rather is a stance that empowers the other to grow to his or her own fullest potential.

When we manipulate another to do things our way, we have forgotten that real love can only be based on mutual respect.

Finally, a willingness to penetrate into the depths of another's life characterizes the fourth sign of love. To know oneself, the ancients said, was the height of wisdom. To know another at the level of his or her hopes and dreams, his or her hurts, sorrows, fears, and pain is only possible when a caring, respectful, and responsible attitude has been established with the other. Knowledge of another builds over time if the other ingredients of love are present. An unwillingness to learn the secrets of another's heart is the opposite of love.

Christian Love

> If I speak in the tongues of mortals and of angels, but do not have love, I am a noisy gong or a clanging cymbal. And if I have prophetic powers, and understand all mysteries and all knowledge, and if I have all faith, so as to remove mountains, but do not have love, I am nothing. If I give away all my possessions, and if I hand over my body so that I may boast, but do not have love, I gain nothing.[3]

In this oft-quoted passage, the Apostle Paul makes clear that nothing exceeds love. Although a person may achieve the highest academic honors, manage the wealthiest and most economically powerful transnational corporation, lead the largest and best-equipped military units in the world, or even balance his or her checkbook—without love, it counts as nothing in the eyes of God. That, indeed, is the real criterion for measuring the value of human life. How well do we love? Are our hearts set on higher things? Paul notes that faith alone is not the gateway to living a good life, for even faith that can move mountains is nothing before the dynamic of love. Too often we admire the person who is single-minded in his or her devotion to a particular cause. But we need only recognize the fanatical tendencies present in any movement to see how easily the pursuit of an objective, without a requisite love for the people involved, can easily degenerate into lunacy. By grounding our beliefs, attitude, and behavior, i.e., our values, in this highest expression of personal dignity and human solidarity, we plumb the depths of human life. To love is to find love.

Despite all the beautiful poetic ways that humans have imagined love, from the sonnets of Shakespeare to the love songs of Barbra Streisand, the real thing is not always dramatic. Paul says "Love is patient; love is kind. . . . It . . . rejoices in the truth. It bears all things, believes all things, hopes all things, endures all things."[4] Patience, which is the initial quality he mentioned in describing love, is not particularly energizing. It takes considerable perseverance for parents to rise night after night to feed or change a diaper for a crying baby. Listening to the fears and anxieties of an elderly nursing-home patient as she worries about someone stealing her blanket takes monumental effort.

Whether it is the daily task of putting up with one's own insecurities, foibles, and shortcomings, or the more difficult job of learning to tolerate, and even accept, the limitations of others, the qualities of patience, kindness, and endurance are the hallmarks of love. So too is rejoicing in the truth, says Paul. Recalling Gandhi's understanding of truth as that which affirms life, we can see readily that love is life-giving; it empowers others to feel secure and wanted. A child or an old woman who is loved has experienced the truth of life.

The evil forces that oppose love need the light of day if they are to be resisted. "Love is not envious or boastful or arrogant or rude. It does not insist on its own way; it is not irritable or resentful; it does not rejoice in wrongdoing."[5] We know, indeed, that all of us have fallen prey, at one time or another, to all of these sins. Cutting off others in traffic, failing to hold a door for the person behind us, crude and boisterous behavior at a party, or making unreasonable demands on members of our family are all evidence of a lack of love on a personal level.

"'Teacher, which commandment in the law is the greatest?' He said to him, 'You shall love the Lord your God with all your heart, and with all your soul, and with all your mind.'"[6] It is virtually impossible to sustain human love without the love of God. Jesus makes it clear that our priorities should be straight. Before we can expect to live out the way of human love with patience, kindness, perseverance, and the avoidance of conceit, irritability, and apathy, we are called to acknowledge in praise and thanksgiving the Creator of the Universe.

The Paradox of Love

Webster's Dictionary defines the word *paradox* as "a statement that is seemingly contradictory or opposed to common sense and yet is perhaps true." "To love yourself, you must die to yourself," is blatantly paradoxical. All of our instincts are aimed at self-preservation and so to die to oneself appears, at first blush, to stand us at the brink of suicide. The paradox of love invites us to appreciate the goodness within ourselves while cultivating our talents and abilities in order to use these gifts for the benefit of others.

The old maxim "You can't give what you don't have" can be applied to love. We need love in our own hearts before we can offer it to someone else. The death to self, on the other hand, is directed at the shadows and dark corners of our hearts. It follows that to love oneself, which should be the first and most important concern in our lives, is to get one's values straight. We mentioned previously that love of self involved care of the body, mind, and heart. Since our soul, or spirit, represents this wholeness of self, we are required to die to those values, those attitudes, beliefs, and practices that are either self-destructive or detrimental to others. Our values are properly ordered when we have died to the false values of power and possessions and learned to live with respect for life and in solidarity with all.

This lesson is not easily learned. Dorothy Day, an American journalist and peacemaker, often referred to love as a harsh and dreadful thing. Mother Teresa speaks of love as painful. Jesus said the greatest love was to die for a friend. Although we are surrounded daily by the false optimism of guaranteed success if we land the right job, go to the best school, or hang around with the "in" group, we know in our hearts that much of the hype in life is just that.

Anyone who has suffered a serious illness, lost a parent or friend through death, or wept tears of contrition over a sinful deed knows the reality of love's hurt. When I say No to a temptation or resist the lure of constantly seeking my own pleasure and satisfaction, when I stretch myself to go the extra mile to reconcile a conflict with someone who has hurt me, when I struggle to accept the limitations of my life and allow for the shortcomings of others—in all of these experiences the pain of love reveals itself.

> Jesus . . . got up from the table, took off his outer robe, and tied a towel around himself. Then he poured water into a basin and began to wash the disciples' feet and to wipe them with the towel that was tied around him. [7]

This act of service toward his disciples at the Last Supper stands as the definitive experience for anyone who would identify themselves as Christian. "I have set you an example, that you also should do as I have done to you."[8]

Among the early Christians three major themes—*kerygma, koinonia,* and *diakonia*—were of paramount importance. *Kerygma* means "gospel" or "good news," *koinonia* is the Greek word for "community," and *diakonia* signifies "service." They preached the good news about Jesus Christ, they shared a common life in friendship and love, and they put themselves at the service of one another. In spite of all of its failings, Christianity has always been marked by its care of the sick, education of the young, sheltering of the homeless, feeding of the hungry, and on and on. Across the globe today, there are hundreds of thousands of hospitals, schools, old-age homes, soup kitchens, shelters, and church buildings caring for millions of people. The hallmark of the Christian faith has always been service. "Do you know what I have done for you?"[9] This is not an invitation to blend in with the environment, but rather a call to transform our surroundings with the service that comes from love.

We noted previously that a look at our calendar and check-book will give us an instant reading of our values. The litmus test for generosity is time and money and talent. Oddly enough, the more we give, the more we get. Jesus spoke about a reward of a hundredfold for even a cup of water given in his name. The recompense of generous service to others frequently shows up in the intangible goods of life: peace of mind, lessening of fears and anxiety, a clear conscience, and the inner joy of knowing that love is its own reward. As we develop habits of generosity, in proportion shall we find contentment of heart.

Love Is a Decision

Begun during the 1960s in Spain, the Marriage Encounter Movement has touched the lives of millions of couples the world over. Many good marriages were enriched; those that were tottering got support. One of the important truths that the weekend experience taught was that love is a decision.

Team couples shared situations in their marriages where walls had been built and barriers erected. Petty feuds and stubborn behavior were only overcome by a willful decision to break down the walls, remove the barriers, and restore the commitment to love. To say that love is a decision simply means that day in and day out we will continue to be faithful to those whom we love.

Recalling the need for self-discipline in order to deal with the difficulties of life, we may draw the same conclusion with regard to love. It is difficult to love. It needs daily discipline. How many husbands or wives wake up each day and ask themselves how they can best love their spouse today? It is a basic question that offers new and creative answers daily. Consequently, a renewed decision for love each day, whether in marriage or to family, friends, and even to enemies, signifies a faithfulness and commitment so desperately needed in a world of infidelity and broken promises.

The natural consequence of fidelity is permanence. But how can this be when times change, people come in to and go out of our lives in rapid succession, and we ourselves are caught in the tides of shifting moods and social upheavals? It would seem that the only permanent reality is change! The friends of childhood and grade school are ancient memories; high-school classmates have gone their own ways; even the new friendships we made in the early days of college tend to be fleeting. It has been remarked that one close friend for life is a rare treasure.

How then can we speak of the permanence of love? We should distinguish first of all between the different forms of love. In marriage, serious promises are made concerning a lifelong commitment to love, honor, and respect each other. "I promise to be true to you in good times and in bad, in sickness and in health, I will love you and honor you all the days of my life."[10] Family love requires an effort on the part of the individual members to help and care for each other because of their common bond of blood. Beyond that, our responsibility toward others is more diffuse.

What requires permanency is an attitude of mind that challenges us to stretch ourselves in an never-ending desire to empower others. Although limitations abound, we need to set our hearts on higher things, as Paul said for "love never ends."[11]

We need to break through the culture block that equates all values. Kindness is better than rudeness; concern is superior to indifference; patience is preferable to churlishness; and love is an improvement over prejudice and hatred. We do not always live as we ought, but only a fool would suggest that the values of Rambo are as good as Mother Teresa's. We need ideals by which to measure our lives. The basic yardstick is how we treat each other. When we fail, let us admit our guilt, repair the damage where possible, and try again to live lives of love.

We have argued that there is a hierarchy of values with love at the summit and hatred at the base. Since each individual person is a unique creation of a loving God, each has a fundamental right to dignity and respect. Since this same God is father and mother for the entire human family, we are united as sisters and brothers in solidarity. Truth-force calls us to respect life; justice invites us to fairness with others and a compassion for the needy; liberation challenges us to develop our potential and enable others to do likewise; and peace is both the way and the end. To work for peace will bring peace to our souls. It is hoped that these reflections on values will provide us with a new way to think about our personal lives and the social issues of our times. Our lives are too precious to chase after worthless and false values. In appreciating our dignity and that of others, we ennoble the human project.

Notes

1 Erich Fromm, *The Art of Loving* (New York: Harper & Row, 1956), 1–4.

2 Ibid., 23.

3 1 Corinthians 13:1–3.

4 1 Corinthians 13:4–7.

5 1 Corinthians 13:4–6.

6 Matthew 22:36–37.

7 John 13:3–5.

8 John 13:15.

9 John 13:12.

10 Paul Covino, ed., *Celebrating Marriage* (Washington, D.C.: Pastoral Press, 1987), 36–37.

11 1 Corinthians 13:8.

29

Judgments/Priorities

More than any other time in history, mankind faces a crossroads.
One path leads to despair and utter hopelessness. The other, to
total extinction. Let us pray we have the wisdom to choose cor-
rectly. I speak by the way, not with any sense of futility, but with
panicky conviction of the absolute meaninglessness of existence,
which could easily be misinterpreted as pessimism.

Woody Allen[1]

On Judging

While we may smile at Allen's zany assessment of the human
condition and our predicament at the close of the twentieth
century, there is a general nervousness that things are out of
control, and God only knows where we are headed. One way
of breaking out of this darkness is to sort out the values in our
own lives and to take a close look at the public policies and
cultural priorities in society for signs of dehumanization.

We have made the argument in the past several chapters
that the key element underlying all worthwhile values is their
humaneness. There are false personal beliefs, attitudes, and

actions that are destructive of my personal well-being, and false social, political, economic, and cultural patterns that deny human solidarity. We cannot avoid the task of judging ourselves and judging the actions of others unless we wish to go blindly through life like the three monkeys seeing no evil, hearing no evil, and speaking no evil. Fortunately, we are far more than monkeys and should be able to tell the difference between right and wrong. That is the task of making judgments.

In judging ourselves, love-hate relationships are often in evidence. On the one hand, we act as judge, jury, prosecutor, defense attorney, bailiff, and key witness when judging our own behavior. Generally, we only allow certain testimony to be heard. We rationalize our questionable deeds by answering ourselves that many others behave as we do. Even if we judge ourselves guilty, we are more likely to plead a misdemeanor than to admit a felony. Furthermore, we are generally predisposed toward fines rather than jail terms. We steal, lie, cheat, manipulate, and copulate with the abandon of Neanderthals, but rarely accept full responsibility for our behavior. Many people who act like 800-pound gorillas think of themselves as kind and gentle. Most other people are terrified!

Conversely, at times we are our own worst enemy. We take on responsibility for others, absolving them of any blame and accusing ourselves for not having done something to prevent someone else's fall from grace. Parents frequently blame themselves for their children's errant behavior. Friends wish they had done more to prevent a suicide. In short, we lack objectivity. Instead of needlessly blaming ourselves for things that we cannot control or absolving ourselves of responsibility when we are at fault, we need to look at the consequences of what we do and judge ourselves on the basis of the criteria previously set forth. If being fully human is my standard, my judgments about myself should be accurate.

The same yardstick of truth can be applied when judging others. Here, however, we are faced with a much more difficult task, because we cannot get inside another's mind to understand why a person believes or acts in a certain manner.

In addition, we have the gospel admonition not to judge others. To further confuse the issue, we have lost our moorings from the natural law ethic of our Founding Fathers. What now prevails is a relativistic morality based more on a misconceived freedom than on the firmness of biblical teaching. Standards of moral judgments such as the Ten Commandments are important prerequisites in determining right from wrong but should not be construed in a harsh or vindictive way. God's judgment includes mercy and forgiveness, and so should ours.

Motivation

In making judgments about right and wrong, good and bad, it is important to bear in mind that no one seeks to do something wrong because they see it as evil. Even the hired killer who commits murder is motivated by the "good" he or she sees in the money earned, or in the perverse joy obtained from killing someone. Furthermore, there are times when we know what is right, but instead, choose what is wrong. Because of bad habits, addictions, and temptations, we drink too much, eat too much, and frequently, talk too much for our own good. The immediate good blocks our vision of the better good down the road.

All this is to say that our motives for doing anything are rarely crystal clear and are usually marked by great ambivalence. We are torn between our instincts and desires, on the one hand, and our knowledge and spiritual values on the other. The junior executive and his attractive secretary are drawn to each other. Yet both are married to someone else. While both of them may realize that playing with fire usually results in getting burned, the immediate good of sexual satisfaction may blind them to the guilt, hurt, and disillusionment that will surely follow.

Pogo, the comic-strip character, once remarked that "we have met the enemy, and it is us!" We are our own worst enemies. We get into situations inimical to ourselves and others, always motivated by an apparent good. We confuse pleasure with happiness, fun with joy, and satisfaction with peace. It follows then that the best way to avoid hurting ourselves and others is to know our destination and keep our compass pointed in the right direction.

The standard way for parents to motivate children is through the time-honored method of reward and punishment. Since there is still a good bit of the child in all of us, we are prone, even as adults, to respond to the same basic motivations. Gandhi fasted to bring his body into submission. Many people turn to the practice of daily reflection in order to center their minds, while it is almost a new religion in the United States to join a health club or workout spa in order to stay in shape. Self-discipline, as we have already indicated, is a fundamental necessity if we are to control our own lives. We can use the motivation of reward and punishment by fasting and controlling our appetites, or disciplining ourselves by staying within the speed limit.

Motivation also comes from remembering our own importance as unique and special individuals. Do we believe that we are created in the image and likeness of God? How often are we aware that an eternal life of happiness has been promised to us? Motivation is not limited to a system of rewards and punishments, but is enhanced on a much higher psychic level when our vision of ourselves as one-of-a-kind is part of our daily thinking.

In recognizing and appreciating our uniqueness, however, we must avoid the danger of hypocrisy. The word *hypocrisy* derives from the Greek word for playacting. This behavior and attitude has a long history and much current practice. The gospels, for example, are filled with incidents of confrontation between Jesus and the Pharisees. The most classic illustration is the story of the woman caught in adultery. Jesus rebukes the crowd for wanting to stone her to death. "Let anyone among you who is without sin be the first to throw a stone at her."[2]

The recent scandals among some televangelists who preached one value, but lived another, shows that hypocrisy is alive and well. Business executives who pad their expense accounts while berating other employees for taking home small amounts of office supplies, parents who smoke and drink while condemning their kids for doing the same, and students who cheat on quizzes and exams while bad-mouthing professors for dull lectures are typical examples of modern hypocrisy. We all have our faults. We are not asked to whitewash behavior that is wrong. We should confront bigots with their racism, but in a way that will respect their dignity as persons. Jesus forgave the sin of adultery; he did not condone it. We can guard against a self-righteous attitude by remembering our own weaknesses.

Public vs. Private Morality

Joan Andrews is a middle-aged woman from Newark, Delaware. Shortly after the Supreme Court decision that legalized abortion, she began lobbying to reverse that judgment. By the early 1980s she saw the futility of verbal protest and joined with others by demonstrating in front of abortion clinics in the hope of preventing women from having abortions. To date, she has been arrested over a hundred times, with seventeen convictions. She was recently released after serving a five-year jail term in a maximum security prison in South Florida for entering an abortion clinic and unplugging the suction apparatus used to abort a fetus. She is a repeat offender, showing no remorse for her deeds.

She and many millions of other people in the United States are absolutely convinced that abortion is murder. They feel obliged in conscience to do everything possible, even breaking the law, in order to prevent the killing of infants growing in their mothers' wombs. They compare abortion to the killing of Jews by Hitler in the concentration camps of Nazi Germany. Those who disagree with their tactics are often vilified for allowing the evil of abortion to remain the law of the land. Joan Andrews is a Roman Catholic. She believes that her Christian faith calls her to stop abortion.

Mario Cuomo is also a Roman Catholic and the Governor of New York State. By profession, he is a lawyer; by practice, a politician. He raises questions about the connection between religious convictions and public policy. He wonders where one leaves off and the other begins, and if the separation of church and state that the U.S. Constitution has established sometimes puts him at odds with his faith. Although he accepts the teachings of his Church about the immorality of abortion, as a public official he is sworn to uphold the law of the land, and that law permits abortion.

He tries to distinguish between private and public morality, seeing the former arising from principles and convictions often embedded in religious teachings, and the latter, especially in the United States, as a consensus within a pluralistic society. Many people believe that a woman has the right to terminate her pregnancy. Others are equally convinced that this is wrong. Cuomo thinks that without consensus, legislating morality is both foolish and dangerous. It was tried during the era of prohibition with the result that more crime and corruption grew out of it. Furthermore, if the tables were turned, and your religious teachings were outlawed, how would you be protected?

> I believe that legal interdicting of abortion by either the federal government or the individual states is not a plausible possibility and even if it could be obtained, it wouldn't work. Given present attitudes, it would be "Prohibition" revisited, legislating what couldn't be enforced and in the process creating a disrespect for law in general.[3]

Although collectively they might have done otherwise, the Catholic bishops of the United States have gone on record that they will neither endorse nor reject particular political candidates for public office because of their political judgments. A few individual bishops have decided to condemn politicians who are pro-choice. Most, however, like Governor Cuomo, believe that law does not determine morality, nor, in a pluralistic society, can particular moral convictions determine the law without a consensus among the population.

Joan Andrews has chosen to carry her convictions about the evil of abortion to the point of civil disobedience. Other honorable women and men have done the same over different issues. They are convinced that, in good conscience, they can do nothing less. Mario Cuomo has chosen to live with the evil of abortion. While agreeing with his Church, he does not think it wise to translate his beliefs into a public policy that would wreak havoc on public order. Who is right?

There is an old saying: "Seek simplicity, but mistrust it." No simple solutions exist for the moral dilemmas that confront us in the political arena. We may have arrived at a morally sound value system for ourselves, yet few of us expect that others will see things the same way we do. Even within particular faith traditions serious differences exist.

As we have stated in several other instances, in the final analysis, we stand alone with our conscience. Joan Andrews and Mario Cuomo are both right, although their response to abortion differs.

Priorities

Since our values determine our priorities, we need to constantly reassess these values, asking ourselves which ones are more important than others. In general, we may say that people have core values for which they would endure suffering; median values, things that are important, but not crucial; and surface values that are of only passing interest. By analogy, lint on your skirt might rate a one, the threat of nuclear war a ten. Are our core values linked to our concern for family, friends, and other people, or are they centered on possessions and prestige? Do our own interests in classical music or travel take precedence over the care of an aged parent? Not long ago, Pope John Paul II made the point that people are more important than money.[4] Would he have bothered to say what appears to be obvious, if, in fact, many people have not misplaced their priorities?

Priorities, of course, have a way of shifting. Things that need attention one day may not need any on the following day. Furthermore, as particular responsibilities are completed, we can rejoice in a job well done, or pick up the pieces if we fail. Parenthetically, failure is not necessarily a total loss. At a recent graduation ceremony, an honorary degree recipient, currently a successful businessman, told how failure in a course forced him to repeat his final semester. In doing so he met his future wife. He asserted that their love, friendship, and family were the richest blessings of his life—all because he had to respond to a failure!

Circumstances surely dictate priorities. The student who can put aside her or his studies to listen to a friend's pain, the professor who allows for interruptions in a tight schedule to hear the problems of students, and the person who volunteers to work with the handicapped instead of spending the day at the beach are examples of rearranging priorities to accommodate a particular need. The Good Samaritan story should set the tone for us. Following rejection by a priest and another official, the injured man is cared for by a stranger. Injuries come in all sizes and shapes, from the more obvious physical kind to the inner pain of loneliness, anxiety, and fear. When we learn to shift our priorities to the needs of people who are hurting, we will surely have imbibed the lesson of the Good Samaritan story.

In sowing justice, we reap peace. This theme, which has dominated our discussion of values, must influence our public life as much as our private one. If we fail to add our voice to the public discourse about the values and priorities of our society, we not only fail our country, but we fail those who have no voice. Because few primary and secondary schools put much emphasis on public and civic values, many college students are abysmally ignorant of even the most simple legislative agendas. For many, writing a letter to their congressional representatives represents a first major step in political involvement. It should be a priority for every citizen to participate in the business of their country, not simply at election time, but throughout the year. Knowledge about particular social issues should not end with a term paper, but should become a vital part of one's public responsibility.

A word of caution is necessary. While zeal is a wonderful quality to develop, and concern for creating a better world a high priority, there is always the danger of acquiring a messianic complex. Crusades are usually charged with excitement as the troops rally around the flag and the charismatic leader excites his followers to climb every mountain, endure every hardship, etc., etc. In real life it is the day-to-day commitment of working diligently and intelligently on the tasks of life that will bring us the most satisfaction. Emotions are an important part of life. They give real clues to our wants and needs, but in the final analysis they are ephemeral whispers lacking the power of endurance so necessary for responsible living.

Option for the Poor

Give me your tired, your poor,
Your huddled masses yearning to breathe free,
The wretched refuse of your teeming shore,
Send these, the homeless, tempest-tossed, to me:
I lift my lamp beside the golden door.[5]

These memorable words by Emma Lazarus, a nineteenth-century Jewish poet, are inscribed at the base of the Statue of Liberty near the entrance to New York harbor, where millions of poor immigrants found welcome in a new land. In a historic sense, a concern for the poor has always been of importance when considering the ideals of liberty.

In recent times, however, a new dimension has been added. It is the question: "Why are people poor?" We have always known that dictators and kings often exploit their subjects. What has been less understood is how whole economic systems and ideological rivalries can also exploit people. If we believe that supply and demand are determining forces within an economy, we will never understand that corporate executives and government officials make decisions based on profit and self-interest rather than on the elementary needs of the general population.

We live in a stratified society where certain economic, political, cultural and religious structures maintain and promote the dominance of the rich and powerful over masses of ordinary people. These structures operate through agencies and institutions that are staffed mainly by middle-class people—those who provide the professional and commercial services of society. Whatever their private loyalties and values, these service people contribute to structural injustice through the kind of work they are doing.[6]

Opting for the poor (*preferential option for the poor* is a term that came out of a Latin American reflection on its own social structures) forces one to ask questions about who the decision-makers are in society, and what values they use in making decisions.

We need to be concerned about the poor, as Mother Teresa reminded us, because they are there. We need to be concerned about the poor, because each of them has the same basic right to life, liberty, and the pursuit of happiness as you and I. We need to be concerned about the poor, because Jesus reminded us that whatever we do to the least among us, we do to him.[7] An option for the poor as a priority value originated in the Hebrew concern for the needy and the identification of Jesus with the least important ones of our world.

In beginning to redirect our values toward the poor, we need to think of new ways to reach out to them. Two examples will help indicate the structural changes necessary to empower others to break the bonds of dependency. The Canadian office for Development and Peace recently gave a $60,000 grant to the Nicaraguan fishing villages of Casares, La Boquita, and Huehuete in order to help local fishermen buy new nets and motors for their boats and to develop a cooperative that drove overhead cost down. Production has increased by 70 percent, with the vast majority of the catch used to meet local food needs without the necessity of costly imports. In a 1979 speech, Pope John Paul II said,

> The needs of the poor take priority over the desires of the rich; the rights of workers over the maximization of profits; the preservation of the environment over uncontrolled industrial expansion; production to meet social needs over production for military purposes.[8]

Pope John Paul II has outlined four major priorities for the years ahead. He is convinced that the arms race is a dead-end street in terms of meeting social needs. He has suggested that if social needs were met, the need for military security would diminish. He notes that acid rain, deforestation, chemical poisons, and other environmental pollutants are continuing to do serious harm to the Earth's ecosystem. Without a change in priorities, the people of the twenty-first century will suffer the consequences of our negligence.

He also stated that millions have lost jobs in the name of profit-taking. Industries have relocated without regard for the workers and families left behind who will suffer from unemployment. Robotization and automation have left thousands jobless and depressed because of corporate decisions made by millionaires with little regard for the workers. In checking the top of the pope's list, we find his option for the poor. It is not an option to be taken lightly, for it involves a serious reordering of our priorities. Do my checkbook and calendar show a concern for the needy? Perhaps as I begin to value my own dignity in its broadest and richest sense, I may come to an awareness of the dignity of the poor.

Notes

1   Woody Allen, *Side Effects* (New York: Ballantine Books, 1980), 81.

2   John 8:7.

3   Mario Cuomo, "Religious Belief and Public Morality." Speech delivered at the University of Notre Dame, September 13, 1984.

4   John Paul II, *Laborem Exercens* (Boston: Daughters of St. Paul, 1981), 28.

5   Emma Lazarus "The New Colossus," *The World Almanac 1991* (New York: Scripps Howard, 1991), 471.

6   Donal Door, *Option for the Poor* (Maryknoll, N.Y.: Orbis Books, 1983), 3.

7   Matthew 25:40.

8   John Paul II, speech at Yankee Stadium, New York, October 1979.

30

Vision/Conversion

The "great" commitment all too easily obscures the "little" one. But without the humility and warmth which you have to develop in your relations to the few with whom you are personally involved, you will never be able to do anything for the many.

Dag Hammarskjöld[1]

Visional Ethics

In chapter 21 we explored the terrain of moral development, especially the reality of how growth occurs in moral reasoning from childhood to adulthood. Kohlberg's studies seemed to indicate that the way people thought about right and wrong changed from a group mentality to a more theoretically principled approach in adulthood, given a commensurate psychosocial maturity. Furthermore, Carol Gilligan noted that women tend to think in more relational terms when making moral decisions. In both cases, the focus was on a morality, or ethics, which may be termed juridical, that is to say, an approach that looks at rules and regulations, rights and duties, and obligations and principles as the governing modalities.

Historically, the Pharisees of Jesus' time represent the epitome of legalism. They prescribed a bewildering array of religious practices, purification rituals, and scrupulous behavior as a way of showing that they worshiped God. Their hypocrisy was condemned because they lost sight of the interior disposition of the heart by replacing it with external appearances of goodness. Plato, however, argued that the good person is not only just, but also wise, temperate, and courageous.[2] In other words, the unity of character in the good person combines several important personality traits that appear simultaneously. Underneath specific issues are attitudes and beliefs that offer different solutions to problems depending on one's point of view. This is the true center of morality and ethics, the vision within our hearts. The Pharisees' concern for regulations masked their desire to control the people. Jesus wished to break with the letter of the law and invite people to look at their personal attitudes and beliefs.

One of the most popular characters in Western fiction is Don Quixote. Immortalized by the sixteenth-century Spanish novelist, Miguel de Cervantes, Quixote found new life in the Broadway production, *Man of La Mancha*. "To dream the impossible dream, to reach the unreachable star . . . that is my quest" are words from a song that captures the spirit of Quixote.[3] After much travail, he convinces a young woman that although she is a prostitute, she is still worthwhile. Quixote's vision of goodness, or morality, had little to do with problem-solving or with rules and regulations. It was not that he believed in anarchy or thought that people should do anything they wished. What mattered most were the things of the heart.

This is the type of thinking characterized in *The Little Prince* by Antoine de Saint-Exupéry. "It is only with the heart that one sees rightly; what is essential is invisible to the eye."[4] Juridical ethics focuses on issues of right and wrong much the same way as a judge might do in a court of law. Visional ethics, on the other hand, depends on how one sees reality and how one responds to it.[5] If the vision we have of ourselves is noble, if the dreams we carry for society are enriching and inclusive, and if the faith and hope in our hearts lift us above the anxiety and pessimism that so often suffocate our highest aspirations, we are living out a morality not limited to the law but driven by the spirit.

The word *character* has several nuances, the best of which indicates those qualities of personality that are noble and good. When we hear words like *trustworthy, competent, generous, likable,* and *honest* used to describe someone's character, we feel assured that the person is decent and possesses moral integrity. Consequently, character-building has to do with those qualities of life to which we should aspire. It is not a function of rules. A person of upright character lives out a vision that expresses her or his ideal of the good life. Conversely, the disreputable character has a vision that leads to destruction of others as well as herself or himself. In short, a conscious decision to mold one's life according to a vision of human dignity for all underlies the best legal codes. When the spirit dies, codes ossify and become bludgeons in the hands of the mighty.

Revelation

The following is a story from a student.

"Yesterday, I was driving down the Atlantic City Expressway in the pouring rain. Cars were almost at a standstill because you couldn't see a thing. Because I had no radio, I began to think of things I had been reading, and I came up with a magnificent vision: I had read about torture lately, especially of the young black children in South Africa. I have a lot of faith in women and children because in general, they are a lot less violent than men. So my vision was that someone would send secret notes to the wives of the big shots in South Africa, both black and white. Presidents', colonels', and ambassadors' wives from both races would come together for a weekend conference. At first, they would be wary of each other, but by the end of the weekend they would be walking out hand in hand, black and white, after having been introduced to the similarities in vision that they had. No one wanted war, everyone wanted their children to be able to grow up, and everyone wanted their husbands to come home alive. They would go back to their regions and share these ideas with women everywhere. They would unite their children with the simple idea that black kids like to play with dolls too, white kids like to play with trucks too.

"The kids would look at each other as friends, not as black or white. After this unanimous change had taken place, they would all march on the capital and demand the release of imprisoned women and children. If someone would try to fire in the crowd, he wouldn't be able to do it because his wife and son would be in there somewhere. The women and children would demand human rights and peace. The children would be set free and the men, seeing how utterly stupid they were, would collaborate with the women to form a new African style for both the black and white races!!

"Just as I laughed and thought how idealistic and utopian this idea was, the rain just about completely ceased, and no kidding—a huge, beautiful rainbow appeared."

Visional ethics demands this type of dreaming, a kind of thinking that pushes our imagination beyond the daily routine of life. Generally, we get so bogged down with a cruise-control life that we hardly ever think of changing speeds, or direction, or even getting a different car! Not all of our dreams will come true, but without dreaming of new possibilities, our brains atrophy.

Flannery O'Connor, a celebrated writer of rural Southern fiction, demonstrated the power of imagination in her short story, "Revelation." Ruby Turpin, a stalwart, class-conscious Christian woman of impeccable reputation (at least in her own mind), is attacked one day by a seemingly demented college girl who calls her a warthog. Ruby cannot shake this image of herself until she gets a vision, or revelation, of many unimportant people going up to heaven before her.

> There were whole companies of white trash, clean for the first time in their whole lives, and bands of black niggers in white robes, and battalions of freaks and lunatics shouting and clapping and leaping like frogs.[6]

Suddenly, she is aware that much of her presumed dignity, common sense, and respectable behavior had little to do with Christianity. We sometimes think that revelation is connected to hearing a voice from God and is reserved exclusively for bishops, priests, and nuns. If that were the case, one could hardly conceive of a God who is Father and Mother to all people. O'Connor, through the personage of Ruby Turpin, dramatically emphasized not only that the handicapped and lowly are first in God's Kingdom, as Jesus himself had said,[7] but she also communicated how the imagined revelation of the last being the first gradually opened Ruby's heart to conversion. While it is the stuff of novels, it is also the reality of human life.

This is again most evident in the life of Jesus. His parables about the rich man and the beggar, the Good Samaritan, the foolish and wise virgins, and many others are simple lessons that reveal the truth about human life. Thus, it is important that we take our own experiences seriously. They surely tell us a lot about who we are and what we are doing with our lives. Naturally, for the reflective person, insights into life abound. They may unfold from stories in the newspapers, films we see, novels we read, people we meet, or any one of dozens of things that happen to us each day. We see then that the Word of God is revealed within the context of our laughter and our tears. As the story of our life unfolds, it need not take on the determinism of a television soap, but it should be self-directed toward wholeness with imagination and creativity.

Dangerous Vision

What he saw in Christian ethics . . . was a democratic effort to curb the egoism of the strong—a conspiracy of the chandala [weak] against the free functioning of their superiors, nay, against the free progress of mankind.[8]

These words of H. L. Mencken, an early-twentieth-century American literary critic, encapsulate the argument of Friedrich

Nietzsche, the nineteenth-century German philosopher, against Christianity. In his work, *The AntiChrist,* Nietzsche deplores the alleged stranglehold that Christianity exerts upon the human race by its claim that all people are children of God. He attacks the values of service, love of enemy, and peacemaking as values of the weak.

We are well acquainted with the consequences of Nietzsche's philosophy of a super-race that was used to justify the slaughter of millions of Jews in the death camps of World War II. It was this dangerous vision, that the strong have a right to dominate and even eliminate the weak, that led to the Holocaust. Christianity, or more precisely the teaching of Jesus, insists that this is not the way to true human life. Advocates of dominative power, in any guise, share the belief that Christian values are worthless.

Other dangerous visions that undercut the responsibility we owe to others are the twin philosophies of objectivism and determinism. On the one hand, we may treat everyone as objects by denying their individuality, acting as though they were merely pawns on a chessboard or toy soldiers in a game. This objectification of people, this dangerous vision that distorts the personal, can be found in education, business, the military, and even within the churches.

Determinism, on the other hand, refuses to deal with meaning and purpose. This fatalist vision of life finds expression in the working routine of many businesspeople who allow little time for personal reflection and much less time for their families and other friends. Friendship is not a particularly desirable goal for them. It is a convenience at best, a liability at worst. In the pursuit of power, money, or a narrowly restrictive sense of success, they will do anything to get their way.

On a more global scale, the vision of the material good life, where everyone has an automobile, air-conditioning, and unrestricted use of the earth's resources, is coming to an end. Modernity began with a promise of unlimited growth by way of the Industrial Revolution. Science and technology, it was promised, would solve human problems and lead the way into a future where all would share in the abundance of wealth and opportunity.

As the twentieth century comes to a close, the consequences of this dangerous vision of unlimited material progress are all too apparent. Environmental pollution of the water, air, and soil has reached epic proportions. Nuclear waste continues to pile up around the globe while waiting for scientists to find disposal sites that will house this lethal garbage for the next ten thousand years! The greenhouse effect and the ozone depletion problem constitute a monumental calamity for our children. If we continue to waste energy and expend valuable resources on superfluous goods instead of life's necessities, the future of the planet will remain bleak.

Finally, and perhaps the worst of all visions, is the vision of no vision. To have no vision or convictions about the meaning and purpose of one's life, to have abandoned or never begun the search for one's unique place in the world, or to have never dreamed about creating a world of peace and justice is to have suppressed our most beautiful gift: the power of vision. We need to be mindful of dangerous visions that harm our planet, our neighbors, and ourselves; we need to dream of new ways to benefit humankind.

Conversion from . . .

Conversion of the heart often begins with conversion of the mind. In an earlier chapter, it was suggested that a moonview of planet Earth helped us to get a broader perspective on the global problems that exist. By analogy, we find that a new vision of how things ought to be should give us the courage to work for reform. If our mind's eye can be converted to seeing new possibilities, our spirit can be energized to build a better world.

The starting point, however forbidding it may seem, is to recover a sense of sin. During the trial of Adolf Eichmann for Nazi war crimes, Hannah Arendt, an American journalist and philosopher, observed that Eichmann's real evil was rooted in the banality of his thoughtlessness. She says that he viewed himself as a cog in a wheel, "an innocent executor of some mysteriously foreordained destiny."[9] This deterministic attitude, that we are not responsible for our behavior, is the polar opposite of the idea that we are free to do anything we want to do.

Late-nineteenth-century Irish writer Oscar Wilde envisioned human freedom as natural and uninhibited behavior.[10] Neither of these opposites, determinism or license, admits the reality of sin, that is to say, a sense that at times we behave badly and are responsible for that behavior. Thus, the first step in the conversion process is to admit our complicity in the evils of our times. If we are not part of the solution, we are part of the problem.

In *Call to Conversion,* Jim Wallis distinguishes between the possessed and the dispossessed. The latter suffer from poverty and the deprivation of material necessities, the former from anxiety and an attachment to their goods. But spiritual poverty is not easy to acknowledge. We are possessed by our possessions, but are blind to the consequences.

> Material goods have become substitutes for faith. It's not that people place their cars on the altar; rather, it is the function of these goods in a consumer society. They function as idols, even though most affluent U.S. Christians, like rich Christians throughout history, would deny it.[11]

For Wallis, the idol of possessions looms as the most paramount sin in the United States. We might begin an examination of conscience by listening to some average conversations. "How's the new car?" "Are you going to Cancun for semester break?" "Did you see the new blouse (or shirt) I just got?" Questions about where to eat and what to buy are part of the daily American dialogue. Answers, of course, are forthcoming from the advertising industry, which continues to entice the voracious animal "consumer" with more and better goodies until it can think of nothing else but the next meal. We should ask ourselves if possessions possess us. If they do, a change of heart is called for.

A change of heart may be self-induced by asking a few simple questions about my needs and wants. Is more money an end in itself? Do I seek my own pleasure with no thought about another's dignity? Am I learned in the ways of the world, but ignorant of the ways of love? Is the bottom line my ultimate goal? Is my prayer for more or for less? Do my political convictions support the needy or are they for my own personal benefit? These and other similar questions challenge us to a conversion of heart that assumes responsibility for the world and joins with others in naming the false idols in our midst.

Wallis also links our lack of concern for the needy with our excessive reliance on weapons. He says that intimately tied to the sins of consumerism and greed is the militarism that seeks to protect the American way of life.

> The sign of the nuclear age is the Bomb. The sign of Christ is the Cross. The Bomb is the countersign of the Cross; it arrogantly threatens to undo the work that the Cross has done. In the Cross, all things are reconciled; in the Bomb, all things are destroyed. In the Cross, violence is defeated; in the Bomb, violence is victorious. In the Cross, evil has been overcome; in the Bomb, evil has dominion. In the Cross, death is swallowed up; in the Bomb, death reigns supreme. Which will hold sway in our times? Will we choose to live under the sign of the Cross or the sign of the Bomb? Finally, which sign will the church choose for its own life? The great evangelistic task before us is to convert our people from the Bomb to the Cross.[12]

Conversion to . . .

"Repent, for the kingdom of heaven has come near."[13] Conversion from sin means a turning toward goodness. Both presuppose that we know right from wrong, good from evil. We have seen how much of the modern world has blinded itself to immorality by hiding it under the cloaks of freedom and determinism. We need to remove these coverings and identify the spiritual decay that is rotting the fabric of society. By doing so, we will have taken a first step in the conversion process, that is, we will have accepted our share of the blame for personal conflicts and the larger ills of society.

The place to start is with personal relationships. Frequently, clashes occur when one person assumes that the other knows what he or she needs. This is an assumption often unfounded. Friendships thrive when both people share their personal hopes and dreams and also their fears and tears. It is crucial that we take the time to hear each other's story. We are each unique genetically, with histories as diverse as Brooklyn and Peoria. In turning toward one another with open minds, and eyes that are willing to look into the heart, we begin the journey of personal love that is a precondition for love of the world.

This second type of conversion, a conversion to the world, is characterized by the development of a social conscience. Within the past few years, more and more stars in the entertainment world have turned their attention to the needy. Bob Geldof's song "Do They Know It's Christmas?" led the way for millions of people to support relief assistance in Ethiopia.[14] Hands Across America raised additional funds for the poor. Students in high schools and on campuses across the country have engaged in service projects as diverse as visiting convalescent homes and washing dishes at soup kitchens.

But service is only one part of the story. An awakened social conscience includes an awareness and understanding of structural sin, as well as personal sin. Many economic and political policies and programs contain within themselves the seeds of destruction for vast numbers of people. While not deliberately setting out to hurt anyone directly, government and business decisions adversely affect the poor. Tax policies, military expenditures, capital investment, and plant relocation decisions impact the lives of society's most vulnerable people. Conversion to . . . , therefore, turns us toward political and social involvement. Our citizenship gives us the opportunity to promote the values of human dignity and solidarity. Consequently, we need to convert our political and economic systems to benefit the least among us.

To young people everywhere I say: let us together create a new future of friendship and solidarity; let us reach out toward our brothers and sisters in need, feed the hungry, shelter the home-less, free the downtrodden, bring justice where injustice reigns and peace where only weapons speak.[15]

These inspirational words of Pope John Paul II call us to conversion. They project for us a vision of the good life in terms of love, justice, compassion, and service. They urge us to put people before products, nutrition before munitions, and care of the poor and oppressed before our own wants and desires. Conversion and vision join hands in the transformation of self-centered values to other-centered ones. It is always a slow and painful process because we are both reluctant to admit our guilt and resistant to change our ways. But change we must if we are convinced that each person, regardless of race, religion, sex, nationality, or economic status, is worthy of respect. Our beliefs must change, our attitudes must be transformed, and our behavior must be brought into line with the values of free-dom, truth, justice, and peace. How to bring this about will be the subject of Part IV.

Notes

1   Dag Hammarskjöld, *Markings* (New York: Ballantine Books, 1964), 112.

2   Craig Dykstra, *Vision and Character* (New York: Paulist Press, 1981), 10.

3   Joe Darion, "The Quest (The Impossible Dream)," *The Man of La Mancha* (New York: Washington Square Theare, 1965).

4   Antoine de Saint-Exupéry, *The Little Prince* (New York: Harcourt, Brace and World 1943), 70.

5   Dykstra, *Vision and Character*, 2.

6   Flannery O'Connor, "Revelation," in *Three by Flannery O'Connor* (New York: Signet Books, 1983), 423.

7   Luke 14:15–24.

8   H. L. Mencken in the Introduction to F. W. Nietzsche, *The AntiChrist* (New York: Alfred Knopf, 1918), 21.

9   Bernard J. Verkamp, "Recovering a Sense of Sin," *America*, November 19, 1983, 305.

10   Ibid., 307.

11   Jim Wallis, *The Call to Conversion* (San Francisco: Harper & Row, 1981), 49.

12   Ibid., 88.

13   Matthew 3:2.

14   Bob Geldof, "Do They Know It's Christmas?" (London: Sarm West Studios, 1984).

15   John Paul II, "Remembering Hiroshima," *The Catholic Worker*, April, 1981.

Part IV

Influence

How Do I Change Things?

Introduction

"Americans have little sense of evil" was a conclusion drawn from a recent study of American life by the French sociologist Levi-Strauss. We are an optimistic people due to a historical consciousness where new frontiers beckoned and all problems could be overcome with muscle and sweat. We are a nation of empire builders, a people who can make things happen, a culture often built around blindness to its own faults.

Currently we live with three great American myths: the myth of no problem, the myth of no pain, and the myth of paralysis. In addressing the first myth, we must admit that there are very big and serious problems in our world today. In many places, violence and hatred are the order of the day. People starve while others gorge themselves. Cruise ships anchor in harbors where poverty is rampant. Something is seriously wrong with a world that has built an arms arsenal large enough to cremate the entire planet several times over.

The second myth of our time suggests that little pain is involved in living a fully human life. Naturally enough, we all experience ailments of one sort or another that cause us pain. But the pain and suffering we are discussing are not the ordinary discomforts involved in the routine of life. We are referring to the suffering taken on when one stands up for the dignity of others and decides to work on behalf of the poor and oppressed peoples of the world.

The final myth is the myth of paralysis. This means that when we look at the enormous array of problems in the world, on both local and global levels, we tend to be so overwhelmed by them that we are incapable of action. Appropriate here are the old saying about Rome not being built in a day and the Chinese proverb "a thousand-mile journey begins with the first step." We must convince ourselves that we share responsibility for the world and can make a difference. Global problems are complex and often appear implacable. But though we tire and feel weary, we cannot afford to quit.

What is essential to keep in mind is that most human problems have human solutions. It is always a question of bearing responsibility for the burdens of another. We need to overcome the paralysis that sometimes invades our minds by using our creative imagination to see new possibilities for change.

In Part IV, we hope to examine some external influences on our lives and find ways to join with others in building a better world. May we be energized enough to see the problems, accept the pain, and respond with our best efforts.

31

Self-Influence

Young people everywhere are aspiring to a world of justice and opportunity. They are seeking remedies to the poverty that hurts much of mankind and an end to the arms race. I believe that no institution or government should ignore the significance of what they are saying.

Javier Pérez de Cuéllar[1]

Moments of Crisis

When we entered the world as babies, we each received the shocks of our lives. Otto Rank referred to it as the "birth trauma." Try to imagine yourself floating around in a bowl full of warm Jell-o. There are a few muffled outside noises and a protective darkness all around you. All of a sudden the bright operating room lights go on, the warmth of the embryonic fluid is gone, and a doctor is slapping your bottom. This earliest influence on our lives may never be remembered, but it was real nonetheless.

This is true about much of our early childhood. Although buried in the subconscious, it still influences us positively and negatively. Parents know that they cannot pick up their child every time she or he cries, or a sense of independence will not develop. They also know that children need to be held and stroked in order to grow up knowing affection and love. The trick is learning how to strike a balance.

As we grow older we begin to make more and more decisions for ourselves. Erik Erikson, whom we discussed in chapter 22 in connection with the epigenetic principle of normal human development, emphasized that growth occurred when the moment of crisis for each stage was successfully resolved. For example, adolescents must understand themselves reasonably well, recognizing their capabilities and limits, before they are ready for young adulthood. Noting that Erikson saw each crisis as a moment of increased vulnerability and heightened potential,[2] it follows that courage is necessary for full psychosocial development.

Courage, or the ability to take risks, is the key to making decisions that will push us toward maturity rather than chain us to childhood. Risk-taking may involve learning how to drive a car, climbing a mountain, or even the simple yet anxiety-producing feat of standing in front of a group and giving a brief talk. Isaac Newton discovered that in the physical world change is produced by external forces; Erikson found that in the inner world of the self, change, or more accurately maturity, comes from internal forces, namely, the taking of risks. Call it bravery, courage, pluck, or chutzpah, in any case, it is an important quality to nourish, if we are to stand against the pressures of conformity that ask us to settle for mediocrity.

Peck's Problem

"Life is a bitch, and then you die; have a nice day" is the logo on Willie Nelson's T-shirt. With a scruffy bandana topping a weathered face, he sings his ballads of love and life. This motto resonates well with people, since most know all too well the hurt and pain of life, yet retain a strong desire to hang tough. M. Scott Peck, an American psychiatrist, in his best-seller *The Road Less Traveled*, also tells us that life is difficult.[3] Although he is well acquainted with a large variety of mental and emotional problems, he is not speaking here about abnormal circumstances. Peck sees the human condition as one long struggle to overcome the vast array of trials and difficulties that beset us. From the Twelve Labors of Hercules, found in ancient Greek mythology, to the present nightmare of nuclear weapons, the human family has been locked in combat with nature and with itself. Our biggest mistake, according to Peck, is to think that life is easy. Admittedly, there is little doubt that just as electricity and water follow the path of least resistance, so do we. Taking the easy way out is a common human phenomenon. So is trying to get the biggest reward for the least effort. But this is often wishful thinking. To accept the premise that life is difficult is to face reality. In spite of the beer commercials telling us "it can't get much better than this," we should not be fooled.

In one way or another we chafe at the control that others constantly try to impose upon us. The teacher who insists on promptness, the police officer with summons book at the ready, and parents who demand that things be done their way, all represent difficulties that we must face from outside ourselves. Add to all of this the constant specter of death, and we begin to get an honest view of the problems we face.

In addition to the inner turmoil experienced, we occasionally do dumb things to ourselves. Have you ever lost your keys, wallet, handbag, or jacket? When was the last time you banged your elbow or twisted your ankle? Is it possible that in a recent conversation you said some things that you now regret? We can all make our own list of the faux pas we commit and the tensions that we bring upon ourselves. This should add up to a realization, if we are to be honest, that life is difficult. Both the external and internal problems of life press upon us. The question is: how do we deal with them?

Solutions to the difficulties of life abound. A common form of handling problems is to go down the drug and alcohol road. Pharmaceutical companies and the liquor industry reap fortunes by assuring people that "they haven't got time for the pain," or that they can't have a good time without booze.

It is common knowledge that drug and alcohol addiction has ruined countless lives, yet millions continue to seek solace in a bottle or a pill.

A close second to substance abuse for handling the difficulties of life is found in playtime. Granted that everyone has legitimate needs for recreation; however, many run from the responsibilities of life by absorbing themselves in the make-believe world of entertainment. The stereotype "Joe" who comes in from work, pops open a can of beer, then falls into his favorite chair to watch television for the evening is not far off the mark for many people. Films, shows, sports, and all of the vast network of activities that are termed recreational distract us from the real tasks of life.

Finally, we have the mechanism of denial. Instead of talking things out, many married couples will sweep their problems under the rug. Students will deny that they themselves are responsible for their low grades. It's easier to blame the teacher. Thus, we have the destructive paths of substance abuse, habitual entertainment, and denial. But is there a better way? Is there a road less traveled?

Peck's Solution

"Discipline is the basic set of tools we require to solve life's problems."[4] This simple, but quite profound truth, says Peck, is the answer we need in order to manage the struggles of life. He agrees with Viktor Frankl that much of life is filled with suffering and would also agree, on a philosophical level, that we need to find meaning in the suffering. Peck's contribution, however, lies not so much in direction, but in providing us with the tools with which we can confront the difficulties threatening to dominate our lives.

Self-discipline is a quality of life that enables us to experience legitimate suffering without resorting to the false solutions provided by drugs, play, or denial. He believes that discipline has four major components: (1) delaying gratification, (2) acceptance of responsibility, (3) dedication to truth, and

(4) balancing.[5] Let us examine each of these in turn in order to understand their importance.

Delaying Gratification

"No dessert until you eat your dinner!" cry moms the world over. Realizing as we do that mothers know best, this bit of homey wisdom characterizes the concept of delaying gratification. Those who seek the pleasures of life without a willingness to work for its rewards fool themselves into thinking that they can obtain good results from poor productivity. Even popular beer commercials tell us the truth when they show the hard work that goes into roping cattle, climbing telephone poles, and constructing buildings before it's "Miller Time." "Miller Time" is a most necessary part of life, but if it comes before the day's work is complete our priorities are disordered.

Delaying gratification, then, is an essential ingredient of discipline. Although many students tend to put off assignments, procrastinate endlessly, and waste time getting ready to study, few would disagree that the right way to do things is to do the studying before the partying, not after. The successful reporter knows that the story will not be well written unless many hours are spent checking out the facts; the rock star commits days and weeks in rehearsal time for one performance; and all sports players will testify to the conditioning and training necessary for athletic competition.

When we learn to delay gratification, we find a richer sense of joy at having done our real work first.

Acceptance of Responsibility

It struck many people as odd when they saw the local chief of police helping to remove garbage from an empty lot. When asked why he was picking up the garbage, he simply said that he felt a sense of responsibility for keeping the neighborhood clean. Many people have developed the good habit of cleaning up after themselves at lunch counters, in rest rooms, in classrooms, and in other public places. They have acquired a sense of responsibility for the common good. Peck believes this sense of responsibility is another essential component of discipline.

When we accept responsibility for our own lives, the tasks assigned to us, and the general welfare of society, we begin to experience the personal satisfaction that comes from contributing to the solutions of life's problems. A responsible person is sensitive to the needs of others, is ready to lend a helping hand, and does not seek rewards. His or her joy comes from doing a good job. How we treat others, how we fulfill our duties, how we care for our health and welfare will indicate the measure of our acceptance of responsibility.

Finally, although responsibilities will shift throughout the course of our lives, if we acknowledge and accept them as times change, we can greatly lessen our burdens. Thus, by taking control of events rather than having them control us, we can decide the direction life will take.

Dedication to Truth

We have already seen the distinction between scientifically measured truth and truth understood as that which gives life. Gandhi's truth-force was not concerned with mathematical formulas or the secrets of the atom, but with discovering the way of nonviolent interaction among people. It is this latter dedication we are to nourish without demeaning the former. We have more than once noted the tendency to stay away from the dark corners of our personality and to deny the disturbing realities within the social orders.

Seekers of truth, however, are not afraid to deal with reality, even in its darkest forms. When we develop the necessary discipline to look honestly at our failings and to affirm our abilities, then we are dedicated to the truth about ourselves. This discipline forces us to find the time, on a regular basis, in which to reassess who we are and where we are going with our lives. Rabbis and pastors often help with this process within the church or synagogue.

In addition, the Arab proverb, "A man who tells the truth must have a fast horse," reminds us that telling the truth can be risky. There is a fine line between honesty and cruelty when we share thoughts and feelings about each other. Our minds may entertain images and expressions about others that we know are false and ones that we know are true (or we think are true), but would hurt others if we spoke them. In these instances truth-telling is harmful. The person who is constantly pointing out the mistakes of others or ridiculing their failures will have few friends. Dedication to truth calls us to honesty with ourselves and life-giving affirmation toward others. It is another essential element in dealing with the problems of life.

Balance

One of the hardest lessons of life to learn is how to let go of previous responsibilities when situations change and new duties come along. It is amusing to see parents still telling their children how to behave even when the "children" are forty years of age. Conversely, it is sad to see a parent driving kids all over suburbia when they are old enough to drive themselves.

The trapeze artist offers us an image of how important the discipline of balancing can be. Just as he or she is helped by a long pole and quality shoes, so too we are often helped by good friends. Balancing our way through life involves the nurturing of our own abilities, care, and attention to our friends, and a concern for the needy of our land. To balance work, play, family responsibilities, assistance to the poor, and all the hundred and one other items that come our way sometimes makes us feel like the circus clown juggling pins. If we go too fast, or pick up one too many pins, they may all fall. Clowns, however, never give up. They may look at the mess for a moment, but before long they pick up the pieces and are back at the task.

Discipline, then, is the secret to a successful life. It is composed of delayed gratification, acceptance of responsibility, dedication to truth, and maintaining psychological and spiritual balance. This is the way we influence ourselves and have a positive influence on our society.

The Quest for Excellence

The White House of the early 1960s was charged with energy. A new president, John F. Kennedy, had surrounded himself with some of the most intelligent, public-minded, and concerned citizens he could find. Consequently, the air was filled with fresh ideas about national policy. Quite naturally, millions of Americans across the country caught the fever. He challenged his generation to dream about a better world: a world where the hungry are fed, the homeless are sheltered, and the weapons of war are silenced. His influence filled people with a deep desire to do their best.

This doing of one's best is the quest for excellence. Since everyone has the ability to influence the world constructively, we need to believe in our own abilities. Far too often we settle for mediocrity, making only half-hearted efforts. This is the attitude of a sluggard. Recently a young boy of only six was cited for bravery because he pushed his injured mother up a fifty-foot embankment to where help could be sought. The boy said that the child's tale about "The Little Engine That Could" gave him the strength to go on.[6] Accounts like this abound. We need to ask ourselves each day if we are prepared to do our best at whatever it is that needs our attention.

Success does not happen overnight. Whether it is a graduation diploma, a good conduct ribbon, or a promotion to regional sales manager, all of these achievements take time and effort. We may describe the quest for excellence not as an accomplished fact, but rather as a journey toward a worthwhile destination. It implies that mountains must be climbed, rivers forded, and underbrush cut away, all the while providing for the mundane needs of body and spirit. It took Magellan's expedition three years to circumnavigate the globe and only ninety minutes for the Mercury spacecraft to perform a similar feat. In both instances, however, enormous preparation and minute planning went into each venture. Only when we become aware that the real test of one's goodness can be likened to the endurance of a long-distance runner will we appreciate that true excellence lies not so much in finishing the race, but in running it well.

Part IV is about influence. The influences that have shaped our lives, especially family and friends, serve as a background. In the present moment we are faced with the influences of our society: positive ones, such as freedom and equality, and negative ones, like individualism and materialism. Family, friends, neighbors, and acquaintances of all sorts continue to impact us.

At the center of this dynamic interaction stands the self. Have we developed the necessary disciplines of delayed gratification, a sense of responsibility, dedication to truth, and the balance to reject destructive influences and to accept constructive ones? Are the values of personal dignity and human solidarity so strongly imbedded in us that no external influences will shake them? Are we in charge of our lives?

The entire project of this text has been to offer the reader a broad overview of life as we move into the twenty-first century and to respond to that reality with conviction, courage, and commitment. The ways in which we mold our own lives and the directions we give to them can have a lasting and positive influence on the world. Let us make the most of the opportunities that come our way and join hands with all who desire to build a better world.

Notes

1   Javier Pérez de Cuéllar, excerpt from statement at United Nations World Conference for the International Youth Year, *U.N. Chronicle*, January, 1986, 2.

2   Erik Erikson, *Identity, Youth and Crisis* (New York: W.W. Norton, 1968), 96.

3   M. Scott Peck, *The Road Less Traveled* (New York: Touchstone, 1978), 15.

4   Ibid.

5   Ibid., 18.

6   *Newsweek,* July 4, 1988, 35.

32

Educational Influence

There is no such thing as a neutral educational process. Education either functions as an instrument which is used to facilitate the integration of the younger generation into the logic of the present system, and bring about conformity to it, or it becomes "the practice of freedom," the means by which men and women deal critically and creatively with reality and discover how to participate in the transformation of their world.

Richard Shaull[1]

From Plato to Bloom

The purpose of this chapter is to awaken in the student a realization that all learning is value-laden. What we learn can direct us toward good or evil. Socrates developed a method of questioning and dialogue as an aid to the ongoing search for truth and goodness. He had the greatest respect for the "autonomy of the individual intellect,"[2] and believed that education was not simply for the sake of gaining knowledge, but rather for the purpose of becoming a good person. Plato, his most renowned student, continued the work of Socrates by emphasizing the importance of civic virtues, that is, those values that promote the good of the whole society.

The educational method of raising and answering questions, of course, is a time-honored practice, but it is most difficult to implement where large numbers of students are involved. Furthermore, the value of seeking the good has been replaced by the value of seeking the practical. Both are values, but we need to ask ourselves which one is better.

Historically, Socrates stressed that learning was directed toward living the good and ethical life; the Church of the Middle Ages saw faith as the goal of learning. These educational values eventually gave way to a new concept, which arose during the Enlightenment. With the continuing warfare among Christians following the Protestant Reformation and the burgeoning of scientific knowledge, it was inevitable that other values would emerge. In the eighteenth century the Age of Enlightenment dawned. It was characterized by a profound commitment to reason alone as the arbiter of truth. Objectivity, bereft of any value considerations, became the norm. Democracy, understood as a breaking away from an arbitrary ruler, and the privatization of faith were the companions of objectivity. In our present day, we find that knowledge for the sake of expediency is the dominant educational value.

In *The Closing of the American Mind*,[3] Allan Bloom takes American higher education to task for its lack of attention to the questions of life that deal with truth, goodness, and meaning. In fact, much of education does not operate in the Socratic method of question and dialogue. The result of a "tank-up" approach to education (pour in as many facts as possible) is that students are hardly given a chance to ask serious questions, much less discuss them. The knowledge explosion is part of the problem since there are so many new and important discoveries in the sciences and arts that it is virtually impossible to know one field of discipline well.

The pursuit of the buck has also affected education. Today, most students indicate that financial success is their primary reason for attending college. This is in contrast to the traditional ideal of education for the sake of understanding and wisdom. If the cultural values of power and wealth dictate the institutional goals for higher education, it is no wonder that students receive little encouragement to get beyond courses that load them up with data but offer little in the way of reflection.

Conscientization

Most of us, no doubt, are familiar with Christopher Columbus and his "discovery" of a "New World." It was a monumental event in the story of civilization. His courage as a navigator and explorer has been praised for several centuries, and we may be sure that the five hundredth anniversary of his voyage (1992) will be celebrated with much fanfare and adulation. Does he really deserve this praise? Quoting from Howard Zinn's *A People's History of the United States,* we read an account by Columbus:

> As soon as I arrived in the Indies, on the first island which I found, I took some of the natives by force in order that I might learn and they might give me information of whatever there is in these parts.[4]

The information he wanted from the natives was simple. Where is the gold? Few of us are taught that the purpose of his voyage was to find the rumored gold and spices of Asia, the original destination. On the first journey he found some gold, but upon his return to Spain he gave exaggerated reports about the wealth of what he thought was Asia. He promised Ferdinand and Isabella "as much gold as you need . . . and as many slaves as you ask" in return for the opportunity to undertake a second voyage.

The awful tragedy that followed upon his return was detailed by Bartolomé de Las Casas in his *History of the Indies,* a multivolume account of the genocide of the Arawak Indians, who were native to the Caribbean. Las Casas wrote that when he arrived in 1508:

> There were 60,000 people living on this island [Cuba], including the Indians; so that from 1494 to 1508, over three million people

had perished from the war, slavery, and the mines. Who in future generations will believe this? I myself who am writing it as a knowledgeable eyewitness can hardly believe it.[5]

Thus, if we read our history from the point of view of the conquerors and the dominant-power people, we accept the exploits of Columbus as normative for the progress of the human race. We are taught that the search for gold or the accumulation of wealth, in its various forms of land and property, is a good thing. Too bad a few million Indians were here before us!

On the other hand, if we begin to read history with a set of values that begins with human dignity and solidarity; if we attempt to read history from the viewpoint of the Indians who shared the land with each other and saw it as a common heritage; if we put ourselves in the shoes of the oppressed and the poor; if we begin to read history from the underside, we are beginning to grasp a new way of learning.

The term *conscientization*, which refers to consciousness-raising or moral awakening, was coined by Paulo Freire, a Latin American educator, in order to help the poor of his own country become aware of their undeserved poverty. He wanted them to change their situation. By working with the poor, he noticed that they were apathetic toward change because they thought that their misery and oppression were the way things must be. Many believed that their suffering came from God. By getting them to talk about their lives and gain a respect for their own humanity, he gradually awakened them to a new awareness of reality. They realized that their poverty and suffering were a result, not of God's curse, but of greed and their exploition by the rich and powerful.[6]

Education for Justice

When we begin to understand education as a way of awakening our consciences to a greater sensitivity about good and evil, we have begun the process of justice education. If we look at

natural phenomena and study other people as objects, we tend
to distance ourselves from what we see. We objectify them. For
example, the voyeur mind that habitually seeks sexual satisfaction through visual stimuli such as *Playboy* photos, romantic
novels, and pornographic films does not see the opposite sex
as real people with feelings and intelligence, ambitions and
dreams, joys and sorrows. We need to understand that "The
relationship between subject and object should therefore be
seen as a dialectical relationship between things separate yet
bound together, where each changes and affects the other while
remaining distinctively itself."[7]

Do we see ourselves in relationship to others? Do not all
relationships imply mutual responsibility? By raising our consciousness to a level where the values of personal dignity and
human solidarity have taken on real meaning, we become
"justice-people." Education for justice is a process of awakening. Our perception of justice is refined, and we become engaged in seeking justice for all.

Ideally, education begins with the subject, namely, the individual unique person who is the learner. She or he should not
be "tanked-up" with information but should be drawn out and
encouraged to wrestle with a problem-posing type of learning
experience. This kind of education respects the individual and
allows for personal growth.

If we focus our consciousness so that it becomes a critical
consciousness, we will continuously question ourselves and re-
make our interpretation of the world. What is being sought is
nothing less than an educational process that aims at the hu-
manization of the individual. This allows the student to learn,
to interpret, and to understand by questioning and dialogue,
rather than by accepting another's "truth" simply on the authority of the teacher. This kind of education necessitates much
give-and-take by students and teachers, but results in a greater
respect for the personal integrity of both learner and learned.
During the 1984 presidential campaign, Ronald Reagan saw
America as a glamorous city upon a hilltop, while Mario
Cuomo looked down the mountain and pointed to America's

crime, poverty, and unemployment problems. Who is telling the truth? The world of the rich and famous may look golden, but the view from down below is more bleak.

Some people are pessimistic by nature; others optimistic. Whatever our backgrounds, previous attitudes, or prejudices, if we are willing to seek truth, we will engage in a learning dialogue. Dialogue implies respect and an attitude of listening. This type of learning sharpens our informational skills and our critical judgments.

Finally, it is unfortunate that many identify education with a classroom experience that, for the most part, is a transmission model. If, however, we come to see education as dialogue, dialogue as communal, and communal harmony residing in justice, we will have grasped the connection between justice and education. Education that is limited to getting ahead in life is shallow. Education for justice, however, seeks to appreciate the uniqueness of each person and strives to create a better world.

Education for Peace

We have grasped the mystery of the atom and rejected the Sermon on the Mount. Ours is a world of nuclear giants and ethical infants. We know more about war than we do about peace—more about killing than we do about living.[8]

No one doubts the United States' war capabilities. Not only do we have two million people in the armed services, but we also have three major college-age military academies, several hundred Reserve Officer Training Corps (ROTC) units on college and university campuses throughout the country, and a few dozen advanced-training war colleges—all ultimately designed to study the art of warfare. Strategies are designed for infiltrating enemy camps, blocking sea-lanes, combating air and sea forces, and disrupting supply lines. Policies and plans for attacking enemy targets, including major population centers, with nuclear weapons are formulated and studied down to the most minute detail. West Point, Annapolis, and Colorado Springs are synonymous with the training of future generals and admirals.

Almost no one questions the need for military preparedness. Preparation for war not only involves having large supplies of weapons and the men and women to use them, but also includes the officers necessary to conduct the battle. They must be well versed in the making of war. They must study past victories and defeats in order to thwart a future enemy and maintain the peace. In short, it is a peace through strength.

But what about the study of nonviolent peace? How much time, energy, and financial resources has our government committed to reducing tension? In comparison to the billion-dollar budget used to fund our military colleges, how much do we spend on peace studies? Too little, you say? Right. And that, of course, is a national disgrace. For the past dozen years, members of Congress and other interested citizens have lobbied for the creation of a National Peace Academy.

Rev. Theodore Hesburgh, former president of the University of Notre Dame, has served as an advisor for the peace academy campaign. He says that a peace academy would serve three distinct purposes. First, it would research both the causes and effects of peace and the techniques of nonviolence and peacemaking. Second, leaders from all walks of life, including the military, would learn conflict-resolution techniques. Mediation, compromise, and consensus management are not whimsical theories, but complex, detailed processes requiring special skill and training. Last, the peace academy would serve as a resource center for policymakers and government officials needing help in conflict resolution.

"Conflict is inevitable," writes Hesburgh. "We need an Academy of Peace, not to do away with conflict but to learn and teach ... how to creatively manage conflict so that conflict can remain constructive rather than destructive."[9] Unfortunately, public sentiment for peace studies lags behind the concern for war studies. Perhaps if more time were spent studying peace, we would have a safer world.

In addition to education on behalf of peace, many thousands of peace organizations have sprung up throughout the country in recent years. The vast majority of these consist of local groups that support nuclear weapons reduction and an end to the arms race. Some of them, notably in the Quaker tradition, have existed for years. Others, mostly nondenominational, have coalesced around a single issue of major importance. For example, the nuclear accident at Three Mile Island near Harrisburg, Pennsylvania, on March 28, 1979, led to the formation of many citizen groups opposed to the proliferation of nuclear power plants.

Although most of these people were originally concerned about safety issues, the companionship that they experienced with people of like-minded values resulted in a networking across the country under the catchall rubric of peace groups.

The *Grassroots Peace Directory*[10] for 1986 listed 9,323 groups in the United States alone engaged in peace activities. Other similar organizations exist throughout the world. This was attested to by the recent (summer of 1988) March for Peace across the United States by several dozen Soviet citizens. No sane person wants war. We need to study more exhaustively the ways of peace and learn to resolve conflicts nonviolently.

Self-Education

Dorothy Day, a journalist by profession and a Christian by faith, suggested that we should go through life with a Bible in one hand and a newspaper in the other. The daily information about life is balanced with the wisdom of God. We should also remember that newspapers, television shows, and films or plays reflect particular values. Nothing is value-free. Where values originate has little to do with place, but much to do with beliefs and attitudes. Self-education, then, involves growth of mind and heart by a continuous reflection on reality.

The key to self-education is asking questions. Students are reluctant to ask questions, partly to avoid the appearance of stupidity, but primarily because transmission education does not readily allow it. Questions must be asked, internally at least, if real learning is to take place. Renaissance philosophers asked a series of questions relating to the circumstances of an act. "Who?" "what?" "where?" "when?" "how?" and "by what means?" were questions that gave flesh to the reasons for a particular action. The all-important question, however, was "why?" The question of "why?" explores the motivating forces behind our behavior. If we develop the habit of questioning things, we begin to gain broader knowledge about ourselves and the world.

An ancient proverb says "I hear and I forget, I see and I remember, I do and I understand." Hands-on education has always been essential to learning a skill or a trade. No one would expect an apprentice carpenter to study measurements, types of tools, and cutting techniques without simultaneously starting to work with wood. Similarly, peace and justice education cannot be limited to a textbook. One may talk extensively about the need to be compassionate toward the homeless and malnourished, but without the experience of working in a soup kitchen or carrying sandwiches to street people, a discussion amounts to little more than intellectualizing.

Ultimately, as we have seen, education involves conscience. It may be a blind conscience, a dead conscience, or a conscience attuned to the values of justice and peace that flow from a sense of one's personal worth and an appreciation of the global dimensions of the human family. Always, it is a process, a willingness to root out, or at least understand, our prejudices, anxieties, and selfish tendencies. One of Jesus' parables talks of the two brothers, both of whom were asked by their father to perform a certain task. One initially refused, but later did the job; the other said yes, but did not do it.[11] At times, we refuse to reach out to others, but we know that we should. Consequently, in overcoming our self-centeredness we grow in wisdom and grace. It follows that we should always seek greater "conscientization."

Notes

[1] Richard Shaull, *Naming the Idols* (Oak Park, Ill.: Meyer Stone, 1988), 150.

[2] *Encyclopaedia Britannica*, vol. 25 (Chicago: Encyclopaedia Britannica, 1984), 336.

[3] Allan Bloom, *The Closing of the American Mind* (New York: Simon & Schuster, 1987).

[4] Howard Zinn, *A People's History of the United States* (New York: Harper & Row, 1980), 1.

[5] Ibid., 7.

[6] Paulo Freire, *Pedagogy of the Oppressed* (New York: Seabury Press, 1968).

[7] Brian Wren, *Education for Justice* (Maryknoll, N.Y.: Orbis Books, 1977), 3.

[8] Theodore Hesburgh quoting General Omar Bradley, "Speakout," *Common Cause*, April 1982, 6.

[9] Ibid.

[10] *Grassroots Peace Directory* (Topsfield, Conn.: Topsfield Foundation, 1986).

[11] Matthew 21:28–31.

33

Culture

The United States is the first country in history to go from barbarism to decadence without ever going through a period of
civilization.

attributed to French critic Georges Clemenceau[1]

Three Idols

The pursuit of money, power, and sex is so much a part of
cultural America that we hardly notice how much we are en-
thralled by them. It is important that we keep in mind that all
three are perfectly good within the context of their rightful use.
Our concern here is when they function inappropriately, that
is to say, they cause harm either to oneself or to others. In
American culture we are graced with music, dance, fine art,
literature, and other pursuits that enhance life; we are "dis-
graced" in our conspicuous consumption, quests for power, and
recreational sex. Let us examine each of these idols in order to
uncover their destructiveness.

The majority of students who read this text are not wealthy;
in fact, many are struggling with summer jobs and bank loans

to stay in college. The issue here is not about the necessity of having and using money in modern society. It is rather about the mentality of shaping one's life around commodities. We know that Americans consume 40 percent of the world's yearly supply of energy and about one-third of the world's food. Yet we are only one-twentieth of the total population. Our culture measures the worth of people by how well they dress, where they live, and how much money they make. Ask yourself how conscious you are about having the right designer jeans or shirts, the best audio equipment, or the nicest-looking jewelry. We pay individuals millions of dollars to perform athletic feats, to entertain us with music and song, and to mesmerize us with television shows and inane films. The medical and legal professions demand exorbitant fees, and, for too many the almighty dollar reigns supreme.

Of equal destructiveness, both personally and socially, is the power idol. Power can be a supportive energy, especially when we help others to be fully human. It is evil when it controls. In the family and among neighbors and associates the power game is played out through manipulation, deception, and overt physical strength. The early history of our continent saw the European exploitation and domination of the Native Americans. Columbus and other explorers marveled at how docile and sharing the Indians were. How easy to oppress them! By the middle of the nineteenth century the oppression of the indigenous population reached its peak with the motto, "The only good Indian is a dead Indian."

The confluence of money and power becomes apparent when we trace the history of United States military dominance in Central America. The United Fruit Company, Gulf and Western, and dozens of smaller, yet equally vocal, American corporations demanded U.S. intervention in order to retain control of the land and the economy of those countries. The worship of money and power was far more important than the welfare of the peasant population.

Lately, it is commonplace in American society to witness sexually suggestive advertising in selling everything from soap to sandals and from autos to lawn mowers. We have become inured to the lingerie ads that affront us in every newspaper and magazine, and in many television commercials. The Playboy mentality has led young people to believe that sexual activity is as natural as enjoying a good meal and is a lot less fattening. From the onset of puberty, teenagers are pressured by the mores of society that equate sex with pleasure.

Sexuality, however, if it is to be experienced in a truly human way, always involves a mutuality which respects the personal dignity of the other. At its most profound level, sexual intercourse symbolizes the bonding and total commitment of one person to another forever. The marriage ceremony is a public testimony of a love that promises to endure. Those who advocate a shopping-around mentality to see "if the shoe fits" or believe that sleeping around will broaden their range of experience often find that a cheapening of personal respect for their own sexuality, as well as others, leads to shallow relationships.

Is there more to life than sex? Fixation on sexual activity ultimately deadens our humanness and leaves us with little chance to experience the subjective richness of another person. I-Thou is more personally fulfilling than I-It. There is a danger that these three idols of American culture—money, power, and sex—may replace the values of sharing, caring, and love. If we allow them to control our lives, we are worshiping false gods.

Individualism

The idols of money, power, and sex are quite obvious in our culture and most thinking people understand that, if they are not idolized, each serves as a normal and natural part of human life. It is a matter of freely choosing to exercise self-control. Meanwhile, at a deeper level, we find another cultural characteristic in American life that exercises enormous influence over the way we see and think. Alexis de Tocqueville, a French statesman and author, observed in *Democracy in America*, written about 1840, that alongside the biblical and republican traditions another trait was equally dominant. He coined the term *individualism* and wrote:

Individualism is a calm and considered feeling which disposes each citizen to isolate himself from the masses of his fellows and withdraw into the circle of family and friends; with this little society formed to his taste, he gladly leaves the greater society to look after itself.[2]

Because the United States was sparsely settled and isolated from the countries of Europe, and because this new nation imbibed the capitalist philosophy contained in Adam Smith's *Wealth of Nations*, in which mutual self-interest would provide opportunity for all, we developed strong individualistic tendencies. The present crop of Rambo films, the enduring popularity of the Lone Ranger, and the exaltation of superstars in the fields of entertainment and sports lend credence to the strain of individualism running through our culture.

Let us examine three manifestations of its influence by considering the nature of success, the meaning of freedom, and the requirements of justice. In a recent work, *Habits of the Heart*, Robert Bellah, an American sociologist, chose these three common human qualities to explore individualism in our present society.

We have previously offered a broad definition of success that includes personal and social goals. American society, however, seems concerned about measuring success quantitatively, not qualitatively. Therein lies the fundamental difference between living individually or living relationally.

We are able to keep score by counting our money; it is not quite so easy to measure our relational success. Often we find men giving material gifts to their wives, but very little quality time; they measure their success as husbands and fathers by how well they provide for their families, but give little thought to the more important dimensions of listening and sharing.

Second, the meaning of freedom for most Americans also is interpreted individualistically. Freedom for many college students means moving away from home, then, after a year or two, getting their own apartment, having their own stereo, car, and, especially, money. Freedom in America often means "being left alone by others, not having other people's values, ideas or style of life forced upon one, being free of arbitrary authority in work, family, and political life."[3] As a consequence this presumed ideal of freedom from constraints offers little or no freedom to be responsible for anyone but one's self. Individualism in our society only allows us to see freedom in a very restricted manner. Trying to get parents to help with Little League, urging neighbors to volunteer for crime watch, and recruiting help for serving meals in a soup kitchen is difficult work. Many Americans want to be left alone.

Finally, the issue of justice has also been tainted by the disease of individualism. Justice in America is usually equated with the opportunity for everyone to pursue his or her own happiness. While equal justice before the law is honored in theory, more often than not those who can afford the best legal representation usually get more justice than others. It is the poor who are driven to crime by lack of education, little opportunity for worthwhile employment, and patterns of discrimination. Because of our individualism many white Americans look down on African-Americans and other minorities who are trapped in the cycle of poverty and welfare.

In America, justice is a legal concept having little to do with a sense of obligation to the needy. Biblical justice, on the other hand, as we noted in chapter 25, attends to the needy.

Give the king your justice, O God . . .
May he defend the cause of the poor of the people
give deliverance to the needy. . . .
For he delivers the needy when they call,
the poor and those who have no helper.
He has pity on the weak and the needy,
and saves the lives of the needy.[4]

Perhaps we need to rethink our understanding of justice in light of biblical teaching. It hardly seems just to live in affluence when others go hungry. If we remain influenced by cultural individualism, our sense of human solidarity will wither and die.

Trivial Pursuits

Communism of the Soviet or Chinese type, together with all that it implies (including control of the population by Big Brother), has been the most feared enemy of Western civilization since World War II. George Orwell's *1984* depicted a worst-case scenario for a world caught in the grip of totalitarian government.

> They were the homes of the four Ministries between which the entire apparatus of government was divided: the Ministry of Truth, which concerned itself with news, entertainment, education, and the fine arts; the Ministry of Peace, which concerned itself with war; the Ministry of Love, which maintained law and order; and the Ministry of Plenty which was responsible for economic affairs. Their names, in Newspeak: Minitrue, Minipax, Miniluv, and Miniplenty.[5]

This classic novel riveted the attention of millions on the need to combat the evils of bureaucracy so prevalent in our time. Arbitrary decisions could be made about what to read, where to go, and how one must think. The memory of the Nazi regime of Adolf Hitler and the present communist, totalitarian states were a reality. Looking back after forty years it is clear that although government bureaucracy is still an intractable problem, Orwell's *1984* drama has not come to pass. What has been realized in some part is the truth of Aldous Huxley's *Brave New World.*[6]

Writing in the early 1930s, Huxley also was afraid of what big government could do. But instead of dominating the lives of people through punishment and repression, in Huxley's book a much more subtle way of control was used. Science and technology, not government, became the sacred cows. Big government controlled the future by coercion, thought Orwell; science directed life toward sober-minded uniformity, thought Huxley.

With the continuing fascination for technological gimmickry as evidenced in the drive for a Star Wars defense system and the endless automation of the workplace and the work force, Huxley's fears have in part been realized. In addition, however, a new and even more frightening control mechanism has developed. As the century comes to a close we are brainwashed by trivia.

There was a time in the not-too-distant past when colleges were popular because of their academic credibility. Today, with a few notable exceptions, the football or basketball ranking determines popularity. From the football Big Ten to the basketball Big East, colleges and universities rely more and more on their sports programs to generate income and attract new students.

Americans, of course, are not fixated only on amateur athletics. Professional sports, primarily the big three of baseball, football, and basketball, gross billions of dollars annually and attract millions of sports fans.

Sports, of course, are far from the only form of entertainment present in modern society. Stage shows, movies, television series and special shows, games from Toys-R-Us, and the old-fashioned vacation at the shore or in the mountains have great appeal. Subconsciously we have been narcotized by the entertainment drug. And it is doing great damage to our collective American psyche.

On the level of politics it is well known that the person with the most glamour, the person who can present the best image will generally receive the majority of votes. Today political candidates do not try to articulate precise positions or policies on anything. The name of the game is showmanship. How the candidates look is much more important than what they say. Because we are fed a steady diet of sports heroes and film stars we begin to lose the distinction between fantasy and reality. We confuse the "reel" world with the real world.

Furthermore, children who were raised on a diet of cartoons generally have a short attention span and have difficulty developing the ability to concentrate for any length of time. This problem can lead to learning disabilities. It is no secret that many students today have difficulty with reading and writing. This is largely due to the impact of television on the culture. In his perceptive analysis of our present situation, Neil Postman writes in *Amusing Ourselves to Death*,[7] that there are two ways in which the spirit of a culture may be shriveled. In the first, the Orwellian, culture becomes a prison. In the second, the Huxleyian, culture becomes burlesque. How much influence these forces exert upon us is a question only the individual can answer.

Culture as Ideology

The ideas of the ruling class are in every epoch the ruling ideas: i.e., the class, which is the ruling material force of society, is at the same time its ruling intellectual force. The class which has the means of material production at its disposal, has control at the same time over the means of mental production, so that thereby generally speaking, the ideas of those who lack the means of mental production are subject to it.[8]

Marx and Engels co-authored this reflection at a time when a clear distinction could be drawn between the owners of production and the workers. In viewing history through an economic prism, they believed that the root of all human problems lay in the alienation of the workers from that which the workers produced. By only receiving a wage and not the full profit of their efforts workers also suffered political, religious, and social alienation. If a classless society could be established and the means of production were controlled by the people, all would benefit. Hindsight, of course, teaches valuable lessons. The paradise of the proletariat became a Siberian gulag, and the children of immigrant laborers became the stockholders of modern corporations. Within a hundred years a large middle class arose from the alienated masses of the nineteenth century.

But is class structure still a reality? And is it true that, to some extent, the popular ideas of our culture are determined by the ruling elite? One need only think back for a moment on the measurement of success in terms of money and financial stability, the concept of justice in terms of legal obligations and equality for all, and the exaltation of power in terms of strength and importance to realize how influenced America is by those who own the country. The alienated masses of the nineteenth century whose children rose to the middle class were quickly replaced by a new generation of immigrants just as alienated and just as oppressed.

If the argument we have previously made about the importance of individualism is valid, and the trivialization of the culture through the entertainment blitz of sports, music, television, films, and the like appears true, then one may assume that, at the very least, the captains of business and all who profit from entertainment support the status quo. It is unlikely that questions about class, race, poverty, and other serious issues will get much attention in a society controlled by that elite.

No one today doubts the influence of economics on our daily life. All people in order to survive must satisfy the basic needs for food, shelter, and clothing. Indeed, most of us spend many hours each day in earning money to provide for the well-being of our families. At issue is whether or not our society has been poisoned by an economic fixation. On the one hand, a drug is needed to dull our sense of right and wrong: the drug of choice is entertainment. Entertainment, however, becomes an end in itself since it is a big money-maker.

Thus, a vicious cycle of work and play robs us of any real time to reflect on the questions of our existence, the place of God in our life, the issues of personal relationship and our growth in love, and the terrible tragedy of vast hunger and malnutrition in a world that most Americans do not see. We do not see it because it is stark, ugly, and depressing. We are fed a bland diet of sitcoms, super bowls, rock concerts, game shows, and a hodgepodge of other trivial pursuits. Is it any wonder that many of us are conspicuous consumers and moral pygmies?

Counterculture

We are again reminded that the concepts of money, power, and sex are not idols in themselves. Indeed, properly understood, each contributes to dignity and solidarity. Money provides us with the material things necessary for decent living; power can support and encourage others; and sexuality brings friendship and love. Our dominant characteristic of individualism, too, is basically good. We are individuals; each person is a unique creation. We can love our children, cherish our freedoms, and appreciate the opportunities that exist in a land blessed with much beauty and natural resources.

But we should not be lulled into thinking that all is well. This chapter has pointed out the major idols that we worship. An obsession with money and possessions destroys our own dignity by negating the spiritual dimensions of life. Misused power creates turmoil, hatred, and communal strife. Likewise, the abuse of sexuality weakens the bond of relationship by equating physical pleasure with commitment and responsibility.

Although an examination of conscience can be disturbing, it provides a remedy against those cultural forces that undercut human dignity. If we find ourselves falling prey to these demons, the best defense, as usual, is a strong offense.

Consequently, when possessions become an obsession, give them away. In spite of the incessant barrage of commercials that bombard the senses, we need to resist the temptations of self-centeredness by developing habits of generosity. Putting aside a healthy portion of one's income to share with the less fortunate produces interior freedom as well as benefiting others. Using our talents and abilities to encourage others instead of finding fault and making judgment focuses our power in healthy ways. Finally, by sublimating our sexual drive into the ways of care and concern for the feelings and sensitivities of others, we relegate the Playboy message to the refuse heap of shallow ideas where it rightfully belongs.

To be counterculture is to swim against the tide. Today, in a society bent on the adoration of fame and riches, the litmus test for the values of dignity and solidarity is attention to the poor. There are many thousands of young men and women who volunteer their services, both personal and professional, to those who are needy. Some will give a year or more with a service organization, others donate a few hours each week to caring for the poor. Many church groups sponsor volunteers for work in Third World countries.

At another level, many people work for political change that will benefit the needy. Training programs for those who have lost their jobs, day-care legislation to assist mothers who are working to support a family, and taxation policies that redistribute wealth are a few of the many ways that the political agenda can help the poor. "The impoverished, as painful as their struggles are, have an unequalled power to educate us to our pretenses, our fears, and the rejection of our humanity."[9] When we learn to identify with those most in need, we have taken a first step in the ways of justice and peace.

In the long run we are responsible for who we become. In spite of the fact that we all succumb at times to the temptations of idol worship, we are capable of picking ourselves up and doing better. Are not the cycles of life filled with falling and rising? The daily motion of the earth on its axis, its yearly cycle around the sun, and the burial of seeds that give rise to new life all remind us of the process of change. Nations and cultures come and go. We need to support the cultural institutions that lift up human life, and reject those things that demean it. We need to let our life be a sign of love for all.

Notes

1   Hans Bendix, "Merry Christmas, America!" *The Saturday Review of Literature*, December, 1, 1945, 9.

2   Alexis de Tocqueville, *Democracy in America*, quoted in Robert Bellah, Richard Madsen, William M. Sullivan, Ann Swidler, and Steven M. Tipton, *Habits of the Heart* (New York: Harper & Row, 1985), 37.

3   Robert Bellah et al., *Habits of the Heart* (New York: Harper & Row, 1985), 23.

4   Psalm 72:1–13.

5   George Orwell, *1984* (New York: Harcourt, Brace Jovanovich, 1949), 6.

6   Aldous Huxley, *Brave New World* (New York: Harper & Row, 1932).

7   Neil Postman, *Amusing Ourselves to Death* (New York: Viking Penguin Books, 1985).

8   Karl Marx and Friedrich Engels, "The German Ideology," in Thomas Sowell, *Marxism* (New York: William Morrow, 1985) 67.

9   John Francis Kavanaugh, *Following Christ in a Consumer Society* (Maryknoll, N.Y.: Orbis Books, 1981), 146.

34

The Relevance of Religion

It has been said that Christianity is a religion designed to "comfort the troubled, and trouble the comfortable." It has also been charged with being the opium of the people. In either case, those who support its influences on society, as well as those who deplore it, would nonetheless agree that Christianity, and indeed all religions, do impact on the habits and customs by which people live their lives.

Owen R. Jackson[1]

Faith: Religion and Politics

In modern times it has become useful to distinguish between personal faith and religion. Faith is concerned with a growing trust in the goodness of life, a belief in one's ability to make a difference, and a willingness to work cooperatively with others in seeking a better future. Faith is generally grounded on a belief or trust in a loving God. Religion, on the other hand, is identified in the public eye with doctrinal beliefs, institutionalized structures, rituals of worship, and social organizations.[2]

Throughout history, religion and politics have had a kind of love-hate relationship. In the early days of Christianity, when the emperor had the status of a deity, Christians suffered persecution. By the time of the high Middle Ages, authority had passed to the pope and kings, and religion and faith were regarded as one cause. Papal contingents marched in the Crusades. Those who disagreed with important Church teachings were at risk of trial and even excommunication. Some were branded heretics and burned at the stake. Later, in early colonial times, as Latin America was taken by the conquistadors, the Church—in allegiance with the Crown—was hard put to escape all blame for the violence and blood visited upon the Native American population. Back in Europe, in Reformation times, armies marched on both sides, Catholic and Protestant, in the name of religious and political unity.

Thus, until the beginning of the modern era, political power was invariably associated with the will of the ruler. However, as modern nations became more secular and democratic, governments and churches drew apart. Today, questions about faith, religion, and politics assume that each field has its own identity, independence, and area of competence. Despite the separation, faith and religion as moral forces still play a vital role in the political order.

Internally, of course, conflicts between progressive and traditional parties still complicate issues of belief and practice in most religious bodies. Traditionalists, who find their values and security mainly in longtime formulations and customs, tend to resist change and new modes of faith formulation and discipline. Applied to the Catholic Church, these internal frictions have been notable in the past twenty-five years, with early post–Vatican II developments favoring the forces of change. More recently, traditional forces may have had the upper hand. Fortunately, one important shift has found near unanimity at the top. Reflecting upon gospel teachings and the growing plight of the poor, especially in Latin America, the Church has finally ranged itself on the side of the disadvantaged. Naturally, not all Catholics accept the "preferential option for the poor."

When faith inspires a belief in human rights and religion supports that ideal, a critical assessment of politics by religious-minded forces is possible. Conversely, when religion ignores social ills, it tends to lose its connectedness with the living God. Religious organizations are healthiest and a positive influence upon society when they uphold the rights of all, not just the rich and well-connected.

Prophecy

Although the most popular understanding of the term *prophecy* has to do with forecasting the future, from a biblical perspective that is a misconception. The biblical prophets were not men who forecast future events, but rather were people who spoke on behalf of God about the present conditions of society. It was the prophetic voice of Moses speaking on behalf of God that demanded a change in the social order of the Jews in Egypt; it was the voices of Jeremiah, Amos, Ezekiel, and Isaiah that harangued the people about their evil ways; and it was the voice of Jesus that challenged the authorities to turn away from self-love to the love of God and neighbor.

If we are to engage in prophetic ministry we are called to develop alternative thinking. "The role of prophetic ministry is to nurture, nourish, and evoke a consciousness and perception alternative to the consciousness and perception of the dominant culture around us,"[3] says Walter Brueggemann, an American biblical scholar. In all places and times, in every age, the dominant cultural patterns need reform. We saw in the last chapter how money, power, and sex play such a forceful role in our society. Brueggemann believes that society's values are always in need of reform. To be faithful to the prophetic tradition we must always seek an alternative life-style.

Because the dominant culture rejects criticism and is rarely open to reform, we need to see prophetic ministry as a process of criticizing and energizing.[4] Indeed, since we are loathe to criticize ourselves, prophetic ministry is all the more important. Do I really love my neighbor? How do I put that into practice? Have I fallen prey to the snares of greed and pride? Do I seek revenge? How have I expressed my concern for the needy? While personal reflection on the direction of one's life is invaluable, we should also develop a corresponding critique of our culture. All too often we acquiesce to the idol worship in society rather than condemning it.

In addition to bringing to light the evils of society we need to balance criticism with affirmation. Very few people are totally depraved. There is always a smoldering ember of goodness in everyone's heart that needs kindling. The sign of a healthy person as well as a healthy organization is one that is in the process of constantly remaking itself. When we keep before our mind's eye the type of goals and vision that express our dignity and humanity, we place ourselves on the peace and justice road. When we encourage others to live rightly and work for a better society, we energize them to walk the same road.

We can look back and point to Jesus as a true prophet. He was courageous enough to stand up to the rulers of the people and call them phonies. "Woe to you, scribes and Pharisees, hypocrites! For you are like whitewashed tombs, which on the outside look beautiful, but inside they are full of the bones of the dead. . . . You snakes, you brood of vipers! How can you escape being sentenced to hell?"[5] He minced few words in attacking the self-protecting status quo of Jewish society.

Yet his anger did not spill over into the lives of people whose failings were obvious. He forgave the woman for adultery, shared meals with tax collectors and other outcasts, and invited a quintuple divorcée to announce his message of salvation to Samaria. The concepts of criticizing and energizing, then, are most clearly realized in the life of Jesus.

The question we need to ask is whether or not this prophetic ministry should be part of every Christian's life. Are we called to criticize and energize? Are there people in our midst today who have taken the task of prophecy seriously, i.e., who speak on behalf of the living God? Jesus called his followers to let their light shine before others and to act as salt. If we season our relationships with the love of God, we live in the prophetic tradition.

Modern Prophets

Who are some of the people in our own times who have spoken on behalf of God? Most of us are aware of the Gandhis, Kings, the Pope Johns, and other well-known leaders who have moved millions to a more profound sense of dignity and unity. Not so famous, yet equally prophetic are others who have committed themselves to criticizing and energizing.

Among the most persistent was an American journalist, Dorothy Day, who cofounded the Catholic Worker movement in 1933 and worked tirelessly on behalf of the poor until her death in 1980. Born into an irreligious family, she decided to become Catholic after giving birth to an illegitimate child. With an immoral past behind her, she chose to live a life of poverty, and established a series of Houses of Hospitality throughout the country to feed the hungry and shelter the homeless. She wrote regular articles in the *Catholic Worker*, a newspaper she founded, about the injustice of meager wages paid to workers. She joined protest marches and walked picket lines to identify with the underprivileged, and she was an outspoken critic of militarism.

Dorothy Day lived her life in service to the needy and inspired many others to do the same. "Poverty is a strange and elusive thing," she wrote. "I condemn poverty and I advocate it; poverty is simple and complex at once; it is a social phenomenon and a personal matter. It is a paradox."[6] She believed that embracing poverty cleansed us of greed and allowed us to walk with the needy.

Dietrich Bonhoeffer was born at Breshau, Germany, February 4, 1906, and executed by the Nazis at Flossenburg Concentration Camp, April 9, 1945. Bonhoeffer was a German Evangelical minister who spoke out against the philosophy of nazism from the beginnings of Hitler's rise to power. During the war he was involved with an underground group helping Jews to escape imprisonment. He too was a prophet who criticized and energized. Bonhoeffer's spiritual classic, *The Cost*

Discipleship, made the distinction between cheap grace and costly grace. The former was a path of ritual, public respectability, and conformity to the established order; the latter took up the Cross by challenging those who espoused evil values. From the time he heard the first speeches proclaiming the National Socialist ideology he knew that he must oppose it. From his prison cell he wrote words of lasting encouragement.

> See what a transformation! These hands so active and powerful
> Now are tied, and alone and fainting, you see where your work
>   ends.
> Yet you are confident still, and gladly commit what is rightful
> Into a stronger hand, and say that you are contented.
> You were free for a moment of bliss, then you yielded your freedom
> Into the hand of God, that he might perfect it in glory.[7]

Bonhoeffer lived his faith and died in prison a free man.

In all walks of life we find prophets, those who speak on God's behalf: the nurse or doctor who offers support and comfort to patients and their families in time of illness; the lawyer or judge who rejects bribery and works to improve the judicial system; the engineer, businessperson, homemaker, or any one of a thousand people who bring to the office, home, and neighborhood a spirit of support for those in need and a willingness to improve society. Recently, the term *whistle-blower* has come into vogue. It refers to someone courageous enough to reveal fraud and illegalities about one's employers. People who are willing to face reprisals in calling attention to acts of dishonesty are the kind of critics desperately needed in a complacent society.

Religious influence, in its best sense, acts as a moral force in society, by bringing to bear its values of justice, freedom, peace, and truth on the conflicts and tensions that abound. Whether it is on a campus or a street corner, in a business office or a factory, the need for criticizing and energizing will always exist. The question is: Who has the courage to prophesy?

Religious Maturity

Because there are different expressions of religious faith, and because religion is considered by many to be a private affair, it is difficult to explore objective standards for its beliefs and practices. Furthermore, each person's uniqueness will lead him or her down a different path toward God. What then can be said about religious maturity? Just as the study of biology and psychology was able to find patterns of growth and development within the person, so is it possible to detect patterns of maturity within a religious context. Gordon Allport, in his classic work *The Individual and His Religion,* indicates three essential characteristics of a mature personality.

First, a mature person will have a variety of psychogenic interests, that is to say, he or she will have developed a thirst for new knowledge about the world and will seek fresh experiences whenever possible.

Second, the individual will have learned to objectify himself or herself. It is a sign of maturity to listen attentively to criticism about oneself and to practice a certain detachment from one's attitudes and behavior in order to judge the quality of one's life from time to time.

Third, the mature individual will have developed a unifying philosophy of life. Although, according to Allport, this wholeness of outlook may be religious in nature, that is, God is understood as the beginning and the end of creation, it need not be so. What is essential is a comprehensive sense of the universe that gives direction and purpose to one's life. Consequently, for Allport there can be no religious maturity without a corresponding psychosocial maturation. Mature religious attitudes correspond to intellectual and emotional growth.[8]

Unfortunately, religious attitudes frequently remain infantile and dwarfed because there is little or no pressure to grow up religiously. While the pressures of earning a living, raising a family, and getting along with one's neighbors force people to grow emotionally, there is little corresponding pressure to develop mature faith convictions. Many people continue to see

God as a fearful avenger or as a "big buddy" in the sky who is constantly in need of placation by superstitious rituals or formalistic, cultic practices. Immature religious attitudes may consist of following particular rules and regulations that have been imposed by clerical authorities, or it may manifest itself in people who have abandoned communities of faith to go it alone, forgetting that, as with most things in life, our richest experiences are found in community.

Perhaps the most serious example of religious immaturity today is found in the phenomenon of the cults. During the past twenty years, cults, ranging from the fashionable New Age beliefs promulgated by Shirley MacLaine to the esoteric fare of the Church of Scientology, have narcotized, confused, and damaged the lives of thousands of young people. On the one hand, cult leaders demand blind obedience from their followers, leaving little room for dissenting opinions, and on the other hand, they often project a life devoid of rationality. "New Age thinking further encourages the belief that what 'feels right' is the best—perhaps the only—measure of human behavior."[9] With the beginning of the third millennium only a few years away it will be surprising if cult groups do not experience many new adherents.

Mature religion is both personal and social. It deals with the common human experiences of suffering, disillusionment, and pain as well as the joys, laughter, and hopes of the whole human family. It does not try to remove the mystery from life; rather it calls people to trust in a higher power than themselves. Religious maturity allows God to touch each person through his or her own uniqueness, yet invites people into community so that they may share their gifts with each other.

Prophetic Communities

Whenever people join together to bear witness to the truth, to act as a leaven within society, they are prophetic. We have already noted that not all religious groups are prophetic. Some, in fact, are antithetical to the will of God, living in the past and clinging to prerogatives. Theologically speaking, the Bible has lost all meaning for them. Their main concern is an institutional church; their only truth is to preserve the past as though it had some intrinsic value in itself and was not simply another part of unfolding human experience. Fundamentalists who refuse to interpret the Bible in its literary and historical context or church officials who remain out of touch with the problems and trials of their people are not prophets. Or perhaps more accurately, they are false prophets, since they speak on behalf of a false god.

In any case, the prophetic community today is a community of conscience. It may be an entire church that is struggling to come to grips with a rapidly changing world, or it may be a parish or group within the larger organization seeking justice on a local level.

Within the American Catholic Church many parishes have attempted to renew and invigorate their members by studying the current social teachings of the popes and bishops and by seeking to engage themselves in works of peace and social justice. Furthermore, just as small groups have formed among the laity to address the issues of family life and spiritual values, so have bishops and priests joined in local and national associations to explore cooperative efforts in rejuvenating the Church and society.

The American Catholic bishops have issued two major documents in recent years, one on the nuclear arms race, and the other on economic justice. A third pastoral letter, on the special role of women within the Church and the larger society, is currently in draft form. Taken together, these teachings represent a major effort on the part of the Catholic community to act prophetically. Of course, some pastors and bishops are reluctant to accept this social gospel.

On the whole, American Catholics have begun to take the lead in pushing for reform. Acting, often in coalition with other church groups, they have brought adversarial shareholder resolutions before corporate boards, marched on Congress to protest everything from abortion to homelessness, and reallocated funds toward social needs rather than church buildings.

For Catholics there is ample opportunity to criticize and energize the pagan culture within the United States, since their leadership has given clear direction.

Christianity, as the quotation that began this chapter reminds us, must comfort the troubled and trouble the comfortable. That is a poetic way of saying that the task of prophetic religion is to energize and criticize. When Christianity aligns itself with the established political and economic powers of the day, as it has so often in the past, it loses its prophetic edge. It may care for the needy, but it hardly empowers them to demand equal voice in the affairs of government and the economy. By maintaining its own respectability within the dominant culture, it helps support the status quo and runs the danger of being co-opted by the culture. This was in part why Marx saw religion as "the opiate of the people."

But this is not the way of Jesus nor the way that God has called his people to live. Both historically and in the present order of things, Christianity has the internal energy to criticize the power structures and energize the human family to build a better world, one that seeks peace with justice. Religious maturity, as we have described it, calls for a dedication and commitment to respect the dignity of every person and to strive for unity with all people. No small order! Let us continue to find comfort from a loving God and the energy to share God's love with our sisters and brothers.

When we speak in a prophetic voice we have forged a solid link between religion and politics.

Notes

1   Owen R. Jackson, from an unpublished sermon, September, 1987.

2   Roger A. Johnson and Ernest Wallwork, *Critical Issues in Modern Religion* (Englewood Cliffs, N.J.: Prentice-Hall, 1973), 9.

3   Walter Brueggemann, *The Prophetic Imagination* (Philadelphia, Penn.: Fortress Press, 1978), 13.

4   Ibid., 19.

5   Matthew 23:27–33.

6   Dorothy Day, "By Little and By Little," *Selected Writing of Dorothy Day*, Robert Ellsberg, ed. (New York: Alfred A. Knopf, 1983), 109.

7   Martin Bailey and Douglas Gilbert, *The Steps of Bonhoeffer* (New York: Macmillan, 1971), 41.

8   Gordon Allport, *The Individual and His Religion* (New York: Macmillan, 1959).

9   Fergus M. Bordewich, "Colorado's Thriving Cults," *New York Times Magazine*, May 1, 1986.

35

Political Influences

Only ideals can light the fires of revolution. People will not die for convenience or utility, but when a cause has been firmly identified with precious ideals, unlimited loyalty and enthusiasm follows.

Daniel C. Maguire[1]

Politics: Yesterday and Today

"Political power grows out of the barrel of a gun,"[2] wrote Chairman Mao Tse-tung, leader of the Chinese communist revolution. This slogan represents the modern-day equivalent of Machiavelli's sixteenth-century idea on political influence. The ruler, he surmised, must be cunning and ruthless in the exercise of power. History, of course, is replete with illustrations of violence, domination, and the use of force to maintain political control. Many despots, warlords, tribal chieftains, clan leaders, kings, queens, and assorted nobles over the centuries have raped, plundered, and pillaged their way through history.

In modern times we find similar examples. "In a thirty-year war against its own people, the Guatemalan military has created a nation of widows and orphans," said a British Parliament report in 1984. "Over 100,000 people have been killed and 38,000 disappeared."[3] Death squads in El Salvador, slave labor camps in Siberia, the genocide in Cambodia from 1977 to 1979, when an estimated four million people were tortured and slain by the communist Khmer Rouge troops of Pol Pot—all attest to the enduring legacy of dictatorship as an expression of political influence.

Plato, however, did not think that the way of the sword was right and proper. In his political philosophy he believed that politics existed for the sake of truth and goodness. He argued that the ruler was to govern the people in a just and noble way, punishing only those who disobeyed the law. Roman law, too, left an indelible mark on Western civilization. Here again we find not an arbitrary justice depending on the whim of a dictator, but a rule of law in which citizenship was respected.

Political philosophers of the eighteenth century, drawing upon a growing awareness of individual liberty, devised a new system of government that began with the premise that people had the right to govern themselves. Many of our Founding Fathers wrote extensively about the structures of government that would allow for the interplay of opposing interests, and yet retain rights for all people. The Articles of Confederation (1781–1789) for the United States failed to provide for a strong central government. They were subsequently replaced with the Constitution, which has served as our central governing document for the past two hundred years. The guiding principle of the separation of powers, in which the legislative, executive, and judicial authority reside within different groups of people, has probably done more to support the idea of justice and respect of individual liberty than any other principle of government. In addition, the principle of subsidiary, that is, allowing local communities to adopt their own ordinances without interference from the federal government, was also an important concept.

Today, political liberty and civil rights are curtailed in many countries. Colonels and generals are paid by wealthy elites to control the population, or they themselves have exploited the people. Dictatorships throughout Africa and Latin America have centralized all authority into the hands of a few. The law-maker is both judge and jury. Occasionally, dictatorships are overthrown, for example, Somoza in Nicaragua and Marcos in the Philippines, but for the most part absolute control is the norm.

Alongside the specter of military rule, a one-party communist system has also stifled individual freedom. Interestingly enough, the policies that Mikhail Gorbachev recently proposed at the Communist party convention in June 1988 have returned some decision making to a local level, and allowed people to choose party leaders in secret balloting. For the most part, however, communism has been and remains a system of political control that makes the economic, religious, cultural, and social dimensions of life subservient to its rule.

Since we Americans can affect, and are affected by, political decisions in our society, let us look at some of the more important areas where we can exert political influence.

Taxing and Spending

The federal government, according to the Constitution, is charged with promoting the general welfare. As such, it has developed over the years an enormous assortment of departments and agencies to regulate interstate commerce, to conduct foreign policy, and to ensure domestic tranquility. Because local, state, and federal government is so enormous, its influence is felt in policy decisions about everything from labeling toxic poisons and tobacco products to dealing with illegal immigrants. Mostly its influence is felt by how and where it spends its money.

The federal budget for 1988 was approximately one trillion dollars. If we include research and development for space programs, retirement, and veterans' benefits, and the usual personnel, procurement, operation and maintenance, housing, and new construction costs, 50 percent of the federal budget is spent on the military.[4] About 25 percent of the revenue is returned in Social Security payments. Contrary to popular belief, food stamps, Medicaid, and Aid to Families with Dependent Children constitute only 7 percent of the federal spending programs. Calling to mind that the Census Bureau places about 20 percent of the population below the poverty level, one begins to wonder if the budget priorities are in line with our values of personal dignity for everyone and a common concern for all.

The influences that affect state and local politics are of a different sort. Most of the major cities throughout the country have sizable populations of minorities. Inner cities are often run-down, drug-infested, and lack the investment capital for growth. There is constant tension between the haves and the have-nots. On the one hand, those who own homes, have good jobs, and live in decent neighborhoods are reluctant to spend tax dollars on revitalizing a ghetto. They want police and fire protection, quality education for their children, parks, and other social amenities.

The poor would like those things too. Unfortunately, racism, high crime rates, inadequate educational opportunities, and the ravages of generational poverty create attitudes of anger and pessimism on the part of the poor. City government must cope with trash removal, public transportation, public safety, and education as well as trying to lure new business for tax and employment purposes. Suburban and rural townships have their own sets of problems and organize political structures to address local needs. The same is true of the various states.

Government spending is predicated on its power to collect revenue. In the early days of the republic, taxes were levied on imported goods and the sale of jewelry and other expensive merchandise. In 1913 the Sixteenth Amendment to the Constitution authorized an income tax for both individuals and corporations. This has remained the primary source of income for the federal government. Many states also impose an income tax on businesses and individuals, but raise sizable amounts of money through consumption taxes. Most municipalities and townships raise revenue through property taxes.

The Tax Reform Act of 1986 was the most sweeping tax legislation in the past fifty years. It attempted to simplify the tax code by eliminating exemptions and creating a mildly progressive tax structure. Corporation taxes were raised, while low-income families were made exempt. Unfortunately, low-income families must still pay the same taxes as the very rich on such items as gasoline, clothing, and food. Furthermore, affluent districts collect high property taxes that generally fund a quality school system. Ghetto children do not have the same opportunity. While it may seem fair to tax everyone equally— our American concept of legal justice—the biblical justice of God demands a different standard. Who speaks for the poor? Can we not structure taxes so that the poor do not have the additional burden of paying sales taxes on the necessities of life?

Watchdogs

Special interest groups and professional lobbyists who persuade, cajole, intimidate, and even bribe public officials have always existed. Politicians, like most people, think of themselves as high-minded and concerned with the general welfare of the populace, yet when sweet-talked or arm-twisted, like most people, they go along with whomever has the most leverage on their reelection. "Money talks," cried Ossie Myers, a Philadelphia politician who was caught taking a bribe in return for political favors.

When one reflects on the power of government officials to allocate millions of dollars for public projects, to grant licenses for highway repairs and road construction, and to issue permits for parking and zoning regulations and a host of other programs, it is little wonder that politicians fall victim to their baser instincts. In some respects, it is amazing that corruption is not more widespread. In other countries, public bribery is so commonplace that few dare suggest that it is even wrong. Fortunately, the public ethics of the United States have generally favored punishing public officials who misuse their trust. A government of the people demands officials who will serve honorably. Most do, in spite of the pressures from special interests.

A two-party system is perhaps the single most important factor in maintaining honest government. Democrats are all too ready to find corruption within a Republican administration; of course, the Republican party is on the watch for Democratic wrongdoing. Even within the respective parties there is pressure not to disgrace the other members of one's party with sleazy behavior. The Watergate scandal during the Nixon administration and the Abscam trials of the late 1970s are but two of the more well-known instances of political corruption, one involving Republicans, the other indicting several Democrats. This two-party system provides a day-to-day partisan check on government officials.

In addition to the two-party system that structurally supports honest government, the media play an equally important role. Few would argue that freedom of the press helps to guarantee public scrutiny of elected officials. For example, the first woman candidate for vice president, Geraldine Ferraro, was subjected to a constant barrage of questions from journalists and reporters about the financial holdings of her husband. In addition, the Watergate scandal mentioned previously did not begin to unfold until an informant began to leak tips to the press about "following the money trail." Media people have been charged with obnoxious behavior in questioning officials—and there is plenty of evidence to suggest that they slant the news toward the sensational—yet they provide an invaluable service to the public. The watchdog behavior of the press has deterred many a politician from venal behavior.

The most well-known and nationally organized watchdog group, after the political parties and the media, is Common Cause. Founded in 1970, it has grown in membership to more than a quarter of a million citizens. The purpose of Common Cause is to promote good government, government that is "clean and lean." It has remained nonpartisan throughout its twenty-five-year history and has lobbied to enact legislation that serves the interest of the general public.

Many other organizations and groups work to protect the public interest. Ralph Nader, who gained a national reputation by challenging the safety of automobiles, founded Public Citizen. This citizens' group alerts consumers to the use of unsafe and hazardous products and has lobbied for product liability legislation. Greenpeace, Physicians for Social Responsibility, the Sierra Clubs, and the National Wildlife Association have stressed the importance of protecting the environment and have worked for laws to contain pollution. What is important to bear in mind is that we get the kind of government we deserve. If we act as responsible citizens and join with others in working for good government, we will see results. Political activism is our right and our duty.

Moral Persuasion

One of the strongest voices on Capital Hill in recent years has been the Interfaith Action for Economic Justice. Composed of such disparate church groups as the Jesuit Social Ministries, the Unitarian Universalist Association, the Friends Committee on National Legislation, and the Board of World Ministries for the United Church of Christ, Interfaith Action has lobbied vigorously on behalf of the poor. On the domestic front they have taken up the fight for low-and moderate-income housing. While upper-income home owners get tax deductions for property tax and mortgage interest, the poor go begging. The National Community Housing Partnership Act (HR3891) hopes to restore some of the funding lost for low-income housing during the Reagan presidency.

Internationally, our government spends far more on security assistance to developing nations than it does on development aid. Instead of alleviating the poverty and misery of Central American peasants we seemingly choose to prop up dictators with military support. Interfaith Action believes "global poverty that fuels violence and political instability poses a far greater challenge to U.S. and global security than the military and strategic concerns that currently preoccupy U.S. foreign aid planners."[5] If this be the case, U.S. funding for many of the United Nations agricultural development programs is long overdue.

Two other well-known moral voices in the halls of Congress are Bread for the World and Network. BFW was begun during the late 1960s as a response to the growing problem of world hunger. Seeing the faces of half-starved children on television and on the cover of national magazines during global droughts demanded a response. American Christians formed a non-denominational coalition with members from each congressional district in order to lobby for laws that would aid the victims of famine abroad and assist the hungry in America. And how effective is it? John Danforth, U.S. Senator from Missouri, said that "in the more than ten years that Bread for the World has been working on Capitol Hill, it has been an effective force in the battle to eliminate hunger."[6]

Network, a Catholic social justice lobby, is similarly organized on a state and congressional district level, but in contrast to BFW they have a much broader agenda. Network tries to effect structural and systemic change in society in order to give the needy a chance at a better life. They have lobbied against aid to the contras in Central America and for a trade embargo against South Africa. Both of these organizations publish reports about current legislation on social justice issues, and urge supporters to write and call members of Congress with their views.

Moral persuasion is not limited to affecting American government policy. For example, the human rights organization Amnesty International was founded in 1961 by a British lawyer who was concerned about the arbitrary imprisonment of two Portuguese students for toasting freedom. By 1977, A.I. was active in 160 countries throughout the world, protesting the torture and execution of prisoners of conscience. Awarded a Nobel Peace Prize in the same year, A.I. continues to insist on humane treatment for all people. Through letter-writing campaigns to prison officials and other government agencies,

A.I. exerts constant pressure on military and political authorities to respect the United Nations Declaration on Human Rights.

Citizenship

"Politics," it is said, "is too important to be left to politicians." While Plato thought that politics should serve the cause of truth and goodness, and Machiavelli believed it should ensure the power of the strong, it is likely that many American politicians get involved because they love it. They enjoy the give-and-take, the push-and-shove, the constant wrangling between the liberal and conservative agendas. Even though politics generates great heat and much bombast, it is an area of social life where real change can take place for the betterment of people.

The great tragedy is that, unlike professional politicians, so few average citizens are inclined to get involved. Statistically, fewer than 50 percent of eligible voters cast ballots in presidential elections, and far fewer vote in state and local ones. Why is this? Perhaps it is because people are too busy with earning a living or too distracted when they have free time. Perhaps it is because they don't see themselves as making a difference or because they don't care. Whatever the reason, the fact remains that politics is important. Civic responsibility should be a sacred duty for everyone. If we believe that our government is of the people, by the people, and for the people, we need to energize ourselves and others into a greater participation in public life. Otherwise, it's just left to the politicians and special interest groups.

Awareness in the social order involves conscientization. It has to do with an interest in the local civic issues of our neighborhood. Are the streets well-lighted? Is the school system adequate? Do police and fire personnel respond promptly in an emergency? Local interest frequently generates state and federal concern. Do I know what congressional district I live in? Who are my representatives? How do they vote?

Experiential learning is important too. You may read all you possibly can about an issue, or know the political process quite well, but unless you put pen to paper by writing a letter on behalf of a political prisoner, or telephone a congressional office with advice on how you want your representative to vote, all the book learning will have been in vain. Political science as a discipline has played a significant role in helping people understand the art of politics. Unfortunately, its academic narrowness has all too often left students with lots of theories, but little in the way of practical knowledge.

We began this chapter by attempting to show the importance of politics in the world. Decisions are made daily that touch the lives of millions for good or ill. Because we are fortunate enough to live in a free society, we tend to take only a passing interest in politics. But that is not good enough. It is not good enough if our indifference allows children to go hungry because legislators ignore their needs; it is not good enough if our apathy permits special interest groups to get the lion's share of tax breaks while the middle class bears a disproportionate burden; it is not good enough if our fear of speaking out on social issues guarantees a continued arms race for exotic Star Wars systems at the expense of welfare expenditures for the poor. We need to stay informed about the pressing social issues of our times and join with others in trying to influence the political decision-making process at the local, state, and federal levels. In assuming a prophetic role to criticize and energize, Mario Cuomo, governor of New York, said:

> We believe we must be the family of America, recognizing that at the heart of the matter we are bound to one another, that the problems of the retired schoolteacher in Duluth are our problems, that the future of the child in Buffalo is our future. The struggle of a disabled man in Boston to survive, to live decently is our struggle. The hunger of a woman in Little Rock, our hunger. The failure anywhere to provide what reasonably we might is our failure.[7]

Notes

1   Daniel C. Maguire, *The Moral Choice* (Minneapolis: Winston Press, 1978), 237.

2   *Quotations from Chairman Mao Tse-tung* (Peking: Foreign Languages Press, 1966), 61.

3   "Bitter and Cruel," in *British Parliament Report*, 1984.

4   *Economic and Budget Outlook: Fiscal Years 1988–1992*, (Congressional Budget Office, 1987), 59–60.

5   *International Development Network* (Washington, D.C.: Interfaith Action, June 1988).

6   John Danforth, cited in *What Can I Do about Hunger* (Washington D.C.: Bread for the World, 1988).

7   Mario Cuomo at the 1984 Democratic National Convention.

36

The Marketplace

We call for a U.S. international economic policy designed to empower people everywhere and enable them to continue to develop a sense of their own worth, improve the quality of their lives, and ensure that the benefits of economic growth are shared equitably.

National Conference of Catholic Bishops[1]

Brainwashing the Consumer

"Caveat emptor" was a common expression among the people of Rome two thousand years ago and it still has validity today. "Let the buyer beware" about the safety, the durability, the quality, and the worth of whatever it is that she or he might purchase. Most Americans are well aware of the hype to which we are exposed daily through television, newspapers, billboards, radio, flyers, catalogs, and fancy coupons in order to get us to buy, buy, and buy whatever it is that is being sold. We are a consumer society to the nth degree.

Never before in the history of civilization has such a wide variety of products been offered in such abundance. Whether we shop at Toys-R-Us or the local supermarket, the shelves are bursting with stock. It may not all be top-quality—and so the Latin maxim should be kept in mind—but the abundance is real and the pressure to purchase is constant.

Beneath this external barrage of salesmanship is the more subtle message that one's well-being is measured in terms of money and possessions. Ivan Boesky, the Wall Street financier who was recently convicted for fraudulent trading on the stock market, boasted that greed was good for society. The advertising agencies of Madison Avenue spare no effort encouraging the public to purchase the best fashions (changed yearly in order to create new sales), to refurnish the house, to drive the latest model of automobile, and to feel good about storing up treasures on earth. The slogan of choice in America, according to the people who bring us Spuds McKenzie beer parties, is "he who has the most toys wins."

Stuart Ewen traced the beginnings of the advertising industry to the early part of the twentieth century.[2] In this country, the conditions of the working class were rapidly improving due to the unionization of millions of factory workers, miners, and transportation employees. The owners and corporate executives saw a chance to expand their industries in the direction of consumer products in order to take advantage of the increasing affluence of the workers. To do this they had to create new tastes. "The functional goal of national advertising was the creation of desires and habits. In tune with the need for mass distribution that accompanied the development of mass production capabilities, advertising was trying to produce in readers personal needs which would dependently fluctuate with the expanding marketplace."[3] In other words, once the struggle of the workers to achieve a living wage had been realized, they were again victimized by the entrepreneurs into thinking that their new freedom was intimately linked to what they possessed.

In chapter 8 we distinguished between wants and needs. There is a normal, and morally sound, need for food, shelter, clothing, and other basic necessities. Unfortunately, there also exists a morally unhealthy desire to possess more and more. When we begin to measure our self-worth in terms of what we have, we are spiritually ill. When we care more about our wardrobes, cosmetics, and investment certificates than about hungry children, homeless and unemployed women and men, the mentally ill, and the elderly, we have lost our vision of God's kingdom; we have imbibed a poison that only the antidote of moral conversion will cure.

Corporations and Owners

While the influence of advertising is apparent to all, the impact of national and global economic dynamics is less obvious but far more influential. Transnational corporations dominate the landscape from supermarket chain stores to the oil conglomerates. These companies both compete and cooperate in the furthering of the economic enterprise. The recent wave of corporate mergers in which energy companies have moved into transportation, filmmaking, and cosmetic manufacturing, and where auto manufacturers have become bankers, brewers, and farmers indicates the extent of the diversity and control exercised on the economic life of the nation and the world by major corporations. Private corporations operate in order to maximize profits for their owners, and it is those owners who direct company policy.

A myth exists that most stocks are owned by vast numbers of people. The opposite is, in fact, true. The top one-half of 1 percent of the U.S. population owns 43 percent of all corporate stock.[4] And the wealthiest 10 percent of our population owns 80 percent of all private property. It is a sobering experience to attend almost any annual shareholders' meeting of a major corporation and find that most of the stock is owned by a half-dozen individuals. The social critic Gore Vidal recently commented that "the genius of our system is that ordinary people go out and vote against their interests. The way our ruling class keeps out of sight is one of the great stunts in the political history of any country."[5] One measure of economic influence is to note that the vast majority of members on the boards of directors for the Fortune 500 (*Fortune* magazine's annual listing of the largest corporations) are white, middle-aged, male millionaires. They exert enormous economic influence from Hong Kong to the halls of Congress.

One particular set of economic players who control vast resources and dominate the destiny of millions of people is the food industry. For example, a few giant food companies, Castle and Cooke, General Mills, and Del Monte, own vast amounts of fertile land throughout Latin America where they grow crops and raise cattle primarily for European and North American markets. This practice, known as cash-cropping, creates severe hardship in the form of malnutrition for the local peoples, who have no land to farm for themselves. In addition to the global corporations, we have a national food-chain gang.[6] composed of the Grocery Manufacturers of America, the chemical giants of Shell, Dow, Monsanto, and Du Pont, and the leading food processors and suppliers, General Mills and Nestle. Together they have repeatedly blocked attempts to curtail the use of pesticides, many of which are cancer-producing.

Government legislation to protect the environment and the public has met stiff opposition. "Standing in the way of Congress's approving a strong bill [controlling pesticides] is a triumvirate made up of the chemical companies that manufacture $6.5 billion worth of farm chemicals a year, the agribusiness giants who use them, and the grocery manufacturers who process the food."[7]

As is often the case, money plays a large role. The food-chain gang collectively donated more than $6.5 million to the congressional election campaigns of 1985–86.[8] Key members of the House and Senate agricultural committees generally side with the business interests since the public and environmental lobby groups have far less money to contribute to election campaigns.

Labor/Government

In addition to corporations, labor unions have also played a dominant role in the economic history of our nation.

Unfortunately, in the last decade the loss of manufacturing jobs brought about by corporations seeking cheap labor in Third World countries has diminished union influence. Furthermore, service industries, which now account for more than half of the work force, have been slow to unionize due to the workers' image as white-collar employees and to the large turnover in personnel. But the flame is not out. César Chavez, who organized many farm workers throughout the Southwest, has kept the promise of workers' rights alive. In the 1970s through the strategy of a national boycott of table grapes and head lettuce, he was able to garner public support for better wages and working conditions for the migrant farm workers, many of whom were women and Hispanics.

More recently, Chavez has campaigned against the pesticide poisoning of crops by charging that the "wrath of grapes" is harming both the consumer and the pickers. (In our appearance-conscious society, table grapes must be unblemished; therefore, we use whatever toxic substance is necessary to kill any bug that might dare to taste the fruit.) Chavez and other labor organizers continue to insist on the dignity of the individual workers and on the rights that are due them. Arbitrary dismissals, meager wages, inadequate working conditions, and lack of safety regulations are the result of a climate of indifference, and even hostility, by employers toward minority workers. Worker influence is usually realized only through labor organizations. This right to organize has often been disparaged and, at times, abused, yet it is a fundamental right, and unions continue to play an important role in the economic life of our nation.

The largest single influence on the American economy, of course, is the federal government. In an economy with a 5 trillion GNP, the government collects and spends about 20 percent of that total. The Tax Reform Act of 1986, in a significant shift toward helping the needy, removed many low-income earners from the tax rolls. Also, tax preferences for the wealthy were scaled back and corporate taxes increased.[9] On the revenue side individuals pay about 45 percent of the taxes, with corporations contributing some 13 percent. Most of the rest is income from social insurance, which is returned through Social Security payments.

Defense spending, which amounts to 300 billion dollars annually, consumes the largest portion of the tax dollar. Although there was no significant threat of war in the last ten years, the defense budget increased by 50 percent. Most of that went for new weapons systems built by corporations eager to do business with the government. The enormous influence of the military-industrial complex on the economic life of the country creates a permanent war economy. Only when people are ready to invest more of their tax dollars in better education, health care, and housing will corporations stop building bombs and start building classrooms, clinics, and homes.

The government also plays the role of regulator within the national economy. The Federal Reserve Board controls the supply of money, the Security Exchange Commission regulates the stock market, and a host of other agencies oversee everything from the quality of food and drugs to the type and quantity of imported goods allowed into the United States. Theoretically, the government acts on behalf of the public to protect us from harmful products and fraudulent practices.

Such, however, is not always the case. For instance, within the last twenty-five years the insurance industry has become one of the biggest industries in America. The McCarnan-Ferguson Act of 1945 exempted insurance companies from federal regulations, since most states wished to retain their right to oversee and tax local insurers. Insurance company mergers, however, have resulted in an "insurance industry so powerful today that, when acting together, it completely overwhelms the regulatory capacity of the states."[10] Although efforts are under way to control them, the insurance companies have contributed substantial amounts of money to both state and federal politicians, making reform highly unlikely.

A Moral Voice

What does the economy do for people? What does it do to people? And how do people participate in it?[11] The answers to these three fundamental questions, the American Catholic bishops believe, will determine the morality or immorality of economic decisions. Although we have looked at the major actors within the U.S. economy, we have yet to explore all the effects of this system. With this in mind, it is important to hear the voice of the bishops as expressed in their 1986 pastoral letter, *Economic Justice for All.* As American citizens and religious leaders, the bishops felt an urgency to raise questions about the economy from a moral perspective. All too often the only questions asked concern efficiency, productivity, and profitability. The call for Catholics at Vatican II was to relate their faith to the political and economic situations of the times.

In their examination of economic life the bishops identify three central motifs for human life. These are creation, covenant, and community. Using the unfolding revelation of God found in the Bible as a guide, they argue that in the final analysis planet Earth, the mountains, seas, and rivers, every plant and animal, each human person—indeed, all creation—owes its existence to the source of life who is God. When people forget their rootedness in God and fail to acknowledge their dependence on God, greed, domination, and oppression are sure to follow.

The same sinfulness occurs when we forget that God created a Covenant of friendship, first through Moses on Mount Sinai, then with Jesus on Calvary. We are blessed with God's friendship, yet often live indifferent to the suffering of each other.

Finally, acknowledging God as creator and appreciating the friendship offered by God through the Covenant with Moses and Jesus, we are led into community. Community implies a discipleship of service that sees concern for the neighbor as a high priority. These three themes, then, creation, covenant, and community are biblical themes that weave the tapestry of dignity and freedom.

But the bishops wish to speak in more than generalities. They place themselves squarely on the side of the poor. "Decisions must be judged in light of what they do for the poor, what they do to the poor, and what they enable the poor to do for themselves. The fundamental moral criterion for all economic decisions, policies, and institutions is this: They must be at the service of all people, especially the poor."[12] We all resonate well enough with a call for human dignity in the abstract, but when we concretize it in the faces of the poor, many people back off.

In chapter 34 we saw how the role of the prophet was to criticize and to energize. We can now see in the actions of the bishops on behalf of the poor the prophetic voice that they raise. Although they are aware of the enormous complexity of the national and global economy and the dynamic nature of production and consumption, they must speak to the simplicity of a minimally decent level of food, clothing, shelter, education, and opportunity for all people. While it is right for union leaders to be concerned about their membership, and it is important that managers and employers run efficient and profitable businesses, both labor and management must also be concerned with the common good.

The bishops are asking all people—consumers, owners, labor, management, and the government—to stop seeing their relationships in an adversarial context. If these groups would begin to shift away from a narrow self-interest and pay more attention to the needy and the poor, the bishops believe that our society would benefit with a renewed sense of mutual respect for all people. This is the Christian vision of economic life.

Problems and Solutions

Having spelled out the Christian vision of economic life, the bishops chose employment, poverty, food and agriculture, and the Third World nations as topics of special interest in their faith reflection on the economy. The first two, employment and poverty, are intimately linked. Because of the high rate of unemployment among blacks and other minorities, frequently due to discrimination or poor educational opportunities, those groups suffer the highest rates of poverty. A minimum wage of $4.25/hour nets approximately $8,500 a year, which, for a family of four, is well below the poverty level set by the federal government (according to the census bureau, the poverty level for a family of four was $13,359 as of 1990). It is estimated that 20 percent to 30 percent of the American people live in poverty. The virtual elimination of low-cost housing has led many families to sleep in city shelters, National Guard armories, and even on the streets.

The bishops point to the enormous inequality between the top 10 percent of Americans who hold more than 50 percent of the net wealth and the bottom 40 percent of the population who share only 15 percent of the annual income. Power generally comes with money, and so it is little wonder that the voice of the poor is weak. In a society where Donald Trump can build luxury hotels and casinos while only yards away children go to bed hungry, one need hardly guess about the judgment of God.

In the areas of agriculture and Third World nations, the bishops also note many serious disorders. More and more farmland in the United States is coming under the control of transnational corporations that follow the dollar. If the family-owned farm disappears, food costs will surely rise. In addition, since corporate "farmers" make economic decisions far from the land, they tend to devalue soil and water conservation, underpay farm workers, and oppose farm workers' unions.

In addition, food corporations have purchased millions of acres of farmland in Third World nations in order to raise cattle or grow flowers for export. Land that once fed indigenous people is now used for exported cash crops. Food is sent abroad and replaced by malnourishment. Statistics on Third World nations numb the mind, the bishops say. "Eight hundred million people live in absolute poverty beneath any rational definition of human decency. Nearly half a million are chronically hungry, despite abundant harvests worldwide. Fifteen out of every one hundred children born in those countries die before the age of five, and millions of the survivors are physically or mentally stunted."[13]

In chapter 4 of *Economic Justice for All*, the bishops suggest a "New American Experiment: Partnership for the Public Good" be instituted. Four particular areas of cooperation demand attention. In the first place, workers, managers, shareholders, owners, suppliers, customers, creditors, and the local and national community should seek ways to contribute to the growth and well-being of all. Capital and labor need each other, not as adversaries, but as good neighbors. Second, local and regional cooperation, through tax credits for businesses investing in urban renewal and retraining programs for the unemployed, are necessary. Government must play a significant role in providing economic well-being. Also, national policies must be judged in the light of concern for the poor and the distortion of defense spending must end.

Finally, the bishops urge cooperation at the international level. We live in a global village where the problems of others are our problems, and our good fortune should be used to help the less fortunate. This leads the bishops to include a final chapter, "A Commitment to the Future."

"As disciples of Christ each of us is called to a deep personal conversion and to 'action on behalf of justice and participation in the transformation of the world.'"[14] We need to see our faith, not as something we dust off and wear on special occasions, but as alive and vibrant each day. We must participate actively through our "faith" decisions about buying and spending, voting, working, and playing. If we raise our consciousness and understand that economic conditions are the result of human decisions, some of them our own, then we can work to improve the lot of the needy. No one has to be poor in a world of abundance; no one should lack shelter where the friends of God are gathered; no one need be lonely where all are in community. The marketplace can test our resolve to build the Kingdom of God.

Notes

1   National Conference of Catholic Bishops, *Economic Justice for All* (Washington, D.C.: United States Catholic Conference, 1986), para. 142.

2   Stuart Ewen, *Captains of Consciousness* (New York: McGraw-Hill, 1976), 37.

3   Ibid.

4   Lester C. Thurow, *The Zero-Sum Society* (New York: Penguin Books, 1980), 169.

5   Gore Vidal, *Monthly Review*, October 1986, 19.

6   Sheila Kaplan, "The Food Chain Gang," *Common Cause* 13 (September/October 1987): 12–15.

7   Ibid., 12.

8   Ibid., 13.

9   *Economic and Budget Outlook: Fiscal Years 1988–1992* (Washington, D.C.: Congressional Budget Office, 1987), 66.

10   Sheila Kaplan, "Hit and Run," *Common Cause*, July/August 1988, 22.

11   National Conference of Catholic Bishops, *Economic Justice for All*, para. 1.

12   Ibid., para. 24.

13   Ibid., para. 254.

14   Ibid., para. 328.

37

Moral Giants

Little Boy: "Mr. President, how did you become a war hero?"

President Kennedy: "It was absolutely involuntary. They sank my boat."[1]

Heroes

What constitutes a hero? From the time we were old enough to admire other people, like the police officers riding in their patrol car, or the nurse at the local hospital who held our hand when we got stitches, or the ball players, rock stars, coaches, etc., who came into our life as we grew up, we've resonated with certain of their qualities or characteristics. Some people admire Beethoven and Mozart for their musical ability; others think of Babe Ruth or Ted Williams as baseball's greatest stars; Generals Patton and MacArthur come to mind as American war heroes; Florence Nightingale epitomizes the nurse of great dedication; Dag Hammarskjöld is remembered as an unselfish statesman; and the Rockefellers are admired for their financial expertise. We all have our heroes, people whom we look up to or admire for some particular talent or ability, some feat of great daring, some extraordinary qualities that lift them just a cut above us ordinary mortals.

On the other hand, we humans have always had our anti-heroes. These are generally people who cut against the grain of society but do so in such a way as to create a kind of perverse admiration in our hearts. The legendary Robin Hood was a thief, after all, yet his feats in tricking the Sheriff of Notting-ham, and his exploits of robbing the rich and aiding the poor have assured his place in history as a "good guy." During the 1940s Willie Sutton, a notorious bank robber and escape artist, became a national folk hero as he outwitted the police in city after city. Mick Jagger and other rockers live on the margin of respectability, yet are admired as much for their iconoclastic image as for their music. Sylvester Stallone has hyped Rambo into a prominent screen antihero. Finally, in many inner-city neighborhoods, it is the local drug pusher who is admired by the neighborhood kids rather than the police who are trying to steer them away from drugs.

What is it about us humans that draws us to admire both the good and the bad in others? Perhaps the problem is that our own values are mixed up. We may understand little kids looking up to a big brother selling dope or stealing cars, but when that type of respect continues into adulthood, one might begin to question the moral maturity of those who look up to the antiheroes.

We see, then, that there are many ways to view the role of hero. Military leaders, entertainers, Hall of Fame sports fig-ures, statespersons, writers, and saints have found their way into our consciousness. The real question for us, however, in the context of peace and justice is: What constitutes a peace and justice hero?

"Moral courage is a rarer commodity than bravery in battle or great intelligence. Yet it is the one essential vital quality for those who seek to change a world that yields most painfully to change."[2] Robert Kennedy spoke those words to a group of South African youth in the summer of 1966. Less than two years later he was shot dead by an assassin's bullets while cam-paigning for the presidency. If we are to look for heroes within the framework of human dignity and solidarity, then the key quality that they must possess is moral courage. As Kennedy noted, bravery in battle and great intelligence are not of themselves particularly worthy of imitation. Presumably Attila the Hun was a brave warrior; he was also a killer of the innocent.

Moral courage may be found in the heart of a politician such as Kennedy, who sought to assist the poor of Appalachia and the ghettos, or an employer who assists minorities, or a student who joins Amnesty International or the Committee for the Homeless, or anywhere, anyplace, and anytime that we stretch ourselves for the rights and dignity of others who are deprived. Moral courage is a belief and an attitude that seeks to create a better world. It is the motivating force for anyone committed to the central values of dignity and solidarity.

Same Fate as the Poor

About 10 P.M. on Tuesday, December 2, 1980, not far from the village of Santiago Nonualco, El Salvador, Ursuline Sister Dorothy Kazel, Maryknoll lay missioner Joan Donovan, and Maryknoll Sisters Ita Ford and Maura Clarke were brutally murdered by five Salvadoran National Guardsmen. They were returning to their mission stations in the Chalatenango province, where they worked with the poor. All were American churchwomen. Their bodies were thrown into a common grave at the order of a local judge who tried to cover up the killings.

Within one day the news leaked out about the death of the women. At noon on Thursday, December 4, United States Ambassador Robert White, several reporters, and other members of the missionary team watched in anguish as the bodies were unearthed and dragged from the grave. The murders caused an enormous outcry in Congress and President Carter immediately suspended economic and military aid. Who were those women? Why were they killed?

Joan Donovan's life has been popularized in the award-winning film, *Roses in December.* She was a young woman, not particularly religious, but with a strong desire to do something meaningful with her life. During her college years she had been challenged by a priest to do volunteer work with the poor and so became a Maryknoll lay missioner. She had plans for marriage after leaving the mission.

Dorothy Kazel had been a high school teacher in Cleveland, Ohio, before volunteering for mission work in Central America. The Cleveland diocese had responded generously to the need for missionary workers and financial assistance in the years following Vatican II, and Dorothy saw herself as one more person willing to share her life with the poor.

Ita Ford and Maura Clarke were Maryknoll sisters. This religious community has a long and proud history of traveling to the four corners of the globe in order to bring the Good News of Jesus to all who would listen. In recent years the focus has changed from teaching the native people American ways to learning the local social and cultural patterns and adapting their customs rather than imposing our own. Ita and Maura, both native New Yorkers, had served for several years in Latin America, but had only arrived in El Salvador shortly before they were murdered.

The most obvious question is why? To understand the murders it is enough to know that this small Central American country has been torn by strife for many years. Most of the land is owned by several wealthy families and it is this elite who controls the military and supports the repression of anyone who tries to reform the present system. The United States government has equipped and trained the military in order to prevent a communist takeover as happened in Cuba. The situation is such that anyone who works with the poor is immediately labeled a communist. Shortly after the deaths of the four church-women, Jean Kirkpatrick and Alexander Haig, well-known American conservatives, suggested that the murdered women brought about their own death by getting too involved with the poor.

The great tragedy of Central America today is that those who want to improve the lot of the peasants, many of whom live in dire poverty, are labeled communists. For some, the label is accurate; for many others it is a lie and a cover-up in order to continue the oppression of the needy. Maura, Ita, Joan, and Dorothy live on in the hearts of the poor of El Salvador, where their pictures have received places of honor in the huts of the poor. Someday they may be canonized as saints for suffering martyrdom in Central America.[3]

It is becoming more apparent in a world divided into rich and poor that those who possess wealth are most reluctant to share with the needy. In fact, as is often the case, the wealth is often accumulated off the sweat and sinew of the poor. The cane cutters and coffee pickers of El Salvador work long hours in the fields for slave wages so that we may have our morning coffee and danish. The millions of acres of ranchland in Honduras and Costa Rica that are used to raise beef cattle for Wendy's, McDonald's, and Burger King deprive many local people of the land necessary to grow beans and other staples for local consumption.

Frequently enough, those who speak out against this kind of exploitation are labeled leftist or "commie" sympathizers. They are accused of being against the American way of life, the free market system where it's "every man for himself."

Fortunately there are people like the four churchwomen who remind us of what we ought to be and where we need to stand. We should be filled, as they were, with moral courage. We should stand, as they did, with the poor. We may be martyred for our convictions, as happened to them.

Voices for the Oppressed

The system of apartheid in South Africa has produced a long list of opponents. Nelson Mandela, who was imprisoned for more than twenty-seven years and his wife, Winnie, are known internationally for their moral courage. Desmond Tutu, who grew up under the oppressive system of separation of the races, became an Anglican priest and eventually was elevated to archbishop of Johannesburg. He received a Nobel Peace Prize in 1984 for his efforts on behalf of his people. Archbishop Hurley, an Irish Catholic cleric working in South Africa, has also been actively opposed to apartheid.

The recent film *Cry Freedom* tells the story of a friendship between Steve Biko, a black South African leader who was murdered while in prison, and Donald Woods, a white South African journalist who investigated the killing. Both men were strongly opposed to the injustice of racism and had the moral courage to resist the government. Woods escaped his homeland while under house arrest and a banning decree that forbade him to write. Along with thousands of others he continues his opposition to apartheid.

Oscar Romero was a quiet and generally conservative Catholic bishop in El Salvador. When more and more of his compatriots were brutally tortured and slain by secret squads of military police in the 1970s, Romero began to protest. Although he was not in favor of a Marxist revolution, he realized that the right-wing policies of the wealthy were equally destructive. After the killing of several lay catechists and a close friend who was a priest, he formed a committee on justice in the archdiocese of San Salvador. He began to make weekly broadcasts about the atrocities taking place throughout Central America and castigated the United States for supplying weapons and training to the military government. On Sunday, March 23, 1980, he made an impassioned plea to stop the violence.

> I would like to make an appeal in a special way to the men of the army . . . Brothers, you are part of your own people. You kill your own campesino brothers and sister. . . . The Church, Defender of the rights of God, of human dignity, the dignity of the passion, cannot remain silent before such an ABOMINATION! . . . In the name of God and in the name of the suffering people whose lament rises to heaven each day more tumultuous, I beg you, I ask you, I order you in the name of God: stop the repression.[4]

The following day Archbishop Oscar Romero was shot and killed while celebrating Mass.

During much of its history, Argentina has lived under one military dictatorship after another, but during the 1970s the brutality of the government reached epic proportions. Mothers of the Disappeared silently walked plazas of the major cities protesting their loss (*disappeared* refers to people who have been abducted from their homes by military or paramilitary organizations and who were never heard from again). One particularly well-known Argentine artist, Adolfo Pérez Esquivel, spoke out against the brutality and was himself imprisoned and tortured for fourteen months. Esquivel was eventually released and received the Nobel Peace Prize in 1980 for his founding of the organization Service of Justice and Peace, which has many chapters throughout Latin America.

Jacobo Timmerman, a Jewish journalist and editor of *La Opinion*, was arrested by the same military junta that imprisoned Esquivel. Timmerman too was tortured by electric shocks and sensory deprivation methods. In his best-selling autobiography of his experiences, *Prisoner Without a Name, Cell Without a Number*,[5] he recounts how the wanton terrorism of both leftists and rightists led inevitably to a fascist government. In Esquivel and Timmerman, as well as the Mothers of the Disappeared, we have more witnesses for the oppressed, people with the moral courage to protest injustice.

Other Voices

Mitch Snyder was an angry man. He was radical-minded enough to castigate college audiences about their insensitivity to the homeless and the affluence of their lives. He asked why college classrooms and administrative buildings that are empty at night could not be used for the homeless who must sleep on the streets. Snyder gained notoriety in 1984 when he demanded the use of federal buildings in Washington, D.C., as shelters for the homeless. In several instances whole families were sleeping on grates and in automobiles for lack of proper shelter. Martin Sheen portrayed him in the docudrama "Samaritan: The Mitch

Snyder Story," which generated much support for the homeless throughout the country. Snyder was a man of strong convictions who was trying desperately to awaken the American public to its responsibility toward the homeless. He knew that unless the federal government constructs more low-cost housing the problems of homelessness will continue. He saw himself as a bridge between the government and the homeless. His untimely death brought an outpouring of tributes for his compassion toward the homeless.

Helen Caldicott, on the other hand, is a bridge builder of a different sort. A pediatrician and native of Australia, she immigrated to the United States in 1977 to work at Howard Medical School, where she had previously studied. As a member of Physicians for Social Responsibility, she became a strong opponent of nuclear power and weaponry, believing that the dangers of radiation are so great that only minimal amounts should be produced. Her cause seemed vindicated by the nuclear accident at Chernobyl in 1986. In addition, Dr. Robert Gale, the American immunologist who traveled to the Soviet Union to assist the victims, has added his name to the list of people opposed to nuclear energy. Both of these physicians are concerned with the high-level risks imposed by nuclear power and are attempting to alert the public to these dangers. Dr. Gale's book, *The Legacy of Chernobyl*,[6] leaves little doubt about his anxiety with nuclear technology.

The voice of Dr. J. C. Willke, president of the National Right to Life Committee, has been heard loud and clear from the time of the Roe vs. Wade decision in 1973, which permitted legal abortions in the United States. Together with millions of other people of various religious denominations, he has spoken forcefully about the rights of the unborn. As pro-life advocates see it, the advances in embryology in the past fifteen years have made it obvious that even in the fetus's earliest stages of development, human life is present. It was his desire to protect this life that brought Willke to champion the unborn. Most recently some pro-lifers have opted for civil disobedience tactics at abortion clinics, hoping to dissuade women from aborting. How far one may go in this direction is highly debatable. Yet one cannot help but admire those who risk ridicule and imprisonment for their support of fetal life. If the respect for all life in our society were higher, abortion would not be an acceptable option.

Many people were brokenhearted over the death of Christa McAuliffe on January 27, 1986. She was a high school history teacher from Concord, New Hampshire. Chosen from among eleven thousand applicants to be the first citizen passenger in space, Christa had been a space devotee since her junior high school days when Alan Shepard made the first American space flight in 1961. When President Reagan announced that a nationwide search would begin to choose an elementary or secondary school teacher for a space flight, she saw an opportunity of a lifetime. Naturally, her students were excited when she was chosen, partly from admiration, but also because they knew she would contribute to the program. Her motto in the classroom was an inspiration to all: "I touch the future; I teach." The Challenger blew up shortly after lift-off because of a faulty seal in the fuel system, killing Christa and the other astronauts. But the memory of a New England schoolteacher who wanted "to get as much out of life as possible . . . to enjoy life and certainly to involve other people in that enjoyment, but also to be a participant,"[7] lives on. Her voice was one of encouragement. We can all reach for the stars.

Models

Throughout this chapter we have met men and women who have contributed positively and constructively to the human enterprise. They are but a few of the millions of people who have had the moral courage to address the wrongs of society and seek ways to assist others in living life to the fullest extent possible. Today we face a real temptation within our society to imitate what is culturally popular. The lives of the rich and famous are portrayed as filled with success and happiness. Rarely do we hear about the values of truth, justice, and peace as the real marks of success. This should not dissuade us, however, from centering our lives on respect for life and looking around for the heroes who are worthy of imitation. Looking good and having lots of toys are poor substitutes for a thirst for justice and a heart of compassion.

Although we are invited to imitate those who seek justice rather than fame and fortune, we need always ground our aspirations in the reality of the self. Each of us has been gifted in different ways and each circumstance of life unfolds uniquely. The real key to the imitation of those who seek to build a better world lies in our attitude. *Attitude*, as we have said before, is the magic word. It is magic insofar as it can transform our lives from despair to hope, from discouragement to challenge, from blindness to vision. The old truism that we act the way we think has been proven many times over.

Healthy attitudes create patterns of honesty and integrity. If we are convinced that personal dignity for everyone is the norm and that we are related to the entire human family, inner signals will alert us when we see violations of justice. When we are tuned in to the respect-for-life frequency, moral courage resonates in our heart. Consequently, we should imitate not the particularity of their lives, but the attitudes of the peacemakers and justice-seekers.

Idealism receives little popular acclaim in a world engulfed in cynicism. Idealism, however, should be a part of our everyday disposition. This is not the same as a longing for utopia where all is bliss. The fulfillment of God's Kingdom will only be realized in eternal life. Here on earth we are called to seek first the Kingdom of God, a kingdom of peace and justice, a kingdom of human harmony and concern for the needy. If we dream these dreams, we will live them out. We will begin to discover new opportunities for listening to the problems of others and new ways to reach out in love.

But we must overcome the ancient enemy, fear. There are several instances in the Gospel where Jesus says to his disciples: "Be not afraid." There was plenty to fear for his followers, then and now. During his lifetime he faced threats to his life on several occasions, and finally he was executed. Throughout much of early Christian history martyrdom was common. With the death of the four churchwomen, Bishop Romero, and hundreds of others who have suffered because they fought injustice, martyrdom has returned. When we think of Gandhi, Martin Luther King, Jr., John and Robert Kennedy, all of whom sought justice and died at the hands of assassins, we are reminded that the pursuit of justice is not easy.

The words of Jesus were meant to offer strength in time of trial. If our life is lived in fear, it is only half lived. We need to convince ourselves that a worthy life that finds its center in the values of personal dignity and solidarity with the poor and oppressed of the world is far more satisfying than one centered on protecting oneself from harm and accumulating more toys. When courage overcomes faintheartedness, we find ourselves standing with moral giants.

Notes

1   John F. Kennedy, *The Kennedy Wit*, ed. Bill Adler (New York: Bantam Books, 1964), 53.

2   Robert F. Kennedy from a speech to the youth of South Africa on their Day of Affirmation in 1966. Quoted in *An Honorable Profession*, ed. Pierre Salinger et al. (Garden City, N.Y.: Doubleday, 1968), 2.

3   Judith M. Noone, *The Same Fate as the Poor* (Maryknoll, N.Y.: Maryknoll Sisters, 1984), 96–97.

4   Ibid., 96.

5   Jacobo Timmerman, *Prisoner Without a Name, Cell Without a Number* (New York: Alfred A. Knopf, 1981).

6   Robert Gale and Thomas Hauser, *The Legacy of Chernobyl* (New York: Warner Books, 1988).

7   Robert T. Hohler, "'I Touch the Future': The Story of Christa McAuliffe," *Reader's Digest*, June 1987, 81.

38

Public Witness

Just Plain Folks

Mary lives in Bogotá, Colombia, where she spends most of her working hours tending to the needs of the poor. She does some begging from stateside friends, accepts donations from other helpful people, and occasionally gets local support. Through her efforts children with physical handicaps have received medical assistance. Infants and poor mothers have gotten milk and other food. Above all, she is a shining example of a woman who cares. Why would an Irish woman seventy years of age continue to live in a Latin American slum when she could return to North America and live in comfort?

John went to a prestigious Ivy League college. Instead of going to weekend booze parties he volunteered his time at a local soup kitchen and became active in a peace group. After graduation he continued his work with the poor and spent much time in nonviolent resistance to the arms race. At the age of twenty-four he died of a heart attack while jogging. He was eulogized as a young man of deep compassion for the needy and a firm believer in the peace movement.

Maureen, who grew up in a rural New England town, was a traditionally conservative Catholic. In her freshman year at college she was angered when a priest showed slides of the bombing of Hiroshima at the Sunday mass. He suggested that the American Catholic bishops were calling their people to resist the arms race. During the course of her next four years she became more and more aware of the connection between faith and politics. Her religious convictions moved from private to public, and she experienced a gradual conversion from a God who was found only in church to a God who was deeply involved in human affairs. She joined the Jesuit Volunteer Corps upon graduation and now works with the elderly in a Philadelphia ghetto.

The influence that the Marys, Johns, and Maureens of this world exert is less well-known than that of Gandhi, King, and Mother Teresa. Yet it is just as important. Indeed, the leaders of organizations concerned about human needs depend a great deal on their ordinary followers for support and encouragement. There are women and men in business, education, executive suites, assembly lines, pulpits, classrooms, driving buses and taxis, and waiting tables who are involved in peace and justice activities. They are young and old, rich and poor, churchgoers and agnostics, of all races and nationalities. All of them, in an infinite variety of ways, are committed to the vision of a better world and are willing to work toward that end.

A mixture of motives attend all human endeavors. Some peace activists dread the thought of nuclear war, others are more concerned about the enormous defense expenditures that result in keeping people hungry because of inadequate funding for domestic needs. The common threads, however, that seem to run through the lives of the thousands upon thousands of ordinary people involved in peace and justice activities consist of three major strands.

The first thread is a conviction that the world is not yet complete; it can change and become a better place. Many people are convinced that they can bring about positive change by applying political and economic pressure on behalf of the poor and needy of the world.

Second, these people are energized by a strong sense of personal responsibility to carry their share of the load in contributing to the well-being of society. Many believe that they have been blessed with talents and abilities that should be used in the service of their fellow humans. Their activism stems from a conviction that "to whom much has been given, much will be expected."

The final strand of thread in the fabric of concern is a remarkable sense of compassion for the stranger. This quality was characteristic of the ancient Hebrews and still runs through the best ethical norms of the major religions.

While it is normal to expect that we will care for our own families and friends, to reach out with compassion, to suffer with, and to assist the stranger is an act of generosity beyond the normal.

Civil Disobedience

One of the most notable forms of public witness in the cause of justice is civil disobedience. It may be defined as "a deliberate, open and peaceful violation of particular laws, decrees, regulations, ordinances, military or police instructions, and the like which are believed to be illegitimate for some reason."[1]

In America, the most well-known exponent of civil disobedience in the nineteenth century was Henry David Thoreau. He was opposed to the war against Mexico (1846–48) and the institution of slavery, and consequently refused the payment of taxes as a protest against U.S. government policies. In his famous essay on civil disobedience he asked rhetorically, "Must the citizen ever for a moment, or in the least degree, resign his conscience to the legislator?"[2] Thoreau, of course, was a poet, author, naturalist, and New Englander. All of these characteristics led to an excessive individualism that caused him to espouse the slogan, "the government is best which governs least."[3]

Some seventy years later, on the other side of the globe, Mohandas K. Gandhi developed a much more sophisticated understanding of civil disobedience and recruited thousands of followers into the movement. As we have seen in chapter 25, Gandhi's concept of truth-force, or satyagraha, was the underlying power behind all his actions. It was crucial in all his behavior that truth be sought. In addition to seeking truth, Gandhi, as a practicing Hindu, had a strong devotion to "ahimsa," the doctrine of refraining from harming any living thing. Civil disobedience, for Gandhi, then, was not simply a protest against unjust laws, it was a way of life rooted in discipline and true love for the opponent in the hope of winning him over. Gandhi made it quite clear in one of his earliest acts of disobedience that he had great respect for the law. The situation involved indigo workers who were unfairly treated by their employers and who asked Gandhi to plead their case. The employers urged local officials to ban Gandhi from meeting the workers. When the government ordered him to leave the area he said, "As a law-abiding citizen my first instinct would be, as it was, to obey the order served upon me. But I could not do so without doing violence to my sense of duty to those for whom I have come."[4] On other occasions Gandhi called off civil disobedience by his followers when they began to attack the government officials.[5] Civil disobedience for him was rooted in nonviolence.

The civil rights movement of the mid-fifties and sixties led by Martin Luther King, Jr., also saw extensive use of civil disobedience. Rosa Parks, a black woman from Montgomery, Alabama, precipitated the movement by her refusal to obey a city ordinance requiring blacks to sit in the rear of buses. Subsequent to her protest, freedom riders, consisting of white and black college students from northern universities and many clergy and nuns, traveled throughout the South, stopping at restaurants and diners where segregation was practiced. Many were arrested and jailed for disobeying laws that forbade blacks and whites to eat together.

In other instances, blacks enrolled in all-white schools, marched and assembled without permission from local authorities, and demonstrated against the racist laws that pervaded many Southern states. King saw in the teachings of Jesus the kind of example he believed was necessary to sustain the civil rights movement. With Gandhi, he was committed to nonviolence not only as a tactic but as a way of life. This inner conviction encouraged him to continue the struggle for racial justice in spite of the setbacks he experienced in many cities. Together Gandhi and King, because of their commitment to nonviolence, gave credibility to civil disobedience. Today, others use this strategy with the same moral conviction that they held.

Saying No to Death

Franz Jaegerstaetter is hardly a household name in the United States, or for that matter, in few places outside of Austria. In December 1984, he was issued a special posthumous Award of Honor by the President of Austria for his bravery in refusing to join the German Army during World War II. Jaegerstaetter was the sacristan of the Catholic church in the village of St. Radegund in a remote part of Upper Austria. When he was inducted by the Nazis he refused to report for training and was subsequently arrested, tried for treason, and beheaded on August 9, 1943.

When Hitler came to power and the Third Reich began its reign of oppression, it openly mocked the gentleness of Christianity. Jaegerstaetter, a Christian Catholic, resolved never to serve a government that he judged to be evil. Although he was married and the father of three daughters, and although the village priest and even the local bishop urged him to serve in the army, he refused. Gordon Zahn, a long-time American Catholic pacifist, said his was a solitary witness. His letters to his wife and his commentaries on the days prior to his execution leave no doubt that he loved his family deeply, but his conscience told him that it was contrary to God's will to fight with Hitler's troops.

Unlike Jaegerstaetter, Dan Berrigan needs little introduction. He is probably the most well-known priest activist in the

U.S. today. He came to national prominence in 1968 when he and eight other antiwar protesters raided an induction center at Catonsville, Maryland. They were arrested by local police after carrying draft records outside the building and burning them. Following his conviction as a member of the Catonsville Nine, he went underground. When caught, he served several years in prison at Danbury, Connecticut.

In 1980, with another group of protesters, Berrigan broke into a weapons manufacturing facility owned and operated by General Electric at King of Prussia, Pennsylvania. The group used small hammers to damage the nose cones of nuclear missiles. Much publicity accompanied the trial, and no jail terms were imposed. Berrigan believes that the U.S. government has created a war-minded culture and that our nuclear arsenal, if unleashed, would be a thousand times more frightful than the Holocaust. He stands as a public witness against the insanity of nuclear war.

Joseph and Jean Gump of Illinois, the parents of twelve children, wound up in jail for following their convictions. Both had been concerned about the threat of nuclear war and had joined protest marches on several different occasions. Jean joined a Midwest antinuclear Plowshares group and subsequently damaged a Minuteman II missile silo outside Knob Noster, Missouri. Although the judge pleaded with her to pay restitution in exchange for a reduction in sentence, she refused, stating that nuclear weapons are evil in themselves and have no right to exist. About a year later her husband demonstrated at another missile silo. He said:

> I believe our government is involved in illegal activities that have no end . . . we were either silent or cheered when the Bomb was dropped, paid taxes to develop more and better bombs and continue to pay taxes to build more to add to our already swollen inventory of death and destruction. In doing this, we ensure either the ultimate destruction of our children and descendants in the worst scenario, or the mortgaging of their future to pay for our insane military expenditures in the best.[6]

The Gumps say that retirement gave them the opportunity to put themselves on the line as public witnesses for peace and protesters against nuclear weapons. They admit that it was a hard decision to choose jail, but "there's a freeing experience . . . they'll never make nuclear weapons in my name again."[7]

Are the Jaegerstaetters, Berrigans, and Gumps of the world all deluded visionaries who are out of touch with the real world, or have they truly gotten in touch with reality? Is it crazy to say No to war? Is it madness to protest the continuation of the arms race? Have they found the courage to get beyond the fears and anxieties of conformity by affirming life in the face of death?

Group Witness

Although most people think of the Religious Society of Friends, the Quakers, as a somewhat distant and exclusive group, the opposite is the truth. Begun in the seventeenth century as a protest against the doctrinaire and formalist Church of England, the Society of Friends suffered persecution for its commitment to simplicity of worship and social concern for the needy. Throughout its history several members achieved notable success in fighting for societal change. John Woolman was a strong voice against slavery; Elizabeth Fry worked for prison reform; Dorothea Dix brought about better treatment for the insane; and Susan B. Anthony was a famous suffragette.

Today, the American Friends Service Committee, a national coalition of Friends based in Philadelphia, administers a wide variety of projects throughout the world. It has been active in refugee placement, assistance to homeless children, and advocacy programs against war. Quakers have generally been pacifists, but because of their disinclination toward imposing rules on their followers, do not insist on this requirement. Although small in number compared to other religious groups, their influence in raising the conscience of people to works of peace has been considerable.

Another group that has had a strong influence on the conscience of the nations is the Fellowship of Reconciliation

(FOR). The Fellowship was begun in 1914 by two friends, Henry Hodgkin, a British Quaker, and Friederich Siegmund-Schultze, a German Lutheran pastor, who met during a conference in Switzerland. Europe was on the verge of war, and the two men promised each other to commit themselves to peace.

Since that time FOR has grown into an organization with chapters in dozens of countries throughout the world. It is an association of men and women who wish to use the power of love and truth in resolving human conflict. While not explicitly proclaiming the title, they are modern-day satyagrahas, fashioned in the likeness of Gandhi and his followers. The Fellowship publishes a monthly magazine with articles as diverse as the story about Finnish women dancing into a nuclear power plant with brooms to sweep away the hazards of nuclear waste to an analysis of conscripting teenagers into the military in Central America. In addition, annual conferences sponsored by FOR bring together peacemakers to discuss new ways to build hope in a time of massive violence. In contrast to building bombs and weapons of war, they build friendship and bonds of peace.

Recently, a new movement has sprung up that attempts to link the issues of economic justice, abortion, and the arms race under the rubric of Just Life. Just Life is a broadly based coalition of Protestants and Catholics committed to educating their constituents on how to work for political change around a consistent life ethic.[8] They believe that if life is precious from the time of conception until death, then human rights should be upheld along the entire spectrum of life. Economic justice requires that all people share in the abundance of the land. The arms race drains away funds necessary to help the needy. A consistent life ethic demands an end to the arms race and a commitment to the poor. Abortion should be seen for what it truly is: the unjust taking of innocent life. The Just Life movement is attempting to bring together people who see the value of personal dignity as a consistent norm for ethical reflections concerning all social issues.

Decisions

Within the context of American society there is sometimes heard an objection about the witness of a particular church or a churchperson, for example, a priest or minister, that they violate the cherished principle of separation of church and state. We should be very clear, however, that separation of church and state means that "religious groups should expect neither favoritism nor discrimination in the exercise of their public, social and religious role."[9] It does not mean that religion must be relegated to the confines of church buildings or exercised only in the privacy of one's home. Although some people complain that the church should mind its own business when it begins to speak about economic and political issues, the reality is that it is minding its business, which is to work within the society to bring about God's Kingdom, which is a kingdom of peace and justice.

Questions and issues about economics and politics are moral because they impact on the lives of people. One of the roles, albeit not the only one, that religion plays is to act as a prophetic voice on behalf of the marginalized people in society. Those who exploit the poor, who are uninterested in bettering the lot of the needy, and who control the political or economic order for their own gain are all too ready to criticize religious groups for meddling in things that should not concern them. But witnesses on behalf of justice know that they have a moral responsibility to engage themselves in working for a better economic and political world.

Among students today there has been a renewed interest in social concerns, although it is not the hyperfrenetic activism of the 1960s, when students stormed administration buildings and took to the streets. Today there is a more methodical commitment that perhaps will endure because it is more cerebral than emotional. Several campuses have established peace and justice centers where students have the opportunities to study and analyze special issues and to develop local chapters of organizations devoted to social change.

Ultimately each of us must face the reality of his or her own life. When all is said and done about the genetic makeup of our personalities and the importance of environmental influences on our life, we are still free to choose the direction of our life. Jordan and Margaret Paul, both clinical psychologists, speak about the option of intention. Our Ego, or self-centered Self, defends its behavior with a protective way of life always ready to blame others for the tensions and conflicts of life. The Higher Self, on the other hand, starts with an intention to learn. There is a desire to be open to new experiences and to learn from the conflicts that inevitably come our way.

The important thing to remember is that we are free to choose. Is our intention to protect ourselves, or are we willing to risk the hurt and suffering that often comes when we stretch ourselves for others? Love, contrary to what the Hollywood mythmakers present, calls for patience, compassion, selflessness, and, most of all, for commitment. If we love justice, which is another way of saying that we love our neighbor, we will be witnesses in a world that desperately needs people to reach out to the poor and needy.

Notes

[1]   Gene Sharp, *The Politics of Nonviolent Action* (Boston: Porter Sargent, 1973), 315.

[2]   Henry David Thoreau, *Civil Disobedience* (New York: W. W. Norton, 1966), 225.

[3]   Ibid., 224.

[4]   Mohandas K. Gandhi, *An Autobiography* (Boston: Beacon Press, 1957), 413.

[5]   Ibid., 470.

[6]   Karen Uhlenhuth, "Peace Activists," *National Catholic Reporter*, September 18, 1987, 19.

[7]   Ibid.

8   *A 1988 Election Guide for Justice, Life and Peace* (Philadelphia: Just Life, 1988), 24–31.

9   Brian Hehir, "Presentation at Network Legislative Seminar, June 1986," *Economic Justice Newsletter* (Washington, D.C.: United States Catholic Conference, 1988), 2.

39

Social Welfare/Social Change

Every human person constitutes something unique; each situation in life occurs only once. The concrete task of any person is relative to the uniqueness and singularity. Thus every person at any given moment can have only one single task.

Viktor E. Frankl[1]

Mother Teresa

Few people alive today have not heard of Mother Teresa of Calcutta. Born in Skopje, a small Albanian village, on August 27, 1910, she rose to fame despite the fact that she never made lots of money, never wrote great books, and never was an entertainment celebrity or political figure. She was awarded the Nobel Peace Prize, the ultimate in global honors, because of her concern for the poor. How ironic—to help the poor and receive popular acclaim. Perhaps buried within our hearts is the realization that the noblest human gesture is the tender touch of love.

A pivotal moment in her life came on September 10, 1946. She was going by train to Darjeeling in the Himalayas for a retreat when she sensed that God was calling her to go and work among the poorest of the poor. She had already committed her life to God with her vows of poverty, chastity, and obedience. She now felt called to go beyond the work of teaching children of upper-caste Indians in convent schools and to spend her life among the needy. One of her first houses was a Home for the Dying in Calcutta. In this country it is hard to imagine hundreds of thousands of people living in the streets of a major city and hundreds of them dying there each day. She began to minister to these dying people, washing their sores, nourishing their wasted bodies, giving each of them the special attention that she felt they so richly deserved.

Mother Teresa's simple, yet remarkable insight was that every person was a child of God and each deserved the best attention she could give. The statement of purpose for her new religious community reads: "To fulfill our mission of compassion and love to the poorest of the poor we go: seeking out in towns and villages all over the world even amid squalid surroundings the poorest, the abandoned, the sick, the infirm, the leprosy patients, the dying, the destitute, the lost, and the outcasts, so that we may care for them, visit them, and awaken their response to God's great love."[2] She knew that God called her to devote her life to the poor.

The Missionaries of Charity are now established in dozens of cities throughout the world. One typical example is the work of the sisters in the South Bronx. Many have compared this area of New York City to the bombed-out cities of Europe after World War II. Block after city block is lined with abandoned tenement buildings, many of them burned out, vacant lots with broken bottles and old tires strewn about, auto wrecks stripped of wheels, bearings, and all salvageable parts, and, saddest of all, many dispirited people living without hope. Within this three-square-mile area the Missionaries operate a soup kitchen, a shelter for homeless families, and a neighborhood pantry for families without food. But their presence is especially felt throughout the area as they daily visit shut-ins and others who are lonely.

"Our poor people are great people," Mother Teresa once told an audience, "a very lovable people. They don't need our pity and sympathy. They need our understanding love and our respect. We need to tell the poor that they are somebody to us, that they, too, have been created by the same loving hand of God, to love and be loved."[3] This is a far cry from the put-downs one often hears about how the poor are shiftless and lazy, and if they'd only help themselves they would get ahead.

Mother Teresa does not blame. In fact she never calls the rich to task for their gluttonous and greedy life-style. She simply calls them to come and visit with the poor. She invites those who are well-off to come and spend time with the disadvantaged. Without condemning, she invites conversion. Her spirituality and that of her missionaries focuses on the care and compassion of the individual rather than on the social problems of the times. With the exception of abortion, about which she has spoken frequently—asking pregnant women to give her their babies rather than abort them—she does not engage in social morality. Her concern is with reaching out to the poor with love, not changing the social order to alleviate poverty. It is the power of mercy.

The Way of Gentleness

The way of Mother Teresa is the way of gentleness. Her deep compassion for the poor comes from her ability to take the words of Jesus seriously when he says that he is to be found in the hungry, homeless, imprisoned, thirsty, indeed, in all those who are considered the least important.[4] We have seen earlier how the ways of the world are quite different. Brute force, power politics, and economic exploitation are generally associated with the ability to gain respect. But in whose eyes? Only in the eyes of those who exert the same kinds of influence.

Mother Teresa believes that in her care for the poor she is following the path God has chosen for her in living a life of faith. In using her gift of gentleness to reach out to the needy, she has literally touched the hearts of millions throughout the world with her example of love. She never sought fame, but it came to her because those around her recognized her commitment and compassion. Her way of life is ascetic, when much of the world is caught up in a race for possessions. She has not tried to change the world by confronting the forces of evil, yet she has changed the hearts of many through the power of love.

The secret to her life lies in her trust of God. Although she is a Roman Catholic nun and daily receives the spiritual nourishment of the Eucharist at Mass, she is not indifferent or hostile to other faith convictions. She believes that there is only one God, the Creator of all things, the Giver of all life, the Healer of all hearts. In choosing to begin her work among the poorest of the poor she went to Calcutta where the vast majority of the population were Hindu. Today her sisters work among Muslims, Buddhists, and many different denominations of Christians, as well as many unbelievers.

She believes that the love she extends to others may help them to see the love that God has for each of them. When someone has been rejected because of illness or disease, as have many of the outcasts in Indian society, it is not surprising to see them respond to her love with a renewed faith that there is a spiritual force in the world concerned with their welfare. Her work with the unemployed, drug addicts, and other urban poor, she believes, attests to God's love for them. In short, God gives meaning to her life. Without that sustaining belief she would hardly have had the dedication and commitment of a lifetime of sacrifice.

In an indirect way, the life of Mother Teresa is a challenge to all. For those who see differently and have far more possessions than they can ever rightfully use, she offers the way of generosity. "Go sell what you have," Jesus advised the rich young man, "and you shall have treasure in heaven." Mother Teresa's message is much the same: If we are generous to God's poor, we will be blessed many times over. Consequently, she has often invited youth to commit their lives to helping the needy.

Is there a spirit of love present in the modern generation that will volunteer at least some time with the poor? she asks. Many young women have joined the Missionaries of Charity because they want to work with the poor. The spirit of commitment runs deep when one has the living example of a saint to lead the way. Her particular charism, her calling, is to minister to the poor wherever they are found. She challenges those who are financially wealthy, yet often spiritually poor, to open their hearts to the needy. In a world where physical poverty has reached epic proportions, where half the human family lives without clean water, decent housing, proper nutrition, and educational opportunities, her message is simple: "Do to others as you would have them do to you."

Martin Luther King, Jr.

Martin Luther King, Jr., was born into a middle-class black family in Atlanta, Georgia, in 1929. Following in the footsteps of his father, he studied for the ministry and began his initial pastoral duties in Montgomery, Alabama, in 1954. At that time racial discrimination was a given. Even water fountains were designated "white" and "colored." Finally, a young black woman, Rosa Parks, broke ranks by refusing to change places with whites on a bus in December 1955. King was persuaded to accept a leadership role in the ensuing boycott and thus began a prophetic odyssey that led to a Nobel Peace Prize in 1964 and his assassination four years later.

During the next several years he faced hostility in city after city, where he traveled because he encouraged blacks to stand tall and work for their rights as American citizens. In Chicago he was stoned and spat at for challenging the segregated housing codes; in Albany, Georgia, he was arrested for leading a civil rights march; in Memphis, Tennessee, he was finally killed while leading a sanitation workers' strike for decent wages. Throughout the civil rights movement he received support from many northern whites who saw the blatant racism of the United States as evil. But when King began to attack the foreign policy of the government over its pursuit of the Vietnam War, many friends deserted him. In addition, he also fell into disfavor with black militants because of his insistence on nonviolent action. While many blacks demanded the use of weapons to resist the racism of "whitey," King was struggling to convince them that violence was self-defeating.

It is hard to overestimate the importance of the black church on Martin Luther King, Jr. During the time of slavery, blacks accepted the Christianity of their masters but formed it into a deeply personal acceptance of Jesus Christ in their lives. They did not believe that slavery was the way of Jesus, but given their situation, were able to draw strength from God's love through Christ. When the civil rights movement got under way, it was religious leaders who spoke the truth about injustice, and it was primarily in church halls that organizational meetings and other rallies took place. Before he was a civil rights leader, King was a man of God. Indeed, it was the latter that led to the former.

The Protestant tradition of emphasis on the Word of God helped King preach the message of nonviolent justice. At the Holt Street Baptist Church in Birmingham, Alabama, during the bus boycott he said, "We are not here advocating violence . . . the only weapon we have in our hands this evening is the weapon of protest."[5] Again, during his imprisonment in 1963 in Birmingham, he wrote:

> In no sense do I advocate evading or defying the law as the rabid segregationists would do. This would lead to anarchy. One who breaks an unjust law must do so openly . . . with a willingness to accept the penalty. I submit that an individual who breaks a law that conscience tells him is unjust, and willingly accepts the penalty by staying in jail to arouse the conscience of the community over its injustice, is expressing the highest respect for the law.[6]

One of his most memorable speeches was given during the Civil Rights demonstration on August 28, 1963, at the Lincoln Memorial in Washington, D.C., before a half million people. In conclusion, he cried out:

> And when we allow freedom to ring, when we let it ring from every village and hamlet, from every city and state, we will be able to speed up that day when all of God's children—black men and white men, Jews and Gentiles, Protestants and Catholics—will be able to join hands and to sing in the words of that old Negro

spiritual, "Free at last! Free at last! Thank God Almighty, we are free at last!"[7]

King was a mighty orator, a man with the gift of eloquence and power. Unlike Adolf Hitler, who used his charisma to dominate and stir up hatred, King spoke words of peace and justice.

Way of Thunder

King followed in the footsteps of the Hebrew prophets. He fully understood that Moses was called by God to liberate the Hebrew people from the hands of Pharaoh. His mission was to lift the oppressive racism from the backs of his people, who lived in white America. When the kingdom was established by David and Solomon, they forgot the ways of God and ignored the cry of the poor. King recognized that Americans had forgotten their own Declaration of Independence, which declared all to be free and equal.

Like Isaiah, Jeremiah, and Ezekiel, he challenged those in authority to give up the ways of injustice. Jesus, too, had criticized the Pharisees and the leaders of the Jewish people in his own day for trivializing religion into a series of ritualistic practices. King saw that he must wake up the Christians in his own land to the evils of racism and economic injustice.

He saw clearly that the structures of society would not change unless there was an awakening on the part of blacks to their power. The initial bus boycott in Montgomery had a twofold purpose: to overturn an unjust law, which forced blacks to sit at the rear of the buses, and to apply economic pressure on the bus company by boycotting the transportation system. Gradually, as more and more of the Jim Crow laws (segregation ordinances) were overturned, King began to turn his attention to the political rights of the blacks. Many cities and towns throughout the South had literacy requirements as well as poll-tax restrictions on voting. Blacks were intimidated by harassment and threats of violence to keep them from voting, much less running for public office. By his constant emphasis on their rights and duties King enabled blacks to overcome their fears and stand up for their rights. In what was to be the final campaign of his life, he had the black sanitation workers of Memphis march in protest wearing signs that read, "I am a Man." Furthermore, the moral power of his message often shamed whites into realizing how they had participated, often times unwittingly, in the nation's racism. He energized many whites to take up the cause of racial equality because an injustice to one group is an injustice to all.

In spite of the thunder of his speech and the radical message of change he preached, he always stood for nonviolent change. He drank deeply of the teachings of Jesus, Gandhi, Tolstoy, and Thoreau and believed that not only was nonviolence a higher moral way to seek justice but the only practical way for a minority to gain freedom. Throughout the years of the civil rights movement much violence was heaped upon blacks. The Ku Klux Klan quadrupled its membership when whites realized that blacks would no longer be subservient to them. Bombings killed little children; police brutality by white troopers in Alabama and Mississippi became commonplace; mass arrests and the fire hosing of demonstrators continued, unabated.

One particularly ugly police action took place on the morning of March 7, 1965, at the Edmund Pettis bridge in Selma, Alabama. On a hot and humid Sunday morning the Alabama state police and local county sheriff deputies, led by Al Lingo and Jim Clark, two racist law officers, stormed into a group of black marchers, many of whom were women and elderly, beating them severely with billy clubs and blackjacks. They then fired tear gas into the group and charged again, this time on horseback. A television crew was on hand to record the mayhem, and the news media dubbed the event "Bloody Sunday."

The pictures of unarmed and peaceful demonstrators beaten by police shook the nation. When millions of Americans witnessed the brutality on their television screens, a cry went up for justice, and within a short time thousands of whites flocked to Alabama for a peace march to Montgomery, the state capital.

Not long afterwards Congress passed the Voting Rights Act, which ensured federal protection in all elections and eliminated poll taxes and literacy requirements. Through it all King preached nonviolence and worked patiently, yet deliberately, to achieve justice for blacks.

Less than two months before his death, perhaps in a moment of prescience, he spoke of how he wished to be remembered. "Yes, if you want to say that I was a drum major, say that I was a drum major for justice; say that I was a drum major for peace; I was a drum major for righteousness."[8] He left behind neither possessions nor property, but a legacy of commitment. The band he led played the music of freedom and the tunes of equality. Its members were mostly the marginalized of society, with other committed people who believed in his message.

Response

How are we to respond to the problems of our age? Do we ignore them? Do we contribute to the problems by deciding that they do not concern us? Or perhaps, like Mother Teresa and Dr. King, we can get involved.

In their lives, we see two distinct approaches to social ills. On the one hand, Mother Teresa responds to the needs of the poor by reaching out in a personal, individualistic way, while, on the other hand, King challenged the systematic injustice of racism found in the political, social, and economic institutions of the United States. Whether responding to a personal need or a social condition, both saw themselves as responsible for their fellow human beings. That is the first step in peace and justice education. We are responsible for each other. We are called to contribute to the betterment of our world.

Mother Teresa and Dr. King shared a conviction that faith in God must be lived out in society. As these two saw it, religion can never be confined to the sacristy. Yet their lives went in two distinct directions. By analogy, if bodies were found floating down a river, Mother Teresa would undoubtedly drag them ashore, clean them, and bury them with dignity. King, on the other hand, might well go back upstream to find out why the bodies were coming down at all. One way is primarily concerned with individual care, the other with social change. While Mother Teresa has been honored by everyone for her gentleness, King was often vilified for his demands of justice. Contrasting these two helps us understand the distinction between social welfare and social change.

The works of social welfare and social change are ongoing. Individuals do make a difference. When Rosa Parks refused to give up her seat to a white man she sparked a revolution. In general, political involvement in the United States is frequently the best means of reform. The work is often tedious, but in a democratic society people can join together for social change. Civil rights legislation helped blacks at least to achieve legal equality. King argued that although we cannot legislate morality, we can legislate desegregation. "It may be true that the law cannot make a man love me, but it can restrain him from lynching me."[9] He was convinced that people coming together in the cause of righteousness could make a difference.

He found the strength for ongoing commitment to racial justice from the support he received from his followers. He stood with millions of people who long for peace and justice. They are the people who believe that the different political, social, economic, cultural, and religious worlds are, in reality, one world—one that continually needs remaking in a spirit of reconciliation and love. At times we suffer the effects of frustration and fatigue. We are tempted to give up, to bury our heads in the sand, or to walk away from the challenges of life. Perhaps the example of a Mother Teresa or a Martin Luther King will encourage us to dream the dream and continue the struggle.

In spite of our human limitations and weakness, there lies within each person a fire waiting to be fanned into life—some would call it the Spirit of God—which when kindled can light a flame that will burn brightly in the cause of human dignity and global solidarity. But it will only sparkle when we resolve to make a difference, when we decide that we count. The tale of the owl and the dove may serve to illustrate the point.

"Tell me the weight of a snowflake," a wise old owl asked the young dove.

"Nothing, less than nothing," was the reply.

"In that case I must tell you an interesting story," the wise owl said. "I sat on the branch of a fir, close to its trunk, when it began to snow, not heavily, not in a raging blizzard, no, just like in a dream, without any violence. Since I didn't have anything better to do, I counted the snowflakes settling on the twigs and needles of my branch. Their number was exactly 2,476,521. When the next snowflake dropped on the branch—'nothing less than nothing,' as you say—the branch broke off."

Having said that, the owl flew away.

The dove thought about the story for a while and finally said to herself: "Perhaps there is only one person's voice lacking for peace to come about in the world."

Notes

1 Viktor E. Frankl, *The Doctor and the Soul* (New York: Alfred A. Knopf, 1960), 47–48.

2 Eileen Egan, *Such a Vision of the Street* (Garden City, N.Y.: Doubleday, 1985), 42.

3 Mother Teresa of Calcutta, address upon acceptance of Nobel Peace Prize, Oslo, Norway, December 10, 1979.

4 Matthew 25:31–46.

5 Martin Luther King, Jr., "Speech, Holt Baptist Church, December 4, 1955," *Life*, Spring 1988, 29.

6 Martin Luther King, Jr., "Letter from Birmingham Jail, April 1963," *Life*, Spring 1988, 29.

7 James M. Washington, ed., *A Testament of Hope: The Essential Writings of Martin Luther King, Jr.* (New York: Harper & Row, 1986), 220.

8 Martin Luther King, Jr., "Sermon Delivered in February 1968," *Life*, Spring 1988, 30.

9 Stephen B. Oates, *Let the Trumpet Sound* (New York: Mentor Books, 1982), 216.

40

Integration

Those who profess to love freedom and yet deprecate agitation are those who want crops without plowing. This struggle may be a moral one, or it may be physical, but it must be a struggle. Power concedes nothing without a demand. It never did, and never will.

Frederick Douglass[1]

Uniqueness

Anna Freud, who founded the field of child psychoanalysis, once reminded a group of her colleagues that "each of our patients is different and those differences matter a lot."[2] We have tried to be sensitive to the many different students who use this textbook. Some come from secure stable family backgrounds, others do not. Some have strong Christian faith identity, others do not. Some are financially independent, many are burdened with college loans. In terms of personality traits, students range from quiet and shy to colorful and loud. They may be politically conservative and religiously liberal, or just the opposite.

Whatever the case, each person is unique. It is this individual uniqueness that has been the central issue in the argument for peace and justice. And it is only when we come truly to appreciate our own specialness that we are able to rejoice in the uniqueness of each other. Adulthood should bring with it a value system rooted in personal worth and a sensitivity to the needs of others. We are called to love ourselves and our neighbor.

This vision of life, of course, should be our polestar. It matters little how old we are, how rich or poor, what the color of our skin may be, or what church we attend. The true measure of maturity is the vision we carry in our hearts. If our values include freedom, truth, justice, peace, and love, then the pathways we journey toward that polestar will be clearly marked. There will be mountains to climb and rivers to forge, deserts to cross and jungles to hack through, but the signposts will be clear and the compass will point due north. Clarity of vision rests on the twin values of worth of every person and our communal destiny. When we lose sight of these values, we are metaphorically mired in quicksand or caught in an eddy. Our fears and anxieties cause us to lash out at others or give up the journey. We need to deepen our understanding of the values in life that are rooted in truth and goodness. In doing so we will have joined ourselves with past and present generations of people who pray and work for peace and justice.

Earlier in this text we mentioned a method of learning that involved human experience, meaning, judgment, and decision making. We may express this process with the axiom: Think-Judge-Act. This phrase was used by French youth in the early part of this century who were involved in social reorganization and is still used by many families in the Christian Family Movement. If we begin to think and judge within the framework of personal dignities and solidarity, our actions will reflect our convictions. When confronted with a moral issue the pragmatist asks: Will it work? The coward asks: Is it safe? The politician asks: Is it popular? One would like to think that the real question to ask about all behavior is: Is it right?

Decisions are right or wrong depending on the degree of sensitivity we exercise toward the rights of others. That should always be uppermost in our minds. Unfortunately, we sometimes act like eagles raised on a chicken farm. Our potential is great, but we fear to take the risk involved in working for justice and living in peace. As we conclude the final chapter of the text let us remind ourselves about the vision of world harmony and our personal responsibility for achieving it.

Community

Tensions between the individual and the group have always existed. The uniqueness of each person, from the individual whorls of fingerprints to the steady flow of creative ideas in the arts and sciences, indicates that everyone is gifted in different ways. This means that each person has the right to express his or her individuality. It is also true that cooperation among people is necessary if harmony is to exist within a group. When one or more individuals assert themselves at the expense of others, conflicts arise. Since we find similar conflict situations in the animal kingdom, with the biggest and strongest beasts dominating the smaller and weaker species, some believe that humans fall into this same social matrix.

In contrast to this view, we have argued that the true uniqueness of humans is their ability to reflect upon their own situation, and thus create for themselves how they wish to live. Freedom of choice is uniquely human. Even in the worst of circumstances (recall the concentration camp experiences of Viktor Frankl), we can still give meaning to life. Individuals, while exercising their basic right to make a unique contribution to human history, can opt to live in harmony with others.

In looking about the world today, with the enormous expenditures on weapons of war, the clash of ideologies among different economic and political systems, the religious and nationalistic rivalry among many nations, and the growing realization of planetary pollution, it would seem that one major concept to work toward would be a community of care. It begins with an attitude of concern for all that is human. It is built around the idea that people are important and that conflict and violence are not the way things ought to be, but rather are the result of misplaced fears and misunderstood intentions.

The great need for building a community of care is most obvious when we look into the faces of children suffering the ravages of hunger and malnutrition, or when we see the hatred and bitterness of Palestinian refugees who live under a harsh Israeli military regime. Naturally a community of care begins with developing a sensitivity to our immediate neighbors, but it must grow beyond that to include ultimately all of the human family. If we develop attitudes of compassion and concern for our world, we may be sure that, at least within our hearts, we will have experienced a true community of care.

But a community of care is not enough. We should also belong to a community of conscience. Throughout this text we have used the term *conscientization* to indicate an attitude of mind that is alert to the social conditions of the human family. Conscientization is a process that makes one aware of the injustices and oppression that exist in society. Many Latin American peasants in the early 1960s stood powerless in their misery, not realizing that this condition was imposed upon them by a wealthy elite. So too are many North Americans unaware that much of the consumerism, militarism, and casual sexuality is imposed upon them by a similar wealthy elite who care little about personal dignity and are interested only in the pursuit of wealth and power.

We have thus come full circle. It is vitally important that we recognize and appreciate our own self-worth. Our life experiences to this point have taught us many lessons and given us moments both of joy and of sadness from which to gain strength and to learn patience. By introspection, we have noticed the differences between our vision and the reality of life. We become more aware of our limits as we grow in wisdom.

The circle is complete when we realize how dependent we are on others. Because we tend to forget the care and attention we received in our lives as infants and children, we often grow indifferent toward those who assist us in everyday life. The farmers, the merchants, the police, the sanitation workers, and millions like them make modern society possible. We are dependent upon them whether or not we realize it. The trick then is not to see conflict between the individual and the community, but to have a vision of harmony. We need not submerge our own identity into a faceless crowd, but rather shape our goals and plans in harmony with others, respectful of their rights. People do need people, and it is only through communities of care and conscience that God's Kingdom will be realized.

Dungeons and Dragons

If we are to live as caring and conscientious people, then we must acquire some knowledge of the things that hinder our progress. High on the list is our instinct to protect ourselves. Not only is this evident in the healthy concern we show for our physical safety; it also manifests itself in the unhealthy ways of paranoia and aggression. We are great at finding fault with others who seem to have abused us in some way, and we are quick to attack at the least provocation. Protective behavior does have a place in human life, but what we are here concerned with is protective behavior that does damage to our own dignity or that of another.

The truth is that beneath our defenses lie a host of fears that provoke our aggressive behavior. Why am I angry when someone cuts me off in traffic? Because I fear that people will think I'm a wimp. Why do I hesitate to take the blame for doing something wrong? Because I fear that people will think that I am stupid. The point is that underlying our hostility, defensiveness, anger, and resentment, are fears about self-worth, respect, honor, and integrity. This is not an easy truth to accept, especially for men, since much of our male cultural imaging centers around the values of macho attitudes and behavior.

Fear is supposedly only for weaklings. The John Waynes and Rambos of our pop culture leave us little room to develop the softer side of our personalities. Fear of heights or of lions may be acceptable, yet fear of a prowler (Dad always goes down the stairs before calling the police), or fear of one's peers is unacceptable. Consequently, we fail to realize that beneath our intention to protect ourselves lie many fears which, if brought to light, might prove to be groundless.

If we open the book on our fears, we will find pages of beliefs about life. Our experiences have taught us some truths; other truths have been fed to us by parents, by teachers, and by social influences. The perennial dilemma, of course, is what is true, half-true, and false? Only by a willingness to learn and rethink our beliefs can we hope to engage in constructive conflict. Defensiveness is a result of fear, which is a result of a conviction about life. We need constantly to see if our "truth" squares with the values of dignity and solidarity.

A final point to make about the dragons of fear hidden in the dungeons of our mind is that each person's dragons are uniquely his or her own. This is another way of saying that each person has his or her own configuration of truth. For example, some people find great fun in going to horror movies. The blood and gore, the tension and suspense, the tongue-in-cheek humor underlying this film genre is seen by devotees as poking fun at the real anxieties of life. On the other hand, many people avoid these films like the plague because they have no desire to be scared half to death, and they believe these films contribute to toleration of violence. Thus, one person's pleasure is another's poison.

In building communities of care and concern, and in respecting the individuality of each person, we need to develop levels of tolerance that allow for a variety of beliefs. But we also need to search for truths that will respect the dignity of all, and condemn the falseness of injustice. Only in a continual quest for goodness will true individuality and community be realized.

The Eighth Stage

Integrity is the final stage in the human life cycle, according to the psychosocial developmental theory of Erik Erikson. For our purposes it is a way of saying that a person has it all together. If in terms of Erikson's theory this is the stage of old age, is it possible to discuss it within the context of young adulthood? No and yes.

On the one hand, the accumulation of life experiences and a concomitant reflection upon them generally add much wisdom to a person as he or she grows older. Some, unfortunately, never grow up and carry unintegrated lives to the grave. Conversely, the process of integration does not begin in old age, and we find that many young people, having gone through their own process of introspection, have a well-developed integrity. As we have previously remarked, facing the problems and challenges of life, whether they are difficult courses in school, family problems, peer pressure, or personal illness, constitutes the clearest sign of maturity. When Freud was asked what he thought a normal person should be able to do well, he answered, "to love and to work."[3] A large percentage of college students have developed good work habits and most have learned to care and respect other people, which are the characteristics of love.

It would be foolish to argue, however, that young adults have the same integrity as the aged. More specifically, older people look back with satisfaction on having lived a productive and decent life, while young adults dream of new tomorrows. It is the dream that essentially characterizes youth. A wide variety of possibilities lies open in terms of where to live and work, who to find friendship and love with, and what objectives and goals to pursue. Of course, many of these possibilities are not determined by cold, hard, rational decisions. More often than not circumstances, luck, chance, or whatever will dictate the direction our life will take. College students frequently switch majors and make new friends at a rapid rate, indicating that no solid game plan has been set. While many possibilities and dreams lie ahead, one hopes that essential values have been established. The integrity of youth is not so much concerned with the wisdom of the ages, as with the ability to say No to phoniness and Yes to honesty.

What *integrity* essentially means is the development of the whole person. We need to appreciate the various dimensions of the self: our intellectual, reflective, rational side; our emotional, sensitive, compassionate side; our spiritual, faith-centered, free, and loving side. Together, these various aspects of personality give our life substance and direction.

The ancients spoke of the cardinal virtues, those strengths of character upon which to hinge our life. They are prudence, justice, fortitude, and temperance. Prudence is the ability to take the proper steps in achieving our goals; justice implies a concern for the well-being of others; fortitude renders us courageous in times of adversity; and temperance gives us a sense of balance about life. Similar in content to Scott Peck's attributes of self-discipline, the cardinal virtues empower us to deal with life in the ways of truth and goodness.

This development of the whole person, naturally enough, is the work of a lifetime. The important thing is to know the direction in which to go. If we build our life on the rock foundation values of personal dignity and human solidarity we will live lives of concern for peace and justice and will be developing our whole self intellectually, emotionally, and spiritually.

The Influence of the Spirit

We have saved the best wine until last. Part IV, Influence, began with an examination of how we can influence ourselves in positive and nurturing ways through self-discipline and a quest for excellence. We then explored the powerful economic, political, cultural, religious, and social influences that impact our lives positively and negatively. Included within the context of societal influences was a sketch of several women and men who have contributed to the betterment of humanity. This chapter thus far has tried to reemphasize the importance of self-influence both on an individual and communal level. The demons we need to exorcise in order to live fully alive were also exposed. Finally, we stressed the need to work toward an integration of our life, especially within the framework of the central values of personal dignity and human solidarity. We would like to conclude the chapter with a brief reflection on the influence of God. In the final analysis, if we are open to the Spirit, God's influence is the greatest of all.

Members of Alcoholics Anonymous speak of turning their lives over to a higher power. They trust that there is a source of energy that can help them resist the temptation of alcohol. Christians, Jews, Muslims, and followers of other religions refer to this power as God. Perhaps an apt generalization might say that this is the God of Creation.

Christians believe that this God became incarnate in the person of Jesus. As a man he experienced all of the fatigue, anxieties, frustrations, temptations, joys, hopes, and pleasures that all humans experience. As the Son of God his divinity gave him the strength to resist selfishness and sin. Christians who accept Jesus in faith are not only influenced by his teaching and the healing power of his ministry but are also convinced that his life, death, and resurrection have brought forgiveness of sins to the human family. Jesus, by dying and rising, influences his followers to live in his Spirit and follow his example. "I am with you always to the end of the age."[4]

The Gospels offer lessons about forgiveness, healing, reconciliation, wonderment, joy, conflict, pain, and suffering. In short, they are typical human experiences influenced by the presence of Jesus. It is crucial for Christians, if not everyone, to appreciate the humanity of Jesus, his love, concern, and care for the needy, and his confrontation with the authorities. Too often people immediately identify Jesus as the Son of God and lose sight of the beauty of his humanity. It is precisely in the humanity of Jesus that we can allow his Spirit to direct our own humanity. "It is the spirit that gives life; the flesh is useless. The words that I have spoken to you are spirit and life."[5]

The psalmist says that when the Lord speaks to his people then "Steadfast love and faithfulness will meet; righteousness and peace will kiss each other."[6] What a romantic image! The Spirit of God does desire to influence us in all the various dimensions of our life. Yet God has created us in freedom and wishes us to use our freedom in life-giving and healing ways.

God has called us to be a people, a people of God. This was one of the images that the Hebrew people cherished and that many Christians are beginning to reappropriate.

People are alive to God when religion energizes them to live out the Gospel in spirit and truth. This is the real challenge of our generation—to build a people of God alive to peace and justice. Do we want to see justice and peace kiss? Do we understand that there is no peace without justice? Can we work to influence our world in the ways of peace and justice? If we do, we can be sure of one thing: We are living under the influence of God.

Notes

[1]   Frederick Douglass, in *Familiar Quotations,* ed. Emily M. Beck (Boston: Little, Brown, 1980), 536.

[2]   Robert Coles, "The Door of Hope," *Sojourners,* April 1988, 19.

[3]   Erik Erikson, *Identity, Youth and Crisis* (New York: W. W. Norton, 1968), 136.

[4]   Matthew 28:20.

[5]   John 6:63.

[6]   Psalm 85:10.

Further Reading

Chapter 1

Dykstra, Craig. *Vision and Character.* New York: Paulist Press, 1981.
Evans, Richard I. *Dialogue with Erik Erikson.* New York: E. P. Dutton, 1969.
Kelsey, Morton T. *Caring.* New York: Paulist Press, 1981.
Powell, John. *Why Am I Afraid to Tell You Who I Am?* Niles, Ill.: Argus, 1969.

Chapter 2

Barnett, Lincoln. *The Universe and Dr. Einstein.* New York: Bantam, 1957.
Sagan, Carl. *Cosmos.* New York: Ballantine, 1980.
Schumacher, E. F. *Small Is Beautiful.* New York: Harper & Row, 1973.
Zukav, Gary. *The Dancing Wu Li Masters.* New York: Bantam, 1980.

Chapter 3

Brown, Lester, ed. *State of the World: 1991.* New York: Norton, 1991.
Buscalia, Leo F. *The Way of the Bull.* New York: Fawcett Crest, 1973.
Garreau, Joel. *The Nine Nations of North America.* New York: Avon, 1981.
Lernoux, Penny. *Cry of the People.* New York: Penguin, 1980.
Peck, M. Scott. *The Road Less Traveled.* New York: Touchstone, 1978.
Speir, Peter. *People.* New York: Doubleday, 1980.
Whitehead, Evelyn E., and James D. Whitehead. *Community of Faith.* New York: Seabury Press, 1982.

Chapter 4

Berne, Eric. *Games People Play.* New York: Grove Press, 1964.
de Saint-Exupéry, Antoine. *The Little Prince.* New York: Harcourt, Brace, 1943.
Fowler, James W. *Stages of Faith.* San Francisco: Harper & Row, 1981.
Goldhaber, Gerald M., and Marylynn B. Goldhaber. *Transactional Analysis.* Boston: Allyn and Bacon, 1976.

Chapter 5

Campbell, Joseph, with Bill Moyers. *The Power of Myth.* New York: Doubleday, 1988.
De Soto, Hernando. *The Other Path.* New York: Harper & Row, 1989.
Iliffe, John. *The African Poor.* New York: Cambridge University Press, 1987.
National Catholic Education Association. "International Youth Year." *Momentum* 16 (1985).

Chapter 6

Berger, Peter L. *The Sacred Canopy.* New York: Doubleday, 1969.
Johnson, Roger A., and Ernest Wallwork. *Critical Issues in Modern Religion.* Englewood Cliffs, N.J.: Prentice-Hall, 1973.
Munitz, Milton K. *The Mystery of Existence.* New York: Meridith, 1965.
Shea, John. *Stories of God.* Chicago: Thomas More Press, 1978.
———. *Stories of Faith.* Chicago: Thomas More Press, 1980.
Smith, Huston. *The Religions of Man.* New York: Harper & Row, 1958.
Weil, Simone. *Waiting for God.* New York: Harper & Row, 1951.

Chapter 7

Berryman, Phillip. *Inside Central America.* New York: Pantheon, 1985.
Freedom in the World: 1990–91. New York: Freedom House, 1991.
O'Malley, Padraig. *The Uncivil Wars.* Boston: Houghton Mifflin, 1983.
Phillips, Kevin. *The Politics of Rich and Poor.* New York: Random House, 1990.

Chapter 8

Alperovitz, Gar, and Roger Skurski, eds. *American Economic Policy.* Notre Dame, Ind.: University of Notre Dame Press, 1984.
Even, Stuart. *Captains of Consciousness.* New York: McGraw-Hill, 1976.
Gilder, George. *Wealth and Poverty.* New York: Basic Books, 1981.
Houck, John W., and Oliver F. Williams, eds. *Catholic Social Teaching and the U.S. Economy.* Washington, D.C.: University Press of America, 1984.

Mintz, Morton, and Jerry S. Cohen. *Power, Inc.* New York: Viking Press, 1976.

Chapter 9

Becker, Ernest. *The Denial of Death.* New York: Macmillan, 1973.
Duska, Ronald, and Mariellen Whelan. *Moral Development.* New York: Paulist Press, 1975.
Golding, William. *Lord of the Flies.* New York: Capricorn, 1954.
Montagu, M. F. Ashley. *Anthropology and Human Nature.* Boston: Porter Sargent, 1957.
Skinner, B. F. *Beyond Freedom and Dignity.* New York: Bantam, 1971.
Stevenson, Leslie. *Seven Theories of Human Nature.* Oxford: Clarendon Press, 1974.

Chapter 10

Brown, Lester R. *The Interdependence of Nations.* New York: Foreign Policy Association, 1972.
McDonagh, Sean. *To Care for the Earth.* Santa Fe, N.Mex.: Bear, 1986.
McGinnis, Kathleen and James. *Parenting for Peace and Justice.* Maryknoll, N.Y.: Orbis, 1982.
Mische, Gerald and Patricia Mische. *Toward a Human World Order.* New York: Paulist Press, 1977.

Chapter 11

Baum, Gregory. *The Social Imperative.* New York: Paulist Press, 1979.
Hammarskjöld, Dag. *Markings.* New York: Ballantine, 1964.
Harrington, Michael. *The Vast Majority.* New York: Touchstone, 1977.
Haught, John F. *The Cosmic Adventure.* New York: Paulist Press, 1984.
Solzhenitsyn, Alexander. *One Day in the Life of Ivan Denisovich.* New York: Bantam, 1984.
Wachtel, Paul L. *The Poverty of Affluence.* Philadelphia: New Society, 1989.

Chapter 12

Brown, Dee. *Bury My Heart at Wounded Knee.* New York: Washington Square Press, 1970.
Fromm, Erich. *The Heart of Man.* New York: Harper & Row, 1964.
Merton, Thomas. *Faith and Violence.* Notre Dame, Ind.: University of Notre Dame Press, 1968.
Niebuhr, H. Richard. *The Responsible Self.* New York: Harper & Row, 1963.
Peck, M. Scott. *People of the Lie.* New York: Simon & Schuster, 1983.

Chapter 13

Fackenheim, Emil L. *God's Presence in History*. New York: Harper & Row, 1970.

Gutierrez, Gustavo. *A Theology of Liberation*. Maryknoll, N.Y.: Orbis, 1973.

Harrington, Michael. *The New American Poverty*. New York: Holt, Rinehart & Winston, 1984.

McElvaney, William K. *Good News is Bad News is Good News . . .* Maryknoll, N.Y.: Orbis, 1980.

Zinn, Howard. *A People's History of the United States*. New York: Harper & Row, 1980.

Chapter 14

Brown, Robert McAfee. *Religion and Violence*. Philadelphia: Westminster Press, 1987.

Cooke, Robert E., Andre E. Hellegers, Robert G. Hoyt, and Herbert W. Richardson, eds. *The Terrible Choice: The Abortion Dilemma*. New York: Bantam, 1968.

Castelli, Jim. *The Bishops and the Bomb*. Garden City, N.Y.: Doubleday, 1983.

Powell, John. *Abortion: The Silent Holocaust*. Allen, Tex.: Argus Communications, 1981.

Rubenstein, Richard L. *The Cunning of History*. New York: Harper & Row, 1975.

Torture in the Eighties: An Amnesty International Report. London: Amnesty International Publications, 1984.

Chapter 15

Hoffman, Nancy, and Florence Hoffman, eds. *Women Working: An Anthology of Stories and Poems*. New York: Feminist Press, 1979.

Kaufman, Linda, ed. *Gender and Theory: Dialogue on Feminist Criticism*. New York: Gasil Blackwell, 1989.

McAllister, Pam, ed. *Reweaving the Web of Life*. Philadelphia: New Society, 1982.

Rothenberg, Paula S. *Racism and Sexism*. New York: St. Martin's Press, 1988.

Spretnak, Charlene, ed. *The Politics of Women's Spirituality*. Garden City, N.Y.: Anchor, 1982.

Chapter 16

Brown, Dee. *Bury My Heart at Wounded Knee*. New York: Washington Square Press, 1970.

Du Bois, W. E. B. *The Souls of Black Folk*. New York: Penguin, 1989.

Garrow, David J. *Bearing the Cross*. New York: Random House, 1988.

Hampton, Henry, and Steve Fayer. *Voices of Freedom.* New York: Bantam, 1990.
King, Martin Luther, Jr. *The Trumpet of Conscience.* New York: Harper & Row, 1967.
Sheehan, Neil. *A Bright Shining Lie.* New York: Random House, 1988.

Chapter 17

Bonhoeffer, Deitrich. *Letters and Papers from Prison.* New York: Macmillan, 1967.
Hillesum, Etty. *An Interrupted Life.* New York: Washington Square Press, 1981.
Speer, Albert. *Spandau: The Secret Diaries.* New York: Macmillan, 1976.
Zahn, Gordon. *In Solitary Witness.* Springfield, Ill.: Templegate, 1986.

Chapter 18

Brockman, James R. *Romero: A Life.* Maryknoll, N.Y.: Orbis, 1989.
Merton, Thomas. *Faith and Violence.* Notre Dame, Ind.: University of Notre Dame Press, 1968.
Nelson, Jack A. *Hunger for Justice.* Maryknoll, N.Y.: Orbis, 1980.
Ramsey, Paul. *The Just War.* New York: Charles Scribner's Sons, 1968.
Shinn, Roger I. *Wars and Rumors of Wars.* Nashville: Abingdon Press, 1972.
Wallis, Jim. *The Call to Conversion.* New York: Harper & Row, 1981.

Chapter 19

Hancock, Graham. *Lords of Poverty.* New York: Atlantic Monthly Press, 1989.
Harrington, Michael. *The New American Poverty.* New York: Holt, Rinehart & Winston, 1984.
Katz, Michael B. *The Undeserving Poor.* New York: Pantheon, 1989.
Myrdal, Gunnar. *The Challenge of World Poverty.* New York: Random House, 1970.
National Commission on Children. *Final Report: "Beyond Rhetoric."* Washington, D.C.: U.S. Government Printing Office, 1991.

Chapter 20

Ferencz, Benjamin B. *Planethood.* Coos Bay, Oreg.: Vision, 1988.
Flavin, Christopher. *Slowing Global Warming.* New York: Worldwatch Institute, 1989.
French, Hilary F. *Clearing the Air: A Global Agenda.* New York: Worldwatch Institute, 1990.
Seuss, Dr. *The Lorax.* New York: Random House, 1971.

Steger, Will, and Jon Bowermaster. *Saving the Earth.* New York: Alfred A. Knopf, 1990.
Taylor, Robert E. *Ahead of the Curve.* New York: Environmental Defense Fund, 1990.
Vogeler, Ingolf, and Anthony De Sousa. *Dialectics of Third World Development.* Totowa, N.J.: Rowman and Allanheld, 1980.

Chapter 21

Frankl, Viktor, E. *The Doctor and the Soul.* New York: Bantam, 1969.
Fromm, Erich. *The Art of Loving.* New York: Harper & Row, 1962.
Leslie, Robert C. *Jesus and Logotherapy.* Nashville: Abingdon Press, 1965.
Peck, M. Scott. *The Different Drum.* New York: Simon & Schuster, 1987.
Teresa of Calcutta, Mother. *A Gift from God.* New York: Harper & Row, 1975.

Chapter 22

de Chardin, Teilhard. *The Divine Milieu.* New York: Harper & Row, 1960.
Dillard, Annie. *Pilgrim at Tinker Creek.* New York: Harper & Row, 1974.
Haught, John F. *The Cosmic Adventure.* New York: Paulist Press, 1984.
Merton, Thomas. *New Seeds of Contemplation.* New York: New Directions, 1962.
Shea, John. *Stories of Faith.* Chicago: Thomas More Association, 1980.

Chapter 23

Erikson, Erik H. *Gandhi's Truth.* New York: Norton, 1969.
Glatzer, Nahum N., ed. *The Way of Response: Martin Buber.* New York: Schocken, 1966.
Gremillion, Joseph, ed. *The Gospel of Peace and Justice.* Maryknoll, N.Y.: Orbis, 1976.
Link, Mark. *Take Off Your Shoes.* Chicago: Argus, 1972.

Chapter 24

Baum, Gregory. *Religion and Alienation.* New York: Paulist Press, 1975.
Brown, Robert McAfee. *Making Peace in the Global Village.* Philadelphia: Westminster Press, 1981.
Coy, Patrick, ed. *A Revolution of Heart.* Philadelphia: Temple University Press, 1988.
Hope, Marjorie, and James Young. *The Struggle for Humanity.* Maryknoll, N.Y.: Orbis, 1977.

Chapter 25

Betz, Margaret. *Faith and Justice.* Winona, Minn.: Saint Mary's Press, 1984.
Brown, Judith M. *Gandhi: Prisoner of Hope.* New Haven, Conn.: Yale University Press, 1989.
Dorr, Donald. *The Social Justice* Agenda. Maryknoll, N.Y.: Orbis, 1991.
Ingram, Catherine. *In the Footsteps of Gandhi: Conversations with Spiritual Activists.* Berkeley, Calif.: Parallax Press, 1990.
Iyer, Raghavan, ed. *The Moral and Political Writings of Mahatma Gandhi.* 3 vols. Oxford: Clarendon Press, 1986.
True, Michael. *Homemade Social Justice.* Chicago: Fides/Claretian Press, 1982.

Chapter 26

Fahey, Joseph, and Richard Armstrong, eds. *A Peace Reader.* New York: Paulist Press, 1987.
Gutierrez, Gustavo. *The Power of the Poor in History.* Maryknoll, N.Y.: Orbis, 1979.
Haight, Roger. *An Alternative Vision.* New York: Paulist Press, 1985.
MacQuarrie, John. *The Concept of Peace.* New York: Harper & Row, 1973.
Musto, Ronald G. *The Catholic Peace Tradition.* Maryknoll, N.Y.: Orbis, 1986.

Chapter 27

Douglass, James W. *The Non-Violent Cross.* London: Geoffrey Chapman, 1968.
Ellsberg, Robert, ed. *By Little and By Little: The Selected Writings of Dorothy Day.* New York: Alfred A. Knopf, 1983.
Guinan, Edward, ed. *Peace and Nonviolence.* New York: Paulist Press, 1973.
Jesudasan, Ignatius. *A Gandhian Theology of Liberation.* Maryknoll, N.Y.: Orbis, 1984.
Sharp, Gene. *The Politics of Nonviolent Action.* 3 vols. Boston: Porter Sargent, 1973.

Chapter 28

Ferrell, Frank, and Janet Ferrell. *Trevor's Place.* New York: Harper & Row, 1985.
Moltmann, Jurgen. *The Crucified God.* New York: Harper & Row, 1974.
Pennington, M. Basil. *The Eucharist Yesterday and Today.* New York: Crossroads, 1985.
Ritter, Bruce. *Sometimes God Has a Kid's Face.* New York: Covenant House, 1988.

Shannon, William H., ed. *Thomas Merton: The Hidden Ground of Love.* New York: Farrar, Straus and Giroux, 1985.
Teresa of Calcutta, Mother. *The Love of Christ.* New York: Harper & Row, 1982.

Chapter 29

Ellis, Marc. *A Year at the Catholic Worker.* New York: Paulist Press, 1978.
———. *Peter Maurin: Prophet in the Twentieth Century.* New York: Paulist Press, 1981.
Maguire, Daniel. *The Moral Choice.* Minneapolis: Winston Press, 1979.
Singer, Peter. *Practical Ethics.* Cambridge: Cambridge University Press, 1979.

Chapter 30

Carr, Anne E. *A Search for Wisdom and Spirit.* Notre Dame, Ind.: University of Notre Dame Press, 1988.
Dykstra, Craig. *Vision and Character.* New York: Paulist Press, 1981.
Kelsey, Morton T. *Caring.* New York: Paulist Press, 1981.
Miller, William D. *All Is Grace.* Garden City, N.Y.: Doubleday, 1987.
Wallis, Jim. *The Call to Conversion.* New York: Harper & Row, 1981.

Chapter 31

Evans, Richard I. *Dialogue with Erik Erikson.* New York: E. P. Dutton, 1969.
Finnerty, Adam Daniel. *No More Plastic Jesus.* Maryknoll, N.Y.: Orbis, 1977.
Ingram, Catherine. *In the Footsteps of Gandhi.* Berkeley, Calif.: Parallax Press, 1990.
Maslow, Abraham H. *Religion, Values, and Peak Experiences.* New York: Viking Press, 1964.
Peck, M. Scott. *The Road Less Traveled.* New York: Touchstone, 1978.

Chapter 32

Bloom, Allan. *The Closing of the American Mind.* New York: Simon & Schuster, 1987.
Boyer, Ernest L. *College: The Undergraduate Experience in America.* New York: Harper & Row, 1987.
Fenton, Thomas, ed. *Education for Justice.* Maryknoll, N.Y.: Orbis, 1975.
Hirsch, E. D., Jr. *Cultural Literacy.* New York: Random House, 1988.
Passell, Peter. *The Best.* New York: Viking Press, 1987.

Chapter 33

Bellah, Robert N., Richard Madsen, William M. Sullivan, Ann Swidler, and Steven M. Tipton. *Habits of the Heart.* New York: Harper & Row, 1985.
Hope, Marjorie, and James Young. *The Struggle for Humanity.* Maryknoll, N.Y.: Orbis, 1977.
Kavanaugh, John Francis. *Following Christ in a Consumer Society.* Maryknoll, N.Y.: Orbis, 1981.
Lappe, Frances Moore. *Rediscovering America's Values.* New York: Ballantine, 1989.
Marstin, Ronald. *Beyond Our Tribal Gods.* Maryknoll, N.Y.: Orbis, 1982.
Postman, Neil. *Amusing Ourselves to Death.* New York: Viking Press, 1985.

Chapter 34

Baum, Gregory. *Religion and Alienation.* New York: Paulist Press, 1975.
Coy, Patrick G., ed. *A Revolution of the Heart.* Philadelphia: Temple University Press, 1988.
Dostoevsky, Fyodor. *The Brothers Karamazov.* New York: Bantam, 1970.
McNeill, Donald P., Douglas A. Morrison, and Henri J. M. Nouwen. *Compassion.* Garden City, N.Y.: Doubleday, 1982.
Sobrino, Jon, Ignacio Ellacuria, and others. *Companions of Jesus.* Maryknoll, N.Y.: Orbis, 1990.

Chapter 35

Anderson, Joanne Manning. *For the People.* Reading, Mass.: Addison-Wesley, 1977.
Brown, Robert McAfee. *Making Peace in the Global Village.* Philadelphia: Westminster Press, 1981.
Gorey, Hays. *Nader and the Power of Everyman.* New York: Grosset and Dunlap, 1975.
Green, Mark. *Who Runs Congress?* New York: Viking Press, 1979.
Schorr, Lisbeth B. *Within Our Reach.* New York: Anchor, 1988.

Chapter 36

John Paul II. *On Human Work.* Boston: Daughters of St. Paul, 1981.
McGinnis, James B. *Bread and Justice.* New York: Paulist Press, 1979.
Morris, Morris David. *Measuring the Condition of the World's Poor.* New York: Pergamon Press, 1979.
National Conference of Catholic Bishops. *Economic Justice for All.* Washington, D.C.: United States Catholic Conference, 1986.

Owensby, Walter. *Economics for Prophets.* Grand Rapids, Mich.: William B. Eerdmans, 1988.
Paul VI. *On the Development of Peoples.* New York: Paulist Press, 1967.

Chapter 37

Brockman, James R. *Romero: A Life.* Maryknoll, N.Y.: Orbis, 1989.
Brown, Judith M. *Gandhi: Prisoner of Hope.* New Haven, Conn.: Yale University Press, 1989.
Miller, William D. *Dorothy Day.* New York: Harper & Row, 1982.
Myers, Ched. *Binding the Strong Man.* Maryknoll, N.Y.: Orbis, 1988.
Noone, Judith M. *The Same Fate as the Poor.* Maryknoll, N.Y.: Maryknoll Sisters, 1984.
Rogers, George L., ed. *Benjamin Franklin's The Art of Virtue.* Eden Prairie, Minn.: Acorn, 1990.

Chapter 38

Berrigan, Daniel. *The Dark Night of Resistance.* New York: Bantam, 1971.
Dees, Morris. *A Season for Justice.* New York: Charles Scribner's Sons, 1991.
Garland, Anne Witte. *Women Activists.* New York: Feminist Press, 1988.
Garrow, David J. *Bearing the Cross.* New York: Vintage, 1988.
Schillebeeckx, Edward. *Ministry.* New York: Crossroads, 1981.

Chapter 39

Day, Dorothy. *The Long Loneliness.* New York: Harper & Row, 1953.
———. *Loaves and Fishes.* New York: Harper & Row, 1963.
McGovern, James. *To Give the Love of Christ.* New York: Paulist Press, 1978.
Nouwen, Henri. *The Wounded Healer.* Garden City, N.Y.: Image, 1979.
Teresa of Calcutta, Mother. *Life in the Spirit.* New York: Harper & Row, 1983.
Washington, James M., ed. *A Testament of Hope: The Essential Writings of Martin Luther King, Jr.* New York: Harper & Row, 1986.

Chapter 40

Berry, Thomas. *The Dream of the Earth.* San Francisco: Sierra Club Books, 1988.
Dykstra, Craig. *Vision and Character.* New York: Paulist Press, 1981.
Küng, Hans. *Global Responsibility.* New York: Crossroads, 1991.
Rice, Helen Steiner. *Gifts from the Heart.* Old Tappan, N.J.: Fleming H. Revell, 1981.
Weiner, Jonathan. *The Next One Hundred Years.* New York: Bantam, 1990.

Index